BEFORE AUSCHWITZ

BEFORE AUSCHWITZ

Jewish Prisoners in the Prewar Concentration Camps

Kim Wünschmann

Harvard University Press

Cambridge, Massachusetts
London, England
2015

Library of Congress Cataloging-in-Publication Data

Wünschmann, Kim, author.
Before Auschwitz : Jewish prisoners in the prewar concentration camps / Kim Wünschmann.
pages cm
Includes bibliographical references and index.
ISBN 978-0-674-96759-5
1. Jews—Persecutions—Germany—History—20th century   2. Concentration camps—
Germany—History—20th century.   3. Germany—Politics and government—1933–1945.
4. Germany—Ethnic relations.   I. Title.   II. Title: Jewish prisoners in the prewar
concentration camps.
DS134.255.W86 2015
940.53'185—dc23
2014030009

To my Grandparents
in loving memory

CONTENTS

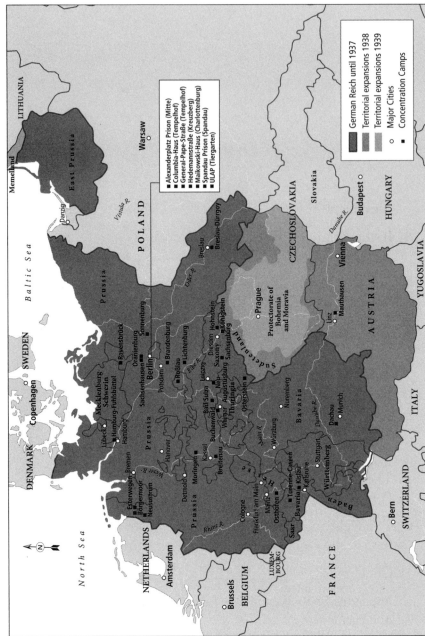

The most important concentration camps for Jewish prisoners, 1933–1939. The German Reich is depicted in its borders of 1937, but the map also indicates the territorial expansions of 1938 and 1939. Mauthausen became a detention site for Jews only during the war; it has been included because in June 1939 it served as a stopover for Jews deported from occupied Czechoslovakia to Dachau.

Legend:
- German Reich until 1937
- Territorial expansions 1938
- Territorial expansions 1939
- ○ Major Cities
- ■ Concentration Camps

- ■ Alexanderplatz Prison (Mitte)
- ■ Columbia-Haus (Tempelhof)
- ■ General-Pape-Straße (Tempelhof)
- ■ Hedemannstraße (Kreuzberg)
- ■ Maikowski-Haus (Charlottenburg)
- ■ Spandau Prison (Spandau)
- ■ ULAP (Tiergarten)

INTRODUCTION

Another [Jewish prisoner] said: "I am not sure yet what they will make of the ruins of the synagogues . . . One day they will identify those ruins and they will commemorate us and we will become the objects of historical research."

[A second prisoner said:] "I think that people, at all times, have found their times particularly fast-moving. In our time it is part of the fast pace of life that, sooner or later, they will make a movie out of us. Well, I shall be curious what those Messrs. film producers will make of our experiences."

[A third one:] "I can tell you that . . . we will become fashionable, they will wrack their brains about special nuances and effects with which to illustrate concentration camp movies."

[A fourth one:] *"Kinder,* don't think too great a deal of yourselves! Do you really think that the world out there cares about our condition? The others are busy with themselves. They see that in here many things have happened to us that can come across as sinister. But they do not want to worry their nations too much. If people out there just have newspapers and radio, then the reports about us will be pushed aside by something new, something that is even more interesting."

Julius Meyer wrote the memories of his imprisonment in Buchenwald concentration camp in 1940, after he had fled from Nazi Germany to England. The lawyer from Frankfurt am Main had been arrested by the Gestapo on November 12, 1938, in the immediate aftermath of the November Pogrom. Together with more than 2,500 Jewish men from his hometown, he was deported to Buchenwald.[1] In the course of the winter of 1938–1939, the catastrophic conditions that prevailed in the camp, and brutal ill-treatment inflicted by the SS, caused the deaths of hundreds of Jewish inmates.[2] Among the victims was the chronicler's brother, Alfred Meyer, who died only days after his arrival.[3] Remarkable in the narrative of Meyer's memoir is the scene cited above, in which he portrays Buchenwald's Jewish prisoners engaged in a vivid discussion about the historical significance of their situation. The inmates wonder how future generations might interpret and commemorate what they clearly recognize as an exceptional historical event. One prisoner finds the mass detention of Jews in concentration camps so sensational that he foresees the world of film dramatizing their fate and framing it with all the necessary tricks and effects. Newspapers and radio are also mentioned as media likely to report on the mass imprisonment of some 26,000 Jewish men. However, as much as Jewish prisoners were sure that the world would learn about their fate, they were also skeptical as to whether people would really care. The sheer monstrosity and brutality perpetrated in the concentration camps would intimidate people, and keep them from paying close attention. The last speaker predicts that soon the extraordinary terror of the November Pogrom would slide into the past, overshadowed by a present simply "more interesting," more dramatic, and—as we know today—even more monstrous.

World interest in the prewar concentration camps was indeed short-lived, soon to be displaced by other shocking news of the Third Reich's domestic terror and diplomatic bellicosity. Many who escaped from Nazi Germany felt the discrepancy between the severity of their personal experience of persecution and its public representation. The circumstances under which Meyer wrote his memoir seem especially poignant in this respect. As a German, and thereby an "enemy alien," the British deported him to the Hutchinson camp in Douglas, on the Isle of Man, in June 1940. Still traumatized by his detention in the Nazi concentration camp, Meyer thus found himself imprisoned yet again: "From Buchenwald to Douglas," reads the sarcastic comment at the end of his account.[4] Thousands of German and Austrian Jewish refugees were interned as "enemy aliens" in the spring and summer of 1940; not a few of them had previously suffered in Nazi concentration camps.[5] But what was haunting to Meyer felt like old news to his contemporaries. History had moved on. The Second World War had started and, after the fall of France, fearful anticipation of German invasion took hold of the British population. The Battle of Britain, waged by the German Air Force, was launched while Meyer was writing, in the summer of 1940.

Informed by the survivor's prediction that one day Jewish concentration camp prisoners "will become the objects of historical research," the historian about to carry out this research must reflect on the task ahead. What does it mean to write the history of Jewish prisoners in Nazi concentration camps in the years 1933 to 1939? With whom are we dealing exactly? What are the particularities and challenges of a study that focuses exclusively on the prewar period? What are the questions to be answered, and what kind of insights can we hope to gain through this research?

First of all, a historical study of the imprisonment of Jews before 1939 demands an understanding of the period in its own right. The concentration camps of the prewar era were different from the wartime camps. They had different forms and different functions.[6] Simply to place them into a seemingly linear development of Nazi anti-Jewish policy, which Raul Hilberg has analyzed as progressing through four well-defined phases of definition, expropriation, concentration, and extermination, would miss the particularity of the prewar period.[7] The development that ultimately culminated in genocide on an unprecedented scale was neither preordained nor the direct result of a single man's long-standing fantasies. Karl Schleunes's concept of "the twisted road to Auschwitz" is more apposite, helping us to grasp a process of gradual development in response to outside influences and internal power rivalries, a process that, at each stage, might have pointed to a different destination.[8]

At the outset, an awareness of historical perspectives—pre- and post-Holocaust—needs to be embraced.[9] How did Jews in the 1930s perceive the concentration camps? How did they react to the threat of the camps, and what were their modes of assessing the overall historical situation? Dealing with these issues poses great challenges to the historian. For us, it is impossible to rewind history and imagine what it must have been like to live at a time when the Holocaust, a crime that was to define national identities after the Second World War, had not happened. However, what we *can* do is be conscious that, as scholars of the prewar era in German-Jewish history, we study a society in motion from the vantage point of hindsight. Fritz Stern emphasized the historian's duty "to try to understand those who had lived at that time, with the enormous resentments that existed then, with the emotions, with the traditions, with the hopes, with the despair, with the humiliation."[10] In contrast to the historian looking at the prewar years with the knowledge of what happened during the war, the perspective of the contemporaries was of *their* past—of the postwar German defeat in the First World War, the downfall of the monarchy, the revolutionary upheavals, the world economic crisis, and the collapse of the Weimar Republic. Experiences of recent extreme situations, of states of emergency, and economic uncertainty shaped the mentalities and behaviors of those living at the time. The future, on the other hand, was veiled to them. In the 1930s, the Holocaust was unthinkable.

Nevertheless, hindsight sometimes condemns Jews in prewar Nazi Germany for not having left in time, or for not having read the supposedly clear "early warning signs" of the catastrophe to come. Accusations of "blindness" and of "not having foreseen the gas chambers of Auschwitz and Treblinka" are made by Jewish and non-Jewish commentators alike.[11] But could Jews in Germany and Austria really "know" that there would be no future for them, and that rather than staying where they felt they belonged, they would be better off facing uncertain prospects and insecure living conditions in exile? The answer is complex. For many Jews in Nazi Germany the day-to-day reality prior to 1938–1939 presented a peculiar blend of unparalleled discrimination and ongoing normal life. In her study of everyday Jewish life in Nazi Germany, Marion Kaplan has cogently analyzed this ambiguous reality as being shaped by "mixed messages," which ultimately "made the assessment of danger so complicated for many Jews."[12]

The question of historical knowledge is, furthermore, closely connected to Jewish identities before the Holocaust. Gershom Scholem's early disillusionment with the "German Jewish symbiosis," in his eyes nothing but a "myth," was by no means representative of German Jewry.[13] Scholem pinned his hopes on Zionism and left Germany for Palestine in 1923, but only a small minority of German Jews identified themselves as Zionists before 1933.[14] Most Jews in both Germany and Austria felt deeply rooted in their fatherland, its history, and its culture. However, Jewish life in a non-Jewish environment was far from "normal."[15] The various Jewish defense organizations installed throughout Europe prove that Jews were vigilant to the antisemitism virulent in many nations as society's "cultural code."[16] In Germany, the Central Association of German Citizens of Jewish Faith (CV) was founded "to fight antisemitism and to foster German patriotism among Jews."[17] Eva Reichmann, who worked for the CV until its dissolution in 1939, continued to have confidence in the "German-Jewish synthesis." In 1934 she reflected upon the "meaning of German-Jewish being" and committed herself to "our German-Jewish future . . . worth building and securing with the best of our forces."[18]

Both Gershom Scholem and Eva Reichmann had close relatives who were interned in the prewar Nazi concentration camps. When her husband was deported to Sachsenhausen in November 1938, Reichmann experienced helplessness and fear, for a long time not knowing his whereabouts or his condition. Ultimately the imprisonment of Hans Reichmann led to the couple's emigration from Germany. In April 1939 they arrived in London, where the released prisoner began to write an eyewitness account of his time in Sachsenhausen entitled *German Citizen and Persecuted Jew*.[19] Gershom Scholem, meanwhile, had made every effort to free his brother Werner from the concentration camp.[20] In contrast to Hans Reichmann, Werner Scholem suffered for many years in various camps, among them Lichtenburg and Dachau. As a prominent political opponent, his name was "on the Nazis' blackest list."[21] Although Werner Scholem had long broken with the religion of his ancestors, his Jewish roots doomed him to especially brutal treatment by the camp guards. He died in Buchenwald on July 17, 1940.

The examples of Hans Reichmann and Werner Scholem alert us to the fact that, in order to reach an understanding of the prewar history of Jewish concentration camp prisoners, it is critical to determine who the subjects of this study are. Jews in the camps did not constitute a coherent group of victims. Even in the prewar period, when they were overwhelmingly German or from German-speaking countries, their different personal backgrounds barely provided any common features for the fostering of a distinct group consciousness.[22] The religious, social, economic, and cultural lives of German Jews in Imperial Germany, the Weimar Republic, and the Third Reich were multidimensional, and their individual self-perceptions were highly heterogeneous. A similar picture holds true for the Habsburg Empire and post–World War I Austria.[23] Jews imprisoned in the prewar concentration camps thus came from many different milieus. Members of the workers' movement, left-wing parties, and trade unions are to be found in significant numbers among the Jewish prisoners of the early concentration camps in 1933–1934. But there were also liberals and conservatives, bourgeois civil servants, entrepreneurs, and the unemployed, "assimilates," Zionists, liberal, or orthodox religious believers, atheists, and baptized Christians. This heterogeneity conditioned particularly diverse manifestations of companionable and conflicting behaviors. As this study will show, underlying political and social tensions were aggravated in the camps' climate of violence, just as a—however distant—common heritage could generate feelings of cohesion and help relieve distress. Taking these considerations into account, the nomenclature "Jewish" or "Jew," to be used in this study, must therefore to a certain extent echo the categorization made by the Nazi persecutors. Individuals we would not refer to as "Jewish" in other contexts, not least because the definition would not be acceptable to themselves or to the rules of Jewish religious law *(Halakhah)*, nevertheless become subjects of this study because they were persecuted, imprisoned, and maltreated as Jews.

Topic and Approach

Jews were among the first prisoners taken into the makeshift concentration camps swiftly established only weeks after Hitler had come to power. Improvisation and a lack of coordination in the practices of arrest and imprisonment characterize the early phase of the history of the Nazi camps. Just as the sites were manifold—police buildings, military barracks, workhouses, prison wings, deserted factory halls, even an old ship—so too were the agencies that administered and ran the early concentration camps. In the absence of nationwide coordination, local and regional authorities tended to empower themselves. Despite the institutional differences that developed in the later SS concentration camps, this study adopts a broad definition and identifies as concentration camps all sites where Jews were held in indefinite detention without trial and without access to legal defense.[24] Documentation is sketchy, but it seems that almost every early concentration camp had its Jewish inmates.[25] A practice of pronounced anti-Jewish violence—from early on referred to by the euphemistic term "special treatment"—is reflected in the camp regulations issued by Dachau's commander Theodor Eicke in 1933. Inmates were grouped into three ranks, with "*Jews* and other persons who have become known as elements harmful to the people's community or as vicious agitators" assigned to the lowest rank and hence subjected to the harshest conditions.[26]

In a process beginning early in the summer of 1934, the diverse topography of the early concentration camps was reorganized under the supervision of the SS. Heinrich Himmler was the driving force behind the expansion of the concentration camp system. In his thinking, the camps played a crucial role as instruments of terror in the struggle against the "Jewish-Bolshevist system"—an alleged threat against which the German people had to be protected, at present and in the future.[27] Accordingly,

Jewish prisoners were always a part of the inmate populations of the camps. In 1938 their numbers skyrocketed through three large waves of mass arrests. In the spring of 1938, Jews were deported to Dachau after the annexation of Austria (the *Anschluss*). In the course of the year, Sachsenhausen and Buchenwald, too, became sites of mass imprisonment. Jews, detained first as "asocials" in June and then again in the aftermath of the November Pogrom, temporarily constituted the largest prisoner group in all three camps.

What was specific to the imprisonment of Jews in the prewar camps? To begin with, camp imprisonment in the prewar years was overwhelmingly a punishment for men. Women generally constituted no more than 4 to 10 percent of all prisoners before 1939.[28] The number of Jewish women in the prewar concentration camp can be estimated at a few hundred, and it is very unlikely that more than 1,000 were interned throughout the whole period. Although Jewish women suffered from the notorious "special treatment," albeit within a less brutal context, there is no documented case of a Jewish woman being killed in the prewar camps. With the mass arrests of 1938 targeting exclusively men, the camps mainly affected Jewish women indirectly. It was their husbands, fathers, sons, and brothers who were hauled away. Thus, women will inevitably be in the background of a historical account of the imprisonment of Jews in the prewar camps. This does not imply, though, that gender cannot be fruitfully used as an analytical category in the present study. Quite the contrary: as Jane Caplan has argued, the "unmarked masculine" of the concentration camps has to be "reconceptualised as more than an unproblematic norm which does not need 'gendering.'"[29] As we shall see when discussing the psychology of terror, masculinity was an important issue for the members of the Jewish prisoner group themselves.

In contrast to the dimensions of the wartime camps, the number of Jewish prisoners in the prewar concentration camps appears to have been relatively low. To date, concentration camp historiography overwhelmingly follows Falk Pingel's estimate for Dachau and calculates the share of Jews in the prisoner populations of all the prewar concentration camps as between 5 and 10 percent prior to the mass arrests of 1938.[30] I shall carefully probe this estimate. In the analysis of prisoner numbers, two important observations can be made. First, Jewish inmates in the camps were at all times conspicuously overrepresented in relation to their share of the population as a whole (which was 0.77 percent and 2.8 percent in Germany and

Austria, respectively).[31] Second, although before 1938 their absolute numbers were low in comparison both with other groups of prisoners and with the wartime figures, their significance was high. As I will shown, "the Jew" from the beginning was an essential entity firmly established in the camps' ecology of violence. Jewish prisoners' constant presence, both physically and discursively, as well as their exposed status as outcasts among the outcasts, structured the "order of terror" and influenced both perpetrators' and prisoners' perceptions and behaviors.[32]

Furthermore, the camps influenced the lives of Jews in Nazi Germany as objects of fear beyond the narrow circle of those who experienced them from the inside. Euphemistic propaganda, disturbing rumors, and in rare cases the shocking accounts of former prisoners who escaped from "the hands of Hitler's hell-hounds" and dared to speak, conveyed torture and murder to the outside world.[33] Paul Moore has pointed to the early concentration camps' visibility and audibility. Where camps were situated within populated environments, evidence of camp violence spread throughout the immediate neighborhoods.[34] Curiosity to see with his own eyes the much talked-about Breslau-Dürrgoy camp prompted Walter Tausk to choose the camp as the destination of a Sunday walk. As the Jewish writer noted in his diary, the sight of the barbed wire "cage" and of the armed *Sturmabteilung* (SA) men (storm troopers) guarding it was oppressing and he returned home with only one wish: "never to end up in this cage."[35] Tausk's words show that to those indirectly affected or living nearby, the deadly peril that radiated from the prewar camps felt real. The symbolic power of the concentration camp in threatening Jews thus cannot be underestimated.

Historians calculate that throughout the regime's 12-year existence, more than 1.2 million of Europe's Jews died in Nazi concentration camps. The overwhelming majority of them were killed in the gas chambers of Auschwitz-Birkenau and Lublin-Majdanek.[36] Whereas in popular perception Auschwitz has long been the *locus delicti* of the genocide of the Jews, research has lagged behind in investigating the connection between the concentration camps and the Holocaust. However, when addressing this desideratum, scholarly attention inherently gravitates to the mass murder perpetrated in Auschwitz and Majdanek—metropolises of death that, due to their "dual function" as concentration camps and extermination centers, do not necessarily represent the camp system as a whole.[37] Other concentration camps cannot compare with the enormous scale and organized nature of the destruction perpetrated there. Seen in this context, the camps of the prewar years, in particular, must pale in significance. It is scarcely surprising, then, that historians who link the concentration camps with the Holocaust tend to pass over the prewar period as a mere "antecedent," to use Raul Hilberg's term.[38] The teleological pull of the wartime genocide seems difficult to resist. Guided by their specific research interest, before even starting their analysis, historians conclude that "prior to 1942, the Nazi concentration camps were much less important for the persecution and murder of European Jewry."[39] Accordingly, the prewar period has sunk into historical obscurity. At most, it represents the "testing ground for the mistreatment of Jews."[40]

To avoid placing the prewar camps into an all-too-teleological development of the murder of the European Jews, scholarly attention must therefore turn to other processes, and to different research questions. Consequently, the epistemological interest of this study does not rest on the genocide as the culmination point of the prewar history of Jewish camp imprisonment. Under scrutiny here is the process of exclusion of Jews from German state and society during the years 1933 to 1939, and in this process, as I will demonstrate, the camps *did* play an important role. The prewar period emerges as a significant phase of transition that affected the living and working together of Jews and non-Jews and violently turned German citizens with Jewish roots into disrespected outlaws. Hence, my main aim is to investigate the role of the concentration camps in the process of marking, isolating, and terrorizing Jews as the prime enemies of German society in the Nazi era. Nowhere was their exclusion as a discriminated minority, their degradation from "German citizens of Jewish faith" to outlawed "Jews in Germany," enacted more radically and brutally than in the concentration camps. The camps' ostracizing effects were evident to the excluded themselves. Julius Meyer realized, "Here in the camp they distinguish between prisoners and Jews. So, we are now officially the Jews."[41] Thus concentration camps, as newly created sites of terror that forcefully sorted "community aliens" from valuable "Germans," contributed to the process of creating a "racially pure" Nazi state. However, this process of exclusion by means of concentration camp isolation, violation, and criminalization was complex. Although we know its outcomes, it requires careful analysis to illuminate the agencies and structures at work. How many Jews were incarcerated at which camps and during which moments of the prewar period? Who were the people involved in the arrests of Jews and their deportation to the camps? What can we say about their motives? What happened to the Jews once isolated in the camps? Where did the guards and overseers who perpetrated antisemitic violence come from? And how did Jewish prisoners react to their confinement and abuse?

The research questions I have outlined can be analyzed with the help of theories of inclusion and exclusion applied in both history and sociology to describe the dynamics and mechanisms of social change at work in German society during the Nazi era.[42] In his social-psychological study of Nazi perpetrators, Harald Welzer stresses that processes of inclusion and exclusion affect not only abstract categories of governance and the body politic but also "concrete people who constitute these societies and realize these forms of governance."[43] When German society in the 1930s was rapidly "national socialized" into privileged in-groups and discriminated-against out-groups, the "process of de-solidarization" between Jews and non-Jews was reflected in many small day-to-day situations, in countless decisions—to tolerate, participate, benefit, or protest—taken by the numerous individuals involved. It is the members of a society and their individual actions that condition the ultimate reformatting of social norms and values.[44]

A useful concept that widens the analytical scope and captures the agency of "ordinary" people within power structures is that of *Herrschaft als soziale Praxis*—domination as a social practice. With its historiographical roots in the history of everyday life, it intends to break open the binary and static opposition of rulers against ruled encountered in traditional theories of power and domination.[45] The concept turns the ruled into actors who themselves have the power to accept domination, obey orders, acquiesce in rule—or not. As Alf Lüdtke argues, the concept of domination as a social practice denotes a "field of forces in which actors relate to and deal with each other even if they sidestep or ignore each other. This field is not of a static size, its dimension as well as its contours change to the extent in which actors become operative or remain passive."[46] In the Nazi dictatorship, the terrorization of the victims was connected to the appeal felt by supporters, abettors, and accomplices of participating in an ultimate "power to kill."[47] Inside the concentration camps the field of forces was, of course, extremely constricted and unbalanced, with prisoners exposed to near-omnipotent guards who were in a position to violently dominate the inmates' every move. Wolfgang Sofsky has described this setting with the term "absolute power"—to all appearances a compelling concept, which nevertheless has to be critically assessed for its applicability as an explanation of the historical situation under scrutiny here.[48] Because in this book I will be concerned with a wider circle of actors involved in the arrests of Jews (including the agency of the victims themselves), as well as with situating the camps within the broader dynamics of social change, a concept as abstract and static as "absolute power" appears, at first glance, to have only limited explanatory potential.

The attempt of some historians to conceptualize the "social practice" of inclusion and exclusion at work in German society under Nazi rule by use of the term *Volksgemeinschaft* (people's community) holds much greater potential.[49] Originally used as a propaganda slogan in political circles of nearly all persuasions from World War I onward, the term "people's community" was quickly usurped by the National Socialist German Workers' Party (NSDAP) as a formula for their vision of a social utopia, "a promise of social community and national resurgence, of overcoming the class society and of political unity."[50] In contrast to other political parties, for whom it served as an integrative model, the NSDAP used the slogan of the "people's community" also in a disintegrative fashion to determine the "community" versus the "racial aliens" who should not belong to it—above all, Jews. The social utopia of the Nazi "people's community" held a destructive potential to be mobilized for the creation of social inequality. Those who succumbed to its appeal agreed at the same time to its inherent antisemitism, even if they might not have been antisemites themselves.[51]

Research on dynamics and mechanisms of social change in German society in the Nazi period is, of course, by no means a new historiographical phenomenon. Here, the recent *Volksgemeinschaft*-approach can build upon earlier studies, such as those of David Schoenbaum or Timothy W. Mason on the intentions and effects of Nazi social policies.[52] In the early 1980s Detlev Peukert analyzed Nazi Germany's "everyday history of racism," in which aspects of "normality" and "criminality" inherent in Nazi social agendas could coexist and affect the behavior and mentalities of both ordinary Germans and persecuted groups.[53] Newer research by Robert Gellately and Eric A. Johnson on the Gestapo and German society also points to the role of "ordinary Germans" in the enforcement of the regime's racial policies.[54] What constitutes the original analytical value of the concept of the "people's community," however, is its potential to expose and explain the enormous mobilizing forces unleashed by the promise of a new social order, involving elites as well as ordinary Germans.[55]

Historiography and Sources

The history of Jews in the Nazi concentration camps remains an under-researched topic. The fate of the Jews in prewar Nazi Germany has been analyzed many times, but historians have rarely given Jews' imprisonment in the concentration camps more than a passing glance. So far, no all-encompassing monograph has brought together the wealth of empirical information unearthed by numerous local studies of individual camp sites and an analytical approach that not only illuminates the bigger picture of Jewish camp imprisonment, but also embeds it in the broader context of anti-Jewish persecution before the war. Those few studies that have explicitly dealt with Jews in the Nazi concentration camps are of limited scope and narrow focus. They can be subdivided into three categories.

First, there are survey articles that establish periodizations and highlight general developments. Besides the article by Dieter Pohl that deals with the concentration camps and the "Final Solution," three additional studies exist. The earliest is Leni Yahil's pioneering work on Jewish prisoners in the prewar camps, based solely on eyewitness accounts, which detects different categories of arrest that brought Jews to the camps.[56] Detlef Garbe studies the history of Jewish prisoners from 1933 to 1945. He distinguishes an initial period of "individual actions" (1933–1938), when arrests of Jews on racial grounds were not of prime importance for the perpetrators, from a later period (1938–1939) characterized by mass arrests specifically targeting Jews "as Jews."[57] Jürgen Matthäus integrates the concentration camps into the history of the Holocaust. He points to dissimilarities between anti-Jewish persecution outside the camps and the abuse inside, and concludes that the practices of maltreatment and murder inside the camps always anticipated the persecution outside.[58]

Second are regional and local investigations into the situation of Jews in a particular camp or during a particular period of imprisonment. Scattered biographical case studies of individual Jewish prisoners also fall within this group. Both genres are characterized by a predominantly empirical approach to their subject, providing rich sources of valuable information for the present study. Detlef Garbe and Sabine Homann have researched the history of Jewish prisoners in the concentration camps of Hamburg.[59] The excellent study by Harry Stein of Jews in Buchenwald analyzes the severe living conditions of this group of prisoners, as well as their attempts to survive and resist the guards' violent excesses.[60] Linde Apel has published an equally well-researched account of Jewish women in the Ravensbrück concentration camp. Although focused, by the nature of the subject, on the war years, she gives an informed overview of the prior history of Jewish women's confinement in Moringen and Lichtenburg.[61] There are also various articles on Jews in Sachsenhausen, compiled by Günter Morsch and Susanne zur Nieden.[62] Finally, recent research has shed light on the history of Jews in the early camps of Osthofen and Oranienburg.[63] The mass imprisonment of Jews in the aftermath of the 1938 November Pogrom has been the subject of research by Barbara Distel, Wolfgang Benz, and Heiko Pollmeier.[64] Christian Faludi has edited a comprehensive source collection on the persecution of Jews branded "asocials" in June 1938 and their deportation to the camps.[65] Biographical case studies of Jewish prisoners of the prewar camps deal with personalities such as Hans Litten, the left-wing lawyer, or Olga Benario-Prestes, a Communist brought to Lichtenburg concentration camp in 1938. Other works, such as Jane Caplan's study of Gabriele Herz, imprisoned in Moringen in 1936–1937, originate from the editing of memoirs. Karl-Heinz Jahnke has published an illuminating study of Heinz Eschen, kapo of the Jewish block in Dachau. Hans-Peter Klausch's monograph on Jakob de Jonge appropriately situates the history of the camp imprisonment of a Jewish merchant from Weener, East Frisia, within the wider context of anti-Jewish persecution in Nazi Germany.[66]

The third category of studies of Jews in Nazi concentration camps approaches the subject from a specific methodological angle, utilizing analytical categories such as religion, gender, or memory. Thomas Rahe investigates religious activities of Jewish concentration camp prisoners in Bergen-Belsen and Auschwitz.[67] Essays compiled by Gisela Bock deal with Jewish women in the camp system, overwhelmingly in wartime camps like Ravensbrück or Auschwitz-Birkenau.[68] The application of gender as an analytical tool for the study of Jewish men in Nazi concentration camps has only just begun, and the uncharted territory ahead appears to have great scholarly potential.[69]

Close readings of survivor memoirs and analyses of collective memorial practices reveal important insights into both the experiences of Jewish prisoners and the remembrance of their histories in postwar narratives. The doyen of the field is James E. Young, whose work identifies Holocaust survivors' accounts as standing in the Jewish tradition of writing as a response to catastrophe—an observation corroborated by the studies of Yosef H. Yerushalmi.[70] Like most scholarly works on memory, however, Young focuses on the wartime period and the "Final Solution." For the prewar camps we are faced with huge gaps in the research. Isolated studies on the camp experiences and memories of the "November Jews," and of Jewish prisoners interned in Osthofen in 1933–1934, reveal that the issues at stake here are very different from those of the later period. The fact that the persecuted had formerly been equal members of the very society that excluded them was particularly painful for the victims. To those who witnessed or participated in bringing about the arrest and imprisonment of Jews in the camp, memory bore great unease.[71]

Looking at the historiography of the Nazi camps more broadly, the focus of the existing literature on the study of Jews in wartime camps and subcamps is striking. The prewar period generally has long been neglected, and has only recently become the object of scholarly interest and debate. Leaving aside Martin Broszat's standard work, based on a specialist report for the Frankfurt "Auschwitz Trial" in 1963–1964, and Falk Pingel's groundbreaking study on prisoners under SS-rule, published in 1978, concentration camp history started to develop into a serious field of research only in the early to mid 1980s.[72] It focused first on general histories of the large, well-known concentration camp complexes located on the territory of the *Altreich* (Nazi Germany in its borders before 1938), such as Dachau, Buchenwald, Bergen-Belsen, Sachsenhausen, and Neuengamme.[73] During the 1990s, historiography turned toward a more institutional and organizational history, with important works by Gudrun Schwarz, Johannes Tuchel, Klaus Drobisch and Günther Wieland, Karin Orth, and others. They all contribute greatly to our understanding of the system of the Nazi concentration camps.[74] The first decade of the new millennium saw an exponential increase in research, which also finally mapped the long-neglected early and prewar concentration camps onto the topography of terror. Important studies, such as those by Carina Baganz on concentration camps in Saxony and Irene Mayer-von Götz on sites of terror in Berlin, both focusing in particular on the time before 1936–1937, make it very clear that the legacy of the early concentration camps left its imprint on the evolution of the later system.[75] Recently, Nikolaus Wachsmann and Christian Goeschel published the papers from an international conference on the prewar Nazi camps organized by Birkbeck College's research project "Before the Holocaust: Concentration Camps in Nazi Germany, 1933–1939," in which this study has its origin.[76]

The relevant source material for this study is of diverse provenance. Firstly, there are what may be called the "perpetrator records," produced by the persecuting agencies and administering institutions of the Nazi state and party. These include the remnants of the mostly destroyed camp files kept in the administration departments of the concentration camps themselves. Fragmentary admission lists as well as "head counts" and prisoner fluctuation records from the large camps of Buchenwald, Dachau, and Sachsenhausen are stored in the archives of the International Tracing Service of the Red Cross (ITS). Although the holdings also contain documentation relating to individual prisoners, such as the camp register (available for Oranienburg) and card indices with basic biographical information, the ITS records are mainly of statistical value. Of greater value in reconstructing prisoner case studies are the sometimes meager, sometimes remarkably voluminous, personal imprisonment files composed by the agency largely responsible for prewar deportations and releases of Jews to and from the camps, the Gestapo.[77] The arrests of Jewish concentration camp prisoners have also entered the records of the other national, regional, and local authorities involved, such as various Reich ministries (Interior, Foreign Affairs, Justice), the Prussian provincial governors (Oberpräsidenten), governmental districts' executives and county executives (Regierungspräsidenten and Landräte), as well as local police stations and NSDAP Gau (district) offices in all other German states.

Given the remarkable publicity for the prewar camps, there are numerous press items that report the imprisonment of Jews. These range from short notes to lengthy articles in the coordinated local or national newspapers, as well as occasional special features in Der Stürmer or Das Schwarze Korps. Foreign press reports, such as those published in the British Manchester Guardian and Times or the French Le Temps, brought the fate of Jewish prisoners to international attention. Many of these reports vigorously denounced camp terror against Jews, as did German exile publications such as Juden in brauner Hölle, the 1934 Konzentrationslager, or the Schwarzbuch.[78] Former camp inmates, both Jewish and non-Jewish, who had reached exile, also helped to spread the word of camp atrocities. Two early examples are the reports, published in 1934, by Max Abraham, religious counselor and teacher, and Werner Hirsch, high-ranking Communist functionary, both of whom suffered in the SA camp at Oranienburg.[79] Their contemporary testimonies belong to the second large group of sources: personal documents and eyewitness accounts handed down in either written or oral form. Testimonies and biographical narration by the persecuted and their family members are of essential value to the present study. Precisely because most of the perpetrator records were destroyed, we depend heavily on the information preserved in survivors' testimonies. These sources not only help to reconstruct and correct the history of events, they also contain the valuable dimension of a history of experience.[80] Personal accounts tell of the effects of oppression and violence, as well as the victims' attempts to assert themselves against acts of camp terror. Highlighting the interplay between the regime's policies and measures, the perspectives and attitudes of the Jews, and the actions and reactions of the surrounding society, I apply an approach that Saul Friedländer has conceptualized as the "integrated history" of the Holocaust.[81] In contrast to his monumental *Nazi Germany and the Jews,* my study also incorporates post-1945 memories to represent the complex experiences of the historical reality.[82]

Postwar trials conducted by the Allied military courts as well as the German state prosecutors' offices form the third source corpus. Atrocities committed against Jewish concentration camp prisoners were a subject matter at the International Military Tribunal in Nuremberg (IMT). The court used documents such as Eicke's camp regulations as incriminating evidence. In the case of Dachau concentration camp, the investigation of early murders, initiated by the head prosecuting attorney of the Munich District Court—closed after his dismissal in 1934—was taken up after 1945 by both the IMT and the German prosecuting authorities that were ultimately responsible for bringing prewar camp perpetrators to justice.

My study assumes a basic chronological structure. I divide the history of Jews in the prewar concentration camps into three broad phases: 1933–1934, 1935–1938, and 1938–1939. Within each period, I focus first on the practices of arrest and release, outlining the motives and rationales for taking Jews into camp confinement. Second, I examine the reality inside the camps, that is, the treatment of Jews, their place in the daily routine of labor and public humiliation, their relationship with the guards and the other prisoners, as well as the distinctive dynamics within the "Jew blocks" themselves. Third, the implications and effects of Jewish camp imprisonment on broader society, and on the formation of the Nazi "people's community," are made apparent. I will close with a short glimpse into the history of Jews in the wartime concentration camps, outlining continuities and discontinuities detectable in comparison with the prewar period.

1

IN THE BEGINNING THERE WAS VIOLENCE

"Protective Custody" and Arrests of Jews, 1933–1934

Accident? Suicide? Murder? When Rudolf S. Mosse died on August 21, 1933, at Berlin's Potsdamer Platz, he had been on a transport from Columbia-Haus to Oranienburg concentration camp. The forty-three-year-old member of a well-known German-Jewish dynasty and nephew of the famous publisher of the same name, traveled to the camp under armed SA escort. He was to be taken to Oranienburg via public transportation. Later that day, an officer of the nearby police department in Vossstrasse described the incident to the deceased's widow and brother as follows: "Rudolf Mosse was to be transferred to Oranienburg concentration camp on the order of the State Police Office and guarded by an SA man . . . In front of the Hotel Fürstenhof building, Stresemannstrasse 130, R. must have thrown himself in front of a passing lorry. It seems that the SA man was unable to prevent R. from doing so without endangering his own life. There must be plenty of eyewitnesses for that."[1] Confronted with this information, the family was shocked yet skeptical of the explanation that Mosse had committed suicide. Dora Mosse remembered her husband reassuring her only a fortnight previously that he would not fear his arrest and neither should she worry about him; in these turbulent times, "all decent people sit in concentration camps."[2] Why should he have suddenly changed his mind? Mosse's lifelong political engagement as a democrat, a member of the German State Party (DStP), and a functionary of the Reichsbanner Black-Red-Gold and of the Reich Federation of Jewish Front Soldiers (RjF), made him everything the new rulers of Germany detested.[3] Would they not have wanted to get him out of the way—if necessary, by using brutal means? In the eyes of the Nazis, political violence meant "taking revenge." What exactly was the nature of the "unsettled scores" in the case of Rudolf S. Mosse? And who were the victim's enemies?

After his return from the Great War, Mosse had become a passionate farmer. Convinced that changing German Jewry's urban-economic profile could undermine antisemitism, he settled on the Stangenhagen estate near Trebbin in East Brandenburg and advocated the education of Jews in agriculture.[4] Although the Mosses had experienced anti-Jewish sentiment before, the National Socialist Krüger family's move from Luckenwalde to Trebbin in 1930 marked the start of an incessant systematic harassment. Both father Krüger and his son Hans were active in building up the local division of SA storm troopers As part of their campaign, they incited the villagers against the Jewish family. According to Dora Mosse, Krüger senior was not motivated solely by antisemitism. Her husband had persistently refused to sell the SA man a piece of land he had set his sights on.[5] In 1932 the family's property was vandalized, and Mosse, on his way home from the fields, was ambushed and beaten up by the Krügers. The situation deteriorated rapidly after January 30, 1933. On April 8 a group of SA militia (Sturmbann) stormed Stangenhagen, frantically searching the house for Mosse, who hid in the bedroom. After the intruders had left without having found him, the family—Rudolf, Dora, and their three children—fled to Berlin. Mosse was forced to give up his farming dreams and Stangenhagen was sold.[6]

On August 19, 1933, Mosse was arrested on the order of the Gestapo. What exactly he had to bear during his two-day confinement in the hands of the SS in Columbia-Haus can be reconstructed only indirectly. In the files of the Institute for Forensic Medicine of Berlin's Charité Hospital, there survives the autopsy report by the coroner who examined the corpse after the incident at Potsdamer Platz. Conspicuously, the examiner makes no direct comment about the fact that Mosse's body bore marks of torture. But when we decipher the report's antiseptic medical language, we find signs of brutal violation of the sexual organs, the anus and underbelly, and the inguinal region.[7] These violations could hardly have stemmed from the "accident" itself, which had primarily affected Mosse's upper body. In other words, the forensic report makes it plain that Mosse suffered extreme violent abuse in Columbia-Haus.

Physically and mentally debilitated as he was, the Jewish prisoner must have been petrified of what would happen to him in Oranienburg—a dreaded concentration camp that had claimed the lives of at least five prisoners by August 1933.[8] There, SA Sturmbannführer Hans Krüger, Mosse's old foe from Trebbin, had made a swift career as the camp's head of interrogations. In the end, it probably was as his widow suspected: "Terrible things must have happened with Rudi and inside of him . . . He could not bear the prospect of getting under Krüger's thumb."[9] Mosse, an otherwise unshakable German citizen of Jewish faith, who had announced before that he was not afraid to be taken into "protective custody" *(Schutzhaft)* and who regarded concentration camp confinement as a kind of badge of honor, must have felt horror and despair when his torturers, after a two-day ordeal in Columbia-Haus, wanted to transport him to Oranienburg. For him, as for many other captives forced to endure brutal abuse, Oranienburg figured as a "camp of revenge," to quote the poignant term coined by Günter Morsch.[10]

The case of Rudolf S. Mosse illustrates many typical features of the particularly violent beginning of the history of Jews in the Nazi concentration camps. It attests, first and foremost, to the outright brutality that radiated from these sites of terror, causing fear and panic not only in those already imprisoned there but also in those threatened with deportation to the camp. Mosse's story, ending between the Gestapo headquarters in Prinz-Albrecht-Strasse, its substation at Columbia-Haus, and Oranienburg, also reveals the diverse nature of the early concentration camps in terms of organization, administrative responsibility, and guard personnel. Located just outside Berlin, Oranienburg concentration camp was run by the SA division 208. By contrast, Columbia-Haus at this time served as a Gestapo prison for captives still under investigation by the political police. Named after its location on Berlin's Columbiastrasse, an avenue in the Tempelhof district, the building of a former military jail was given a new use as a detention center in the summer of 1933. Officially, it was declared an SS concentration camp only in December 1934.[11]

In addition to the diversity of the camp sites, the variety of actors involved in the arrest and deportation of Jews to the early concentration camps is also worth emphasizing. As the implementation of camp imprisonment was initially a regional matter and there were no attempts at nationwide coordination prior to April 1934, many early concentration camps were originally established on the initiative of local powerholders, some of them representatives of the state, others activists of the Nazi party and its paramilitary units. As we saw in the Mosse case, the SA was very active in pressing for "protective custody." The brownshirts were supported and sometimes rivaled by the SS, the Gestapo, and the police. There were also other, less predictable agents at work in bringing Jews to the early camps. As I will demonstrate in detail below, the participation of individual members of the public is especially striking in arrest cases in 1933–1934. Moreover, the motives for the denunciation, arrest, and imprisonment of Jews were not limited to the strictly "political." Quite often we find racially inflected economic or other private interests lying at the heart of an arrest.[12]

We also can see that there are difficulties in judging camp violence juridically. Mosse's death cannot be unambiguously classified as a suicide. Nor can we speak of it as an accident. The act must rather be situated in a distinct legal grey zone characteristic of many deaths occurring in the context of the concentration camps. Where brutal force was wielded against defenseless prisoners, the boundaries between suicide and murder often blurred.

Finally, Rudolf S. Mosse died in brightest daylight at the Potsdamer Platz, one of the busiest, most crowded places in Berlin. As the policeman who reported the incident to the family remarked, "there must have been plenty of eyewitnesses." Kurt Jakob Ball-Kaduri, a contemporary resident of Berlin, testified about the public effects of Mosse's death. According to the tax lawyer, who after his emigration to Palestine became a historian of German Jewry, the incident caused a stir. Berlin's Jewish Community, in particular, was severely shaken by the death, coming as it did at a critical time when German Jews hoped that the Nazis' initial antisemitic onslaught, launched in the spring of 1933, had come to an end. In April the Ball family itself had been hit by camp terror when Kurt Jakob's brother Fritz was abducted to the SA torture site in General-Pape-Strasse.[13] An entry in Thomas Mann's diary dated September 13, 1933, proves that Mosse's death also attracted international attention. Mann had learned from the French paper *Le Temps* that Mosse, a decorated war veteran, had been returned to his family in a coffin that had been soldered to conceal the crime.[14] Finally, the stark and lasting impression that Mosse's death made on Jews all over Germany finds its expression in the memoir of Otto Blumenthal. When together with other Jews from the Lake Constance region he faced deportation to Dachau in November 1938, Blumenthal contemplated committing suicide to evade the horrors of the camp—"as Rudolf Mosse had done." To German Jews, Mosse had been a symbol for successful acculturation; was his violent death a portent for the death of German-Jewish coexistence as a whole?[15]

This chapter investigates the arrests of Jews and their deportation to the early concentration camps. After analyzing the institution of "protective custody," I will introduce different groups of Jewish prisoners and re-construct their various paths into custody. The investigation will start with radical political activists and then turn to left-wing politicians and political journalists. I will discuss in detail the persecution of Jewish jurists, and then, focusing on a more rural milieu, I will analyze the arrests of "ordinary Jews" who fell victim to camp terror on the basis of economic or private conflicts. My aim is to clarify who those Jews were that fell victim to early camp terror, and who instigated and carried out their arrests.

"Protective Custody"

The National Socialist assumption of governmental power on January 30, 1933, marked the starting point of a political process that transformed what had remained of the parliamentary democracy of the Weimar Republic into a one-party dictatorship, divided German society into friends and foes, and ultimately led to world war.[16] The initial process saw a massive wave of terror sweep through the country. Its main perpetrators were SA and SS men who, together with members of the Steel Helmet paramilitary organization (Stahl-helm), were elevated to the status of auxiliary policemen by Prussian Min-ister of the Interior Hermann Göring. With his decree of February 22, brutal paramilitary activism became state-sanctioned.[17] Long withheld, the mo-ment of reckoning with the Nazi movement's enemies had come. Concen-tration camps quickly became the new rulers' sharpest instruments of op-pression. There emerged a diverse landscape of hundreds of detention sites established on the initiative of local state authorities and Nazi potentates and activists practiced in the use of political violence.[18] It was not until the summer of 1934 that these early camps were reorganized under the super-vision of the SS—a process overseen by Theodor Eicke in his capacity as Inspector of the Concentration Camps.[19]

Underlining the importance of the concentration camps for the con-solidation of totalitarian power and the making of the Nazi "people's com-munity," I focus on the hitherto unexplored antisemitic dimension of early camp terror. Beyond the general conclusion that Jews had been among the camps' first prisoners, scholars do not seem to have gone very far in their interpretation of this phenomenon. Most historians of the early concen-tration camps ascribe the reasons for the imprisonment of Jews either to their Communist or left-leaning political activities, or to a vague set of "ra-cial reasons" that are regarded as self-explanatory and generally not ana-lyzed any further.[20] Historians of the initial phase of Jewish persecution, in turn, acknowledge that Jews were taken into concentration camps from early on, but they, too, do not dwell systematically on this specific form of discrimination.[21] Other forms of exclusion, such as street violence, day-to-day discrimination, anti-Jewish legislation, economic boycotts, and expropriations, dominate the historiographical picture.[22]

This study aims to bring together these seemingly independent campaigns of terror: the suppression of political opponents and the initial antisemitic onslaught. Under investigation here is the role of the concentration camp in the societal transformation process launched in spring 1933—the effort of "national socializing" German state and society by marking, isolating, and terrorizing those considered harmful to the "people's community" in the making. Along the way to seizing total power, the Nazi party not only had usurped the state through administrative-constitutional transformations on a structural level, but also, on an ideological level, had redefined the enemies of the Nazi movement as the enemies of German society at large. A telling example of this is the process by which the institution of "protective custody" gradually became antisemitically charged.

The emergency decree issued by President Hindenburg on February 28, 1933, constituted the basis for the use of "protective custody," and ultimately for the establishment of the concentration camps. This so-called Reichstag Fire Decree suspended central constitutional rights and gave the executive the right to impose detention without trial.[23] Although detention in early concentration camps was also implemented without official orders, the institution of protective custody served as the legal-administrative foundation for most of the early arrests. Vague and ambiguous in its definition, protective custody became "the embodiment of the political fight against the opposition in the Third Reich."[24] It served as an instrument that ex post facto "legalized" the illegal features of Hitler's "seizure of power."[25]

Jane Caplan has pointed out that although, in a triad with concentration camps and an independent political police, protective custody became a "foundation stone of the new extra-constitutional order" in Germany, the National Socialists did not "invent" indefinite detention without trial.[26] Its roots stretched back into the mid-nineteenth century. From the first implementation in Prussia in the wake of the failed revolution of 1848–1849, the power of detention without trial served as an instrument of political repression beyond judicial control for governments in Imperial Germany and the Weimar Republic.[27] Judging from the highly ambiguous term itself, it is unclear who was to be protected and from whom—the detained individual from the danger of their own safety, as the literal meaning suggests, or the state and the public from the unwanted insurgent. The detention practice, however, was clear: protective custody prisoners suffered from disfranchisement and from arbitrary, violent treatment. They were held against their will and not for their protection.[28] A significant discontinuity between pre- and post-1933 lies in numbers and in treatment of prisoners: Whereas protective custody affected only a few hundred during the First World War and a few thousand during the Weimar Republic, the National Socialists would build on their interpretation of protective custody a large-scale and brutal system of police detention and concentration camps ultimately affecting millions.[29]

On the evening of February 27, 1933, the Reichstag in Berlin went up in flames. Both the circumstances and the question of who exactly set fire to the plenary chamber still remain unresolved. What is clear, however, is that the Nazis were quick to blame the radical left for the attack. A large-scale arrest action was launched that very night.[30] With national elections just a week away, the extensive manhunt was aimed at left-wing political parties and organizations, first and foremost the Communist Party of Germany (KPD). Formally, protective custody orders were based on the Reichstag Fire Decree's explicitly posited aim to "ward off seditious Communist acts." This enemy conception, however, was quickly expanded when, on March 3, Göring declared that the police measures should "target also those . . . who collaborate with the Communists, and, even indirectly, support and foster their criminal intentions."[31] Around 5,000 people were taken into protective custody between February 28 and March 5, 1933. An unknown number of these prominent left-wing activists were of Jewish origin.[32] Who, then, were these prominent Jewish political activists arrested at this very early stage immediately after the Reichstag Fire? What happened to them once they were captured? And how were their cases used to construct the antisemitic profile of "the Jewish enemy" as a threat to the Nazi "people's community" in the making? I will answer these questions with an analysis of four individual case studies, looking at Werner Scholem, Werner Hirsch, Erich Mühsam, and Hans Litten.

In contrast to the pervasive political myth that "Jewish Bolsheviks" dominated the Communist party, not a single KPD member of the German Reichstag in 1933 was Jewish. Even in 1924 the party had sent only six delegates of Jewish roots to the national parliament.[33] One of them was Werner

Scholem, who belonged to the Reichstag until 1928. Being a founding member of the KPD, Scholem quickly figured as one of the party's most influential leaders. A dramatic break with the KPD came in 1926, after his ultra-left-wing position had become incompatible with the party line.[34] In the night of the Reichstag Fire, he was among the Nazis' very first captives. His mother reported, "This night, Werner has been arrested again! . . . At 4.30 this morning, a constable and two men appeared and after they were not let in, they opened the door with a lock pick, nice isn't it? They searched the place for one hour . . . but they did not find *anything*, because Werner does not have anything forbidden in his apartment, but they arrested him nevertheless, because they had the order . . . he is also mentioned again in every paper, I do not understand why they are so interested in Werner! Was he so important then? Evidently."[35] Betty Scholem's observations are not only illuminating with regard to the apparent orderliness of the early arrest procedures, carried out by policemen. We also learn that the regime did not keep silent about the arrests. Reports in the papers made Scholem's capture a public affair.[36] The unfolding events confirmed his mother's suspicion that Scholem was, indeed, a very important catch for the new rulers. Incarcerated in the Moabit prison, under the authority of the German legal system, an indictment for high treason was constructed against him. It accused Scholem and his wife of having participated in Communist activities to undermine the Reichswehr through agitation among soldiers. In their interrogations they both denied any involvement in such conspiratorial activities. His wife was released in November 1933 and escaped to Great Britain; Scholem was kept in prison for two years awaiting his trial.[37]

After one and a half years of prison, Scholem was first deported to Lichtenburg concentration camp, then to Dachau, and later to Buchenwald. All efforts to effect his release with the necessary visa failed, and after having suffered in the concentration camps for more than five years, Scholem was killed in Buchenwald on July 17, 1940.[38] What difference did his Jewish origin make in the persecution? In a letter to Walter Benjamin, Gershom Scholem points to his brother's significance as a prototypical Jewish enemy of the Nazis: "Göbbels [*sic*] needs a few Jews there, with whom he can demonstrate that he has crushed bolshevism, and this, among other things, is what my brother is destined for."[39] Werner Scholem himself understood that his Jewish ancestry was an additional factor in his suffering. In October 1933 he wrote to his brother: "You will have heard about my fate from mother. I am affected in two respects, as a Jew and as a former politician." He signed this letter "your brother Job," identifying himself with the biblical character punished despite his righteousness.[40]

Whereas Werner Scholem broke with the Communist party in the mid-1920s, Werner Hirsch remained committed and held a senior position. Hirsch worked as the chief editor of the party paper *Die Rote Fahne* (The Red Flag) and as right-hand man to the Moscow-loyal party leader Ernst Thälmann. Engaged in the establishment of the KPD from its foundation in January 1919, he was crucial in building up party infrastructure. His political activities brought him into conflict with the legal authorities, and Hirsch was arrested and taken to trial at various times during the Weimar years. When the immediate manhunt for leading Communists began in the night of the Reichstag Fire, Hirsch was one of the top targets. He was arrested together with Thälmann on March 3, 1933. He was kept in several early concentration camps, among them Brandenburg, Oranienburg, and Lichtenburg. Eventually, on the intervention of his mother, who used her personal contact to Göring's wife-to-be, Emmy Sonnemann, Hirsch was released from Lichtenburg concentration camp in late 1934.[41] Via Prague, he was able to escape to Moscow, where he joined the exiled leaders of the KPD. After difficult years in the Soviet Union, he fell victim to intrigues and the Stalinist purges and died in the Lubyanka prison in October 1941.[42]

Shortly after his release from Lichtenburg, Hirsch authored two pamphlets on the Nazi camps.[43] Both are suffused with political idealism, interpreting the concentration camp as a school for the workers where they learned that only a united front of Socialists and Communists could stop Hitler. In his writings, Hirsch described the tortures he had to suffer and gave a detailed account of the crimes perpetrated by the Gestapo, SS, and SA. As a fellow inmate in the Brandenburg concentration camp later attested, Hirsch's "non-Aryan" status aggravated the violent treatment he had to suffer: "The SS had an infinite anger for him, because among all those who were there, he was the only one who in the eyes of the SS was considered a Jew, and he, of all people, proved to be very courageous and steadfast."[44] Similarly, KPD party functionary Rudolf Bernstein, who was also imprisoned in the early concentration camps, was abused first and foremost as a Jew.[45] When Hirsch recorded that the prisoners of Brandenburg's "Jew section" (*Judenstation*) became victims of "ill-treatments in the most bestial form," he remembered one fellow sufferer in particular: Erich Mühsam.[46]

Mühsam embodied everything the Nazis hated: he was one of the few surviving leaders of the Munich Republic of Councils that had emerged in the Bavarian revolution of 1918–1919 as a short-lived attempt to establish a socialist state in Germany; he was a radical anarchist fighting for independent, self-organized socialism and the abolition of any kind of rule; he was a Bohemian intellectual who had denounced National Socialism and satirized Hitler in the most eloquent ways—and he was a Jew.[47] The Nazis held Mühsam responsible for the more violent chapters of the Bavarian revolution. In particular, Nazi propaganda persistently accused Mühsam of involvement in the detention and execution of ten political captives held hostage in Munich's Luitpold Gymnasium by guards loyal to the second Munich Republic of Councils. Seven of those shot on April 30, 1919, were members of the Thule Society, a forerunner of the NSDAP. The Red Army's so-called murder of hostages became a topos widely dispersed in right-twing-*völkisch* circles. Saul Friedländer stresses that "the executions . . . became the quintessential illustration of Jewish Bolshevik terror in Germany." Gradually, Mühsam—although completely innocent and absent from the scene due to his own imprisonment—was made responsible for the bloodbath.[48] Once the Nazis assumed power, the myth was cemented. Nazi propaganda drummed it into concentration camp guards. According to his wife, the guards were handed photographs of him captioned "The Hostage Murderer Mühsam."[49] The false narrative served as a pretext for both verbal and physical abuse in Sonnenburg, Brandenburg, and Oranienburg.[50] Upon her first visit to Sonnenburg on April 8, 1933, Kreszentia Mühsam found that "Mühsam was terribly mauled. I could hardly hide my horror. He sat on a chair, did not wear glasses—they had crushed those—his teeth were knocked out, and his beard was cut by the barbarians in such a way that the Jewish type had become a caricature."[51]

Mühsam's death coincided with the SS takeover of the concentration camps. On July 6, 1934, only days after the "Röhm purge"—the regime's violent strike against the SA leadership—an SS squad composed of storm troopers from Württemberg and a small unit from Dachau took over the Oranienburg camp. They marked the end of SA rule with violent assaults on the inmates.[52] On the morning of July 10, 1934, Mühsam's body was found hanged in the latrines. His fellow prisoners were sure that the alleged suicide was in fact murder.[53] When Kreszentia Mühsam confronted the former deputy commandant SA Sturmführer Hans Stahlkopf—whom she found drinking with other sacked SA men in a tavern opposite the camp on the day of Mühsam's death—and accused him of killing her husband, he, to no surprise, denied any involvement in the act. To her utter disgust, he pulled out from his pocket a photograph of her husband that showed him wounded, maltreated, and with a completely shaven head. The picture was captioned: "The Hostage Murderer Mühsam."[54]

Hans Litten is our fourth example of an individual of Jewish background who was a prominent political opponent of the Nazis and was arrested in the immediate aftermath of the Reichstag Fire. As a left-wing lawyer, Litten had fiercely fought the Nazi movement and publically exposed the NSDAP's essential dilemma: how to balance the revolutionary radicalism of the SA, manifesting itself in political violence and street terror, with the tactical legalism of the party leadership, who were determined to come to power through electoral successes. Before his death in Dachau in February 1938, Litten suffered a five-year ordeal in numerous prisons and concentration camps, where he encountered not only Scholem, Hirsch, and Mühsam but many other Jewish and non-Jewish prisoners, who later told of the horrendous outbursts of violence Litten had had to suffer.[55]

The mere mention of Litten's name in Hitler's presence is said to have provoked the Führer into outbursts of rage. Those who tried to intervene on her son's behalf told Irmgard Litten that "Hitler's face went purple when he heard the name."[56] What had the lawyer done to incur Hitler's personal hatred? On Litten's request, a Berlin court, in May 1931, summoned Adolf Hitler as a witness to testify in a trial against members of the SA Storm 33 who had attacked the Eden Dance Palace—a place frequented by socialist workers and left-leaning groups. The nighttime riot, one in a series of violent street battles waged between Communists and the SA, left some twenty people injured. Four members of the SA Storm were subsequently tried for attempted murder. Litten, in his effort to make a crucial political point in the trial, was determined to prove that "the violence committed by Storm 33 was an essential element of the Nazi program, carried out on orders directly from Hitler."[57] Examined by the lawyer, Hitler insisted that the NSDAP, in its striving for political power, operated solely through constitutional methods. The lawyer's searching questions on the Nazis' intentional use of violence soon cornered Hitler, who struggled to maintain his line of argument. This examination was nothing less than a threat to Hitler's political career. Litten was marked as an enemy; Nazi characterizations of his oppositional legal activities were infused with antisemitic stereotypes.[58]

Figure 1.1 Aerial view of the Sonnenburg prison, early 1930s.
Herder-Institut, Bildarchiv.

The first concentration camp to which Litten was deported after being taken into protective custody was the Prussian state concentration camp of Sonnenburg near Küstrin (today Poland). The camp was installed in a large penitentiary, which had to be closed in 1931 due to poor sanitary conditions. Within the building's three wings, prisoners were held in single cells or in larger dormitory cells. Besides Mühsam and Litten, KPD functionaries Rudolf Bernstein and Georg Benjamin, brother of Walter Benjamin, suffered from Sonnenburg's regime of terror. For Litten, the choice of location could not have been worse. Members of SA Storm 33 had been deployed as camp guards in Sonnenburg. The lawyer, who had once accused their comrades in the courtroom, was now tortured by them in the most horrific ways.[59]

The four men introduced here—all arrested in the week between the Reichstag Fire and the national elections on March 5, 1933—were outright opponents of Nazism. They had exposed themselves through their political work against Hitler and his movement. To be sure, their fight for their revolutionary ideals did not make them supporters or defenders of the Weimar Republic. They were radicals prepared to apply illegal means to overcome the parliamentary-democratic order, and their actions had repeatedly brought them into conflict with the law before 1933. Once captured after Hitler's seizure of power, Scholem, Hirsch, Mühsam, and Litten were trophies whose maltreatment satisfied a long-held lust for vengeance on the part of the Nazi movement's paramilitary units, first and foremost the SA. The arrest of these prominent protagonists was also used to convince conservative elites and the broader public of the legitimacy of the new rulers' violent "fight against Marxism." The regime exploited their left-wing sympathies to construct a Jewish-Bolshevist threat, from which the nascent Nazi "people's community" had to be defended by means of protective custody and concentration camps. Propaganda Minister Joseph Goebbels evoked the names of Mühsam, Litten, and Scholem in his 1935 speech at the Nuremberg party rally as belonging to those Jews who pulled the strings in the Communist attempt to poison the world.[60] In the camps, Scholem, Hirsch, Mühsam, and, Litten were tormented to present an example of Nazi power and to initiate guards into a practice of brutal antisemitic conduct. Three of them lost their lives in the Nazi concentration camps.

Arrests of Social Democrats and Political Journalists

Despite the massive terror campaign launched after the Reichstag Fire, the Nazi party did not gain a majority of the votes in the national elections of March 5, 1933. After the elections the Nazis quickly increased their levels of persecution and political violence. The number of arrests and kidnappings skyrocketed to figures of between 45,000 and 50,000 by the end of April 1933.[61] Prisons, police jails, and court arrest facilities reached their capacity limits, and new detention sites were established. Protective custody was expanded beyond the arrests of Communists, and the wider circle of captives now also included large numbers of members of the Social Democratic Party of Germany (SPD), the trade union movements, and smaller left-wing parties like the Socialist Workers' Party (SAP). Furthermore, representatives of professional guilds identified with the "Weimar system," such as journalists and lawyers, were arrested. The share of Jewish protagonists within these groups of prisoners is much higher than among the Communists and political radicals initially targeted.

The persecution of SPD functionaries, members of the Reichstag and the parliaments of the German states (*Länder*), reached its peak with the banning of the party on June 22, 1933. In the course of the twelve years of the Nazi dictatorship, thousands of Social Democrats were taken into protective custody and hundreds lost their lives.[62] Among the arrested were a significant number of Jews. Active as local politicians and engaged in social work, many of them were well known in their communities. Alfred Kantorowicz, for example, served as SPD deputy in the Bonn Municipal Council. He was also a renowned professor of dentistry and a member of the Association of Socialist Physicians. Arrested on April 1, 1933, Kantorowicz was deported first to Börgermoor concentration camp and later to Lichtenburg. His fellow prisoners remember him providing most needed medical service in the camp infirmary.[63] Jewish Social Democrats also took part in active resistance to the Nazi dictatorship. Kurt Eisner, whose film and photo studio in Berlin was used by an SPD resistance group for their conspiratorial work, was arrested on March 7, 1933. His status as a prominent prisoner derived not least from his father's fame as a leading activist of the Bavarian revolution. Eisner junior was held in various prisons and camps until he was killed in Buchenwald on August 26, 1942.[64]

The two most prominent Social Democrats of Jewish descent who fell victim to early Nazi terror were Ludwig Marum, a leading representative of the SPD in Baden, and Ernst Heilmann, the charismatic chairman of the party's parliamentary group in the Prussian Diet.[65] Given their status as influential leaders of the labor movement, the Nazis staged their deportation to the concentration camp as a public spectacle to reinforce the stereotype of the Jewish *Bonze* (bigwig) who betrayed the workers. These performances were meant to impress, deter, and ultimately win over the workers, who might, the Nazis calculated, disassociate themselves from their humiliated leaders and shift their allegiance to National Socialism instead. Paul Moore has discussed the deportations of prominent political enemies, Jewish and non-Jewish, enacted in ritual punishment processions as a favored tactic of the regime's public display of the concentration camps in the early phase. As "consensus-building exercises in *Schadenfreude*," the pleasure derived from the misfortune of others, these exhibitions had the dual function of allowing the Nazi movement and its supporters to revel in the downfall of the Weimar system and its representatives, and simultaneously shocking and deterring others from resistance and association with the bygone democracy.[66]

On June 26, 1933, four days after the banning of the SPD, Gestapo officials captured Ernst Heilmann in Café Josty at Potsdamer Platz. His deportation to the SA camp in Oranienburg on August 8 was staged as a great media event. Together with party comrade Friedrich Ebert Jr., son of Germany's first president, and four leading representatives of broadcast radio, Heilmann was photographed standing at attention in front of the brown-shirts. These pictures were then circulated widely in the press. It was claimed that the arrest of the SPD politician was grounded in his "spiteful attitude toward the new Germany" and his "misconduct," which had, so it was emphatically claimed, aroused the anger of the population.[67] Inside the camp, rituals of degradation were enacted. The men's hair was shaved off, and they were forced to strip in front of the other prisoners to exchange their clothes for rags. According to Gerhart Seger, a non-Jewish SPD politician and witness to the scene, their suits were given to Communist prisoners, some of whom "turned away in disgust while others enthusiastically accepted the suits from the National Socialists."[68] In staged confrontations like this, long-standing conflicts between Communists and Social Democrats were stirred up to intensify the humiliation of the victim and to prevent solidarity among political prisoners. The consequences of the ordeal for Heilmann personally were devastating. He became the victim of constant abuse by SA and SS guards. In Börgermoor camp, where Heilmann was shipped from Oranienburg on September 13, 1933, the SS introduced him to the inmates as an SPD *Bonze*, a "swine" and a "criminal" whom the workers could "'thank' for the fact that you had to give up so much in your lives" and "to whom you owe it that you are now in the concentration camp."[69] The guards ridiculed the politician by locking him in a kennel. Heilmann was forced to bark like a dog while carrying a crown of thorns that another Jewish prisoner had to bind for him.[70] As a politician Heilmann had been a controversial figure who had polarized the political left. In the camp these "pre-concentrationary" conflicts further aggravated his situation and isolated him within the prisoner society.[71] Carrying the double burden of being a prominent politician and a Jew, Ernst Heilmann was not released from the camp, unlike the other five prominent captives in the group that arrived with him in Oranienburg in August 1933.[72] The Gestapo kept him imprisoned, and after almost seven years in custody he was murdered in Buchenwald on April 3, 1940.

Like Heilmann, Ludwig Marum lost his life in the concentration camp. In the early hours of March 29, 1934, he was killed at Kislau, a castle turned into a protective custody camp located some 30 kilometers north of Karlsruhe. Most likely he was executed on the order of his archenemy, Gauleiter and

NSDAP Reich Governor of Baden, Robert Wagner. Reports of the murder—poorly camouflaged as a suicide—were scrupulously twisted and abused for propaganda purposes.[73] *Der Stürmer* reported that the "swindler of the workers" Ludwig Marum had seen "his only way out" in the cowardly act of hanging himself. The article portrayed the politician's life as one of "heartless" deception of credulous German workers and claimed that Marum was deported to the Kislau camp "in the face of the vengeance of the Baden working class," which, "finally awakened, wanted to beat him to death."[74] These slanderous lines invoked their readers' memory of Marum's spectacular transport to the concentration camp on May 16, 1933—a remarkable public event, witnessed by thousands and talked about well beyond the borders of the state of Baden.[75] In reality, of course, it had been the Nazis, and not the workers, who paraded Marum and six other high-ranking SPD representatives on an open truck through the streets of Karlsruhe and, as Marum's daughter Elisabeth later remembered, "through all the little villages between Karlsruhe and Bruchsal and Heidelberg." Witnessing the event from her father's office, where the staged procession briefly stopped, she saw "people who yelled and screamed . . . there was an enormous upheaval both for and against it."[76]

As Michael Wildt has shown, public spectacles were constitutive enactments of the Nazi "people's community," unequivocally drawing the line between "national comrades" and excluded "community aliens." The onlooking crowd, including all those who did not publicly show their dissent, automatically acted as an agent of "collective violence" bound to the instigators of the scene in "situative complicity."[77] On May 16, the people of Baden watched as Marum, the "leader of the workers" who used to enthuse the masses, was now exposed to an agitated mob calling him a "traitor of the workers."[78] To the SPD politician, who, according to his associate Albert Nachmann, was the "beloved leader of the Baden working class" and "knew most of his voters personally," the event was, as the victim himself termed it, a "trauma."[79] Much to the new rulers' concern, however, the crowd was divided. As Marum's daughter remembered, some people showed solidarity with the prisoners and voiced protest that disturbed the Nazi demonstration of power. Those who shouted "Red Front!" were arrested on the spot and put on a second truck closely following the prominent Kislau deportees, in a public demonstration of how quickly acts of dissent could land one in a concentration camp. The Nazis calculated that the labor movement would soon realize that the "Jew-republic of the SPD" was finished,

Figure 1.2 Together with other Social Democrats, Ludwig Marum is paraded along Karlsruhe's Kaiserstrasse on May 16, 1933. He is seated on the backbench of the open truck and guarded by SA and SS men.
Stadtarchiv Karlsruhe 8/PBS oVI 38.

as one paper put it, and that today they were living "in the Germany of Adolf Hitler."[80] But however hard they tried to vilify Marum's name, his case is also an example for the resistance of the labor movement to the new powerholders' attempts to enforce a de-solidarization from their leaders. Marum's funeral, held on April 3, 1934, and carefully watched by the Gestapo, was attended by a large crowd. An estimated 3,000 made their way to the graveyard with flowers and wreaths hidden in plastic bags. They turned the burial into a solemn and impressive demonstration of solidarity.[81]

Acts of resistance and political solidarity attest to the limitations of the Nazi effort to create a racially pure people's community fatefully bound together by the struggle against common enemies. Similar to Marum's funeral, workers of Breslau paid their last respects to a Jewish representative of the labor movement whom they continued to hold in high esteem after his arrest. Like Marum, the Nazis had paraded Ernst Eckstein through the streets of the Silesian city in an open wagon—a most humiliating spectacle.[82]

On May 8, 1933, the SAP politician and attorney lost his life while held in protective custody. By turning his gravesite into a place of pilgrimage, the workers created a visible memorial to Eckstein.[83] Through this form of counterpublicity his ordeal was reinterpreted as a most honorable sacrifice for the socialist cause. The Nazis' attempt to win over the working class by turning their Jewish leaders into disempowered and publically humiliated villains was rendered futile. Likewise, when Reichsbanner leader Hans Alexander, who had been killed in the Esterwegen camp on September 2, 1933, was laid to rest at Breslau's Jewish cemetery, thousands of workers turned out and held a spontaneous demonstration crying "Hail freedom!" and "Revenge!"[84]

Protective custody and camp terror were also used to reinforce the antisemitic stereotype of Jewish journalists, whose articles were said to spread "atrocity propaganda" harmful to the German people and to the nation's image abroad. In 1933 a number of political journalists of Jewish descent were taken into protective custody together with many non-Jewish journalists. The arrest of Fritz Solmitz on March 12, 1933, in Lübeck was staged as a spectacle. The editor of the local SPD paper *Lübecker Volksbote* was paraded through the Hanseatic town on an open truck. In May 1933 Solmitz was deported to the Fuhlsbüttel concentration camp in Hamburg, where he died a violent death on September 19, 1933.[85] Ludwig Pappenheim, SPD deputy in the provincial parliament of Hesse-Nassau and editor of the *Volksstimme*, was arrested on March 25, 1933. His journalistic work was defamed as "Jewish spiritual terror" *(Jüdischer Geistesterror)*, and the mayor of his hometown of Schmalkalden, who had helped bring Pappenheim into protective custody, hoped that the journalist would remain "imprisoned in Breitenau concentration camp for the rest of his life."[86] Earlier Pappenheim had protested fiercely against his unlawful imprisonment. Laying bare the twisted nature of protective custody, he informed the provincial governor in Kassel: "The arrest warrant against me is maintained on the grounds that I would be in need of protection. I am touched by this concern for my person and declare: I forego the protection, no decent people are threatening me . . . I wish not to be kept here as the object of primitive feelings for revenge. I further complain about being put under the control of the auxiliary police without any participation of orderly police. In fact, it is them, in whom I see the only danger for my own person."[87] This note of protest reads as a striking testimony of courage. Pappenheim truly did not mince his words. He openly condemned the erosion of the constitutional legal order and accused state authorities of taking part in the Nazi onslaught of terror. Pappenheim's treatment worsened after he had been transferred from Breitenau to Börgermoor concentration camp, where the guards constantly ridiculed and beat him. The fact that an article critical of religion, not authored by him but published in the SPD paper under his editorship in December 1932, had led to a conviction for blasphemy served the SS as a pretext for abuse. On January 4, 1934, SS man Johann Siems shot Pappenheim dead, allegedly because the prisoner had "tried to escape from the camp."[88]

On August 7, 1933, in a forest near Warburg, SS and SA killed Felix Fechenbach, who was on a transport from the Detmold court prison to Dachau concentration camp. The journalist, who wrote for the SPD paper *Volksblatt*, was taken into protective custody on March 11, 1933. Fechenbach's enemy status was determined by his involvement in the Bavarian revolution as Kurt Eisner's right-hand man in 1918–1919.[89] In the Weimar years, Fechenbach had challenged the Nazi party's rise to power. As a journalist he had access to confidential information about the NSDAP in Lippe, and he had named and shamed their secret intentions and scandals in a column he regularly published in the *Volksblatt* under the pseudonym "Nazi-Jüsken."[90] After the Nazi seizure of power, the *Lippischer Kurier* reframed Fechenbach's investigative journalism, which aimed to unmask the Nazis' questionable methods, as directed against the workers instead. The swiftly coordinated paper claimed that "for years, the Jewish editor Fechenbach [had] systematically poisoned the minds" of the workers. An "enormous outrage" allegedly prevailed because "the Jew Fechenbach is still allowed to shoot his poison arrows in the hearts of the German workers."[91] This stirring of hatred led to verbal abuse against the journalist in public. Children are remembered to have accosted him by calling out "Fechenbach, perish!" Before that the whole town had laughed with him about the Nazis.[92]

Protective custody and early concentration camp imprisonment silenced the critical voices of left-wing journalists and intellectuals. When dissent became a punishable offense and the German people were stripped of their freedom of expression, Jewish journalists in particular were threatened by censorship, professional bans, and violent persecution. Although of course writers of Jewish descent were not alone in publicly denouncing the Nazis' illegal schemes and violent methods, Nazi antisemitism and the ideology of the "people's community" identified and defamed them as the originators of "atrocity propaganda" harmful to the nation. When on May

10, 1933, students and Nazi activists in Berlin burned books considered "un-German," one of the ceremonial slogans shouted while writings were thrown into the flames was "Against a journalism of democratic-Jewish imprint alien to the people! For a responsible cooperation for the work of national construction!"[93]

Jewish Jurists in the Early Concentration Camps

Those who could protest professionally against illegal measures of arrest and imprisonment were in great danger of becoming themselves the targets of Nazi terror. In the spring and summer of 1933, a remarkably high number of German jurists of Jewish origin were taken into protective custody. Hans Litten is but one prominent example. Others, too, had used their legal proficiency to challenge the Nazis' unlawful political methods. Max Tschornicki from Mainz, whose activities as an advocate of the political left had earned him local prominence, published an article in the *Mainzer Volkszeitung* on March 6, 1933, in which he criticized the Reichstag Fire Decree as "the most severe and outrageous intrusion into the private and political freedom of the German citizen." The decree, he firmly believed, would "not be granted a long life": "no German court will recognize the new will of the state to punish offenders not according to their deed but according to their worldview."[94] Tschornicki was repeatedly taken into protective custody—twice in the prison of the Mainz District Court and for a third time in the Osthofen concentration camp. His admission to the bar was withdrawn.[95]

Hundreds of Jewish jurists fell victim to early Nazi terror.[96] What stood behind this violent persecution? Why were so many members of this professional group attacked, kidnapped, imprisoned, and sometimes even killed during the phase of the Nazi takeover of power? For the most part, the literature only mentions the facts and points to a few prominent arrested lawyers engaged in political opposition. An analysis of their persecution is mostly situated within a discussion of the early economic boycotts against German Jews and the restrictive anti-Jewish legislation of spring 1933.[97] What is missing is a critical analysis of terror and violence as the most powerful forces of the exclusion of Jews from the legal profession and from society at large. In the following, we will examine the role of protective custody and the early concentration camps in the persecution of Jewish jurists.

The function assigned to the legal system in Germany after 1933 was to support Nazi rule by assisting in the elimination of its opponents. Jurists thus played a critical role in the Nazis' seizure of power.[98] Those judges, state prosecutors, and lawyers from whom resistance was to be expected were persecuted. That jurists' Jewish heritage made a crucial difference in their discrimination was already suggested at the time. The 1934 *Schwarzbuch*, an exile publication documenting early Nazi discrimination against Jews, asked whether the treatment of Joachim Günther and other Jewish colleagues would have been "equally catastrophic, if they had carried out the same political or politically colored activities but would, at the same time, have been Aryan?" Through his work as an advocate of left-wing activists Günther had frequently clashed with Nazi radicals in the Weimar years. On March 18, SA men arrested the Berlin lawyer. After being held in a detention center in Jüdenstrasse, Günther was brought to the infamous ULAP-camp in Tiergarten, where he was beaten to death by the SA on March 29, 1933. In view of such violent excesses perpetrated against Jewish jurists, the *Schwarzbuch* stated: "One can guess that they would have gotten off more lightly, had they not, through their characteristics of being Jewish, attracted the ill will of the party now in power."[99]

Antisemitic stereotypes of "the Jewish lawyer," who corrupts the law and focuses only on the selfish individual interests rather than the common good of the people, were propagated widely by the Nazi press. Racist views of the legal profession were shared by Hitler himself, whose hatred for Jewish lawyers can be identified as "the culmination point" of his "scorn for law and justice."[100] To drive out Jews from the judiciary was, as Peter Longerich emphasizes, "an old keystone of anti-Semitism."[101] The practice of law was a popular occupation for Jews in Germany, and Weimar's bar association had a remarkable number of members who were of Jewish descent. Of the 19,208 lawyers registered in the beginning of 1933, some 5,000 — over 25 percent — were regarded as "non-Aryan." In relation to the Jewish share in the population as a whole, which amounted to only 0.7 percent, this constituted a stark overrepresentation. The majority of Jewish lawyers, around 3,500, were registered in Prussia. A great number of Jewish lawyers practiced also in the big cities of Frankfurt (278, or 45.8 percent, of this city's lawyers were Jewish), Hamburg (215, or 31.6 percent), and Munich (225, or 50 percent).[102]

For some Jewish lawyers, practicing law was not merely a craft but a question of identity. Ludwig Bendix, for example, a lawyer from Berlin who will figure prominently in this book because he suffered in the prewar concentration camps for over two years and authored a unique account of his experiences, described himself as a "legal fanatic." As his son later recalled, "His commitment to the law was more than the choice of a career. It was a dedication to German culture and society, more specifically, to the development and reform of German law in place of his family's traditional commitment to Judaism. The practice of law became his way of life."[103] Many Jewish lawyers tended to advocate progressive ideas of democracy and social emancipation. But only very few could really exert political influence. Hugo Sinzheimer was one of them. As a member of the 1919 national assembly he was involved in the promulgation of the Weimar Constitution. In March 1933 Sinzheimer was taken into protective custody. After his release, he gave up his admission to the bar, his post in the German Legal Association, and his professorship at the University of Frankfurt and fled to Holland.[104]

In her research on Jewish lawyers in Nazi Germany, Simone Ladwig-Winters distinguishes an initial wave of "exclusion by terroristic means" from later waves of "exclusion by 'orderly,' bureaucratic means" which finally ended in late 1938 with the professional ban. Exclusion by terroristic means, according to Ladwig-Winters, was practiced in the period between the Reichstag election and the coming into effect of the Law Regarding Admission to the Legal Profession (Gesetz über die Zulassung zur Rechtsanwaltschaft) on April 7, 1933.[105] Taking a closer look at the persecution of Jewish lawyers in 1933 and especially at those cases in which protective custody and camp terror were used to catalyze exclusion, we find, however, that violent action cannot be so clearly separated from legal and economic discrimination. As the following analysis will show, boycotts, professional bans, and protective custody measures were intertwined and mutually reinforcing. Where legal discrimination proved ineffective, the exclusion of "unwanted" Jewish lawyers was achieved by illegal means; kidnapping, torture, and murder in protective custody were not restricted to the period before the promulgation of the 1933 law.

Along the lines of the Civil Service Law, which affected Jewish judges, state prosecutors, and those who worked in state institutions of juridical bureaucracy, the Law Regarding Admission to the Legal Profession also had exemption clauses. Lawyers who had started working before August 1, 1914, could continue their practice, as could those who had served as combat soldiers in the Great War or had close relatives killed in action. On the whole, the effects of legal-bureaucratic measures to restrict the professional activities of Jewish lawyers were limited. While the Reich Ministry of Justice (RMJ) reviewed thousands of applications for readmission to the bar—a laborious bureaucratic process that dragged on from April until September/October 1933—it became clear that many Jewish lawyers qualified for one or both of the law's exemption clauses and would have to be allowed to continue their practice.[106] In this situation, discrimination against Jewish lawyers radicalized as the authorities began to "look for other ways to deny Jews admission to the bar." The Ordinance of the Reich Law Regarding Admission to the Legal Profession, decreed in Prussia on April 25, 1933, allowed for the possibility to draw on information about alleged "Communist activities" in order to banish Jewish lawyers.[107] In the Nazi effort to construct political crimes that ultimately led to professional bans, protective custody and camp imprisonment played a pivotal role. In the intimidating presence of the SA and SS, lawyers were forced to resign "voluntarily" from the bar. Counselor of Justice Karl Schulz from Frankenthal in Bavaria, for example, held in protective custody from April 25 to June 2, 1933, had been so affected by his imprisonment that, in the end, he revoked his admission to the bar.[108]

Martin Rosenthal, a judge at the Altlandsberg District Court, was deported to Oranienburg on June 28, 1933. Denunciations by the head of the local Nazi party group and Altlandsberg's Mayor Funke, whose office functioned as the small town's police authority, had instigated Rosenthal's protective custody. They accused the judge of being opposed to the new government, invoking an incident from early March 1933 when Rosenthal had ordered the removal from the local court building of a swastika flag put up by Nazi radicals. The convinced democrat had further prohibited hanging pictures of Hitler in the courtrooms.[109] On the Boycott Day of April 1, 1933, a nationwide act of discrimination targeting Jewish professionals and Jewish-owned businesses, Rosenthal was suspended from office temporarily. According to the subsequent Civil Service Law the judge would have had to be allowed to continue working, as he was a war veteran. While the juridical authorities were reviewing his case, Rosenthal's opponents from the local NSDAP and SA strove to prevent his return to office by portraying him as a state enemy. Their campaign ended with Rosenthal's imprisonment in Oranienburg. His official protective custody order, issued *post factum*, gave "suspicion of actions hostile to the state" as the reason for his imprisonment.[110] His wife fiercely protested against this accusation and told the police in her appeal for his release that Rosenthal had never been a member of any political party. She stressed that he was a patriot and as a judge had always ruled with utmost impartiality.[111] Mayor Funke, now under pressure to legitimate his actions to the County Executive, his superior authority, offered new and graver accusations against the judge: "If it is argued . . . that Rosenthal would have a patriotic attitude, then this declaration does not correspond with the truth. Rosenthal is a Jew and he is suspended from office since April 1, 1933. He had always spoken out against the national movement and the government . . . The local population could not help but get the feeling that Rosenthal sympathized with left-wing circles and came to their defense. Understandably, this fact has also created uproar."[112] The construction of Rosenthal's enemy profile draws on arguments that would not qualify at all if brought forward as evidence in a constitutional state. The strongest of them—that he is a Jew and thus banned from office—is, in fact, drawn directly from Nazi antisemitic discourse, which rapidly permeated the bureaucratic modus operandi in the German state administration. By suggesting that Rosenthal sympathized with the Communists and that his behavior caused public outrage, Funke touched upon the key prejudices applied time and again in the reasons given for Jewish jurists' protective custody. However flimsy and weak, these formulas quickly became self-explanatory and needed no further evidence. For the responsible County Executive they translated into "suspicion of hostile acts against the state"—a reason sufficient for arrest and imprisonment.

What the accusation of being an enemy of the state who worked for the Communists meant for the SA guards in Oranienburg is not difficult to imagine. Shortly after his arrival in the camp, Rosenthal declared that upon release he would not only give up his post as a judge but leave Altlandsberg altogether.[113] Although we do not know the exact circumstances under which this "decision" came about, it is safe to assume that it was not reached voluntarily. It is highly likely that the aforementioned Hans Krüger, Oranienburg's dreaded head of interrogations, had forced Rosenthal into this renunciation. For months before he was deported to the camp, the Jewish judge had resisted the political pressure directed at him. In the campaign for his expulsion from his occupation and residence, camp terror had finally effected what could not have been reached by legal-bureaucratic means. With camp imprisonment now lending a criminalizing taint to his record, Rosenthal was banned from the legal profession on July 27, 1933.[114]

The history of Jewish jurists who fell victim to early protective custody measures concludes with the remarkable case of Ludwig Bendix. Like his colleagues, the fifty-six-year-old lawyer was imprisoned in the summer of 1933 to enforce his expulsion from the Berlin bar. Unlike other cases, however, in which a jurist's reaction to persecution can be reconstructed only indirectly from petitions for release or the reports of fellow prisoners, Bendix left a unique testimony that provides invaluable insights into his personal experience of camp terror and exclusion.[115] Based on the exemption clause of the Law Regarding Admission to the Legal Profession, Bendix, who had practiced as a lawyer since 1907, would have had to be readmitted to the bar. On June 2, 1933, however, he was arrested in his home by the police. During his three-week spell in the Alexanderplatz prison, Bendix sent countless petitions to the Berlin Gestapo demanding to know what was held against him. He never received an answer. It was only weeks after his transfer to the protective custody wing in the Spandau prison that the lawyer was informed of the "reason" for his arrest and imprisonment, namely, that he was regarded "a secret leader of the Proletarian Freethinkers' Society"—an allegation that could not have been more absurd.[116] In restless efforts to make sense of his predicament, he then remembered that two of his former clients had been Communists, and one of them also had been a member of this Society. Still he could not understand why this would be interpreted to his disadvantage. As his son later described it: "The ethics of his profession demanded that a lawyer accept a client in need"; but "in the eyes of the Nazi authorities, this action made him vicariously a Communist."[117]

The fact that the Nazis openly mocked the legal system, attacked its representatives and its most sacrosanct principles and symbols, and made a travesty of all legal procedures shocked many persecuted jurists, both Jews and non-Jews. Bendix admitted feelings of deep humiliation, shame, and self-pity stemming from the profoundly upsetting experience "that an outrageous injustice was done to me."[118] After his release from protective custody in late September 1933, though, the Jewish lawyer, who could not imagine living and working anywhere other than in his German homeland, decided to stay. He undertook enormous efforts to clear his name from the criminalizing taint of camp imprisonment. According to his son, "he explained whenever possible that his protective custody had been based on false assumptions."[119] Like other lawyers with Jewish roots who had been disbarred, Bendix could now work only as a legal counselor. His family, too, was affected by the criminalizing aura of the concentration camp. Bendix's son Reinhard remembered how they became increasingly socially isolated: "All of us seemed marked by my father's earlier disbarment and imprisonment."[120] Reinhard was expelled from school as a result of this discrimination. When his father had been arrested, the agitated boy confided in his teacher and told him that from now on he would abstain from giving the Hitler salute at the beginning of the class. A few days later Reinhard was asked not to attend classes anymore pending further consideration of his case. He would never return to this school. A classmate later reported to him how the teacher had announced that "it was considered best for me to leave . . . because it would be asking too much of the class to tolerate the presence of someone whose father had been taken into protective custody. Under the circumstances of the day, that hinted at communist activities."[121]

To coordinate the legal sector was crucial to the Nazi effort to assume and secure power. Both terror and legal discrimination were used to attack, defame, and exclude from the profession jurists who represented the detested Weimar system. In cases when their exclusion could not be effected with discriminatory laws and economic boycotts alone, juridical authorities worked together with agencies of violent oppression to reach what was intended. Protective custody affected hundreds of Jewish lawyers who were pushed to give up their membership in the bar in the intimidating presence of the SA and SS. Many of those who would have otherwise qualified for exemptions from the professional ban were criminalized as agents of Communism and deported to camps. In turn, their alleged political offenses, supposedly "proven" through their imprisonment, became the determining factor in the juridical authorities' decision to banish them from work in the legal sector. This reinforced antisemitic stereotypes of "the Jewish lawyer." The effects for the persecuted were devastating. Protective custody measures destroyed not only their careers. Given the high degree of identification of many Jewish jurists with the legal profession, it destroyed their personalities and social lives as well as the lives of their families. Some, like Bendix, eagerly sought to clear their reputations by openly confronting the injustice done to them. Others, like Rosenthal and Sinzheimer, fled from Nazi Germany. Still others, like Alfons Kalter from Grünstadt in Bavaria, felt so deeply humiliated and uprooted by the experience of imprisonment and exclusion that they committed suicide.[122]

Camp Terror against "Unpolitical" Jews

Many Jews fell victim to early concentration camp terror even though they neither saw themselves as political activists nor formally belonged to any party or political organization opposed to the Nazi movement. The tendency of stretching the vaguely defined arrest category of protective custody beyond its official political scope to use it for the exclusion of Jews from certain professional sectors has already become evident in the persecution of Jewish jurists. Protective custody was used in various ways also to exclude "ordinary" Germans of Jewish origin from the envisaged Nazi people's community. Research has demonstrated how antisemitic violence radicalized the breakdown of social ties between Jews and non-Jews in early Nazi Germany.[123] The role of protective custody measures and camp terror in this process of building and cementing the enemy category of "the Jew," on the other hand, remains unclear. This might have to do with a lack of general public awareness that, from the spring of 1933 onward, nonpolitical Jews were being arrested, imprisoned, and taken to the camps alongside politically active Jews. Striking examples of these very early arrests of Jews who were not members of the KPD or SPD are the violent raids on Berlin's Scheunenviertel in spring 1933. On March 9, the SA rioted in this impoverished neighborhood, which had a large Jewish population including a high proportion of migrants from Eastern Europe. A month later, on April 4, members of the police division Commando Wecke—infamous for their brutal tortures in the Friesenstrasse barracks in Berlin-Kreuzberg—captured numerous of these Eastern European migrants, the so-called *Ostjuden*, and abducted them to illegal detention sites. The attacks, which overwhelmingly targeted politically uninvolved individuals, gave vent to a violent hatred of Jews and were intended to drive Eastern European Jews out of Germany. One of the first victims of SA brutality in Berlin's Scheunenviertel was eighteen-year-old Siegbert Kindermann, a Jewish apprentice in a bakery, who was murdered on March 18, 1933, in the early camp in Hedemannstrasse 31.[124] Around the same time in Kreuzberg, SA men kidnapped the young writer Leo Krell, whom his widowed mother and sisters characterized as "a harmless Jewish man without any political exposure." After days of brutal abuse, Krell was murdered in the concentration camp in General-Pape-Strasse.[125]

Before proceeding, we must ask a general question: Where is one to draw the line between the arrests of "real enemies" and the arrests of nonpolitical men and women, including Jews, who were also taken into protective custody from early on? Given that in a dictatorship every prisoner in a camp is ultimately held for political reasons—just as concentration camps themselves are essentially political entities, the "true central institutions of totalitarian organizational power," as Hannah Arendt put it—this might at first glance seem to be a distinction without a difference.[126] But if we understand political arrests in the narrow sense, as cases in which a person has been arrested because of active, conscious, and declared opposition to the Nazi movement, a distinction between "political" and "nonpolitical" arrests becomes important. For only in this way does the place and function of the concentration camp in the rapidly increasing antisemitic atmosphere sponsored by the new regime become fully palpable. Historians who have studied Nazi terror in the initial stages of the dictatorship have often not fully grasped *why* Jews were taken into protective custody. Approaching the subject from a close examination of the Gestapo—an agency of terror still under development in 1933–1934—they conclude that it was overwhelmingly "politically active Jews [who were] threatened with being send to a concentration camp."[127] Here, the concentration camp figures merely as the terminus of Gestapo-ordered deportations. The picture becomes more complex, however, if one drills down to the initial events that triggered the detention of Jewish prisoners. In doing so, the involvement of a broad range of agencies beyond the political police becomes visible. Especially during the phase of the early concentration camps, a variety of actors instigated and carried out arrests. Their practices were mostly uncoordinated. Their motives for imprisoning Jews were highly complex and need to be carefully probed. The notion that only Jews with political affiliations were imprisoned in concentration camps of 1933–1934, however, is invalid.[128]

Beyond the Cities

In what ways did protective custody and camp terror affect the lives of Jews who resided in small towns and villages?[129] A brief survey of early protective custody cases from rural Bavaria shows that a considerable number of arrests of Jews were in fact based on nonpolitical grounds. Listed in the Bavarian State Ministry's register of protective custody prisoners is, for example, Hermann Rothschild from Hörstein in Lower Franconia. The authorities justified his arrest and detention as follows: "He is considered the worst Jewish bloodsucker in the district of Gerolshofen. Recently, a resident of the town of Veitshöchheim has cut his own throat after he had become penniless due to Rothschild's ploys."[130] Here, the suicide of an insolvent client served as a ground to implement protective custody, and the Jewish businessman was arrested on March 14, 1933.[131] In the case of Julius Schuster from Brückenau in Lower Franconia, arrested on June 7, it was Reinhard Heydrich who gave the reasons for the Jewish merchant's protective custody. According to Heydrich's report, Schuster had not only "supported Communist groups"—in which ways exactly remains open—but he was also, and this clearly serves as the main argument, "one of the most scheming and cunning businessmen of Brückenau," driven by an "unscrupulousness"; a "great profiteer and cutthroat" whose practices aimed at "unfair competition."[132] Through reasoning like this, antisemitic stereotypes of Jewish businessmen were not only codified as enemy conceptions but rendered punishable offenses. Take also the case of Selmar Oppenheim, whose company, the Oppinwerke in Bayreuth, dealt in footwear. By ordering his arrest on April 4, 1933, the authorities seized the opportunity to rid themselves of someone they perceived as an uncomfortable and annoying nuisance: "For years, he had, in a way utterly devoid of any decency and morals, pestered the police, the tax authorities, and the prosecution authorities with petitions." Officials of self-declared "nationalistic conviction" who had not forgotten that the Jewish entrepreneur once denounced them to their superiors in order to advance his own interests were now able to turn the tables. "Objections of a principal nature" were raised against Oppenheim's release from Dachau concentration camp: "O. belongs to the race of cheaters and exploiters of the people."[133] Another clearly nonpolitical charge was alleged harassment of non-Jewish women. Emblematic is the case of Korman Rosenbusch from Dettelbach in Lower Franconia. According to the entry in the ministerial register, his arrest on March 24, 1933, and his subsequent two-year imprisonment in Dachau were ordered "for his own protection": "Through his behavior as a Jew toward the female sex, he had outraged the public."[134] No mention of any political offense whatsoever was needed to justify his arrest.

All four cases show how rapidly the vocabulary of Nazi antisemitism entered the bureaucratic modus operandi. That these arrests of nonpolitical Jews from Bavaria were no isolated cases can, in turn, be concluded from the records of the highest offices of party and state, which voiced sharp criticism of such "abuses" of protective custody. Several complaints brought forward by officials and authorities of the regime serve as the strongest proof that the early practice of arrest and detention went far beyond the regime's propagated "fight against Marxism" and targeted also "ordinary" Germans, among them Jews. In a letter of April 18, 1933, to all police departments and other agencies responsible for protective custody, the Saxon Ministry of the Interior noted: "It has become known to the Ministry that in some cases prisoners taken into protective custody were arrested only because they belong to the Jewish race. The police departments are alerted to the fact that affiliation to the Jewish race *alone* is not a reason to impose protective custody. If today there are still Jews held in protective custody solely because of them being non-natives [*Fremdstämmigkeit*], their protective custody is to be suspended immediately."[135] Arbitrary arrests that brought politically nonactive Jews into detention without trial could entail indefinite imprisonment, as Nazi officials sometimes ruled over the equally random practice of release from protective custody. On April 19, 1933, Josef Bürckel, the leader of the Bavarian Rheinpfalz NSDAP party district proclaimed in autocratic fashion that "those political prisoners for whom the most appeals were presented should be the last to be released . . . In the future, Jews can be released only if two petitioners or the physicians who had issued their sickness certificates are willing to replace them and serve their sentence."[136]

A note sent on April 26, 1933, by Vice Chancellor Franz von Papen to Hermann Göring in the latter's capacity as Prussian Minister President points in a similar direction. Von Papen reported a conversation with Lord Newton, a member of the British House of Lords, who had expressed his suspicion that "in the concentration camps Jews, too, would be imprisoned and that it would be planned to deprive Jews of their private property." The vice chancellor's answer mirrors the euphemistic image the Nazis tended to propagate about the concentration camps: "Naturally, I enlightened him of the fact that only Communists who must be kept busy [with work] are to be found in these camps."[137]

These various statements from the spring of 1933 attest to the arbitrariness of the early arrest practices. They tell us that a significant number of Jews were among the arrestees and that they were detained not only as political enemies but also because of their "race." Although high-ranking authorities tried to deny that Jews were arrested for racial reasons—mostly out of concern for the regime's public image—the practice on the ground was different. Arrests based on the denunciations and self-empowered actions of local Nazi party activists expanded and stretched protective custody beyond a strictly political category. In the process, an antisemitic line of attack was fixed onto one of the emerging regime's sharpest weapon of terror.

A case study of the early concentration camp in Osthofen, in existence from March 1933 to July 1934, will demonstrate that the majority of the Jews in protective custody there were, in the strictest sense, not political prisoners but "unwanted" for other reasons.[138] The camp was located in Rhenish

Figure 1.3 Osthofen Concentration Camp, April 1933.
NS-Dokumentationszentrum Rheinland-Pfalz/Gedenkstätte KZ-Osthofen.

Hesse, a rural region with an agelong tradition of Jewish settlement, culture, and trade. Typical for the early concentration camps, it was not purpose-built but provisionally set up in an empty paper factory located in the middle of the small town. The new powerholders confiscated the vacant estate from its legal owner. A large, very visible sign reading "Konzentrationslager Osthofen" was painted on the building's front.

The camp had been in operation for almost two months when the newly appointed State Commissar for the Police in Hesse, Werner Best, decreed on May 1, 1933, that the former factory should serve as the official state concentration camp of Hesse. SS Sturmbannführer Karl d'Angelo was nominated camp commander. Subordinate to him were more than fifty auxiliary policemen recruited from the SS and SA.[139]

An analysis of Best's Decree on the Establishment of a Concentration Camp in Osthofen offers an important perspective on the enforcement of the Jewish enemy category by means of camp punishment. Intentionally or not, his ordinance embodies the very ambiguity—the tension between political intention and racial practice—that colored the early arrests of Jews.

Best, who later acted as deputy to Reinhard Heydrich in the Reich Security Head Office (RSHA) and masterminded countless anti-Jewish measures, explicitly defined the circle of persons to be imprisoned in Osthofen as "everybody taken into police custody for political reasons." But this restriction of arrest on political grounds was undermined when, in a *pro forma* to be used for the official admission of the arrested to the camp, the state commissar named his hypothetical political prisoners "Salomon Rubinstein" and "Moses Grünebaum."[140] The use of these stereotypical Jewish names suggests that for Best the discrimination against Jews was an integral part of the first conception of the Nazi concentration camp. Although he does not explicitly declare Osthofen to be a weapon of anti-Jewish policy, the antisemitism inherent in his depiction of the enemy is obvious: the Nazis' political and ideological opponents coincided in "the Jew" as the archenemy of the German "people's community."

Among Osthofen's Jewish prisoners were a number of businessmen interned after being denounced by former trading partners for alleged criminal business practices. Take the cases of the cattle dealers Josef Wachenheimer and Richard Hirsch. Both of them lived in villages not far from the camp: Wachenheimer in Biebesheim and Hirsch in Gimbsheim. In the end of June 1933, Wachenheimer was deported to Osthofen and interned there for two weeks. His detention must be understood in the context of police investigations following a denunciation for illegal usury brought forward by his client, the farmer Karl Ludwig Volz. As can be learned from surviving police and court files, Volz had bought fertilizer and fodder from Wachenheimer in 1927–1928. Payment for these products was still outstanding in the spring of 1932, when the Jewish seller filed a complaint to the Rhenish Hessian Cattle Dealer Association and asked for the confiscation of Volz's money.[141] A year later, when Nazi power was established in the region and the new rulers were openly acting against Jewish citizens, the situation had changed in favor of the client in arrears, who must have felt that he now stood a good chance of getting rid of old debts. Volz reported his Jewish supplier to the police and claimed that the cattle dealer had invoiced him at excessive interest rates for the outstanding payments. On the order of the Hessian Central Police Authority, Wachenheimer was deported to Osthofen.[142] We do not know what he experienced inside the camp. While police and party officials had quickly reacted to what was an essentially private economic conflict by locking up the accused in a concentration camp, the legal apparatus simultaneously processed the incident and came to very different results: the Jewish cattle dealer was found not guilty of usury.[143] It remains unclear whether Wachenheimer ever received his money. Furthermore, Osthofen concentration camp was only the first station in his history of persecution. After his imprisonment in Buchenwald in November 1938, he emigrated from Germany with his family and found exile in the United States.[144]

A similar constellation of joint interests of "ordinary Germans" and the new rulers occurred three months earlier. The case of Richard Hirsch is a key example for the involvement of the local populations in profiting from a Jewish citizen's protective custody. Hirsch was first brought to Osthofen in March 1933, suspected of having delivered weapons and munitions to the Communists—an allegation that was never proven. He was interned twice in the spring of 1933 and finally released upon his sister's intercession with the Central Police Authority in Darmstadt. When the SS came looking for him a third time, Hirsch escaped by crossing the border to the Netherlands in early May, leaving family and business behind. When the Germans occupied his exile country during the war, Hirsch was again caught up in the Nazi persecution. From Westerborg he was deported to his death in Auschwitz in 1943. In his testimony, he remembered that people who owed money to him came to see him in the concentration camp. In the intimidating presence of the SS, they demanded cancellation of their debts. Hirsch, however, refused to agree to that.[145]

After Hirsch and Wachenheimer had been arrested and imprisoned in a concentration camp, "national comrades" believed that they were "officially" disenfranchised and their situation could be exploited for personal profit. The involvement of various party and state agencies—SA, police, SS concentration camp officials, and traditional judicial authorities—especially in the case of Wachenheimer, is typical of the improvised and arbitrary procedures of arrest and imprisonment practiced during the Nazi dictatorship's initial phase of "revolutionary violence." This arrest practice began to undermine the traditional constitutional state's methods of investigation and punishment.

When transcending the case study of Osthofen to look into the economically motivated persecution of Jews in other rural areas, we find similar examples that back up the observations made: Protective custody and early camp terror were used to oust Jews from their professions and to forcefully disentangle business relations between Jews and non-Jews. In some instances the authorities even openly encouraged a profit from the Jews' persecution. After Jakob de Jonge, a shopkeeper from the small town of Weener in Friesland, had been taken into protective custody on July 27, 1933, the local Kreislandbund, the organization of the local farmers, called on "everybody who feels they have suffered a damage due to the business practices of de Jonge to come forward."[146] Through this appeal, the authorities, not least, hoped to find grounds for a *post factum* justification of his arrest. For although the public was informed about de Jonge's capture and turned out in large numbers to watch him being transported to the court prison, no reason for this act could officially be given.[147] An inspection of de Jonge's business records did not yield any liable delinquency. However, it did reveal the names of his customers, some of whom adhered to left-wing parties, so the dangerous remark "closely associated with the Communist party" entered his police records.[148] Jakob de Jonge was deported to Börgermoor concentration camp on August 12, 1933. His brutal ill-treatment and weeklong confinement in the notorious "arrest barrack 11" have been recorded in the memoirs of fellow prisoners as exceptional examples of camp violence. From Börgermoor he was brought to Lichtenburg and imprisoned there until the beginning of June 1934.[149]

The frequent use of protective custody as an extreme measure of deterrence and punishment demonstrates not least how difficult it was for the Nazi regime to disentangle business relations between Jews and non-Jews. To enforce boycotts and economic exclusion, the concentration camp functioned as both a symbolic and a real menace. On the nationwide Boycott Day of April 1, 1933, local Nazi activists set up in the center of Kassel a barbed-wired cage with a donkey inside. According to a newspaper report, the enclosure, which was positioned directly opposite the Jewish-owned Tietz department store, was marked by a sign reading "Concentration camp for stubborn citizens who do their shopping at the Jews."[150] For Georg Bolte from Ochshausen in the Kassel district, this theatrical enactment—observed by crowds of excited spectators—became a real threat. For "shopping in a Jewish business" he was interned in the nearby Breitenau concentration camp in the summer of 1933.[151] Even though drastic measures like this remained the exception, they nevertheless made an impression and branded people who dealt with Jews as offenders against the Nazi people's community. Apart from public shaming in newspapers and display cases of *Der Stürmer*, it was terror that most effectively excluded Jews from the economy and disrupted Jewish-Christian business relations by scaring people into compliance.[152]

From economic relations between Jews and non-Jews, I will now turn to an investigation of social relations and the Nazi powerholders' attempts to forcibly break them apart. The most striking examples for the use of protective custody as a political category of imprisonment ringing hollow are early "race defilement" (*Rassenschande*) cases. Long before the promulgation of the Law for the Protection of German Blood and Honor on September 15, 1935, police and local Nazi activists targeted relationships, friendly or sexual, between Germans of Jewish heritage and their non-Jewish friends or partners. This early phase of the persecution of "race defilers" involved public humiliation of the victims through pillory processions—a symbolic practice of exclusion that took place in many towns and villages throughout Germany. These mortifying spectacles were often followed by a significant number of arrests that landed the defamed in protective custody. Aggressive reports published in the press accompanied these arbitrary acts of terror.[153] Although no detailed figures are available, the number of Jews arrested and imprisoned as "race defilers" before September 1935 must be estimated at hundreds, possibly over 1,000.[154] An unknown number of them were deported to concentration camps. Camps in which Jews were detained as "race defilers" included, among others, Dachau, Breitenau, Osthofen, and Lichtenburg. Ludwig Bendix, who was deported to Lichtenburg in early August 1935, reported on a whole separate company of "50 to 60 race defilers" that existed in this Prussian camp before the promulgation of the Nuremberg Laws, an act of antisemitic legislation that classified Jews as "non-Aryan" and deprived them of their German citizenship.[155]

From early on, the arrests and imprisonment of Jewish "race defilers" differed from other protective custody cases of Jews in one crucial point: these persecutions were based on, and openly justified with, racial reasons. In contrast to other cases, authorities here did not have to bend underlying antisemitic motives into more publicly acceptable offenses of political opposition. In fact, it is striking that already in the spring of 1933, with the earliest cases of "race defilement" leading to camp imprisonment, prisoners' "Jewishness" sporadically entered the official records. In the transport lists for deportations from local Bavarian prisons to Dachau concentration camp, compiled by the police and the responsible district offices, a prisoner's "religion" is indicated only in isolated cases.[156] Remarkable exceptions are the cases of prisoners accused of having sexually assaulted non-Jewish women, for whom the entry "Jew"—printed spaced, in capital letters, or highlighted with exclamation marks—was added to the names, as if it was a synonym for their offense. Take the examples of Hans Stein from Kitzingen and Louis Schloss from Nuremberg. Stein, who was deported to Dachau on May 13, 1933, was identified to camp officials as a Jew ("*J u d e*") who, according to the local SA leader in his letter to the camp leadership, had "chastised a female employee in his shop . . . after having abused her for animalistic indecencies [*Viecherei*]."[157] Schloss, too, was identified as a Jew, and his fate tells us that Jewish prisoners defamed as race defilers suffered extremely harsh treatment once inside the camp. When he arrived in Dachau on May 15, 1933, SS guards attacked and beat him so brutally that he died of his injuries on the following day.[158] Postwar juridical investigation into his death determined that Schloss "was a Jew who apparently had relationships with Aryan women, because of which he had repeatedly been attacked in the 'Stürmer.' Schloss was therefore no stranger to the Dachau guards, who were aware of his arrival."[159] Attacks on Louis Schloss in the Nazi press go back to 1926 when the Upper Franconian paper *Der Streiter* defamed the Jewish merchant on its front pages as a "desecrator of girls and women."[160]

Strong language full of antisemitic abuse was applied to brand Jews as "race defilers" and to communicate their abduction to the camps. For example, a report in the *Mainzer Warte*, a local National Socialist weekly, from May 26, 1934, reads: "For quite some time, the twenty-five-year-old Jew Erich Scheier from Mainz maintained sexual relationships with girls of Aryan descent. Shortly before Whitsun, he was observed raping a seventeen-year-old Aryan girl in his father's apartment. The inhabitants of Mainz were seized by such an outrage against the race defiler that he voluntarily went into protective custody." Scheier was brought to the Osthofen concentration camp for four weeks.[161] The story of the Jewish race defiler lusting after innocent Aryan maidens, reported in this drastic and sensationalist way, invokes an old and persistent antisemitic myth. At its core lies xenophobia combined with suppressed pornographic fantasies of the sexually potent Jew slyly "penetrating" into the (Christian) communal body by seducing naive Gentile women—the weak and seducible members of a male-dominated society.[162] The persecution of "race defilers" also satisfied very private jealousies generated when Jewish rivals outdid their "Aryan" competitors. The Nazis could effectively draw upon this dual mechanism of serving both collective and individual interests.[163]

The deportation of the branded Jewish "race defiler" to a concentration camp was an important component in the Nazis' attempt to remove Jewish citizens from the "people's community." An investigation into cases of race defilement connected with the Osthofen concentration camp shows that this region was not excluded from such early manifestations of anti-semitism. The above-mentioned Erich Scheier was interned in Osthofen from May 22 until June 20, 1934.[164] By taking the Jewish "lechers" to a place in which the public could be sure they would receive what was announced as their deserved punishment, Jews were castigated and dishonored. At the same time, an image of the concentration camp was disseminated as a pseudo-penal institution necessary to purge society of harmful enemies.

Denunciation lay at the root of another Osthofen case. By 1933 Isak Krieger and Anna Uhrig had been a couple for six years. Their friends and neighbors knew about the love of the trained engineer from Worms and his non-Jewish fiancée, who lived in Leiselheim. Nevertheless, already in the early days of Hitler's rule, the couple had to put up with humiliations and discriminations inflicted upon them by both Nazis and members of the public, some of whom they had, until then, counted among their friends. In his postwar memoir, Krieger described the attacks they had to suffer: "Immediately when Hitler set off the new times, nobody knew us anymore, in her [his fiancée's] village and in our street, she was just a Jew whore. The landlord forbade my wife to live in the house; before we had been very good friends with him, now he got the police on to us . . . over night they branded us as criminals . . . Because of this girl I was sent to Osthofen right at the beginning, in 1933. I was there for over four months, badly beaten up by a friend from school; I had to clean the toilets with my bare hands and sand.[165]" After he had been denounced in the summer of 1933, Krieger had to serve an exceptionally long sentence of four months in the concen-tration camp.[166] Thanks to a distant relative of his fiancée, a member of the criminal police who intervened on Krieger's behalf, he was eventually set free. As soon as he was released, he heard about the threat of another arrest. To escape from it, he left Germany with his family for Biala (Bielitz), Poland, in October 1933. His fiancée accompanied him; they married and survived the war.[167]

The brutality described in Krieger's testimony is striking. His words make it very clear that detention in the early concentration camps of Jewish "race defilers" suited the Nazi state's general aims: the construction of a clearly defined "Aryan" racial society. Often it was "ordinary" citizens who through their denunciations had set off protective custody measures. As Robert Gellately has shown, individual members of the public, by reporting "race-defilers" and "slaves of the Jews" (Judenknechte), significantly aided the political police, which "on its own could not enforce racial policies designated to isolate the Jews."[168] As with the imprisonment of the Jewish cattle dealers, the motives for arrests and camp detention of "race-defilers" can be traced back to a noxious mixture of voyeurism, antisemitic prejudices, personal gain, and political opportunism in line with the new National Socialist morality.[169] Take as a final example the imprisonment of Arthur Braun in Osthofen, which was triggered by a denunciation by his former lover. After the termination of their relationship and her dismissal as a maid from the household of the Braun family in Flonheim, Katharina Heinrich reported the twenty-year-old man to the police and accused him of rape.[170] While Braun was imprisoned in the early concentration camp from April 18 to May 10, 1934, the State Prosecutor's Office in Mainz examined the case and, after having put all the evidence together, declared: "There is not sufficient proof for a rape in the light of § 177 RStGB [Reich Criminal Code]."[171] This had not stopped the police and SS from putting the falsely accused man into a camp, however.

Among all the instances of persecution that Jews in Nazi Germany had to suffer, race defilement cases are especially haunting because persons from the accused's immediate environment were often actively involved in bringing about an arrest. With their gossiping, spying, and denunciations, neighbors, colleagues, friends, and, in not just a few cases, even family members intruded into the most intimate spheres of others' lives. According to Alexandra Przyrembel, it was more out of personal rather than political reasons that they acted as police informers and triggered investigations, which could then lead to concentration camp imprisonment.[172] Particularly in rural areas with communal structures of strong social control, like the ones under investigation here, terror and camp imprisonment destroyed earlier bonds of Christian-Jewish coexistence.

Finally, violence and terror that radiated from the concentration camps contributed to the suppression of a critical public discourse in Nazi Germany. Expressions of dissent and discontent vanished from the media and were displaced to more private spheres. With the so-called *Heimtücke* decree of March 21, 1933, and the subsequent Law against Malicious Attacks on State and Party from December 20, 1934, the new rulers implemented punitive legal norms for the persecution of "slanderers."[173] In each juridical district a Special Court was set up. In 1933 the Special Courts convicted 3,744 individuals for making "malicious attacks" against the regime.[174] As Bernward Dörner points out, the accused, at each stage of the persecution process, were in danger of being deported to a concentration camp, and although this happened de facto only in every twentieth case, the rate was still high enough to have a deterrent effect on the population.[175] Interacting with the threat of being put on trial and sentenced to regular prison, camp terror facilitated the criminalization of dissent.

The records of *Heimtücke* trials provide valuable information about the fact that, despite massive repression, people *did* talk about the arrest and imprisonment of Jews in concentration camps. Some voiced their condemnation and their horror. Alois Halbig, for example, a fifty-five-year-old waiter from Berlin, was accused of having told other customers in a shop in September 1933 that the SA "would murder Communists in all quarters of Berlin. The prisoners in the concentration camps would be beaten black and blue." He had also heard "that many Jews were sent to the concentration camps."[176] Halbig was sentenced to three months in prison. Rumors about the gruesome ill-treatment of Jews by the SA, even the belief that Jewish girls would be raped in camps, can be found in other trial records.[177]

Jews punished for alleged or actual criticism of the regime mostly fell victim to denunciatory reports brought to the authorities' attention by members of the public.[178] In a number of cases they were taken into protective custody, and some were deported to a concentration camp. Rabbi Max Dienemann, for example, was sent to Osthofen in December 1933 for "attitudes hostile to the state." A history lecture he delivered to the Jewish community of Offenbach had been monitored by two policemen who later claimed that by drawing parallels between the era of King Herod and the present times, the rabbi had gravely insulted German authorities. Although Dienemann, his wife, and several other witnesses tried hard to rectify the authorities' twisting of words, the local police president had him deported to Osthofen.[179]

There are also cases in which the concentration camps themselves were the subject of criticism. Some former Jewish camp prisoners were re-arrested for talking about the severe conditions they had experienced inside a camp. Striking is the case of Eugen Kahn, deported to Osthofen twice within the course of a few months. In a local inn in his hometown of Wöllstein he had allegedly not only danced with "Christian maidens" but also showed photographs documenting scenes of the beating of prisoners in the camp. The pictures were confiscated and Kahn, branded as a race defiler *and* a slanderer, was imprisoned in Osthofen in September 1933.[180]

How far the emerging antisemitic model of "the Jew" as the proto-typical enemy could be stretched in practice is ultimately made clear by the case of the arrest of forty-one children and teenagers residing in the Jewish Youth and Educational Home in Wolzig, Brandenburg. The youths, between the ages of thirteen and nineteen, were sent to the SA concentration camp Oranienburg and imprisoned there from June 7 until July 10, 1933.[181] Their detention was the culmination of a campaign that started before 1933 when followers of the Nazi movement in Wolzig had openly insulted and attacked the Jewish boys. Within a short time the inhabitants of the Youth Home became isolated in the village.[182] Several violent raids on the Youth Home took place in the spring of 1933, when local businessmen envisioned using the property for tourism. The graduate engineer Hildegard Harnisch, in a letter to the Reich Commissar for the Provision of Employment on March 17, 1933, tried to further such business plans by denouncing the Youth Home for promoting Communist activities. The institution's "sick pupils" and "doubtful elements," she wrote, were "an annoyance" to the region and they would often hold "intimate, Jewish folk-festivities, in many cases in the Hebrew language."[183] When these complaints were not resolved by the authorities, the local SA storm raided the Youth Home on June 7, 1933, on the pretext of fighting Communist subversion. Its inhabitants were brought to Oranienburg.[184] Incriminating material, such as Communist propaganda literature and weapons, had been deposited in the boys' closets and desks and under their mattresses by the SA men themselves.[185] Once the teenagers had been taken away to Oranienburg, the Youth Home was expropriated—a very early example of camps being used to facilitate the "Aryanization" of Jewish properties.[186]

At Oranienburg, the youths from Wolzig joined the camp's "Jew company," then consisting of approximately fifty-five men.[187] One of them was Max Abraham, a Jewish cantor and teacher from Rathenow. He characterized himself as "a person who has not acted politically," but nonetheless had been arrested as a "state enemy." Abraham reported on the gruesome interrogations the teenagers had to suffer in Oranienburg and the traumatic effects the camp imprisonment had on the adolescent prisoners.[188] Inside the camps the Jewish enemy stereotype, created with the help of the pseudolegal instrument of protective custody, was cemented through extreme violence, sometimes resulting in death. Jewish prisoners' paths into the camps were diverse: they were arrested for active political resistance to the Nazi movement, for criticizing the regime, or due to antisemitic distortions of their economic or private activities. Inside the camps, this heterogeneous assemblage of individuals was turned through violence into "Jews." Chapter 2 will investigate the day-to-day realities of antisemitic discrimination and violent punishment.

2

INSIDE THE EARLY CONCENTRATION CAMPS

Abuse, Isolation, and Murder of Jews, 1933–1934

At a press conference held in Munich on March 22, 1933, acting Police President and Reich Leader SS Heinrich Himmler announced the foundation of the Dachau concentration camp. According to his plans, up to 5,000 prisoners should be detained in the detention center swiftly established at the site of a dilapidated former munitions factory on the outskirts of the town of Dachau, located some 20 kilometers northwest of Munich. The first guard force was provided by the Bavarian State Police (Bayerische Landespolizei) but Himmler soon ordered their replacement by the auxiliary police, a political formation of Nazi paramilitaries, in this case members of the SS, elevated to the status of policemen.[1]

The SS marked the beginning of their rule over the Dachau camp with the murder of four Jewish prisoners. On April 12, 1933, Rudolf Benario, Ernst Goldmann, Arthur Kahn, and Erwin Kahn were shot in the woods adjacent to the improvised camp site. The first three men died immediately; Erwin Kahn initially survived the shooting. He was brought to a hospital in Munich where, on April 16, he succumbed to his injuries. The frightened and appalled Dachau inmates who had heard the gunfire and screams did not believe the explanation given to them afterward by the SS: that the four had been "shot while trying to escape." They were sure that, as Kasimir Dittenheber put it in his memoir, "a naked brutal murder had been committed against defenseless prisoners . . . The four had been selected; they had never voiced thoughts of escape. Now we knew it and we knew that this murder would be followed by others."[2]

In the early concentration camps, the first killing of prisoners was an event of enormous significance. It constituted a radical break in the camp experiences of both inmates and guards, a point of no return after which nothing was as it had been before. Karin Orth, in her study of the concentration camp personnel, aptly terms these brutal incidents "a collective watershed of applied terror and group identity formation."[3] To the prisoners, the first murder signaled that, inside the camp, they bore the real risk of losing their lives. From this point on, they knew that the guards would not stop their abuses at the ultimate border of death. The SS and SA men, on the other hand, for the first time tasted the overwhelming and unbound "power to kill." More than before, the camp personnel were now held together by a shared criminality.[4] Guards covered up for each other to thwart the threat of punishment by a not-yet "coordinated" judiciary. Those who perpetrated the killings irrevocably stepped outside the conventions of civilized society and committed themselves to a camaraderie of crime structured by its very own codes of honor and morality.

It is surely no coincidence that the first victims of Dachau concentration camp were of Jewish origin. Historians agree that camp guards were driven in their violent behavior toward inmates by an aggressive hatred of Jews. Garbe asserts that Jewish camp prisoners were "the selected victims for ill-treatment"; Orth detects a "racist and antisemitic consensus among the concentration camp SS, reflexively governing the actions of its members"; and Matthäus notes perpetrators' "ideological fixation" on the Jews, ultimately rendering the concentration camp "the first institution in which the Nazi slogan 'Jews, perish!' was officially put into action."[5] While these observations without a doubt hold true in general for the history of Jewish prisoners in Nazi concentration camps, they appear rather static, blanket, and circular when one inquires into the initiation of this violent antisemitic behavior. When we turn scholarly attention to anti-Jewish violence in the early concentration camps, we must not forget that what might seem "normal" or "common sense" at later stages of camp history evolved out of deeply unsettling and "abnormal" first-time situations—origins and precedents whose consequences and impacts were entirely unclear.[6]

The case of the first murders in Dachau is a suitable point of departure for an investigation of the specific situations, imprisonment conditions, and experiences of Jews inside the early concentration camps. In this chapter I shall reconstruct the watershed killings in Dachau, and introduce both victims and perpetrators by evaluating juridical files and survivors' memoirs. Based on this detailed empirical analysis, light can be shed on how Jewish victims of ill-treatment were identified and selected, whether the choice was arbitrary or deliberate, whether the guards strictly acted out orders or had some room for maneuver, and finally, how the crime was communicated within the circle of the SS as well as to the inmate population and to the German public beyond the barbed wire.

The day the Bavarian State Police handed over command of the Dachau prisoner camp to SS Oberführer Hilmar Wäckerle and his deputy SS Sturmführer Robert Erspenmüller—Tuesday, April 11, 1933—coincided with the arrival of the first transport of "protective custody" prisoners from Nuremberg and Fürth.[7] Among the sixty men on this transport were Benario, Goldmann, and Arthur Kahn. Wilhelm "Willi" Gesell, another man on the transport, remembered their arrival in Dachau: "When we entered the camp, about 100 characters in green drill uniforms, armed with guns and pistols, who loitered sitting on the ground, rose up. They beat us randomly and called on the Jews to step forward. Those were severely mistreated in front of our eyes."[8] The procedure of identifying and ill-treating prisoners of Jewish origin immediately upon their arrival in the camp was to repeat itself with future transports. Besides Jews, the Dachau SS also selected prominent KPD and SPD functionaries, the *Bonzen* ("fat cats," "bigwigs"), for special abuses.

For Benario and Goldmann, the racial stigma was aggravated by their political profiles. In his student years Rudolf Benario led the student movement at Erlangen University. He campaigned for a broad alliance of left-wing and republican groups to fight the Nazi German Students' League (NSDStB). Through his friend Ernst Goldmann he retained close links to the Young Communist League of Germany (KJVD) in his hometown of Fürth. To all appearances, Benario also held party membership for some time. In July 1931 the political police of Fürth had arrested him at a demonstration in front of the local employment office. He was put on trial a few months later. After the Nazi takeover of power, Benario continued his resistance work against the Nazis. On March 10, 1933, the *Fürther Anzeiger* reported that "the notorious Communist malcontent and Jew Benario" had been taken into "protective custody."[9] Ernst Goldmann was captured along with him. An active member of the KPD, he was also well known to the authorities. After he had been tried in 1931–1932 for "participation in an illegal political assembly," his name entered the police records with the crucial annotation "political troublemaker and Communist agitator."[10] Arthur Kahn, who studied medicine in Würzburg, held no official position in any left-wing organization. Politically interested but altogether rather "harmless," he seems to have fallen victim to the anti-Jewish agitation of the NS-

Figure 2.1 Inmates march out of the fenced-in prisoner compound in the early Dachau concentration camp, May 24, 1933.
KZ-Gedenkstätte Dachau.

DStB that strove for universities "free of Jews."[11] Unaware of the individual prisoners' political profile, the Dachau camp SS learned from the transport list, prepared by the police, that like all the men deported from Nuremberg and Fürth, Benario, Goldmann, and Kahn were to be addressed as "Communist protective custody prisoners." The deportees' religious affiliations were generally not indicated.[12]

After their violent initiation into the camp, Benario, Goldmann, Kahn, and the other men from the transport were sent to the second "company"—the military term for one of the ten single-story stone structures that housed Dachau's first prisoners. Enclosed by barbed wire, the prisoner barracks formed a separated fenced-in compound within the larger walls of the camp. For meals in the dining hall and in order to perform forced labor in the nearby gravel pit, the workshops, or the road construction detail, the prisoners left the barracks compound. The arrival and registration room as well as the prison, the *Bunker*, were also located in outside buildings. The camp site was situated 3 kilometers away from the small town of Dachau in a forested area.[13]

The SS man commanding the second company was Hans Steinbrenner, who rapidly came to epitomize the brutal "Dachau spirit," in spite of the fact that he served in the protective custody camp *(Schutzhaftlager)* for a mere five months. Numerous memoirs and survivors' accounts denounce his extremely violent conduct, relentlessly mocking and torturing the inmates. They agree that Steinbrenner was the most feared and violent man in the early Dachau SS.[14] Born in 1905, Steinbrenner was socialized in the reactionary paramilitary circles of Munich's Steel Helmet organization, the emerging SA, and the SS. On March 9, 1933, he enlisted in the newly formed auxiliary police. Two weeks later he arrived in Dachau.[15]

In the early hours of April 12, 1933, a group of drunken SS men led by Steinbrenner stormed the second company and woke its prisoners by firing several shots. The terrified Franconians had to line up outside for a count and endure threats and insults. The abuse continued in the morning after this sleepless night. At the roll call, when the work commandos for the day were formed, Benario, Goldmann, and Kahn were called forward and Steinbrenner grouped them together with the KPD functionary Gesell. The four men had to load debris onto a large wheelbarrow and push it to the gravel pit, throughout which they were maltreated with beatings. Their ordeal lasted until noon.[16] The grouping together of high-ranking politicians with Jewish prisoners in so-called punishment details *(Strafkommandos)* soon became common practice in Dachau, as well as in other concentration camps. Dachau's dreaded road-roller work detail was called "JuBoWa" *(Juden-Bonzen-Walze)*, a nickname that derived from the fact that it was mainly Jews and high-ranking representatives of the labor movement who had to haul it.[17]

The Communist prisoner Gesell was exempted from the dangerous punitive labor in the afternoon, when the Jewish businessman Erwin Kahn was suddenly assigned to work with the trio from Franconia.[18] Erwin Kahn had no affiliation with the labor movement whatsoever. He was an "unpolitical" Jewish prisoner. As we learn from the letters he sent to his wife, an SA man had arrested him in the streets of Munich without giving any reason. Kahn was confident that once he had been interrogated, all misunderstandings could be cleared up and he would soon be reunited with his family.[19] By the time the first prisoner transport from Franconia arrived in Dachau, Erwin Kahn had been in the camp for almost three weeks, the period in which it was overseen by the Bavarian State Police, whose treatment gave Kahn "in general nothing to complain about."[20]

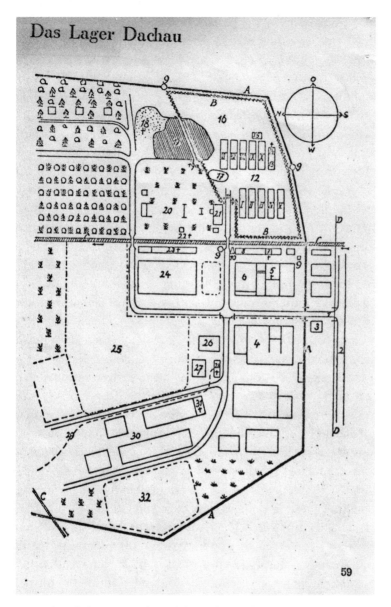

Figure 2.2 A hand-drawn site plan of the early Dachau concentration camp shows the fenced-in prisoner compound with its ten barracks in the upper right-hand corner (12). It also indicates the roll call square (16), the gravel pit (18), the prisoners arrival and registration room (6), as well as the SS accommodation (30) and their drilling and sports grounds (25 and 32). Sites where prisoners were maltreated or killed are marked with a cross (+).

Konzentrationslager: Ein Appell an das Gewissen der Welt (Karlsbad: Graphia, 1934)

After they had finished their afternoon's work, all prisoners returned to the inner enclosure of the barracks camp. As dawn was breaking, they assembled to receive their mail, handed out by camp administrator Anton Vogel, an "old fighter" who had joined the Nazi party in 1922 and, at forty years of age, was one of the oldest of the early Dachau SS.[21] This procedure was interrupted when Steinbrenner appeared on the scene and called out the names of Benario, Goldmann, Arthur Kahn, and Erwin Kahn. The four were told that they were to perform additional punitive labor in the gravel pit and were led away.[22] Why Erwin Kahn was grouped with the other three cannot be fully clarified, but it seems that elements of arbitrariness and accident influenced the choice, possibly stemming from his sharing the same family name with Arthur Kahn.[23]

To reconstruct the murder itself, historians confront a meager and biased source base. Except for the witness statement of Police Lieutenant Emil Schuler from the Bavarian State Police, who rushed to the scene after he heard the first gunshots, the only witness accounts are postwar judicial interrogations of former SS men, who of course had a vital interest in distancing themselves as far as possible from the crime. The evidence identifies deputy camp commander Erspenmüller, and the SS men Hans Burner and Max Schmidt, as the murderers of Benario, Goldmann, and the two Kahns.[24] Schuler encountered Erspenmüller at the scene of the crime and managed, just in time, to prevent him from "finishing off" the mortally wounded Erwin Kahn.[25] Rejecting all responsibility for planning the murder, the former Dachau guards blamed the camp leadership in their postwar interrogations, in particular Erspenmüller, who conveniently could not be questioned, as he had died in the war, as had Wäckerle.[26] Before the killing Erspenmüller had apparently shown off in front of the state policemen, announcing that "in the next [few] days he would kill some Jews" and that a "trial of strength" was due.[27] The Bavarian State Police, although removed from the duty of guarding the prisoners, were still responsible for training the SS in weaponry during the first months of Dachau's existence. Police Lieutenant Schuler, a more credible witness, also attested to the nervousness of the SS in the days preceding the crime, and speculated that Wäckerle, "in his rage and fear of a Communist revolt," had ordered the murder of the Jews.[28] Piecing together all the information, it is clear that the killing was a premeditated deed insofar as Jews had been deliberately chosen as victims. They were called up by name, and it seems likely that the decision as to whom to select—Jewish representatives of the Communist left—had been made beforehand, with Steinbrenner then altering the choice by ordering Erwin Kahn to join the three men from Franconia.[29] By the time of their selection, guards and inmates "knew" the chosen Jewish prisoners, as they had been singled out for two days of brutal humiliation—the likes of which Dachau had not previously seen and which must have had a shocking impact. Steinbrenner's disturbing appearance in the inmates' sleeping quarters on the evening after the murder further aggravated their horror. The SS man is said to have threatened them that soon all the Jews would be executed but non-Jews would remain unharmed.[30]

During the roll call the next day, camp administrator Vogel officially informed Dachau's prisoners that Benario, Goldmann, and the two Kahns had been "shot while trying to escape."[31] Former prisoner Martin Grünwiedl reported that a Communist inmate was ordered to read out a list of "Marxist Jews in the Reichstag," followed by an address from Vogel telling the prisoners that the Jews who had tried to escape were cowards, like all of the leaders of the labor movement who had fled Germany after the Nazi assumption of power.[32] This ideological connection between left-wing politicians and their Jewish roots, which in the eyes of the SS made them particularly dangerous and harmful, was not, however, made in the reports of the deaths circulated outside the camp. From the Nazi-controlled press as well as from a leaflet composed by left-wing resisters, the German public learned that those shot had been "Communists."[33]

Within the Dachau SS, the murder was communicated as a "trial of strength," signaling to its members the kind of "tough" behavior that was expected of them. According to Steinbrenner's memoir—penned in prison after his conviction by a postwar court—they were told about the "dashing" performance of the SS men who shot the Jewish prisoners. The camp leadership was full of praise for those "who were the first to prove themselves."[34] Embedded into a highly ideological discourse that identified camp prisoners as "state offenders" and "race defilers" who would "deserve no other punishment," the killing was presented as a test through which the men would become "hard as Krupp steel," in order to "finally avenge all the misdeeds committed by Communists, Social Democrats, and Jews [during the Weimar years] from 1918 to 1933."[35]

Taking explanations given by SS perpetrators seriously is a challenging enterprise, as it harbors the danger of unwillingly transmitting their agenda of self-vindication. On the other hand, dismissing these sources, and favoring instead abstract and ahistorical condemnations of "evil," does not advance any real understanding of the Dachau "school of violence" that produced such brutal antisemitic behavior. As Christopher Dillon has shown, powerful civil war imagery crucially influenced the early violence in Dachau. Evoking a fear of an imminent Communist insurgency, it was constructed and permanently reinforced by leading personalities such as Wäckerle, Erspenmüller, and the commander of the SS Standarte Munich, Johann Erasmus Freiherr von Malsen-Ponickau—men whose biographical background as *Freikorps* fighters and early SS members had provided their formative political experiences.[36] The narrative of civil war, in Dillon's analysis, served as a "rhetorical pretext" and "helped furnish a cultural architecture and rationale" for the early violence in the camp, representing the prisoners as the very personification of a feared and even genuinely expected counterrevolution.[37] If not stopped by the Nazis, Communist and Jewish insurgents would "have made sure our heads rolled in the dust," as Malsen-Ponickau is reported to have told SS guards in Dachau.[38] Here was evoked the potent topos of the Luitpold Gymnasium massacre, which, as we saw in Chapter 1, played a decisive role in the Nazi vilification of Erich Mühsam and others.

This extremely violent habitus, sponsored by a paranoid fear of a counterrevolutionary strike of the political left, also manifested itself when Steinbrenner confessed to killing KPD activist Karl Lehrburger from Nuremberg on May 25, 1933—the only murder he could ever be legally charged with. The SS man claimed to have shot the Jewish prisoner in an arrest cell on direct orders from Wäckerle, who had allegedly exposed Lehrburger as "a Soviet agent trained by the Cheka in bacterial warfare"—an outlandish claim that Steinbrenner, however, seems not to have questioned.[39] Lehrburger had indeed hidden a crucial part of his identity from the Dachau terror regime, namely that he was of Jewish origin. Brought in along with Benario, Goldmann, and Kahn, he had witnessed but escaped brutal illtreatment and murder by not disclosing his Jewish identity upon arrival. Protected by his comrades, he remained undiscovered—though reportedly living in fear—until the camp was visited by Chief Inspector Paul Ohler from Nuremberg's political police, who knew Lehrburger personally and blew his cover.[40]

While in 1933 the investigating Munich juridical authorities, headed by the persistent Senior Public Prosecutor Carl Wintersberger and First State Attorney Josef Hartinger, had had to accept Steinbrenner's claims of having shot Lehrburger in self-defense—the case against him was closed in June

1933—a postwar court found the former SS man guilty of murder.[41] Although in the 1930s the legal authorities that tried obstinately to bring the criminal early Dachau SS to justice ultimately failed, mounting political pressure forced Himmler to dismiss camp commander Wäckerle in June 1933.[42] The gruesome balance of his reign in Dachau counts twelve dead prisoners in only six weeks—eight of the victims had been of Jewish origin.[43]

The man who came to succeed Wäckerle as the commandant of Dachau was SS Oberführer Theodor Eicke. Chosen by Himmler personally, and remaining forever indebted to his Reichsführer for rehabilitating him from disgrace as a patient in a psychiatric hospital, Eicke would, within a short time, carve out a nefarious career as Inspector of the Concentration Camps and Leader of the Death's Head SS. Dachau became the springboard for this career. Replacing Wäckerle's Special Regulations with no less tokenistic Disciplinary and Punishment Regulations, he gave the impression of introducing order and professionalism to the camp.[44] For the prisoners, however, his taking office as camp commander brought no improvement in their precarious condition. As before, they endured wanton violence and terror. The murders continued and by the end of 1933 the death toll had risen to twenty-two, with victims of Jewish descent still starkly overrepresented (eleven men, or 50 percent).[45] This abysmal statistic marks Dachau as the most lethal of the early concentration camps, comparable, in terms of the number of deaths, only with Oranienburg, Hamburg-Fuhlsbüttel, or the early Emsland camps. The former is estimated to have claimed at least sixteen lives—among them two Jews—throughout its sixteen-month existence.[46] In Fuhlsbüttel, at least fifteen inmates died between June 1933 and June 1934.[47] Up to the dissolution of Börgermoor and Neusustrum in April 1934, a minimum of seventeen prisoners died in the Emsland camps. Three of them can be identified as having been of Jewish origin.[48]

A Statistical Survey

Insofar as they were kept at all, official records of the administration of the early concentration camps provide almost no information that can answer our research questions. They do not satisfactorily clarify the status of Jews in the camp hierarchy, or the conditions of their detention, especially when it comes to questions of housing, labor, or the supply of food and medical care. They also do not illuminate the ways in which Jews fell victim to violent "special treatment," or their relationship to the guards and to other, non-Jewish prisoners, let alone their own experiences of the camp. As the case study of the first murders in Dachau has demonstrated, historians cannot do without the accounts and memoirs of former prisoners, as well as judicial documents, when they want to reconstruct the reality of the imprisonment of Jewish inmates.

The historiographical challenge lies in striking a balance between the particular and the general, that is, between the detailed analysis of biographical and geographical case studies of individual prisoners and camp sites, on the one hand, and the illumination of the overall picture of early camp imprisonment of Jews, on the other. A balance needs to be struck between a depiction of extraordinary events like public beatings or murders, and the less spectacular routine and monotony of Jewish prisoners' day-to-day life inside the camps. Sociologist Paul Martin Neurath, one of the earliest analysts of the Nazi concentration camp and himself a Jewish former prisoner of prewar Dachau and Buchenwald, detected in survivor testimonies a tendency to give an account only of unusual occurrences such as extreme manifestations of violence. He warned that these accounts thereby put across "a completely distorted picture" of the camp, whose reality lay rather in "the 120 loads of gravel and the roll call and the construction of the bed and other routine jobs, which dominated the prisoner's life."[49]

There are no definite figures for the absolute number of Jewish prisoners in the early concentration camps, just as there is no definite total of how many people altogether were unlawfully detained in 1933–1934. For Bavaria, official records added up to just under 20,000 protective custody prisoners captured by August 1934; about 6,300 of them were detained in Dachau.[50] The topography of early terror was institutionally extremely diverse, and not all of the arrestees were, in fact, deported to a concentration camp. Many were kept in local police or court prisons, especially when there was no concentration camp located in the vicinity.[51] Furthermore, official statistics do not record the innumerable "wild" arrests and kidnappings carried out by the SA, SS, and other Nazi party formations, often without authorized protective custody orders. Historians therefore estimate the actual number of arrests and imprisonments to have been much higher than the officially documented protective custody cases of about 100,000. The latest calculations assume that nationwide 150,000, or probably even 200,000 people were detained in 1933, including state prisoners convicted for political offenses.[52]

How many of these detainees were of Jewish origin? Unable to come up with absolute numbers, historiography generally assumes that before the mass imprisonments of 1938, Jews made up 5 to 10 percent of all concentration camp inmates.[53] A translation of this share to the cited absolute minimum figures of official protective custody cases results in a range of at least 5,000 to 10,000 Jews imprisoned in 1933, and probably 7,000 to 12,000 during the whole period from February 1933 to July/August 1934.[54] But 10 percent of Jewish prisoners, however, appears too high a proportion even for the early concentration camps, so I shall adopt as a working hypothesis the minimum of 5 percent.[55]

The most significant sources for a calculation of prisoner numbers would be the administrative records of the various camps detailing prisoner arrivals, transfers, and dismissals. Unfortunately these records have for the most part not survived. For Oranienburg there exists a relatively complete set of prisoner dossiers.[56] In the case of Dachau, we have the arrival books of prisoners as well as the police lists documenting confinements and transfers of prisoners to the camp.[57] For the period after March 24, 1936, there are also the camp reports, which detail daily changes in the numbers of prisoners, the so-called *Veränderungsmeldungen*.[58] For Osthofen, Breitenau, or the Emsland camps, no such documentation exists.

To complicate matters further, the fragmentary administrative records only very seldom identify a prisoner as Jewish.[59] More telling are official reports, documenting the background of individual arrest cases, which were kept in the registries of various state institutions such as the police, the political police, the ministries of the Reich and the individual German States, as well as the responsible district authorities.[60] In addition, Jewish prisoners are sporadically mentioned by name in survivors' testimonies or in contemporary press items. Together with the information generated from the primary sources, existing biographical research conducted by historians and memorial sites can be used to reconstruct individual case studies.[61] Finally, when trying to determine the number of Jewish prisoners in the early concentration camps, we must account for an unknown proportion of inmates who, like Karl Lehrburger, may have tried to hide their Jewish roots from the Nazi perpetrators. Hence, the following statistics can only be approximate. They aim at providing reliable minimum values.

Taking into account both the source base and the location of the camp in relation to the share of the Jewish population living in the region, five camp locations were chosen as representative samples: Dachau in Bavaria, Osthofen in Hesse, and the Prussian camps in Oranienburg, Breitenau, and the Emsland. Of the 499,682 Germans defined as Jewish, who were counted in the census of June 1933, a total of 421,653, or 84.4 percent, resided in these territories. The percentages of the population who were Jewish in Hesse (1.25 percent) and in the administrative districts of Kassel (1.18 percent), Middle Franconia (1.12 percent), and Lower Franconia (1.07 percent), were above the nationwide average of 0.77 percent. Munich had a Jewish population of more than 1 percent, and 160,564 Jews (3.78 percent of the city's population) were counted in Berlin alone.[62]

At least 112 prisoners of Jewish descent were deported to Dachau before the "Röhm purge" on June 30, 1934. While in total around 6,000 men passed through Dachau as prisoners during this period, the average number of detainees held in camp at any one time is estimated to have fluctuated between 2,000 and 2,500 men.[63] Some survivors make statements on the number of Jews interned in the camp. Erich Braun, who arrived in Dachau in early July 1933, counted "around 50 Jews." Hugo Burkhard, who was brought to the camp at around the same time, gave a figure of 64. Siegmund Herz attested to 90 Jews of whom 57 were accommodated in his barrack room. And Ferdinand Kapelner wrote of 60 Jews detained in Dachau by October 1933. In an official letter to the Reich Ministry of the Interior, the National Representation of the German Jews (Reichsvertretung der Deutschen Juden)—the umbrella organization founded in September 1933 to confront Nazi persecution and to represent Jewish interests at a national level—stated that "still over 50 Jewish protective custody prisoners" were interned in November 1934. This figure accords with a report published in the *Manchester Guardian* around the same time that speaks of 50 Jewish prisoners in Dachau.[64] All this points to an average of 60 to 80 Jewish prisoners constantly present in Dachau in 1933–1934. In relation to the above-mentioned total figures of Dachau prisoners (2,000–2,500), this would amount to a share of 2 to 4 percent of the inmate population.

Making similar calculations for the other camp locations, we find that Jews were 4.67 percent of prisoners in Breitenau,[65] 2.9 percent in Oranienburg,[66] just under 1 percent in the Emsland camps,[67] and 4 to 5 percent in the Hessian camp of Osthofen.[68] Although all proportions are minimum values, the figures clearly remain under 10 percent and thus confirm the hypothesis that an average of 5 percent or less of prisoners interned in the early concentration camps were Jewish. Judging from the results, Osthofen was the camp that not only had the highest share but also held the largest number of Jewish prisoners of all the early camps; 119 cases of Jews interned in the Hessian camp could be found.

Further statistical information can be provided on the age profile of Jewish prisoners, their places of origin, and their various professions. Prisoners with Jewish roots were mostly of a mature age—in their thirties or older—when they arrived in the early concentration camps. As table 2.1 details, almost one-third of them were over the age of forty.[69]

The inmates' average age differed from location to location: Jews deported to the Dachau camp were on average 34.86 years old, in Breitenau the average age was 36.5 years, and in the Emsland camps, 37.62 years. The exceptionally low average age of 27.43 years for Oranienburg can be explained by the presence of the forty-one teenage prisoners who were deported to the camp from the Jewish Youth Home in Wolzig, Brandenburg. The youngest of them was only 13 years of age, the oldest 19, when they arrived in the camp in June 1933. Leaving this exceptional group out of the calculation, the average age of Oranienburg's Jews was 39.47 years. The Jewish prisoners in the Osthofen camp were clearly the oldest, with an average age of 41.16 years. This might be due to the location of the camp, in a rural region with a generally older population.[70]

The overall average age of Jewish inmates in the early camps was 34.26 years, or 37.43 years when excluding the boys from Wolzig. Qualitative figures for other groups of prisoners do not exist in a comparative sample, but considering Dirk Lüerssen's figures for the Emsland prisoners, we can cautiously assume that, on average, Jewish prisoners were among the oldest

Table 2.1   Age Groups of Jewish Prisoners in the Early Concentration Camps

Age Group	Born before 1870	1871– 1880	1881– 1890	1891– 1900	1901– 1910	After 1910	n.s.
Dachau	3	5	13	28	38	5	20
Oranienburg	1	5	11	6	8	44 (3)*	11
Breitenau	0	3	5	4	6	4	0
Emsland	0	2	5	5	8	1	13
Osthofen	4	8	10	11	13	3	70
Total	8	23	44	54	73	57 (16)*	114
Percentage	3.09	8.88	16.99	20.85	28.19	22.01 (6.18)*	—

* Calculation omits the 41 teenagers deported to Oranienburg from the Jewish Youth Home in Wolzig.

camp inmates.[71] Moreover, they were significantly older than the guards, whom prisoners of the early camps usually describe as "young lads" of "between 20 and 25 years of age."[72] Dillon has established that the average age of the Dachau SS was 25.7 at the final handover of the camp from the Bavarian State Police on May 30, 1933, and that it declined constantly to reach 20.7 in December 1939.[73] Assuming similar figures for other camp sites, this means that Jewish prisoners, on average, were ten to fifteen years older than the young men who guarded and abused them—a fact not unimportant to bear in mind when analyzing their conflicting relations.

Information about Jewish inmates' places of residence helps to shed light on the relationship between the camp and the locality, and on the social dynamics between prisoners and guards, as well as within the prisoner group itself. It surely made a difference to its threatening reputation if a camp detained mostly captives from the immediate vicinity, or if it had a broader "catchment area" that spread its terrorizing name to more distant localities. As we learn from survivors' memoirs, a common local heritage could be a unifying and strengthening factor for the prisoners. Shared local ties could even transcend political or ideological differences.[74] Erich Braun, from Coburg in Upper Franconia, remembered that his violent initiation to the Dachau camp was somewhat alleviated by his caring reception by other Jews from his region.[75] Ludwig Bendix felt some relief when he found among the hundred prisoners on the transport to Brandenburg his "dear old friend and now fellow sufferer" Kurt Eisner Jr. from Berlin.[76]

Personal acquaintance also affected the treatment of prisoners by the guards, but at times in a reverse way. Isak Krieger, who was deported to Osthofen from the neighboring town of Worms, encountered in the camp a former schoolmate who now served as a guard. The man he knew from his teenage days became his worst tormentor. He severely beat Krieger and made him clean the latrines with his bare hands.[77] When Karl Steiner and Justin Wilmersdörfer from Weiden arrived in Dachau in July 1933, they fell victim to the most brutal abuse, perpetrated by Josef Wolf and the brothers Franz and Max Liebwein. Originating from the same faraway town, the three SS men had anticipated the transport with great excitement, preparing "welcoming weapons" and declaring that "the Weideners were the real *Bonzen* and that they would be given the right kind of reception."[78] Anonymity, on the other hand, could afford protection, as we have seen in the example of Karl Lehrburger. As none of the SS knew him personally, he could conceal his Jewishness until a personal foe from his hometown of

Nuremberg visited the camp. On the whole, however, it seems that the abuse of Jewish inmates was not driven—as it was the case of many political prisoners—by a personal acquaintance of the SS and SA guards with their victims. The label "Jew" would often expose an otherwise unknown person to severe maltreatment.

Survivors' statements to the effect that the overwhelming majority of Jewish prisoners in Dachau came from Franconia can be confirmed by the statistics. An evaluation according to Bavaria's administrative districts results in the geographical distribution shown in table 2.2.

More than half of Dachau's Jews were deported to the camp from Franconia (53 percent), in particular from the populous administrative districts of Lower and Middle Franconia, which traditionally had the largest Jewish populations within the state of Bavaria.[79] Franconia was also the region in which Julius Streicher, the *Gauleiter* (Nazi Party district leader) of Middle Franconia (later Franconia), stirred up hatred of the Jews through violent antisemitic publications and an aggressive political culture. Of the early Dachau SS, however, only a handful of men came from Franconia. Most of them were drawn from the SS Standarten in Munich and its surroundings, from Augsburg, or from Landshut in Lower Bavaria.[80] In Dachau, therefore, most Jewish prisoners did not previously know the SS men guarding and abusing them inside the camp.

Table 2.2   Local Origin of Jewish Prisoners in the Dachau Concentration Camp, 1933–1934

Local Origin according to Administrative Districts (*Regierungsbezirke*)	Number of Jewish Prisoners
Lower Franconia (incl. Würzburg, Kitzingen, Schweinfurt)	24
Middle Franconia (incl. Nuremberg, Fürth)	22
Upper Bavaria (incl. Munich, Ingolstadt, Rosenheim)	17
Upper Franconia (incl. Coburg, Bamberg)	14
Upper Palatinate (incl. Regensburg, Amberg, Weiden i.d. Oberpfalz)	10
Bavarian Swabia (Augsburg)	5
Rhine Palatinate (incl. Pirmasens)	3
Lower Bavaria (Furth bei Landshut)	1
Not from Bavaria	5
n.s.	11

This was different in the case of Osthofen, where the camp was located in a rural area from which not only many prisoners but also the great majority of the guards came. Every day, an average of fifty-five auxiliary policemen, recruited from Osthofen, Worms, and the immediate vicinity, were on guard duty in the camp.[81] They were confronted with prisoners from the same region. The majority of Osthofen's Jewish prisoners came from Hesse's province of Rhenish Hesse, in which the camp itself was also located. When looking at the places of origin, we find a number of Jewish prisoners deported from the Hessian cities—sixteen from Mainz, seven from Worms—but mostly the inmates were from small towns and villages in the areas near the camp.

Oranienburg's Jewish prisoner population, in contrast, had a more urban profile. Leaving aside again the special case of the teenagers from rural Wolzig, the majority of the Jews had their homes in Berlin.[82] The others were deported from Potsdam and various smaller towns in the district of Niederbarnim—termed by camp commandant Werner Schäfer "the politically most dangerous district bordering Berlin"—in which the Oranienburg camp was located.[83] The picture looks similar for the Breitenau camp in the Prussian administrative district of Kassel. About half of its Jewish prisoners were residents of big cities like Kassel, Fulda, or Berlin. The others were brought to the camp from small towns and villages rather distant from Breitenau.

Börgermoor, Esterwegen, and Neusustrum mark a special case in terms of prisoners' geographical origins, because for many of the prisoners it was not their first concentration camp. About one-third of Jewish inmates were transferred to the Emsland camps from other Prussian camps in the second half of 1933, when the Interior Ministry pursued plans to build up a central camp complex in this region and systematically exploit prisoner labor for the cultivation of the peat bog.[84] Most of the Jews came from towns and villages in Westphalia, the Ruhr, or the Prussian Rhine Province. A few also came from Silesia.[85]

An evaluation of the databases of Jews in the early camps for the prisoners' various jobs and professions results in the occupational distribution listed in table 2.3.

These figures broadly mirror the general occupational structure of Jews in the German economy.[86] Almost half of Jewish concentration camp prisoners, 44.05 percent, worked in commerce or trade. Among them were entrepreneurs and proprietors of companies, factories, and department stores, as well as owners of small shops or medium-sized businesses, like cattle dealers

Table 2.3   Occupations of Jewish Prisoners in the Early Concentration Camps, 1933–1934

	Dachau	Osthofen	Oranienburg	Emsland Camps	Breitenau	Total
Clerical workers & civil servants	8	1	6	3	2	20 (7.94%)
Industry & crafts	8	8	11	2	5	34 (13.49%)
Commerce & trade	41	46	8	7	9	111 (44.05%)
Independent professions (doctors, lawyers, journalists)	8	8	12	7	3	38 (15.08%)
Professional politicians & functionaries	—	1	1	2	1	5 (1.98%)
In training/ education	4	3	31	—	2	40 (15.87%)
Unemployed	–	2	2	–	–	4 (1.59%)
n.s.	43	50	15	13	–	121

or merchants. Together with those employed as civil servants and clerical workers (7.94 percent), those occupied in the industries and crafts (13.49 percent), and those practicing independent professions, such as lawyers, doctors, journalists, or pharmacists (15.08 percent), they, for the most part, economically belonged to the middle class. Only a very small minority of Jewish prisoners (1.98 percent) made their living as professional politicians.

Jewish inmates differed from SA and SS guards in terms of both class and culture. Members of the early Dachau guards mainly had lower-middle-class and working-class occupations before they joined the camp SS. Of the general rank-and-file SS of the early 1930s, a large part can be identified as lower-class.[87] These observations seem to support survivors' testimonies that characterized the Dachau guards as uneducated and simple country lads—"Bavarian swains," as former prisoner Wenzel Rubner perceived them.[88] Perpetrators in Oranienburg are described as "simple S.A.-men, almost all young untrained workers, unemployed since years . . . proletarian lads aged 19 to 20 years."[89]

To be sure, former prisoners' statements carry their own agenda of devaluing the adversary. Still, they are instructive when it comes to the victims' perception of their tormenters and their interpretation of violent encounters as sociocultural clashes. Prisoners who wore glasses often provoked abuse, because they bore "the fatal insignia of the intelligentsia."[90] Branded as "Jewish intellectuals," inmates lived in constant danger of falling victim to acts of violence; as Bruno Bettelheim phrased it: "to enter the camp with horn-rimmed glasses was tantamount to a death warrant."[91] Not least in the discrimination against spectacle wearers, it became manifest that the SS and SA bore class resentments and regarded well-educated members of the middle class and the intelligentsia as idlers who would shy away from "honest"—that is, hard physical—labor. Although further research into the social profile of both camp guards and inmates is needed, it can be noted that class differences and the acting-out of social envy influenced the violent relationship between overseers and Jewish prisoners.

The Birth of the "Jew Company"

To lock up their opponents in concentration camps once the Nazi Party came to political power had been a long-standing demand of Hitler and his followers. As early as 1920, Jews were included in the circle of enemies who should be taken into protective custody and deported to detention camps (*Sammellager*).[92] In a lurid article on the treatment of supposed traitors to the nation, published in the *Völkischer Beobachter* in March 1921, Hitler himself made the following claim: "Traitors to the national cause of the people should be strung up once and for all . . . Let us stop the Jews from undermining our nation, if necessary by keeping their germs safely in concentration camps. In short, clean our nation of all poison above and below."[93]

The National Socialists' aggressive political rhetoric, however, remained vague when it came to the practical implementation of these intentions. When, in the spring of 1933, rhetoric suddenly had to be put into action, the new powerholders, by and large, stood unprepared. Hence, there was also no concrete plan for what to do with Jews once they were held in captivity. Eicke's camp regulations are the only known document that attempted to determine the status and treatment of Jewish prisoners. Still rather abstract, the source merely stated that Jews rank in the lowest category of prisoners, to be subjected to the harshest living conditions.[94]

Another unforeseen problem occurred: except for a few foreign nationals—who could sometimes hope that diplomatic pressure on the

German Reich would result in their release—most Jews in the early concentration camps were German citizens.[95] They were acculturated and "modernized" men who, by their looks, were indistinguishable from other Germans, including the guards. Instead of conversing in Yiddish, German was their mother tongue, and some spoke it in the local dialect. How, then, could the SS and SA guards recognize Nazi Germany's supposed Jewish enemies? Procedures of selection had to be developed. Ordering Jews to step forward upon arrival was one strategy of identification. I will focus on two other practices: permanent separation in "Jew companies" and special work detachments.

Identification of Jews inside the camp, and their vilification as enemies of the German people, became easier for the perpetrators when individual prisoners were forced together into a group. Blanket treatment as a separate group facilitated generic attribution as well as collective punishment and reprisals that could then, in turn, effectively enforce the racial stigma. A permanent segregation of Jewish inmates through spatial separation and separate work details, a practice well known from wartime, was, however, not commonly applied in the early concentration camps. In 1933–1934 it was rather an exception. Doing justice to its label as the "model camp," Dachau marks the most definite exception. Beginning in about mid-April 1933, Jewish prisoners were housed in separate barrack units quickly dubbed the "Jew company."[96]

Dachau's prisoner camp initially consisted of ten companies (barracks) with five halls or platoons (*Korporalschaft*) each. Each hall was designed to have 54 beds, a total of 270 beds per barrack.[97] Strictly speaking, the term "Jew company" is misleading, as the number of Jewish prisoners in early Dachau was too small to fill a whole barrack. Only after February 1937, when Jews from all other concentration camps were brought together in Dachau, did they occupy an entire block. In the early years Jews shared a barrack with prominent politicians and high-ranking functionaries of political parties and organizations, the so-called *Bonzen*. These "bigwigs" had to bear violent "special treatment" like that given to the Jews. The barrack in which they all were housed was also known as the "punishment company" (*Strafkompanie*).[98] In the topography of early Dachau, this was barrack 7, and Jewish prisoners were quartered in halls 2 and 3, with the latter also partly populated by Social Democrats. A few years later—in all probability between 1935 and 1936—it was renumbered to be barrack 6 of Dachau's ten barracks.[99]

Each barrack had an SS man as a company leader, who commanded a company senior or sergeant (*Feldwebel*), a vice company senior, and five platoon seniors (*Korporalschaftsführer*), all from the ranks of the prisoners. As the leader of the seventh company, prisoners remember the notoriously violent SS man Johannes Kantschuster. Together with Johann Unterhuber, Kantschuster, who came to Dachau in April 1933, also oversaw the camp's arrest section, the *Bunker*, in which inmates were tortured and a significant number of them were murdered.[100] Non-Jewish prisoner Max Dankesreiter is remembered as the company senior. Burkhard describes him as "a decent, honest political prisoner."[101] Siegmund Herz, a Jewish merchant from Pirmasens, who arrived in Dachau in early June 1933, testified that he served as the senior of the second hall, the "Jew-*Korporalschaft*." He had been transferred to Dachau after the dissolution of the only other early concentration camp on Bavarian territory, the Turenne-Kaserne in Neustadt a.d. Haardt, located in the Rhine Palatinate.[102] Living conditions in the "punishment company" were especially severe, as prisoners had to cope with a number of restrictions not applied to the occupants of other barracks. They were forbidden to smoke, received smaller rations of food, were given dirty and torn gowns instead of prisoner uniforms, and, as I will show more systematically below, were forced to perform the hardest and most degrading labor.[103]

As in Dachau, Jewish prisoners in the Oranienburg concentration camp were also separated into a distinct "Jew company"—sometimes referred to as "Jew division" (*Juden-Abteilung*) or "Jew platoon" (*Judenzug*).[104] Like many of the early concentration camps, Oranienburg's topography did not resemble the seemingly classical structure of a barrack camp. In February 1933, the SA Standarte 208 took over a disused factory site in Berliner Strasse, located in the center of town and known to locals as The Old Brewery. Roll calls were held in the courtyard of the old factory, where prisoners had to stand at attention in rows guarded by SA men. Until the camp administration distributed worn-out police uniforms, inmates had to dress every day in the same civilian clothes in which they had arrived in the camp.[105]

Oranienburg's prisoners were quartered in the clammy former cooling cellars of the brewery, initially sleeping on the bare floor or on damp piles of straw. In his 1934 book, the escaped prisoner Gerhart Seger described them as "long, narrow rooms that open out into a dark hallway, with a small window located at the opposite narrow side (with entirely insufficient ventilation possibilities). Into these tubular cellars they then built bedsteads on the right and on the left sides that reached, at a stretch, from the hallway to the window. On these bedsteads the prisoners lie to this day, on three

Figure 2.3 Roll call in the courtyard of the Oranienburg concentration camp, August 1933.

bpk, Bayerische Staatsbibliothek, Archiv Heinrich Hoffmann.

levels one upon the other."[106] Dubbed "rabbit hutches" by the prisoners, the official camp language referred to these cellars as "companies." There were seven companies, each divided into two platoons *(Züge)*, and each company accommodated 100 to 150 prisoners.[107] As in Dachau, Jewish prisoners in Oranienburg were too few to constitute a whole company. They were, however, grouped together and separated from the other inmates at one end of the sleeping hall, as Stefan Szende remembered: "The Jews lived at the rear wall of the barrack [*sic*], somewhat aside but still in the same room as the other prisoners."[108]

In contrast to Dachau, Oranienburg's "Jew company" did not exist continuously throughout the whole period of the camp's operation from March 1933 to July 1934. Seger, who was detained in Oranienburg from June 14 until his escape on December 4, 1933, stated that "the so-called Jew company" had existed only "for a while."[109] In fact, in the history of the camp, one needs to speak of an early and a later Jew company. The former existed from mid-June to early September 1933 when most of Oranienburg's Jewish prisoners were transported to Börgermoor concentration camp.[110] According to camp commandant Schäfer, the Jew company was first established after the arrival of the teenagers from the Jewish Youth Home in Wolzig. Max Abraham stated that it consisted of some fifty-five prisoners officially assigned to the fifth company, first platoon.[111] The Potsdam lawyer Ludwig Levy, imprisoned in the camp from June 28 to July 24, 1933, served as the leader of the early Jew company.[112] The second Jew company, consisting of some twenty men, was established in early January 1934 after Jewish prisoners were transferred to Oranienburg from Columbia-Haus and the Brandenburg camp upon the latter's dissolution.[113] Both Max Fürst and the SAP activist Paul Walter are named as leaders. In the early period, a strict spatial segregation of Jews was also enacted during the day, but social isolation seems to have been somewhat less rigorously enforced in 1934.[114]

In Oranienburg, the existence of a Jew company was conditioned by the presence of a critical mass of Jewish prisoners in the camp. Although in the intermediary period from September 1933 to January 1934 the camp had never been completely "free of Jews," the few individuals who remained were apparently not grouped together under the racial stigma.[115] Numerical strength thus constitutes an important factor in explaining the establishment of Jew companies in the early concentration camps. In the Lichtenburg camp, the grouping together of Jews started after a large transport of prominent political and Jewish prisoners from the Emsland in October 1933 brought thirty to forty Jews into the camp. The Social Democrat Fritz Kleine reported that after the arrival of the transport, prisoner housing was rearranged: "Functionaries of the old state, all the members of the Reichstag and the state diets, and all Jews came to station III, called the station of the 'prominent.'"[116] In the Sachsenburg camp, a Jew company was established in mid-1935 when the number of Jewish inmates increased to about forty; they were housed together, worked together, and had to line up as a separate group during roll call.[117]

While the presence of a larger group of Jewish prisoners facilitated the establishment of Jew companies in the early concentration camps, numerical strength alone cannot explain the practice of spatially separating Jews from other prisoners. In the rather small Saxon camp of Osterstein castle in Zwickau, for example, where Jewish inmates were few, they were nevertheless kept in strict isolation from the rest of the prisoners. Paul D., a textiles salesman from Aue, gave the following account of his incarceration in Osterstein from March 10 to May 6, 1933: "We Jews were kept in total isolation from the other inmates and never even saw them. We washed ourselves separately, used a different toilet and had our daily walks at different times."[118] In contrast to the spatial segregation practiced in Osterstein, there was, remarkably, no separate housing of Jewish prisoners in the Hessian state concentration camp of Osthofen, and this despite the fact that here we find the largest group of Jewish inmates in the early camps. As a result of the uncoordinated practices of imprisonment in 1933–1934, living conditions varied from place to place, as did the way Jewish prisoners were treated.

Although it is hardly possible to compare camp terror prevailing at different locations, Dachau under the command of Wäckerle and Eicke stands out through its extreme degree of violence, most strikingly reflected in a death toll of at least thirty-nine prisoners in 1933–1934. With at least fifteen of the dead having been of Jewish descent, it is self-evident that Jews in Dachau, the flagship SS camp, were exposed to particularly lethal treatment.[119] Their forced grouping together as a visible Jew company, housed at a fixed location and thereby available for abuse at all times, was an outgrowth of these harsh imprisonment conditions and, in turn, promoted the most severe collective treatment. This is true also for Oranienburg under SA Sturmbannführer Schäfer, a camp that claimed the lives of at least sixteen prisoners.[120] Spun as it was for the purpose of public presentation, Schäfer's self-vindicating *Anti-Brown Book* nevertheless clearly exposes the camp commandant's antisemitic worldview, which directly influenced his perception of the prisoners. The teenagers from the Wolzig Youth Home, for example, he described as "depraved human beings," "degenerate, downright asocial Jews, criminal and previously convicted for political reasons."[121] His subordinates, most notoriously Krüger and Stahlkopf, are remembered for translating this racial ideology into violent anti-Jewish behavior.

While commandants such as Wäckerle, Eicke, or Schäfer are unanimously remembered as cruel leaders, Osthofen's SS Sturmbannführer Karl d'Angelo seems to have been a more ambiguous figure. Acting the "kind old daddy" and the "good ordinary citizen" when dealing with the inmates, he is said to have demonstrated a "rare human impulse." Former inmates stated that he often did everything he could to effect early releases from the camp.[122] But d'Angelo's occasional leniency did not extend to Jewish prisoners. A committed party comrade and antisemite, he lectured non-Jewish prisoners and tried to convert them to Nazism.[123] While ultimately responsible for the crimes committed in the camp, it remains to his relative credit that no prisoner lost his life inside the Osthofen camp—although the Jewish inmate Adolf Sondheimer died shortly after his release from the consequences of ill-treatment inflicted upon him in the camp.[124]

In 1935, about half a year after the dissolution of the Osthofen camp, Karl d'Angelo was assigned to Dachau where, under then-commandant Heinrich Deubel, he held the influential position of leader of the protective custody camp *(Schutzhaftlagerführer)*. In contrast to other SS concentration camp officers from the early period, d'Angelo did not make a career in the camp system. Disqualified as too soft, with a "weakness of character," Eicke soon declared him unsuitable "for any political activity in a concentration camp."[125] His dismissal from camp service had been instigated by the new commandant Hans Loritz, who found that discipline was down at Dachau when he took office in April 1936. In order to prevent imprisonment conditions from further "deteriorating," Dachau had to be "cleansed" of d'Angelo, whose "disgustingly humane treatment of the inmates" disturbed other camp SS men, too.[126] Among other charges held against him when he was forced to leave Dachau, in spring 1936, was the accusation of having approved the appointment of a Jew to the rank of prisoner functionary.[127] The fact that d'Angelo obviously "failed to evince the hatred and brutality of many of his peers in the concentration camp environment" would also explain to some extent why he refrained from institutionalizing a punitive Jew company in Osthofen despite the camp's large presence of Jewish inmates.[128]

Through the creation of Jew companies, camp officials forced diverse personalities into a collective amenable to the projection of generic ideological stereotypes. Spatial separation can thus be understood as a tool for provoking the guards and facilitating the blanket perception of Jewish inmates as evil, dangerous, and criminal enemies of the regime.

Camp Labor

The second means of permanently segregating Jewish prisoners from others was to assign them to separate work details. Labor in the early concentration camps was more punitive than productive. As a means to enforce discipline, to humiliate the prisoners, and to break their will, it tormented them and kept them occupied throughout the day. Most of the "real"—that is, productive—work was devoted to the construction, maintenance, and furnishing of the makeshift camp sites. While some of the early camp labor did also have a commercial aspect, it was not until 1937–1938 that economic factors came into play and camp officials began to seriously exploit the prisoners' workforce for more profitable enterprises, beyond merely covering the camps' own requirements.[129]

The stereotype that Jews refused to dirty their hands with "honest" physical labor was pervasive among SS and SA men. As it was with prominent political prisoners or Jehovah's Witnesses, camp labor became an instrument to torment Jewish prisoners. The harsh maltreatment one injured Jew in Dachau had to suffer is exemplary for this practice of violence, and scenes like the following were witnessed many a time: Despite the camp doctor's order to let him rest and be exempted from labor, Max Hanns Kohn, a junior lawyer from Nuremberg, was ordered to work at the road roller. As his SS-inflicted injuries were not recognized as disqualifying him from work, Kohn was beaten by the SS work deployment supervisor (Arbeitsführer) and berated thus: "You shirker, you dirty Jew! I will teach you how to work!"[130] Instead of being "taught how to work," however, Jews were frequently singled out for punitive and pointless jobs. Forced labor was thus advanced as a form of "special treatment" that affirmed the prevailing antisemitic stereotype of "work-shy Jews." As a result, qualified skilled workers like the carpenter Max Fürst were often not deployed for artisan work but ordered to do punishment work: "I would have worked in the camp carpentry, if I had not been a Jew."[131] Dachau prisoner Hugo Burkhard distinguishes "slave labor"—the work under constant abuse and severe conditions, in the open, whatever the weather—from the "professional work detail" for skilled craftsmen inside the workshops. Very few Jewish prisoners managed to secure a place in these details. Even if they were highly qualified, the camp rule that Jews should not perform "noble labor" or benefit from moderate working conditions in sheltered places blocked their entry into these units.[132]

To which work detachments, then, were the Jewish prisoners assigned? In general, these were work details deployed exclusively inside the camp perimeters and mostly occupied with cleaning, construction, or maintenance work. The reason for this practice is not officially documented. However, it can be assumed that because the details that worked outside the camp perimeter were exposed to the public eye, it would have been difficult, if not impossible, to inflict brutal "special treatment" on Jews if they worked in those groups. Furthermore, these external details mostly performed construction work, renovation, clearing, or forest operations for the local communities—all of which were "worthy," productive forms of labor from which Jewish inmates were excluded according to Nazi ideology. In the following I shall introduce work details set up in Dachau, Oranienburg, and the Emsland camps.

Prisoners in Dachau were forced to work nine to fourteen hours per day.[133] During the morning and noon roll calls, SS work deployment supervisor Max von Dall'Armi, assisted by prisoner Josef "Sepp" Zäuner in his function as the labor sergeant (*Arbeitsfeldwebel*), read out prisoners' names and assigned them to their daily work details. Always the last on the list were the inhabitants of the Jew company.[134] They were mainly deployed in two work detachments: the gravel pit detail and the roadwork detail, both of which also employed non-Jewish inmates. Prisoners sent to the gravel pit had to labor under especially harsh conditions. Some had to quarry out gravel with pickaxes, while others had to shovel it away. Using a light railway, the gravel was transported from the pit to various construction sites. The men had to push the heavily loaded roll cars while being ordered to constantly move around on the double. Prisoner foremen supervising the workers instructed them and hurried them along. A chain of SS sentinels was positioned around the rim of the pit. With work constantly interrupted by insults and physical abuse, Dachau prisoners feared the gravel pit as a gruesome torture site. It was located in a secluded area remote from the prisoner compound but still within the larger camp perimeters.[135] Like the gravel pit detail, the roadwork detail was also considered a punishment detail for Dachau's Jews and prominent political prisoners.[136] Forced to construct camp roads, a team of forty to fifty inmates had to push and pull the heavy road roller, which was filled with water. Others worked in small formations around it, loosening the ground and shoveling it away. Still others mixed newly delivered materials with the loosened rubble and spread the matter back on the ground. Afterward the road roller and sprinkler were applied to give the new road layer the necessary consistency.[137]

In Oranienburg too, Jewish prisoners worked only in details inside the camp. Fürst remembered that "as a Jew one was not allowed to work outside."[138] During his time of imprisonment in early 1934, about 100 of the estimated total of 800 Oranienburg inmates remained inside the camp while the others "marched out" every day to labor in the town and its vicinity.[139] Jewish prisoners' work mainly consisted of cleaning the camp latrines and washroom. In what was euphemistically termed the "bathing house" there stood a disused railroad engine that had to be fired with cordwood to pro-

Figure 2.4 In the Dachau concentration camp an SS man guards a work detail of prisoners forced to level a street with a road roller, May 27, 1933.
Bundesarchiv, Bild 152–01–26 / Friedrich Franz Bauer.

vide hot water. Prisoners Fürst, Szende, and others had to keep clean the approximately forty showers and fifty plate-bowls that were installed on benches and served as toilets. Besides the bathing house commando, Jewish inmates also worked in the camp kitchen or in the details responsible for cleaning the courtyard and the sleeping quarters.[140]

The plan to use prisoner labor for the cultivation of the Emsland marshes had been a decisive factor in the choice of location of the large complex of camps established in the region since the summer of 1933. According to the calculations of the state institutions involved, a contingent of 5,500 prisoners could reclaim 11,000 hectares of land.[141] From the beginning, however, the work input was neither cost-effective nor economically justifiable. Prisoners of the moor detachments, the "peat bog soldiers" (*Moorsoldaten*), described their work as extremely hard. Under the instruction of civilian workers, they ploughed up the moor. Equipped with inadequate tools and maltreated by their SS overseers, they were by no means able to fulfill their daily target of 10 square meters per man. The SS had no respect for the injured or the disabled. Hans Litten, for example, whose physical condition was critical due to severe maltreatment and a heart condition, was forced to carry out the same excruciating labor as everybody else.[142]

As in Dachau and Oranienburg, Jewish prisoners in the Emsland camps, too, had almost no chance of being selected for work in their original professions.[143] Sharing the fate of prominent politicians and Jehovah's Witnesses, Jews were mostly assigned to the so-called special work details assembled to execute various unpleasant tasks of maintenance and construction works—including a funeral column that had to take care of dead bodies. Prisoners in the special detachments were subject to harsher working conditions and longer hours; sometimes they also had to work during the night. Every job had to be done in a constant hurry.[144] Survivors of the Emsland camps who testified in the criminal proceedings against former SS man Fritz Vogel in 1950–1951 described such a special detachment that existed in Esterwegen in late summer 1933 as a punishment detail: "In the early days, while other prisoners did not yet have to do any real work and mostly still lingered in the barracks, the special detachment, from the outset, was deployed for heavy labor . . . It might have been 30 to 40 men strong. To my knowledge, all the Jews were in the special detachment."[145] The Esterwegen special detachment worked in and around the camp compound where the prisoners had to construct paths, plots, and flower beds. It was occasionally also sent to work in the no-man's-land of the marshes—outside the camp but far away from any curious or protective gazes of the local population.[146]

Former prisoner Rudolf Münch, a bricklayer from Koblenz, told the examining magistrate how Vogel, who oversaw the special detachment, forced him to drive around a Jewish prisoner in a pushcart loaded with turf. He had to dump the man in a trench and then to fill it as if to bury him alive.[147] It seems that the victim was a Jewish textile merchant from Düsseldorf named Meyer (or Meier). Several other survivors remembered him not only as Vogel's selected object of ill-treatment but also as the kapo, the prisoner foreman, of Esterwegen's special detachment.[148] This is confirmed by former SS man Wilhelm Heitmann, himself a defendant in the trial, who stated that he had once remonstrated with Vogel on his selection of a Jewish prisoner as kapo: "Vogel legitimized this before me and said that he had only wanted to ridicule the Jew."[149] Cases like this make very clear that the boundaries between forced labor and ill-treatment were fluid, especially when Jewish prisoners were concerned.

In almost every camp, Jews were ordered to do the most dirty and repulsive of tasks. Dachau's "commando 4711," sarcastically named after a well-known German brand of eau de cologne, consisted exclusively of Jewish prisoners. It was also the only work detail in the camp that temporarily had a Jewish kapo. Its members had to clean the cesspit underneath the toilets. In Esterwegen, Jews had to clean the sewage barrel with their bare hands. Bendix reported that Jewish prisoners in Brandenburg were forced to do "especially filthy jobs," and he himself became the "minister of the latrines." Finally, the Jews in Osthofen also had to empty the toilets with their own dishes or tins. The SS pressed them ahead and watched that nothing was spilled from the brimming-over buckets. When someone stumbled because the guards had tripped him up, he immediately fell victim to further mockery and beatings.[150]

For the prisoners it was vital to keep busy, or at least appear to be busy, with a job, so as to not attract the attention of the guards and provoke ill-treatment. When there was no work to do, punitive drill emerged as a means to control and terrorize prisoners. In Dachau, all those who were not assigned to a work detail remained behind on the mustering grounds to do "sport." Driven by threats, insults, and beatings, both Jewish and non-Jewish inmates were forced to perform gymnastic exercises and endurance runs, and had to prove themselves on an improvised obstacle course with a 5-meter-high climbing wall.[151] Oftentimes Jews in particular were singled out for "camp sport." Roman Praschker, a former prisoner of Brandenburg, described a similar so-called *Judenexerzieren* (exercise for Jews) held in this Prussian camp: "We had to run, do leapfrogs, jump up and down like frogs until we collapsed. We were spurred on by cane strokes."[152]

Keeping inmates occupied and bound to the rule of camp terror were not the only functions of punitive drill. Research by Veronika Springmann compellingly analyzes "camp sport" as a specific everyday practice of violence, and illuminates its overall purpose as a means to effectively "produce differences" between guards and inmates.[153] Springmann rightly points out that "camp sport" encoded rituals and principles practiced in the military. But whereas in the context of the army, drill should ultimately inscribe individuals into the fighting community by hardening their bodies for the battle and by instilling into them discipline, attitude, and order as well as obedience, exercise in the concentration camp was disintegrative, humiliating, and violating in effect. Prisoners were forced to mimic the rituals of becoming manly soldiers only to prove that they could never do so. Jewish prisoners, in particular, whom ideology excluded from the Nazi people's community, were exposed to excruciating "camp sport" in order to brand their bodies as weak and degenerated. Their inevitable failures in accomplishing the exercises were taken, not least, as a demonstration that Jews were unfit for military service. This insulted Jewish prisoners' male pride, because they mostly adhered to the ideal of the soldier.[154] Hence, torture through "camp sport" was a means to publicly demonstrate the essential differences between the prisoners and their overseers. This practice of violence affirmed antisemitic stereotypes and images of the Jewish body. While it insulted Jews (and non-Jews) in their masculinity and denied them participation in the prestigious national institution of the German military, it simultaneously enabled SA and SS guards to identify themselves with the soldierly ideal.[155]

Jewish Prisoner Functionaries

There were almost no Jewish prisoner functionaries overseeing work details in the early concentration camps. Those who were made a kapo, like Jewish prisoner Meyer/Meier in Esterwegen, suffered from the position and received additional distress instead of the privileges normally also granted. Although the prisoner functionary system was not firmly established until the mid-1930s, its roots are clearly visible in the organization of the early camps, where SA and SS were quick to delegate power and responsibilities to a selected circle of auxiliaries recruited from the ranks of the inmates. Installed as a "perfidious measure" to co-opt prisoners in the implementation of terror and violence, the kapo system developed into a parallel organizational structure of "divide and rule" that ensured the running of the camp on a day-to-day basis. At the top of the prisoner hierarchy stood the camp eldest and his deputies.[156]

Prisoners who held posts of influence and exerted power over fellow inmates can be divided into those who performed disciplinary tasks and those who performed administrative tasks. Among the first were the labor supervisors who headed work details. Larger details were led by several prisoner foremen, who themselves were overseen by a chief kapo. Kapos had to push prisoners to work and to ensure that a set task was fulfilled to the satisfaction of the camp leadership—often an almost impossible thing to do with SA and SS giving out unachievable assignments and work-output quotas. Apart from the labor supervisors, there were also prisoner functionaries who enforced order and discipline in the inmates' living quarters. Each housing unit had a barrack elder *(Blockältester)* aided by room elders *(Stubenälteste)* and table elders *(Tischälteste)*. Together they distributed foods and other goods, and made sure that the inhabitants of their block adhered to the strict routine of the day and kept their quarters spotlessly clean. Each block also had a clerk *(Blockschreiber)* whose task was administrative rather than disciplinary. He had to keep track of all changes in the composition of the block, registering new arrivals, releases, and prisoners transferred to other places, including the infirmary. Prisoners who worked as scribes in the camp administration fulfilled similar tasks and helped to issue reports and to keep the records and statistics for the camp as a whole. Besides the scribes who performed the paperwork in the various offices of the camp leadership, prisoner functionaries deployed in the kitchen, laundry, storerooms, and infirmary performed administrative tasks that kept the camp's supply and service facilities running.[157]

Jewish prisoners rarely held administrative posts in the prisoner functionary system, because their racial status prohibited them from gaining influence over "Aryan" inmates. Truly exceptional in this sense was the status of a few doctors of Jewish origin who were allowed to work in their occupation. The medical help these orderlies provided was much needed because official camp "doctors," often recruited from the ranks of the SS or SA, were either incompetent or absent altogether, or acted in such a way as to harm rather than cure. As the following examples will show, Jewish medics' influential position did grant them certain advantages, but it also caused them great difficulties as it put them into the impossible situation of negotiating between their own interests to survive, the demands of the perpetrators, and the needs of the other prisoners.

Dr. Hamburger from Tirschtiegel in Posen, West Prussia (today Trzciel, Poland), who had been arrested as a race defiler, served as a dentist in the early Lichtenburg camp. Commander Edgar Entsberger and his SS men exploited him and his skills to the utmost, and according to prisoner accounts, they were quick to overcome their ideological principles and had the Jewish specialist repair their teeth free of charge. As a reward, the doctor was granted various freedoms that his fellow prisoners viewed with disgust. They defamed Hamburger as a sponger who made common ground with the camp SS and let himself be invited to the guards' nightly carousal. Unlike the SS, Lichtenburg prisoners had to pay for dental treatment.[158]

In contrast to Hamburger, the memory of Jewish doctor Alfred Kantorowicz is more balanced. In the Börgermoor camp, Kantorowicz worked in the infirmary, were officially he only assisted two untrained SS men who acted as camp doctors. On occasions, Kantorowicz incurred the wrath of fellow prisoners when he refused to attest that they were unfit for work. Rather than recommending the desired respite, he often sent them to their work details. Signing a prisoner off as sick who did not really suffer from any severe illness could have had serious consequences for him. Not least because of this dilemma, Kantorowicz assumed a rather isolated position among the prisoners. After some time, he lost his job in the camp infirmary and was sent to the peat bog for work.[159]

Doubtless the most dramatic case of a Jewish physician in an influential position is that of Delwin Theodor Katz. The forty-five-year-old Nuremberg doctor and specialist in skin diseases arrived in the Dachau camp on April 13, 1933. Katz was a member of the KPD but never held any representative public function.[160] Once in camp captivity, he volunteered for service in the *Revier*, the infirmary, where he provided medical care for ill and injured fellow inmates—at times also in secret. For reasons of double bind similar to those that troubled other Jewish camp medics, Katz assumed an outsider position among his fellow prisoners. Separated from the rest of Dachau's Jew company, he was granted the privilege of living and sleeping in the infirmary.[161]

Katz's cautious and seemingly uncomradely behavior might have stemmed from the fact that, through his special position, he had gained deeper insights into the camp's regime of terror. A former Dachau inmate, who remembered that the "small, broad-shouldered man with the fencing scar in his face did not have everybody's sympathies," suspected that the doctor's "unsociability" stemmed from the fact that "he knew too much."[162] Indeed, Katz treated many victims of SS abuse. He "saw all of them, the tortured, the shattered, the trampled down."[163] Within a short time the Jewish doctor had become an unwanted and dangerous witness to the crimes of the early Dachau SS. Following the arrival of a letter from his family announcing that Katz could hope to soon be reunited with his loved ones on the occasion of his son's upcoming Bar Mitzvah, Judaism's coming-of-age ritual, his living conditions in the camp suddenly worsened. Pressured by the threat of having to release a "bearer of secrets," the SS began to oppress Katz. He was dismissed from working in the camp infirmary and sent to the overcrowded quarters of the Jew company, where prisoners who did not get a bed had to sleep on the barrack's cement floor.[164] Sent to the road-work and gravel pit details, he suffered humiliation and especially harsh physical abuse. Katz is said to have reacted nervously to his degradation, "his face was pale, his eyes showed a fear of what might come."[165]

Delwin Katz was murdered by the SS in Dachau on October 18, 1933. His death was brought about in the context of one of the most brutal acts of collective reprisal against Jewish prisoners documented in the history of the early concentration camps: the "atrocity propaganda" affair. When, on the morning of October 17, 1933, those Jewish prisoners who were assigned to barrack-room duty suddenly heard their SS company leader yelling "Jews out!," they were completely unprepared for what would happen to them over the next few days. An estimated fifteen men had to stand at attention at the "rondel," a sitting area surrounded by trees inside the prisoner camp compound, where they were confronted with Theodor Eicke and a large assembly of his staff. The commandant ordered the prisoners to dig up the whole area in order to unearth a can, which, he was convinced, "the bold Jew pack" secretly used for smuggling out atrocity reports about the camp. Although the search for the incriminating *corpus delicti* remained without result, Eicke did not allow the Jews back into the barrack. They had to stand at attention in the cold until around 7 p.m. The depressing effect of the horrors of the day was still lingering, when in the evening SS man Lutz, who was in charge of sending inmates to the camp prison, appeared in the Jew company and led Delwin Katz away. Jewish prisoner Martin Stiebel, a Communist from Kitzingen, had already been thrown into the *Bunker* earlier that same day.[166]

The collective ordeal, called "the great Jew action" by one of the witnesses, went on for several days.[167] Isolated from the other prisoners, the Jewish inmates were continuously threatened and mistreated. Abused as hostages held responsible for occurrences in the outside world that could harm the Nazi regime, the "atrocity propaganda" affair established a fatal reprisal pattern that was to be repeated in the later stages of the history of Jewish camp prisoners. Altogether seven prisoners were jailed in the camp's arrest block. Five of them were killed: Katz, Stiebel, Albert Rosenfelder, and two non-Jewish prisoners, Josef Altmann and Wilhelm Franz.[168] The extremely violent incident forced Bavaria's Political Police Commander Heinrich Himmler to report to his superiors. Himmler maintained that the deceased had pulled the strings in a large-scale conspiracy to smuggle reports about Dachau to Czechoslovakia, where, according to information available to him, exiled Communists planned to produce a film about the camp's alleged atrocities. On October 17, according to Himmler, the camp leadership had been able to uncover a communication channel between Dachau prisoners and their connections outside the camp.[169]

As we learn from prisoner memoirs, this secret connection between the camp and the underground resistance operating in its surroundings was not just a paranoid fantasy on the part of Himmler and Eicke—it really existed. Survivors reported that through a "splendid connection with Munich," all the important events of Dachau were known in the Bavarian capital, mostly "within hours and certainly on the day after." Secretly produced leaflets helped to spread the gruesome news.[170] To what extent did Jewish inmates participate in these actions? Hugo Burkhard reported that in September 1933, shortly before the "atrocity propaganda" affair, he was approached by a fellow inmate and asked to translate into shorthand an unspecified document. When he enquired after additional information, he learned that this document was a list of names of all those prisoners murdered or severely mistreated in the Dachau camp—his own name was on it. He was told that on the following morning the information would be smuggled out of the camp "so that it could be published abroad." Burkhard was anxious at having become privy to a plot that, as he stated, had worked a few times before its cover was blown.[171] The possible involvement of Jewish prisoners in the smuggling out of Dachau information about SS crimes raises the larger question about the resistance of Jews in the concentration camps.

Resistance and Self-Assertion

Jewish resistance against Nazism has emerged as one of the most heatedly discussed subjects in the historiography of the Holocaust. Scholars, when disagreeing about its virtue and reach, tend to base their arguments on different definitions of resistance. In the immediate postwar period, armed resistance in the style of the Warsaw ghetto uprising of the spring of 1943 was considered the only legitimate reaction to oppression if Jews did not want to go "like sheep to the slaughter."[172] However, it was soon found that the heroism of ghetto fighters and partisans was not the only manifestation of Jewish resistance. Today many historians also acknowledge nonviolent, "quiet," or "spiritual" resistance.[173] The Hebrew term *amidah*, which literally means "to stand" or "to stand up," came to signify these no less weighty struggles to maintain human dignity in the face of persecution.[174] Since the 1990s, broader definitions of Jewish resistance have been accepted, such as that advanced by Roger S. Gottlieb. He defines acts of resistance as those "motivated by the intention to thwart, limit or end the exercise of power by the oppressor over the oppressed."[175]

Historians of the Nazi concentration camps correctly point out that camp resistance needs to be understood in its own right, that is, against the backdrop of the camps' unique conditions of extreme violence and the overwhelming powerlessness of the prisoners vis-à-vis their oppressors. To organize armed struggle inside the camps was almost impossible. In general, inmates had little hope that their actions could bring about the collapse of the regime.[176] Moreover, camp resistance in the period before 1939 differs from resistance in the wartime camps, when Jewish prisoners were threatened with systematic biological annihilation on a massive scale.[177] Jewish prisoners' resistant behavior in the camps took different forms and worked on different levels.

One form of protest against camp terror has been referred to already throughout this chapter: the courageous acts of publicly denouncing the crimes committed by SS and SA guards through writings that brought the horrors of the camps to the attention of a larger audience, in Germany and abroad. After they had reached exile, liberated Jewish prisoners such as Max Abraham, Kurt Hiller, Max Tabaschnik, Werner Hirsch, and Marcel Ludwig Baron published their experiences of protective custody. Because their publications sooner or later became known to the Nazis, the authors had to live with the responsibility of having put their fellow sufferers, as well as their friends and families, into the great danger of becoming victims of reprisals. A witness who, because of this risk, preferred to publish his report anonymously, stated that there were discussions among the Dachau prisoners about how a freed person should act. Some were convinced that everything needed to be done so that the world would learn the truth about the Nazi camps; others, and according to his testimony especially Jewish prisoners, thought that the released should instead keep silent, as every publication of "atrocity propaganda" would only result in violent reprisals against prisoners. Pondering this dilemma, the anonymous author found that "only a complete and truthful enlightenment will be able to put an end to the barbarism of the German concentration camps, for I had to experience long enough that the SS does not need any special reason for their ill treatment and torture."[178]

Clearly the most spectacular forms of resistance were escapes from the camps. Besides Gerhart Seger's flight from Oranienburg and the breakout from Dachau by Bavarian KPD leader and Reichstag deputy Hans

Beimler, the escape of Jewish prisoner Max Tschornicki from the Osthofen camp on July 3, 1933, likewise mocked the Nazis' claim to absolute power. Tschornicki's flight could only succeed on the basis of the far-reaching support of fellow prisoners organized in the "illegal camp headship" and trusted people positioned outside the camp. Former prisoners remembered how an advance plan was carefully devised in order to save the Jewish lawyer's life, which was under severe threat from constant abuse by the guards. Christof Weitz, a Reichsbanner man from Bürstadt who served as the concentration camp's cook, had organized as an escape vehicle the supply truck of Osthofen's grocery store, which, in the company of an SA man, he regularly called on to obtain food for the camp kitchen. On the day of the flight, fellow inmates were on the lookout when Tschornicki climbed the wall in the rear part of the camp courtyard and entered the truck waiting for him on the other side. Speedily he was driven away from Osthofen. Like many other Nazi opponents, Tschornicki took refuge in the Saar, a part of Germany governed under a League of Nations mandate. When the region was restored to the Reich in March 1935, he fled to France. Arrested after the German occupation, Tschornicki lost his life in a Dachau subcamp only days before the liberation.[179]

Jewish prisoners were further involved in acts of solidarity that materially aided others by mitigating severe imprisonment conditions. These acts of solidarity could result in easier working positions, such as Max Fürst, responsible for Jewish work details in Oranienburg, was able to arrange for a fellow prisoner.[180] They could also consist of medical help, which Jewish doctors like Delwin Katz, in a pinch, provided also in secret. Furthermore, as is known, for example, of Max Laskin in the Neu-Augustusburg camp in Weissenfels located in the Prussian province of Saxony, Jewish prisoners organized additional food rations and distributed them to the needy.[181] Erich Mühsam, too, is remembered to have shared his food supplies with fellow prisoners in Oranienburg.[182] In Dachau, Lichtenburg, and probably also other camps, well-to-do prisoners supported with money those who were poor so that these could buy additional goods from the canteen to supplement their meager food rations.[183]

Besides organized acts of material aid, there are also documented cases of spiritual resistance or *amidah* by Jews in the early concentration camps. These assertions of self-worth manifested themselves either in open confrontations with the oppressors in front of an audience of witnesses, or in more indirect or concealed strategies of endurance and defiance applied on an individual level. The aims, however, were the same: prisoners sought ways to survive the extreme situation of the camp both physically and mentally. They strove to withstand attacks on their dignity and autonomy and to fight off that state of self-abandonment and apathy that later came to be embodied in the term *Muselmann* or "walking corpse."[184]

Prisoners who defined themselves as Jews and observed their religion were the most vulnerable to harassment and mockery of Judaism. Some continued to practice their beliefs even under the most adverse conditions of the camp. On Yom Kippur, the highest holiday in the Jewish calendar, the observant Jew Ernst Katz from Hungen, who was detained in Osthofen in 1933, insisted on not breaking the fast and refused his lunch. The camp guards, who were initially unaware of both the holiday and its custom, beat him up severely when they learned about the religious reason for Katz's refusal. When the prisoner regained consciousness after the violent assault, his tormentors forced him to eat the first pork he had consumed in his whole life.[185]

Max Abraham testified that he had originally planned to ask the Börgermoor SS to exempt Jewish prisoners from work duty for the period of the high holidays. However, after having consulted with his co-religionists, he decided that it would be better to not mention the upcoming festivals so as not to provoke additional antisemitic violence. The SS, however, learned about the holidays through Jewish prisoners' relatives, who meant well and sent their best wishes for the New Year into the camp. Abraham did then ask the commandant for permission to celebrate a religious service—a request that was first denied and later taken up as a cause for abuse. When he was forced by SS Scharführer Everling to hold the service in a manure pit, Abraham refused: "Inside me, I felt a strong resistance against having our belief literally be dragged in the mud. I kept silent. Everling: 'You refuse to carry out the order?' 'I do not hold a service in a manure pit!'"[186] The religious counselor was badly beaten up for this defiant attitude. He lost consciousness and was admitted to Börgermoor's hospital block. There he made a point of fasting on Yom Kippur despite his critical state of health—a condition in which he normally would have been relieved from the commandment by Jewish religious law.[187]

Just as religious Jewish prisoners were prevented from keeping the Sabbath or observing the dietary laws, the perpetrators also refused them the opportunity to celebrate religious services. The Dachau SS initially allowed the local priest Friedrich Pfanzfelt to hold a catholic mass on Sundays, which was attended by both prisoners and guards, but nothing comparable was offered to Jewish prisoners.[188] In a letter to the Reich Ministry of the Interior the National Representation of the German Jews complained that "religious support or services, if only on the high holidays, are not permitted." In view of the "large number of deaths" in the Dachau camp, the Reichsvertretung bemoaned in particular the practice of cremation of the bodies, which was "incompatible with Jewish religious law and is considered an insult to the religious feelings of many of our co-religionists." In the cases of the deaths of Erich Gans and Julius Adler, both killed in the "Röhm purge" massacres, it was found unacceptable that relatives were informed only three months later that the cremations had already been performed.[189]

Osthofen, again, represents an exception, as religious Jewish inmates in this camp could from time to time find spiritual support provided by the Mainz rabbi Sali Levi. He had obtained the permission from the Nazi Party district leader and Reich Governor Jakob Sprenger to visit the camp to give to Jewish prisoners some comfort.[190] Offenbach rabbi Max Dienemann, imprisoned in Osthofen in December 1933, wrote in a letter to his family of the uplifting effects of practiced religiosity in the camp: "My Dears! Dr. Levi was here earlier to hold the first religious service. It was a great refreshment for the soul, many cried their first tears."[191] Max Abraham, too, tried his utmost to console fellow believers in the Oranienburg camp with religious counseling. At one point he was able to turn into an act of spiritual self-assertion something that had been intended by the SA as a humiliation. Stahlkopf ordered Abraham to hold religious lessons "to lead back to Judaism" dissidents like Ernst Heilmann in particular. The SA Sturmbannführer then "had to listen to me saying that there is a God who supports the fallen, who heals the sick, who redeems those who are enchained, who had bestowed grace and reason upon humanity."[192]

The last form of Jewish prisoners' self-assertions to be discussed here concerns more-indirect efforts and concealed strategies to withstand camp violence, applied mostly on an individual level. The narration of an encounter between prisoner Burkhard and SS man Steinbrenner serves as a telling example of this kind of defiance. After Burkhard had been badly beaten upon arrival in the camp, he was brought to the infirmary. Although it was very difficult for a Jewish inmate to be admitted there, he received treatment. When he awoke the next morning, he saw himself confronted with his tormentor, who stood by his bed and "simply stared at me without saying a word; this time I resisted his intimidating glare and sharply looked him back into the eye; he hung his head and left my bed. What might have gone on inside him? Who knows? . . . As I later learned from comrades, he could not bear the gaze of a prisoner, he used to get nervous and let go of his victims."[193] In his memory of the incident, Burkhard reassured himself of his courageous act of withstanding the threat of terror. Through his defiant behavior, the former prisoner had regained autonomy and self-worth. Burkhard mastered the trauma of being helplessly exposed to his perpetrator—he lay wounded, asleep at first, while Steinbrenner loomed over him—both in the moment and in retrospect.

An examination of other prisoner memoirs reveals many similar recollections of defiant encounters with camp violence. Precious in their source value, testimonies tell what would have otherwise been unknown: Jewish prisoners' intellectual responses to the oppressors' attempts to vilify, humiliate, and terrorize them. Evaluated for manifestations of masculinity, specific survival strategies can be exposed that aimed not only at physical endurance but also at preserving one's personal integrity. The need was urgent because, as we have seen not least in the analysis of "camp sport," male self-understanding was constantly attacked by guards who strove to affirm their own fragile manliness at the cost of emasculated Jewish prisoners in particular.

Depending on the social profile of the group of Jewish inmates, different manifestations of masculinity emerged throughout the course of the prewar years. In the early concentration camps, where many prisoners had a pronounced left-wing political identity, these manifestations reproduced a male ideal of the revolutionary, the tough fighter for the class struggle.[194] Political Jewish inmates not only identified with the theories of Marx, Engels, and Lenin, but also, somewhat more unconsciously, took over dominant images of manhood bound to physical strength, hardiness, resilience, and an unconditional commitment to the political cause.[195] In their writings some styled themselves, as KPD functionary Werner Hirsch did, as representing these "steely, fearless front soldiers of the political class struggle" who remained unbroken and immune to the Nazi assault.[196] These manifestations of masculinity, which also radically oppose antisemitic caricatures of "the Jew," become evident most strikingly in accounts of torture and experiences of extreme violence. In an abstract and distant tone, Hirsch described how he was several times beaten unconscious, but managed, in a moment of utter presence of mind, to protect his genitals from maltreatment so that he "at least was not castrated." Thanks to the mobilization of "all my energies" he was further able to repress all thoughts of suicide.[197] Erich Drucker, too, emphasized his physical strength in the face of violent oppression. In his prison cell in Columbia-Haus the SAP activist was "working out" because he wanted "to become tough and even tougher." Under torture he exercised self-command: twenty-five or even fifty lashes he "should be able to bear." If he was forced to commit suicide, he would not do it out of despair but as a calculated act: "I wanted rather to die than reveal something."[198] Hirsch advised his fellow sufferers to bear torture silently so as to not become "a rascal and traitor of their class."[199] The suffering was seemingly easier to bear when it could be understood as embedded in a higher logic of the antifascist class struggle. SAP functionary Stefan Szende emphasized that working for the Socialist cause was similar to fighting a "war," the activist being a "soldier." Operating underground, one had to always anticipate arrest and torture. To withstand the camp was possible for him only "because I had trained my mental-psychological apparatus for months to face torture."[200]

When prisoners were largely unable to affirm their self-worth by the classical male strategy of fighting back, they had to rely on the group of fellow sufferers to esteem them. Among themselves, political prisoners developed certain behavioral codes and concepts to assert their gendered identities. These patterns remained valid also in later stages of camp history. Paul Martin Neurath, who was deported to Dachau as a Jewish political prisoner in April 1938, discussed "honorable" versus "shameful" reactions to SS abuse, and provocatively asked: "Why didn't they hit back in the concentration camps? Weren't they men?" To answer this burning question, he distinguished between the concept of honor in "civilian society," where the degraded man feels impelled to defend himself if he does not want to be considered a coward, and the "prisoner society," where hitting back was considered unwise, even "suicidal." No prisoner was expected to hit back at his perpetrator; however, what affected a man's status was the way he took the beating: "If he cries and weeps, he is considered a weakling" and loses his honor. Enormous social pressure was put upon him to "remain silent and solid, both before, during, and after the beating."[201] Adherence to this code of male behavior was constitutive for a political prisoner's status in the camp society.

From the beginning, Jews in the early concentration camps were exposed to an extreme degree of violence, manifested most strikingly in a stark overrepresentation of Jews among the deaths. Despite their relatively small numbers—estimated at a maximum of around 5 percent of the prisoner population as a whole—the presence of Jewish inmates was constitutive for the camps' evolving rule of terror. Perpetrators developed ways of identifying their Jewish victims. Jews were deployed into special work details and, in camps like Dachau and Oranienburg, they were housed in special Jew companies. All these measures made Jewish prisoners visible and thereby more vulnerable to abuse. The camps served to make Jews pariahs, to break down any solidarity among the prisoners, who would turn against their Jewish fellow inmates, and, not least, to confirm antisemitic stereotypes that influenced the guards' violent conduct. The statistics demonstrate that the group of Jewish inmates was, in fact, a most diverse assembly of individuals who came from different social backgrounds, were of different age groups and localities, and thus, in general, did not have much in common when they were forced together under the racial stigma. Much coercive power and violence was needed to collectivize them into a seemingly coherent enemy group corresponding to antisemitic stereotypes.

3

HER TRANSPORT TO THE CONCENTRATION
CAMP HAS BEEN ORDERED

Arrests and Imprisonment of Jewish Women, 1933–1939

In his report to the Berlin Gestapo dated December 21, 1934, Hugo Krack, the director of the Moringen concentration camp for women, complained about the insubordinate behavior of sixteen-year-old protective custody prisoner Eva Mamlok. When questioned upon arrival, Mamlok "showed such arrogance and impertinence, that I had to seriously reprimand her. In view of her youth, her attitude is even more deplorable." In order to make the rebellious prisoner realize "the gravity of the situation," Krack deemed it appropriate to postpone her release for as long as possible. As a result, Mamlok had to spend half a year in protective custody.[1] Who was this young woman, categorized by the authorities as a volatile teenager who had yet to learn about the seriousness of life? What had brought her into the camp, and how did the isolation she experienced in Moringen influence the future course of her life? What does Mamlok's case tell us more generally about the imprisonment of Jewish women in the prewar concentration camps, a topic hitherto conspicuously absent from this study? How was their persecution different from the persecution of male Jewish prisoners?

Contrary to Krack's conception of camp imprisonment as a pedagogical measure to educate an immature and recalcitrant girl, Mamlok was serious about her resistance to National Socialism. Politically socialized in the labor movement, she had been active as a member of the Socialist Workers' Youth (SAJ) until the organization was banned in June 1933. Committed to fighting the Nazis, she turned to underground activity. Mamlok is remembered by her friends for having put up anti-Hitler slogans on the roof of a department store at Berlin's Hallesches Tor.[2] She also publicly demonstrated her opposition to the regime by decorating the grave of Rosa

Luxemburg with flowers—officially the act for which she was arrested.[3] As a young Jewish woman opposed to the Nazi dictatorship in an atmosphere of growing state repression and social exclusion of Jews, Mamlok took great risks that imperiled not only herself. Her resistance also endangered her family. After she had been deported to Moringen, her mother and sister appealed to the authorities for her release. Their letters to Hugo Krack attest to the profound worries felt by many relatives of concentration camp prisoners. Eva's sister, Hilde, described their mother as "being at the end of her tether, a nervous wreck due to the affair." Martha Mamlok herself told Krack that she "had lost all real lust for life while hoping and waiting and waiting" for her daughter to be set free.[4] Apparently Eva's political activity also did not conform to the expectations the family had of her role as a young woman. The mother informed the authorities of her intention to "take her out of the improper environment in Berlin" and send Eva to a school for young women near Frankfurt "where she should be properly educated in housekeeping."[5] In his response, the camp director informed Martha Mamlok of her daughter's rebellious conduct in the camp. Eva would stick with imprisoned Communist women "to show thereby that she identifies with Communist ideas." In a patronizing tone, he added that he had warned her several times and reminded her of her youth and, especially, of her responsibility toward her parents. To calm the family's concerns, Krack indicated that the girl's behavior had recently improved and that they could hope for her release.[6]

On May 8, 1935, Mamlok was free to return home to Berlin. Unbroken by her camp imprisonment, she continued her resistance work against the Nazi regime. She became the leader of a group of young Jewish women who concentrated their illegal activities mainly on distributing anti-Fascist leaflets. Following a denunciation, the women were arrested in September 1941, accused of subverting the war effort, and sentenced to death without trial. In January 1942, Mamlok was deported from Berlin to Riga. She died in the Stutthof concentration camp on December 23, 1944.[7]

Eva Mamlok's case points to the importance of gender and generation for the investigation of arrest and imprisonment of German Jews in the prewar concentration camps. Conservative estimates count more than 3,000 German Jews as having been actively involved in the resistance movement. The number of women among them is unknown. The extant research calculates that 15 to 20 percent of individuals involved in underground activities against the Nazi regime were women, Jewish and non-Jewish.[8]

There were exceptions: in the Herbert Baum Group, the most prominent German-Jewish resistance organization, women made up nearly half of the members. A similarly high proportion of women, 14 out of 37, can also be found among the members of the German-Jewish agitprop-troupe Das Rote Sprachrohr.[9] The share of women who had held membership in the KPD and SPD was comparatively lower, 12 percent and 22.8 percent, respectively, in 1932.[10]

Like their male comrades, Jewish women in the organized political resistance either came from the ranks of the labor movement and had opposed the Nazis already before 1933 or they were, as Eva Mamlok was, socialized in the left-wing youth movement. When in 1936–1937 the KPD excluded Jews from its remaining illegal cadres so as to not jeopardize non-Jewish comrades in cases of arrest, Jewish Communists were forced to form their own underground networks.[11] Growing antisemitic pressure radicalized especially young Jews like Marianne Prager (later Marianne Joachim), who was driven to fight the Hitler regime when she could no longer bear the many restrictions inflicted daily upon Jews in Nazi Germany. At age sixteen she joined Herbert Baum and his circle.[12]

As has been established most convincingly by Marion Kaplan, gender made a difference in the enactment, as well as in the experience, of persecution. As anti-Jewish agitation and violence targeted Jewish men above all, women, at least in the early years of the regime, were mostly spared brutal forms of abuse. Nazi propaganda vilified first and foremost the male Jew; public perceptions of the Jewish enemy stereotype were to be gendered male.[13] Precisely because their bodies were not associated with this stereotype, Jewish women often "passed" as "Aryan," especially when they were young and had physical features such as blond hair, blue eyes, or light skin color. Young Jewish women who engaged in underground political activities took full advantage of this gendered enemy perception, which reflected both conservative antifeminism and the Nazi view of women in general as "essentially passive in the little world of the family household."[14] Like Eva Mamlok, who owed her release from the Moringen camp to the authorities' perception of her as an immature teenager rather than a resistance fighter, other Jewish girls, too, were able to disguise their illegal activities through their youth. Helga Beyer (born 1920), who was organized in the Breslau group of the Communist Party of Germany Opposition (KPO), a splinter group of the KPD, used her "Aryan" looks to work as an underground courier. Unrecognized, she even frequented SA taverns. When Beyer's sister was arrested in 1935, their stepmother achieved her release from Gestapo imprisonment by characterizing the young woman as an "imprudent, innocent but kindhearted girl."[15] Helene Hüttner of Das Rote Sprachrohr evaded long years of imprisonment that threatened the lives of her male comrades. When in the spring of 1936 the resistance group was tracked down and arrested by the Gestapo, Hüttner walked free from Alexanderplatz prison after seven weeks of detention because she was thought to be uninvolved. Her husband of later years recalled: "She acted the naive and totally innocent Jewish girl."[16]

To be sure, female gender did not always serve as a "natural" protection from unlawful imprisonment and physical abuse. There is evidence that female Jewish Communists were severely mistreated at the hands of (male) Gestapo agents and SA men. Lilly Salm, a former member of the Jewish youth group Schwarzer Haufen (Black Mob) who held an important function in the KPD, was taken into a three-month protective custody in Cologne in 1933. To extort information from her, she was beaten up and suffered severe injury to her liver and kidneys.[17] KPD functionary and underground activist Käthe Baronowitz of Berlin was arrested following a denunciation by her landlord, who was a member of the SA. She provided a haunting account that took the form of a reported, third-person testimony of the tortures inflicted upon her in the SA camp located in Charlottenburg's Maikowski-Haus: "[She] had to undress completely. A howling pack goaded on by alcohol surrounded her. They stuck pens in her vagina as well as paper flags which they burned so that they could gloat over the tortured woman's screams of pain." An SA Sturmführer called Baronowitz a "Jew whore" who was to suffer now for the "Commune."[18] When perceived to be Communist agents, female political activists, in these cases, were treated no less brutally by the Nazis than were their male comrades. Judging from the available sources, however, most female Jewish activists did not suffer such violent excesses as those perpetrated against Salm and Baronowitz.

Gisela Peiper (later Gisela Konopka) endured a terrible solitary confinement in the Fuhlsbüttel concentration camp in Hamburg. As a particularly harsh form of punishment she was kept day in, day out, in a cell without contact with other people, forbidden to read, write, or occupy herself with needlework. The twenty-six-year-old Peiper had been arrested in December 1936. As a member of the Internationaler Sozialistischer Kampfbund (International Socialist Fighting League) she fought the Nazis and did everything to denounce their claim to be backed and supported by a broad consent of the people. When the regime exploited the Olympics for propaganda purposes, Peiper and her friends—many of them non-Jews—sought "to let those foreign guests know that Germany was not the wonderful country that it was meant to appear." The resistance fighters distributed anti-Nazi leaflets and marked the streets with slogans reading, "Germany's peace is the peace of the graveyard."[19] Incarcerated in Fuhls-büttel, Peiper had to mobilize all her strength to survive the terror of the notorious concentration camp installed within a large prison complex initially overseen by the judicial administration. While the political police of Hamburg at first used parts of the buildings to only hold men in protective custody, a special detachment for women was opened in Fuhlsbüttel in August 1934.[20]

Despite the fact that a handful of prewar concentration camps had separate sections for women, one must agree with Sybil Milton, who correctly pointed out that prisons were the first and, until 1939, the most important sites of female detention. Most women activists and female political prisoners served their protective custody in arrest cells of police departments or in women's sections of prisons.[21] Margot Fürst, for example, was sent to the women's prison in Berlin Barnimstrasse while her husband Max was deported first to Columbia-Haus and later to the Oranienburg concentration camp. The couple had been arrested together in December 1933 after a failed attempt to free their friend Hans Litten from the Brandenburg camp.[22] The absolute number of women in detention remained relatively low. While 40,000 to 50,000 men were taken into protective custody in spring 1933, the number of women detained in the camps during the same period is estimated at between 300 and 400; that is, fewer than 1 percent of those detainees were women.[23] However, as clear-cut delineations are difficult when dealing with periods of uncoordinated political violence, research on the prewar concentration camps has classified as concentration camps a number of prisons with protective custody wings for women, most importantly the prisons of Gotteszell in Baden, Stadelheim in Munich, and the aforementioned Fuhlsbüttel in Hamburg.[24] Taking these into account, historians estimate that, up until 1939, between 6,000 and 8,000 women were detained for political offenses, and 3,000 to 3,500 of them were detained in the camps. Milton's assessment that almost 25 percent of all female protective custody prisoners were Jewish, however, seems exaggerated.[25] The following case study of the Moringen concentration camp will probe her estimate and carefully analyze the number of Jewish inmates in this camp. A research focus on Moringen is justified not only by the fact that it operated as a women's camp for the longest period during the prewar years (1933–1938). For Moringen, historians can also draw on a very favorable source base, containing at its core a set of 327 prisoner dossiers.[26] Moringen's institutional successor, Lichtenburg, functioned as a rather short-term transition camp before female prisoners were brought to Ravensbrück from May 1939 onward. I will not therefore analyze the imprisonment of Jewish women in Lichtenburg in equivalent detail. The history of Jewish prisoners in Ravensbrück, the first purpose-built women's camp, will not be treated in this study, as the Second World War and the Holocaust significantly determined the composition of Ravensbrück's group of Jewish inmates and their living conditions.[27]

Moringen Concentration Camp

Among the concentration camps of the prewar era, Moringen assumes a "special status."[28] The camp was located in center of the small town of Moringen, northwest of Göttingen in the Prussian province of Hanover. Established in the spring of 1933 as a separate section within the large building of an existing state workhouse, the camp initially detained some 1,000 male protective custody prisoners. A small section for women was opened in June 1933. In October the Prussian Ministry of the Interior decided that in the future Moringen should function solely as a women's camp—per decree institutionally on equal terms with the Prussian state concentration camps.[29] Officially the camp was never subordinated to the IKL, but was administered by a civilian director, Hugo Krack, who simultaneously functioned as the director of the Moringen workhouse. The male and female "correctional inmates" of the workhouse, who were clearly recognizable by their black uniforms, were strictly separated from the concentration camp prisoners. The female correctional inmates lived on the first floor of so-called women's house while the concentration camp detainees occupied the second floor before they moved to a bigger space in the long house in 1937. Camp director Krack headed a small staff of female overseers recruited from the local National Socialist Women's Association (NSF). SS men merely guarded the outer perimeters of the camp. Due to these obvious differences with the camps under SS administration, historians initially hesitated to term Moringen a "real" concentration camp. Newer studies, however, recognize its equal status among the concentration camps of the prewar period.[30]

Figure 3.1 Aerial view of the Moringen concentration camp and workhouse, early 1930s.

Massregelvollzugszentrum Niedersachsen (MRVZN).

In total, some 1,350 women were imprisoned in Moringen throughout the women's camp's five-year existence.[31] Pioneering research by Hans Hesse identifies almost half of Moringen's female prisoners (45.9 percent) as Jehovah's Witnesses.[32] My statistical evaluation yields an approximate share of 10 to 15 percent of Moringen's female prisoners categorized as Jews. Of the surviving 327 prisoner dossiers, which represent about a quarter of the estimated total number of female inmates, 43 (13.15 percent) concern cases of Jewish women.[33] Widening the empirical sample by adding the 514 women whose names can be identified through the transport lists for Lichtenburg in 1937–1938—70 of whom were of Jewish origin—I arrive at a figure of 113 Jewish prisoners within a sample of 841 women, a proportion of 13.44 percent.[34] Evaluating memoirs and combing through additional official documentation, a total of 123 names of female Jewish prisoners in Moringen can be compiled.[35] With the exception of female Jewish "race defilers," Jewish women interned in Moringen were officially not arrested on racial grounds. In 59 of the 123 cases, spanning the period from March 1934 to March 1938, the reason for arrest and imprisonment can be reconstructed and classified according to the categories in table 3.1.

The statistics, first of all, confirm that only a minority of Jewish women in Moringen were imprisoned as active members of the political opposition. Their relative absence can be explained by the fact, outlined above, that female political offenders were detained mostly in prisons and penitentiaries, following sentences by judicial courts. Among the Jewish political prisoners of Moringen was Lizzy Hirsch, a thirty-two-year-old photographer from Cologne arrested in November 1933 for distributing Communist propaganda. She was brought to the camp on March 12, 1934. Her case marks the earliest documented imprisonment of a Jewish woman in Moringen.[36] Other politically active Jewish women included KPD functionaries Marie-Luise Hirsch from Hamburg and Herta Kronheim from Würzburg. Both were arrested in 1933 but arrived in Moringen only in 1935 and 1936, respectively, after having served prison sentences for "preparing for high treason."[37] In a number of cases concerning political activists, protective custody was applied as an instrument to "correct" a court decision. Elisabeth Blättner, for example, who was engaged in the Red Aid in Hamburg, was tried for "preparing for high treason" in the summer of 1935. After the trial, which resulted in her acquittal, she was arrested by the Gestapo and deported to Moringen. Ilse Rolfe (née Gostynski), a KPD activist from Berlin arrested in March 1936, also fell victim to Gestapo-ordered

Table 3.1 Composition of the Group of Jewish Prisoners in Moringen, 1934–1938

Reason for Arrest	Number of Cases	Percentage
Return from emigration	33	56%
"Race defilement"/prostitution[a]	11	18%
Political opposition	7	12%
Criticism of regime	7	12%
Fraud	1	2%

a. Two different offenses in essence, the practice of arrest shows that the accusation of having committed "race defilement" was held against Jewish prostitutes, too. Boundaries between the two categories are often blurred, and in some cases the sources do not allow us to clearly identify a female Jewish prisoner as either a prostitute or a woman persecuted for an extramarital relation with one "Aryan" partner.

deportation to the camp when legal authorities withdrew her charge for lack of evidence.[38]

Cases of arrest and imprisonment of women on the grounds of critical remarks about the regime, frequently initiated by denunciations, largely parallel the persecution of male Jewish offenders against the *Heimtücke* ordinance against "malicious attacks on the state." Instead of analyzing those female cases, I will discuss the arrest and imprisonment of Jewish women accused of race defilement, cases in which notable differences from the persecution of Jewish men can be established, as well as the arrest category of "return from emigration."

Arrests for "Race Defilement"

It is striking that the great majority of women interned in Moringen for an alleged "pollution of race"—twenty-two persons, or two-thirds of all these cases—were non-Jews; in other words, they were non-Jewish women accused of intimate relations with Jewish men. In fourteen of the twenty-two cases the arrest of the non-Jewish female "race defiler" dates from the months from July to early September 1935, the period immediately preceding the promulgation of the Nuremberg Laws when persecution of mixed-race couples peaked amid a major campaign of violence and boycotts against German Jews. During this summer, Nazi party activists aggressively pushed for the implementation of far-reaching racial legislation. Julius Streicher's weekly *Der Stürmer* further fueled the campaign with antisemitic propaganda on race defilement. Hence, the high number of non-Jewish women detained in Moringen in the summer of 1935 vis-à-vis the almost complete absence of female Jewish race-defilers in the camp at that time represents the nature of the persecution as it manifested itself in the early years of the regime. The sources, in fact, document only one case of a Jewish woman imprisoned in Moringen during this period. On July 30, 1935, the Berlin Gestapo arrested the twenty-four-year-old sales clerk Hildegard Berlowitz and accused her of having "sexual relations with an Aryan man, which had destroyed his marriage." She was brought to the camp on August 8, 1935, and imprisoned there for almost one month.[39] In contrast to the scarce number of female Jewish race defilers, a significant number of Jewish men were imprisoned in the early concentration camps for their relations with "Aryan" women, who in turn were defamed as a "Jew's sweetheart" (*Judenliebchen*) "forgetful of her race." In some cases, a couple's deportation to a concentration camp was reported by newspapers in a sensationalist fashion.

Through publicity like this, camp terror helped branding as a racial crime any form of social contact between Jewish men and non-Jewish women.[40]

The Nuremberg Racial Laws, adopted on September 15, 1935, forbade future marriages, and outlawed extramarital intercourse, between Jews and "citizens of German blood." While both sexes were punished for violating the bar to marriage, the law explicitly decreed that in the case of extramarital intercourse only men were to be penalized with sentences in prisons or penitentiaries.[41] This exemption of the woman in principle from punishment had its roots in a complex mixture of racial and gendered stereotypes—Hitler himself was against any legal prosecution of women involved in race defilement—as well as criminological-juridical calculations that aimed to avoid a situation in which a woman, out of the fear of being punished herself, would refuse to give the evidence necessary for a conviction of the man.[42] Only weeks after the adoption of the law, courts issued the first verdicts against men accused of race defilement. Jews and non-Jews were more or less equally charged, but Jews were convicted more often and, on average, received longer sentences than non-Jews.[43]

Although the implementation of the Nuremberg Laws rendered racial offenses a crime liable for trial in court, the political police continued to impose protective custody against alleged race defilers whenever it felt the need to "correct" legal decisions. In a directive given out immediately after the promulgation of the Laws, the Gestapo ordered its local desks to "refrain in general from taking into protective custody persons engaged in race defilement." However, the option was kept open to "continue and issue protective custody" in "particularly serious cases" whose precise nature was left unspecified.[44] Officially exempt from legal persecution, Jewish women, in particular, were exposed to police sanctions. In the case of Moringen it is notable that, whereas the number of non-Jewish women deported to the camp for the alleged offense of race defilement declined noticeably after September 1935, over 90 percent of the Jewish women imprisoned as race defilers arrived in the period after the promulgation of the Nuremberg Laws. In a secret directive dated June 12, 1937, Reinhard Heydrich ordered that in a case of race defilement between a non-Jewish male and a Jewish female tried before a court, the Jewish woman "in any case" was to be taken into protective custody immediately after legal proceedings were completed.[45] In practice this meant imprisonment in a concentration camp for an indefinite period. Female race defilers of "German blood," on the other hand, were deported to the camp only in exceptional cases.[46]

One of the women imprisoned for race defilement in Moringen in 1937 was Charlotte Goldmann, who later became famous as the artist Lotti Huber. She was arrested in Berlin together with her non-Jewish partner, Hillert Lueken. While Lueken was held in investigative custody and, as she found out much later, was killed in prison, Goldmann was deported to Moringen and from there transported to Lichtenburg concentration camp. Thanks to her brother's leading position in the Youth Aliyah movement, a lifesaving opportunity to emigrate could be arranged for her. In late 1938 Goldmann was released from the concentration camp on the condition that she leave Germany for Palestine within ten days.[47] In her memoir she remembered another woman who shared a similar fate, Annemarie Münzer from Magdeburg, one of the youngest of the Jewish prisoners in the camp.[48] Aged nineteen, she was arrested on March 9, 1936, and arrived in Moringen two months later. The Nuremberg Laws had rendered impossible her planned wedding with an "Aryan" man, a young police officer. Although initially her fiancé would not part from her and the couple made plans to emigrate together, he then broke the engagement and accused her of perjury. When she was finally released from Lichtenburg concentration camp on February 4, 1939, she had spent almost three years in protective custody. Her entry in the Central Name Index of the International Tracing Service records that she fled Germany in May 1939 for Shanghai.[49]

The prosecution of race defilers also criminalized Jewish prostitutes who had "Aryan" clients. Accused of having committed race defilement in multiple instances, cases of Jewish prostitutes differed markedly from those of non-Jewish prostitutes interned in Moringen. The determination to impose social discipline on sexually delinquent women, which drove the arrest and imprisonment of non-Jewish prostitutes, played only a small role in the persecution of their Jewish counterparts. With the racial category overruling other forms of delinquency, Jewish prostitutes' offenses were not primarily defined by transgressions against state-imposed requirements of regular health checks, mandatory registration, observance of curfews, or restrictions on their movements. As a result, neither did the persecution of Jewish prostitutes fall under the jurisdiction of the criminal police (Kripo).[50] Accordingly, Jewish prostitutes were not taken into preventive police custody (polizeiliche Vorbeugungshaft), as was the standard procedure, but instead received protective custody orders issued by the Gestapo. In only one documented case, concerning twenty-four-year-old Anni Krümmel, the Hamburg Kripo took into preventive police custody the "full-blooded Jew" who "continued to have illegal sex with male citizens of German blood . . . for money." Shortly after her arrest, however, the Gestapo took over the case and changed the charge to "protective custody for prostitution." Krümmel was deported to Moringen on September 30, 1937.[51] As a poor woman from a lower-class social milieu who suffered from physical and mental illnesses, she had no chance to escape Nazi terror. Curtly, camp director Krack informed the Gestapo: "Due to her ailing condition she does not want to emigrate." After her camp detention was temporarily interrupted by hospitalization in a psychiatric clinic in Göttingen, Krümmel was transferred to Lichtenburg concentration camp and from there to Ravensbrück. She was murdered in the T4 "euthanasia" center in Bernburg (Saale) on April 2, 1942.[52]

On May 5, 1937, the Breslau Gestapo sent Hedwig Hirschel, a fifty-one-year-old blue-collar worker who earned her living as a packer, to Moringen as a prostitute guilty of race defilement. Her case is a rare exception among the cases of Jewish women accused of race defilement: in the prisoner dossier her own contemporary testimony has survived and can be contrasted with the authorities' version of the story. Hirschel's response to her persecutors, sent in the form of a letter to Hugo Krack, is a vehement repudiation of the allegations brought against her: first and foremost, against her stigmatization as a prostitute, which she declared to be "a total defamation, severe insult and untruth." In her view, her arrest followed a denunciation by her (Jewish) landlady, who had made a "revengeful report" to the police after Hirschel terminated the tenancy of her room in the shared apartment.[53] The urge to affirm her innocence and to refute false allegations was prompted by Hirschel's shock at the publication of her picture in *Der Stürmer*, a copy of which Krack had presented to her during an interrogation in his office. In the paper, Hirschel and two other Jewish women from Breslau—Charlotte Cohn and Charlotte Droste, both interned in Moringen in 1935–1936—were decried as "women of Satan" and "the Jew whores from Breslau."[54] *Der Stürmer* used their Gestapo mug shots to brand the women as criminals. In the related article, the paper warned of the dangers and of the harmful influence of Jewish prostitutes, who were "afflicted with terrible diseases" and would "strive to enervate the male German youth to wrest them away from their people's community." Men who got involved with them could easily fall victim to blackmailing and exploitation.[55] Hence, without their knowledge, Hirschel, Cohn, and Droste were publicly abused for an antisemitic propaganda campaign that pushed for a suspension of the exemption from legal punishment of women involved in race defilement as codified in the Nuremberg Laws. The Gestapo, concentration camp officials, and *Stürmer* journalists had worked hand in hand to construct this libel. According to a Gestapo order from April 1937, "material about criminal and other offenses of Jews" gathered by the secret police was to be made available to *Der Stürmer* so that the newspaper could use it for its "educational work."[56]

To the victims, the campaign was a painful and embarrassing exposure. As can be learned from her letter to Krack, Hedwig Hirschel was outraged and disgusted to see the publication of "this horrible picture which publicly pillories me."[57] The camp director, on the other hand, did not seem to feel any doubts or regrets about the public vilification. Quite the contrary, the *Stürmer* article apparently confirmed his image of Hirschel. In his correspondence with the Gestapo, Krack refers to her as "an inferior, asocial Jewess," "a textbook example of her race: dirty, garrulous, negligent and, of course, 'completely innocent.' I enclose a picture of her."[58] An antisemitic enemy stereotype had been cemented that negatively influenced the fate of Jewish women categorized as prostitutes and race defilers. Imprisoned in a concentration camp, the victims were dishonored and disenfranchised. Their lower-class social background further aggravated their situation. As the Moringen statistics show, Jewish women detained for race defilement and illegal prostitution, on average, served longer terms of imprisonment and had fewer chances (and oftentimes greater reluctance) to emigrate than other Jewish inmates had. The overwhelming majority of those whose further life histories can be reconstructed perished in the Holocaust. Hedwig Hirschel was discharged from Moringen in March 1938 on a trial basis. Her traces are lost afterward, but the entry of her name in the German Federal Archives' Memorial Book indicates that she did not die a natural death on August 28, 1940.[59]

The camp authorities' broad categorization of who was to be considered a Jew included so-called *Mischlinge*—persons of both Jewish and "Aryan" ancestry. In the case of the "half-Jew" Elsa Conrad, born to a Christian father and a baptized mother of Jewish origin, the racial stigma finally overruled all others in the complex enemy profile constructed by the authorities. Her protective custody in Moringen followed a fifteen-month prison sentence for "malicious attacks on the state" imposed on December 18, 1935, by the Special Court of the Berlin District Court. Conrad had been denounced by her lodger, who reported that Conrad had pretended to be

"Aryan" and concealed her homosexuality. The Gestapo quickly found out that, during the Weimar years, Elsa Conrad had been very active in Berlin's lesbian scene. She managed the club Monbijou des Westens, a renowned venue frequented by actresses, female artists, and many other women from the Bohemian world.[60] However bothersome to the Nazis, Conrad could not be criminalized for her sexual orientation. The laws against homosexuals prosecuted only men. Cases of lesbian women in the camps are rare and, as becomes evident at Conrad's persecution, the women had been officially arrested mainly for other offenses.

In Moringen, Elsa Conrad became "the Jew Conrad." After camp director Krack initially still referred to her as "the half-Jew (by her own account)," he quickly adopted the Gestapo characterization and classified her as a "Jew." Accordingly, her release was tied to the condition that she leave Germany for Palestine or oversees.[61] Discharged from the camp on February 4, 1938—after more than a year in protective custody—Conrad managed to escape to East Africa. There she made a living by running a milk bar in Nairobi. In the circle of German emigrants, "Elsa Conrad had been an authority who was respected by everyone and who did not tolerate any contradictions. She . . . was the only Berliner in the group, and she was the only one who was not Jewish."[62] Freed from Nazi oppression, Conrad thus immediately freed herself of the racial stigma that her persecutors had violently forced upon her and that her concentration camp imprisonment was meant to cement.

Return from Emigration

Most of the Jewish women detained in Moringen fall into a category of arrest and imprisonment newly created in 1935. As "returning emigrants" *(Rückwandererinnen)* they were sent to the concentration camp for "instructive custody" *(Schulungshaft)*. In contrast to the gendered persecution of so-called race defilers, both sexes suffered similarly from police sanctions imposed on Jews after their return to Nazi Germany from longer stays abroad. As we will see, it was, in fact, not so much gender that made a difference in the imprisonment of returning emigrants, but race.

More than 50,000 Jews left Germany in the first year of Hitler's rule. Among the escapees were many who cherished hopes that the political situation in Germany would soon quiet down so that they could come back to their native country.[63] And following the relative lull in state-sponsored anti-Jewish measures in 1934, several thousand emigrants did indeed return to

Germany. Their decisions might seem naive in hindsight, but they were less so at the time, given their poor and insecure living conditions abroad and the widespread notion that the Hitler dictatorship would not last. The writer Kurt Hiller, for example, states that he initially perceived Hitler as "a cranky ideologue full of complexes and hunger for power. A dictator who, so I believed, would moderate his dictatorship after the brutal phase of establishment has come to an end."[64] His contemporary testimony echoes assessments made by many German Jews in the mid-1930s. The decision of whether to stay in Germany or leave the country was difficult and often painful. Like many others, Hiller felt rooted in his home country. Strong commitments to loved ones whom he would not be able to take with him, as well as a lack of the economic resources needed to make a fresh start abroad, further complicated the situation. Hiller called "fools" those "clever critics" and "smart true cosmopolitans" who later reproached him for not having emigrated without delay.[65] Although he was taken into protective custody and detained in the more moderate Spandau prison for five weeks in spring 1933, the writer continued to hope for a modus vivendi in Germany: "I told myself that they are starting to make differences, I dreamed of a permitted opposition literature . . . and of limited freedom of press."[66] But as a left-leaning critic he was soon again caught up in the Nazi web of terror. What followed his arrest in July 1933 was a nine-month odyssey through the concentration camps of Columbia-Haus, Brandenburg, and Oranienburg. Upon reception of another dreaded summons from the Gestapo and in shock at the murder of his colleague Ernst Mühsam, Hiller escaped to Prague in September 1934. His reflections about the dilemmas of emigration help explain why some of those who went into early exile returned to their country of origin.

The phenomenon of remigration did not go unnoticed by Nazi party and state authorities. In the spring of 1935, the *Völkischer Beobachter* warned of 10,000 emigrants who would stream back into Germany.[67] As Herbert Tutas shows in his pioneering study on the topic, "the exile"—a term that signifies political emigrants actively opposed to National Socialism abroad—became a declared enemy of the Nazi state. Starkly overestimating the emigrants' scope for action, the new rulers feared that the emigrants would influence foreign nations against Germany and plot to overthrow the regime. Perceptions of "the exile" merged with antisemitic fantasies of "world Jewry" as the originator of "atrocity propaganda" harmful to the German people. Soon the enemy conception extended beyond the political emigrants and included anybody, Jews and non-Jews, who had left the country for any reason.[68]

The SD and Gestapo, too, turned to the issue of Jewish remigration. As early as May 1934 the strategists of the "Jewish Question" in the SD (the SS security service) issued a memorandum that declared: "The aim of Jewish policy has to be the complete emigration of Jews."[69] The return of large numbers of Jewish emigrants to Germany undermined this central aim of the regime's evolving anti-Jewish policy. The Gestapo issued its first ordinance for the persecution of returning emigrants on January 28, 1935. In a striking fashion this decree draws a clear line between Jewish and non-Jewish returnees: "Lately, a continuous increase in numbers of returning emigrants is to be observed, of which the Jewish returnees mark by far the largest percentage. The return of these elements, who are to be regarded as unwanted in principle, has already led in several cases to anti-Jewish riots whose cause was to be found in the arrogant behavior of the returnees."[70] In contrast, non-Jewish returnees are described as "human material that, with appropriate guidance and instruction, can be reincorporated into the national body." The Gestapo ordinance established a practice of arrest and persecution that systematically targeted all returning emigrants. It introduced the term "instructive camp" (*Schulungslager*) to denote the place where the arrestees would have to spend their "instructive custody," and it decreed that "in the absence of adequate instructive camps the returnees are to be transferred to a concentration camp." Depending on the location of the border crossing, they were to be sent to the SS camps of Esterwegen, Sachsenburg, or Dachau.[71] A supplementary order, dated March 9, 1935, designated Moringen concentration camp as the site for "instructing" female returning emigrants.[72]

In the course of the implementation of "instructive custody," the Gestapo sharpened the distinction between returning emigrants "of German blood" (*deutschblütig*) and Jews. Each Gestapo desk had to keep accurate records of the arrested indicating their "race" as well as statistical information on the number of cases in which the mere threat of concentration camp detention had successfully prevented remigration.[73] The rules for the release of returning emigrants from "instructive custody" in concentration camps were first codified in a Gestapo order of June 13, 1935. The decree gave Jews two weeks to leave the Reich after they had been discharged from the camps. Release from "instructive custody" was thereby tied to emigration. This discharge procedure was utterly different from the treatment of non-Jewish emigrants, who were often simply released from the camps within weeks or months if nothing incriminating had been uncovered, and who, of course, were not forced into emigration.[74] On August 31, 1937, Himmler reflected: "The institution of instructive custody, which had a deterrent effect on those emigrants inclined to return, was necessary to stop the unwanted stream of, particularly, Jewish emigrants returning to the Reich."[75] Noteworthy in the analysis of the practice of deportation of returning emigrants is thus not only the differentiated treatment of Jews in "instructive custody," but also the Gestapo's instrumentalization of concentration camp confinement to force Jews to leave Germany long before it became the government's official solution to the "Jewish Question." Many Jewish returning emigrants, on the other hand, had decided to return to their fatherland because they felt German. Their sense of patriotism and an identification with German culture stood in painful contrast to their criminalization in the concentration camps.[76] Quite contrary to the Jewish "politicals" of the early concentration camps, they generally came from middle- and upper-class backgrounds, and many of them had not previously been in conflict with the police.

Returning emigrants were unaware that their action—crossing the border back into their native country—was considered an offense that could ensure concentration camp imprisonment. The various ordinances quoted above that defined their "crime" and its punishment were not made public and remained unknown to the arrested. In fact, as we learned from the investigation and intrigues that led to the dismissal of SS Standartenführer Karl d'Angelo from Dachau in spring 1936, all orders that laid out the rationale and practice of "instructive custody" were to be kept secret. While SS officers were informed about these regulations, they were strictly forbidden to reveal them to the prisoners. When a former prisoner stated under duress in a Gestapo interrogation that he had discussed the "legislation regarding emigrants" with d'Angelo, Theodor Eicke, the Inspector of the Concentration Camps, considered taking the Dachau camp compound leader to trial before an SS court, so grave was the alleged infraction of his duty.[77]

Gottfried Fischer, the released inmate who unintentionally incriminated d'Angelo, had been detained in Dachau for more than a year. He was in the first group of thirteen Jewish prisoners categorized as emigrants who arrived in the camp on March 18, 1935. Shortly before their arrival, SS Scharführer Christian Guthardt, the block leader of the first prisoner company, was ordered to evacuate his barrack "because the five halls were to be kept clear for this new category of prisoners." The Jewish emigrants, who occupied the fourth hall of the block, were initially strictly isolated from the rest of the prisoners. Uncertain of how to treat this new category of inmates, the camp SS made sure that "the emigrants" would not "come into contact with other prisoners" and locked them into their barrack room, probably for a few months.[78] As the Fischer/d'Angelo case shows, the prisoners, too, were puzzled about the newly invented category of enmity into which they were classified. The nearly fifty-year-old Fischer, who worked as an interpreter and for decades had frequently traveled abroad, suspected that he "should not have been considered an emigrant." Seeking clarification, he spoke with d'Angelo about the regulations regarding "instructive custody." This remarkable incident, in which the SS officer, according to Fischer, was "helpful" and was "willing to provide information" on the "legislation regarding emigrants," took place in d'Angelo's office and is said to have lasted for one hour.[79] The former prisoner's positive depiction of what sounds like an unusually fair and open consultation must, however, be understood in the context of the threatening atmosphere of the Gestapo interrogation. Out of the fear of being re-arrested and sent to the camp again, Fischer might have carefully cut out of his statements the terror of Dachau, emphasizing instead his "correct treatment" by the SS. D'Angelo, for his part, was ultimately spared a trial "due to his long-standing services to the Protection Squad [SS]." Gottfried Fischer did not survive the Holocaust. He was deported to Sachsenhausen concentration camp on March 4, 1940, and died there eleven days later.[80]

The category of arrest and imprisonment with the highest percentage of women was "emigrants." Because migration was often a family project, there are cases of couples taken into instructive custody. The women were sent to Moringen, their husbands were imprisoned in Esterwegen or Dachau. The separation of spouses in different camps was extremely hard to bear. Communication over strategies to secure release was restricted to the utmost minimum and became entirely impossible during phases of mail embargos. When in the summer of 1937 Dachau's Jews were prohibited from writing or receiving letters, Moringen prisoner Gertrud Glogowski did not hear from her husband, Arnold, for weeks. She was on the verge of collapse: "So far, his letters have held me up. Now, because there is no news at all, I am completely done for."[81]

In 1935 and 1936, when their persecution peaked, returning emigrants constituted the great majority of the Jewish inmates in the Moringen camp.[82]

Frieda Sherwood (formerly Redelmeier), imprisoned from May to September 1935, counted some twenty-five Jewish "emigrants" in the camp during the summer. She herself had been sent to Moringen after she came back to Germany from a one-year stay in Italy.[83] Jewish women's personal backgrounds, and their motives for returning from abroad, were many: economic, private, professional, political, or a mixture of these. Else Lindner and Frieda Cassel, both incarcerated in Moringen in April 1935, had been unable to make a living abroad.[84] The same is true of Charlotte Schwarzenberger, whose husband's shoe shop in Paris became insolvent after one year. As an unwanted "remigrant" she was sent to Moringen on March 21, 1935.[85] Amalie Benjamin and Erna Muszkat, also interned in the spring of 1935, returned to Germany after they had separated from their spouses.[86] Hedwig David's husband died in exile in the Netherlands. Widowed and suffering with illness, she returned to her family in Mönchengladbach in January 1937.[87] Bella Liesel Jacob and Gerda Lissack, both from bourgeois families, had been studying abroad. They arrived in Moringen in July 1935 and December 1936, respectively.[88] Herta Eichholz, who had visited relatives and worked as a nurse in Barcelona, fled the erupting Spanish Civil War on a transport of refugees organized by the German Consulate.[89] Gabriele Herz, whose memoir of imprisonment in Moringen in 1936–1937 is one of the most important accounts of female camp detention in the prewar era, returned home after having investigated how her family could make a new life in Italy. She was taken to the women's camp on October 8, 1936.[90]

It is very likely that it was the sizable influx of Jewish returning emigrants to Moringen from March 1935 onward that led to the accommodation of Jews in the "Jews' Hall" (*Judensaal*), separate from other prisoners. The sources do not allow us to determine when exactly it was established. Centa Herker-Beimler, wife of fugitive KPD functionary Hans Beimler, recalled that the "Jews' Hall" existed by the time she arrived in the camp in early 1936.[91] Gabriele Herz remembered as her roommates in the Jews' Hall the Communist activists Herta Kronheim and Ilse Rolfe, the young race defiler Annemarie Münzer, as well as several Jewish women interned as returning emigrants.[92] Moringen's Jews' Hall was therefore not merely a "Remigrants' Hall," as Hesse mistakenly assumes in his otherwise meticulous study of the camp.[93] Like the Jew companies of the male camps, the Jews' Hall concentrated all prisoners who bore the racial stigma, regardless of the varying reasons that had led to their arrest.

Conditions inside the Women's Camps

The majority of all Moringen prisoners—Herz counted some eighty during her time in 1936–1937—were installed in the Great Hall. The small Jews' Hall contained only a handful of prisoners in October 1936; Herz described it as "a small space that offers its five occupants only very limited domestic facilities. A long, unfinished table, four stools, one chair, five narrow blue cubbyholes mounted on the wall for soap, toothbrush, and towel compose all of the 'furniture.' Our few belongings are stored in cartons, cardboard boxes, and suitcases, stacked up under the table for lack of any other storage space. The only window faces the courtyard and is, of course, fitted with iron bars."[94] In this small space, the women ate, worked, and passed idle time, often with nothing meaningful to do. The exhausting monotony was interrupted by exercise periods in the courtyard twice a day. The prisoners' sleeping quarters were located in the attic of the building. When shortly before 9 p.m. a bell signaled bedtime, the women were ordered "to undress downstairs and walk upstairs in our nightclothes." In contrast to their separation throughout the day, all of the women prisoners shared the same crammed quarters in the night.[95]

The prohibition against "Aryans" entering the Jews' Hall and against Jewish prisoners visiting the other day-rooms, was circumvented in practice when "urgent reasons" could be found to obtain from the neighbors a necessary tool for work, a dress pattern, knitting sample, and so on. However leniently the racial separation was exercised when such trivial day-to-day issues were concerned, the camp director forbade in principle all contact between Jewish and "Aryan" prisoners when he heard that women from the Bavaria Hall went to the Jews' Hall regularly to participate in English classes organized by Gabriele Herz. The teacher was told that "members of the Jewish race have recently been forbidden to give instruction to Aryans." Nevertheless, Herz managed to receive Krack's permission to continue instructing her "Aryan" students while walking in the courtyard during the exercise periods.[96]

Article 7 of Moringen's "Service and House Regulations" allowed "Jewish protective custody prisoners . . . to observe the holidays according to the commandments of their religion."[97] In December 1936 they were granted a two-day leave from work to celebrate Hanukkah, Judaism's festival of lights. In joyful anticipation the women prepared for the ceremony. The Jews' Hall was cleaned and decorated, a festive meal was prepared, and small presents were laid out. Herz described the uplifting effect of the celebration: "We who had been expelled from the German 'national community,' felt within us the ancient Jewish solidarity, a community with neither spatial nor temporal boundaries . . . and the hope for the fulfillment of that ancient prophetic dream of justice, peace, humanity, brotherhood."[98] With the exception of the spiritual support provided by Rabbi Sali Levi in Osthofen in 1933–1934, such relative freedom to observe a Jewish holiday and practice religion in the concentration camp was never officially granted to male Jewish prisoners. When in 1933 they witnessed members of their congregations being arrested and detained in the newly established camps, individual rabbis, cantors, and religious counselors quickly requested permission to care for Jewish protective custody prisoners. Rabbi Heinrich Guttmann, for example, formally asked the commandant of Sonnenburg to allow him to provide religious services to a number of Jewish men from his community in Landsberg an der Warthe (today Gorzów Wielkopolski, Poland). In October 1933 he was informed that the Prussian Ministry of the Interior denied him the permission to visit the camp.[99] Jewish communities in Munich, Leipzig, Potsdam, and Papenburg received similar rejections. By the end of 1933, Jewish organizations campaigned on a national level for the right to administer religious services in the concentration camps and also reached out to representatives of other confessions who faced the same problem. The CV was particularly active and emphasized the "exceptional urgency of the matter as appeals are brought forward by family members every day."[100] Concentration camp administrations and state bureaucracies overwhelmingly denied these claims.

In Moringen, Jewish prisoners' freedom to practice their religion came to an end when Rabbi Schwarz, the spiritual head of the Jewish communities in the governmental district of Hildesheim, appealed to the camp director and asked permission to care for Jewish inmates.[101] The response was succinct. Krack informed the Rabbi that "due to an order from above," religious counseling for Jews in the camp could not be permitted. At some unknown date the whole paragraph on the practice of religion, which had also granted permission to Christian pastors to visit the camp, was crossed out from the House Regulations.[102]

The sources do not suggest that female prisoners in Moringen suffered extreme physical violence. Instead, inmates, both Jewish and non-Jewish, suffered primarily from their isolation in the camp, the uncertainty of release, and constant worries about their families. Ilse Rolfe remembered,

"It was the thousands of little humiliations, the being cramped together in the narrow space, constantly hanging around together and many other things which constituted the tragedy of the concentration camp."[103] Apart from the mental strains, the drafty and insufficiently heated quarters harmed the prisoners' health. Hygienic facilities were poor and far too few. The camp infirmary is described as "completely unsuited to proper medical treatment."[104] Women like Frieda Sherwood, who arrived in the camp in a weak condition, collapsed under exhausting work assignments.[105] When Moringen became overcrowded in the spring of 1937, prisoners suffered hunger caused by acute shortages of food. When the occupants of the packed Jews' Hall could no longer stretch a leg without bumping into each other, an extra cell for Jewish prisoners was opened.[106]

The daily monotony and the uncertain prospects for the future weighed heavily on the women. Long-term prisoners and those who were mentally unstable particularly saw their situation as utterly desperate and developed anxiety disorders and depression. Frieda Sherwood reported, "Many of us went mad and one could hear them screaming day and night."[107] There were no deaths in Moringen, but we know of at least two Jewish prisoners who attempted to commit suicide. One was Anni Krümmel, the prostitute from Hamburg, whose mental condition was critical. In her prisoner dossier it is recorded that she suffered a nervous breakdown when disciplined for insubordinate behavior, and then tried to kill herself.[108] Long years of imprisonment had also preyed on the morale of Herta Kronheim. The KPD activist had been arrested in a police crackdown on the Communist resistance in Würzburg in autumn 1933.[109] Her friend Hedwig Laufer (later Hedwig Regnart), a Communist from Nuremberg, remembered Kronheim's suicide attempt. After the Jewish prisoner had remained behind alone in the sleeping quarters in the morning, telling Laufer that she wanted to rest, she slit her wrists with nail scissors. The friend became suspicious and alerted a warden, who found Kronheim covered in blood but alive.[110] Her desperate act was probably triggered by the Gestapo's denial of her request for release, which she had filed in late 1936. Herz reported that when Kronheim learned from Krack that she would have to remain in custody indefinitely and that "any further appeal would be pointless," she collapsed.[111] Kronheim was transported to the Lichtenburg camp on March 21, 1938. She was eventually released and left Nazi Germany for Paraguay in November 1938.[112] With a total of five years spent in prisons and concentration camps, Kronheim's confinement was exceptionally long compared to that of other female victims of Nazi persecution in the years 1933 to 1939. Even Centa Herker-Beimler, undoubtedly one of the most prominent female prisoners of the prewar era and, like Kronheim, at the mercy of one of the harshest organs of persecution, the Bavarian Political Police, did not spend such a long time behind bars. Held hostage for her fugitive husband, Herker-Beimler was freed from Moringen in February 1937 after almost four years of protective custody.[113] Because Kronheim was not only a Bavarian KPD functionary convicted of "preparing for high treason," but also a Jew, it seems that the racial stigma crucially aggravated her fate.

Practices of Release from the Concentration Camp

In the women's camp, director Hugo Krack evaluated prisoners' behavior and filed a conduct report to the Gestapo every three months with recommendations either for or against a release.[114] In principle this procedure also applied to camps for male prisoners. Most Jewish prisoners of the prewar concentration camps eventually *were* set free; generally, release was still the rule rather than the exception. A perusal of the Moringen prisoner dossiers suggests that the first attempts to systemize the release of Jews from the camps were made in 1935 with the arrival of the larger group of "remigrants." In his correspondence with the Gestapo in early August 1935, Krack indicated that "according to the judgment of the Gestapo [headquarters] in Berlin, Jewish returning emigrants should generally remain in the camp for six months."[115] A survey of the cases of Jewish emigrants interned in Moringen confirms this trend, revealing an average detention period of slightly more than five months, with spells rather shorter in 1935–1936 and rather longer in 1937–1938.

The practice of a six-month period of detention of emigrants soon filtered through to Jewish aid organizations, which supported prisoners and their families in their efforts to effect release from the concentration camps. In a report from January 1936, Salomon Adler-Rudel, who held a leading function in the emigration department of the National Representation of the German Jews, noted that while measures of arrest were tightened as more and more Jewish returning emigrants were caught up in the Gestapo's web of terror, the organization was now at least able "to inspire some hopes in relatives as to when they will be reunited with their arrested [family members]." Such attempts on the part of the Jewish organizations to make out and rely on rules and regulations were, however, often rendered futile by the inherent arbitrariness of the Gestapo's practice of arrest and release.

In his 1937 report, Adler-Rudel frustratedly records the case of "a woman who has been in an instructive camp [i.e., concentration camp] for ten months, has not been released and there was no chance of her being released in the future." Hence, any interpretation of Nazi policy by reading its visible—and often contradictory—"symptoms" remained guesswork ultimately unable to predict and influence the fate of concentration camp prisoners.[116]

The decision for or against the release of a protective custody prisoner rested, in the last instance, with the headquarters of the Secret State Police in Berlin. Conduct reports filed by the camp director or commandant, and reports from the local Gestapo desk that had executed the arrest, were important but not ultimately decisive.[117] In a number of instances, Krack's recommendation to release a prisoner was ignored by the Gestapo headquarters, which instead extended the imprisonment.[118] In 1936 Himmler made the release of Jewish prisoners from the concentration camps a matter for his own personal decision. A circular from the political police dating from August 18, 1936, decreed, "From now on, Jewish protective custody prisoners are to be released only on the authority of the Reich Leader SS and Chief of the German Police."[119] This decree was preceded by a discussion at the highest level of the Nazi state. From a note that has survived in the Gestapo file of a Jewish prisoner who was not released from a prewar concentration camp, we know that Himmler had secured Hitler's backing in the affair. On March 21, 1936, Himmler issued an instruction to the Gestapo leadership saying, "I have reported to the Führer, who has left the release of Jews to our discretionary power."[120] Hitler therefore was not only informed about the evolving "special treatment" of Jewish prisoners, he himself gave Himmler full powers to decide on their release. In dossiers of remigrant prisoners in Moringen from 1936–1937, Gestapo authorizations for release invoke Himmler's personal approval in increasingly standardized formulations. Moreover, release from instructive custody was soon tied to a guarantee that the prisoner in question would leave Germany permanently.

Initially Jewish prisoners detained in Moringen for reasons other than return from abroad were not always forced to emigrate from Germany upon release. For example, political prisoner Eva Mamlok was permitted to return home to her family when discharged from the camp in May 1935. Jewish prostitutes and their release provide a particularly interesting case study. Although they were officially categorized as protective custody prisoners, the women were, in practice, treated like non-Jewish prostitutes held in preventive police custody when it came to release. Most prostitutes were discharged from Moringen after about three months on the condition that they could be placed in a steady, regular job.[121] Krack applied the same procedure to Jewish prostitutes and searched for employment for them, too. When, for example, he reported to the Breslau Gestapo that, with the help of the local welfare office, he had found Edith Unger a post as a housemaid with a Jewish family in Clausthal-Zellerfeld, the political police approved of his initiative and set the prisoner free.[122] In addition, the Gestapo itself became active in other cases of Jewish prostitutes. It contacted the local Jewish Labor Welfare and found jobs as housemaids for Charlotte Cohn and Charlotte Droste. As "their offenses were not political in nature," Krack in turn agreed to discharge them before the six-month minimum term set for Jewish prisoners. The women's conduct in the camp had been "orderly" and, although he found them "a little unclean," the camp director hoped that they would "overcome this in the future possibly through education by their Jewish employers."[123]

Gradually, however, release of all Jewish prisoners from the concentration camp was tied to their leaving Germany permanently, preferably for Palestine or overseas. On the occasion of his visit to Moringen on May 28, 1937, Himmler decreed that "Jewish protective custody prisoners would be released only if their emigration is guaranteed."[124] In the same year, Jewish organizations understood that the persecution of returning emigrants with concentration camp terror "has led to a real system of deportation." Proceeding in a brutally arbitrary mode of action, the Gestapo threatened with detention even people who had not spent time abroad. Numerous cases were made known to the National Representation of the German Jews in which "Jews, who are residing in Germany, have been asked to report to the police, where they have been told that they have been away from Germany longer than three months, although this was not the case, and that their only choices were either to emigrate immediately or to go to a concentration (instruction-) camp."[125] The persecution of returning emigrants, which had started in the spring of 1935, thus gradually turned the concentration camp into a powerful weapon to force Jewish emigration from Nazi Germany. During the second half of the prewar years, Jewish prisoners' chances of surviving the camps increasingly depended on their ability to leave the country if released. In January 1939 Himmler ordered that in principle Jewish prisoners were to be released from the camps provided that "they have not previously come to the attention of the police on criminal or political grounds and are willing to emigrate." The only exemption from the rule concerned Jewish "Communist functionaries, in particular leading intellectuals, whose release even for the purpose of emigration is not permissible."[126] The outbreak of the war would radically alter the policy of release. In April 1940 Himmler ordered a stop to releases of Jewish concentration camp prisoners. Only those whose emigration was imminent were still discharged.[127]

As already mentioned, Jewish concentration camp prisoners and their families were assisted by Jewish welfare and aid organizations in their attempts to find opportunities to emigrate. Apart from efforts to provide religious counseling to protective custody prisoners, it was this help to seek ways out of Germany and thereby out of detention that brought Jewish organizations into close contact with concentration camp terror. From the mid-1930s on, they were confronted with hitherto unknown pressure from the Gestapo, which increasingly thwarted all well-planned and cautiously implemented measures of "orderly emigration." Previously, issues of Jewish emigration were negotiated with the Reich Office of Migration (Reichswanderungsamt), an authority located within the Reich Ministry of the Interior. Arthur Prinz, a leading functionary of the Aid Association for Jews in Germany (Hilfsverein der Juden in Deutschland), in retrospect described this cooperation as based on a mutual recognition that "Jewish emigration had to take place only after the most careful preparation for which an adequate period of time had to be allowed." Leading officials in Reich Office of Migration "were extremely accommodating and did everything they could to make our work easier." Not so the Gestapo, whose forceful interference with matters of Jewish emigration not only disturbed these most sensitive relationships between the Jewish organizations and the state bureaucracy, but also eventually rendered futile all efforts "to pursue a productive and efficiently directed Jewish emigration policy." In contrast to the Reichs Office of Migration, the attitude of the Gestapo to Jewish emigration "appeared to us inconsistent, unclear and torn between two opposing trends," the speeding up of emigration on the one hand and the imposing of countless obstacles on the other hand.[128]

In 1935 the National Representation of German Jews set up an emigration department to coordinate the work of individual Jewish organizations that aided German Jews in their attempts to leave the country.[129] One of these organizations was the Aid Association of Jews in Germany. Until the end of 1939, the Aid Association advised a total of 90,000 clients in questions of emigration. It provided linguistic support, job training, and assistance with the bureaucratic obstacles to and practical challenges of moving abroad. Some 31,000 Jewish emigrants were granted financial support. While the Aid Association helped German Jews to escape to countries other than Palestine, the Palestine Office of the Jewish Agency (Palästinaamt) allocated the immigration certificates given to the organization by the governing British Mandate. Until 1936 Palestine absorbed the majority of Jewish emigrants from Nazi Germany. The Jewish Women's League (Jüdischer Frauenbund, JFB) worked closely with the Aid Association. When Moringen prisoner Annemarie Münzer, for example, informed her family that the only way out of the camp for her was through emigration, her brother turned to the Aid Association for help. The organization transferred the case to the JFB and on August 16, 1937, its president, Hannah Karminski, appealed to Hugo Krack for a visit to the camp in order "to make enquiries whether the responsibility can be taken to send A. M. oversees where she would be completely on her own and exposed to the uncertainties of a foreign country." Krack consulted with the Gestapo headquarters in Berlin, which approved Karminski's request. In the following months, the leading representative of the JFB paid frequent visits to Moringen. Her last visit to the camp was on February 14, 1938. Her organization supported female Jewish prisoners in their efforts to prepare for emigration—Erna Rittel, for example, received foreign-language dictionaries and stationery—and it also organized charitable donations of clothing to be sent to the camp.[130] Once the camp director had secured approval from the Gestapo as the superior authority, he seemed to have collaborated rather smoothly with the JFB.

Historians of the Moringen concentration camp agree that an evaluation of Hugo Krack's personality, political attitudes, and motives reveals ambivalences and ambiguities. Krack became a member of the NSDAP and the SA in 1933—during the Weimar years he belonged to the liberal German Democratic Party.[131] Was Krack a convinced National Socialist? Did antisemitism shape his relation to Moringen's Jewish prisoners? How do we judge his role as a perpetrator active in the implementation of the regime's racist principles? Bearing in mind his opinions on some of the Jewish women, Krack emerges as an antisemite. Anni Krümmel, for example, he viewed as "descended from a Jewish family of criminals, herself the type of an asocial human being. Despite her relative youth she is completely debased in character."[132] On Jenny Berzinsky (from whose prisoner file comes this chapter's title), Krack reported: "She is the exemplar of the type of a Jew involved in shady businesses, trading credits and carrying out other money dealings besides running her boarding house." Berzinsky had been arrested for criticism of the regime and nonconforming behavior. Krack interpreted the fact that she still owed wages to her employee as "antisocial behavior of a Jew toward a German."[133]

These negative statements in which classical antisemitic stereotypes abound must, however, be contrasted with former Jewish prisoners' positive characterizations of Krack. The Quaker archives holds a letter from the Jewish physician Milli Beermann sent in November 1935 from her exile in New York. In it Beermann attributed her release from Moringen to Krack's personal intercession with the Gestapo in Berlin. She attested that he was no Nazi and begged that the Quakers "should neither mention the name of the camp direktor [sic] nor praise him. Because if the Nazis knew about his kindness, they would dismiss him at once. The loss of his position would be very bad . . . for all the women in the camp."[134] Frieda Sherwood, detained in Moringen from May to September 1935, testified after the war that Krack had "cared for the Jewish prisoners in a self-sacrificing way." He saw to it that they could "secretly receive packages from the outside world and he helped in any possible way." Sherwood was convinced that she owed her life to Krack.[135] Also illuminating with regard to these seemingly conflicting traits is the memoir of Lotti Huber (formerly Charlotte Goldmann), who regarded neither Krack nor the female overseers of Moringen as Nazis. Rather "they were social workers used to dealing with prostitutes and the 'work-shy.' What should they do with the wife of a professor or a [female] member of parliament or a harmless housewife? It would not have taken much for the director to address us as 'ladies.'"[136]

Apparently, it was a prisoner's class rather than "race" that influenced Krack's perception of her. He treated with relative respect those women equal to him in social status but disregarded those socially inferior to him as well as those who, like young Eva Mamlok, disobeyed his authority and behaved "arrogantly" and were "unruly."[137] Women from a lower-class milieu, socially deviant women, so-called asocials, "professional or habitual criminals," Krack viewed as morally "unfit." The majority of the Jewish women in Moringen, however, came from middle-class backgrounds. During the few occasions when they saw the camp director—for example, when summoned to his office—the impression they got of him must have been close to the one gleaned by Ilse Rolfe: "In his narrow-mindedness he once told me: 'To me it makes no difference which government happens to be in power, I will always have to stand behind the government. I serve the fatherland.' Obedience was his first duty. He did not treat the women inhumanely."[138] Historian Matthias Kuse has characterized Krack as the "type of the Bildungsbürger," a member of the educated classes, who co-operated with the Nazis, albeit with some inner reluctance. Kuse states that in his position as camp director Krack remained, first and foremost, loyal toward the state and holds that, perhaps somewhat unwillingly, Krack be-came complicit in state-sanctioned acts of repression.[139] This interpretation must be revised, especially when contextualizing it with new research that stresses the importance of civilian administrators for the implementation of Nazi racist policies. In her paradigmatic case study of Udo Klausa, the Chief Executive of the county of Bedzin, Mary Fulbrook has explored the role and responsibilities of a civilian functionary who got caught up in the system of the Hitler dictatorship and his crimes. Like this county executive, Krack was not a committed perpetrator driven by a genuine belief in Nazi ideology. He, too, was "mobilized rather than motivated."[140] At the time, Krack went along with the regime. When he understood that his institution, which was underused by the end of the Weimar period, would benefit from the admis-sion of protective custody prisoners, he seized the opportunity.[141]

There can be no doubt that, as camp director, Krack ratified inhumane policies that caused great suffering. Like other civilian administrators in Nazi Germany he served a system that degraded and terrorized the women of Moringen and aimed at "destroying their physical and psychological ca-pacity for resistance or escape."[142] He was also responsible for the forced sterilizations perpetrated against women in Moringen after 1933.[143] Hence, despite his apparent empathy for individual female prisoners of middle-class backgrounds, the historical picture of Krack is that of one of those "many hundreds of thousands of low- und middle-level functionaries and facilita-tors of the racist policies of the Third Reich," who—"whether willingly or unwillingly—ultimately helped pave the way for genocide."[144] After the war, he could stylize himself as a "decent" German who had, based on a self-conception as teacher and social psychologist, merely extended his peda-gogical commitments from the treatment of correctional inmates in the workhouse to the protective custody prisoners of the concentration camp. To the concentration camp he attributed an "educational character" and thought of it as "an interesting psychological experiment" whose setup and course he could actively influence.[145]

Krack's "experiment," which lasted until spring 1938, was ultimately sanctioned by Himmler. In his capacity as chief of all state political police forces, Himmler nominally oversaw also the Moringen concentration camp, which, unlike most other concentration camps of the mid-1930s, was not run directly by the SS but instead was run by the civilian provincial administration of Hanover. It is precisely because Moringen appears as a kind of relic of the period of the early concentration camps that it was chosen for in-depth analysis. The case demonstrates that female and male camp imprisonment differed not only in terms of numbers. The historical development of the system of concentration camps for women and men was also divergent.[146] As a result of this asynchronicity, it took the SS until 1937–1938 to secure full control over the camp detention of women. With the decision in autumn 1937 to continue using the male concentration camp of Lichtenburg, in the process of being dissolved, for the imprisonment of women, the course for the future development was set. The Renaissance castle in the Prussian province of Saxony functioned as a "hinge," an intermediary stage, between Moringen, the civilian-administered relic of the early concentration camps, and the "modern," purpose-built barracks camp of Ravensbrück opened in May 1939.[147] The Lichtenburg castle complex, which included a sixteenth-century church, had traditionally served as a widows' seat of the Saxon Electors. Starting in 1812 it was used as a prison, and over the years the site, on the outskirts of the small town of Prettin an der Elbe, turned into an important detention center in Prussia. Prisoners were accommodated in the converted palace rooms. In the 1870s, the authorities added a prison building with small cells that held three to six inmates each. The prison was closed in 1928 due to sanitary problems and the insufficient hygienic conditions in the worn-out, cold, and damp buildings. A concentration camp was officially opened on the site in July 1933. The palace courtyard now served as the place for roll calls and excruciating "camp sport."[148] Female prisoners transported from Moringen to Lichtenburg, some of them later deported on to Ravensbrück, faced a grim deterioration in their imprisonment conditions. Their accommodation, either in the overcrowded halls under the damaged roof of the castle or in the small cells of the prison building, was completely inadequate, sometimes without heating.[149] The women's camp of Lichtenburg was now subordinated under the IKL.

Previous research has not uncovered the fact that the female Jewish prisoners of Moringen were sent to Lichtenburg as one distinct group with

Figure 3.2 Aerial view of the Lichtenburg castle in Prettin an der Elbe, 1930s.
Private collection of Stefan Hördler.

the transport of March 21, 1938. This transport consisted of 168 prisoners, whose names have been compiled on four separate lists.[150] Fifty-seven of the women are officially labeled "professional criminals."[151] The other names on the lists, labeled merely as protective custody prisoners, have not hitherto been identified as belonging to a particular group or prisoner category. With personal record cards missing for this transport, information on the women's arrest categories and "racial descent" cannot easily be checked.[152] By consulting the ITS Central Name Index, the German Federal Archives' Memorial Book, and other sources, I was able to identify seventy names compiled on one separate transport list as the names of Jewish inmates. My results prove that Moringen's Jews were held back in the camp until March 21, 1938, and then transported to Lichtenburg as one distinct group. To all appearances, the seventy women from Moringen who arrived in Lichtenburg in late March were among the first Jewish female prisoners in the new camp.[153]

What conditions confronted Jewish women in Lichtenburg? Ilse Rolfe, interned in the camp until its dissolution in May 1939, reported that in contrast to Moringen, a "completely different atmosphere" prevailed in Lichtenburg. Although extreme physical violence was still the exception, many "cruelties" and "torments" were inflicted on the prisoners.[154] Upon arrival, both Jewish and non-Jewish women had to endure death threats while standing at attention in endless roll calls. A militaristic daily routine provoked conflicts with the female overseers, whose number gradually rose to more than fifty.[155] The women's camp of Lichtenburg was first led by SS Standartenführer Günther Tamaschke. In the end of 1938, he was followed by SS Hauptsturmführer Max Koegel. Similarly to Moringen, the enforcement of labor was limited in Lichtenburg. A report of April 1938 registers only 22 percent of the prisoners deployed in work detachments—Jews were not among them. As a means of punishment Jews were initially not "allowed" to work but kept locked in small cells without any variety in their daily routine.[156] Later on Jewish prisoners were ordered to do hard and filthy labor. According to the testimony of a non-Jewish former prisoner, they were forced to work as drainers in the sewage system in autumn 1938, performing "work that was not easy even for men . . . only one of the delicate women received rubber boots and these were still too short. These Jewish prisoners came back every evening covered in mud and dirt up to their hips."[157]

A total of 1,415 female prisoners were registered at the Lichtenburg camp; 1,115 of them are identified by name.[158] The exact percentage of Jewish women is unknown but can be estimated also to have ranged between 10 and 15 percent. The names of 155 Jewish female prisoners could be identified for this study.[159] As was the case in Moringen, Jewish inmates in Lichtenburg were housed together as one distinct group. Their unit was termed "Jew Station" (Judenstation), "Jew Building" (Judenbau) or "Station VII" and was located in the camp's prison building, where the SS also kept prostitutes and so-called criminals and asocials, as well as Sinti and Roma women persecuted as "gypsies."[160] Olga Benario-Prestes functioned as the "eldest" of the Jew Station. As a prominent political prisoner, the Communist had to bear especially harsh conditions of chicanery, isolation, and punishment. Arriving in Lichtenburg in the spring of 1938, she was initially kept in special solitary arrest in the "bunker," the part of the castle building that had been converted to a jail.[161]

Release from Lichtenburg concentration camp became increasingly difficult for Jewish women. Almost half of the seventy inmates transported to the camp from Moringen in March 1938—thirty-three women—were shipped on to Ravensbrück in May 1939. A number of the Jewish women originally deported to Moringen could not escape Nazi persecution and lost their lives in the Holocaust. Some of their names are to be found among the first group of Ravensbrück prisoners selected for death in the gas chamber of the T4 "euthanasia" center in Bernburg (Saale) in the spring of 1942. "Action 14f13," the official code for the "euthanasia" murders of concentration camp prisoners, claimed the lives of Anni Krümmel, Charlotte Cohn, and Olga Benario-Prestes, among others.[162]

Although analyzing female Jewish prisoners in the prewar concentration camps has established important differences between the detention of men and women, it has also yielded a number of results that apply to the persecution of both sexes. First, it has shown how, in the mid-1930s, the function of camp terror was expanded to new enemy categories. Most importantly, return from a longer stay abroad came to be considered an offense hostile to the Nazi state, and hundreds of returning emigrants were taken into so-called instructive custody. Officially targeting both Jewish and non-Jewish Germans, the practice of arrest swiftly took on an antisemitic cast. Second, the authorities developed a particular practice for the release of Jewish prisoners from the concentration camp. Gradually, their release became tied to the condition that they emigrate, and depended on Himmler's personal consent. Third, the fatal entwinement of police sanctions with legal prosecution brought to the camps of the mid-1930s men and women discharged from prisons or found not guilty of any legal offense. With self-styled "corrections" of court decisions, the Gestapo detained all those they perceived as Nazi Germany's ideological enemies. The divergence in the development of the male and female concentration camp system requires a brief jump back in time to the summer of 1934, when Himmler and Eicke started to transform the diverse topography of the early concentration camps into the later system of SS concentration camps.

4

CEMENTING THE ENEMY CATEGORY

Jews in the Evolving SS Concentration Camp System, 1935–1938

In May 1934, Dachau commandant Theodor Eicke was commissioned by Himmler to reshape Nazi Germany's concentration camps in the style of the Bavarian "model camp." Starting with the reorganization of Lichtenburg, Eicke, who was officially appointed Inspector of the Concentration Camps and Leader of the SS Guard Units in early July 1934, gradually secured SS control over the existing sites of terror and standardized their administration and guarding along the lines of Dachau's organizational structure. Smaller camps like Osthofen and Rosslau were dissolved. After the brutal purge of the SA leadership in the "Night of the Long Knives" on June 30, 1934, the SS Brigadeführer also closed down the SA camps in Oranienburg and Hohnstein. On December 10, 1934, the Inspectorate of the Concentration Camps (IKL) became officially institutionalized under the authority of the Secret State Police Office, a state institution by then under Himmler's control. By the end of the year Eicke had reorganized the Prussian camps of Esterwegen, Lichtenburg, and Columbia-Haus, as well as the Saxon camp of Sachsenburg.[1] The camps of Fuhlsbüttel in Hamburg and Kislau in Baden never came under the jurisdiction of the IKL. Like Moringen they assumed a kind of "special status" and existed parallel to the evolving system of the SS concentration camps until their inmates were eventually transferred to SS camps in the late 1930s.[2]

By April 1936 the SS controlled six concentration camps: Dachau, Esterwegen, Lichtenburg, Columbia-Haus, Sachsenburg, and Bad Sulza.[3] With the exception of Dachau, which was completely rebuilt in 1937–1938, all of these camps were closed down until the outbreak of the war. In their place the SS established new structures that were, as Nikolaus Wachsmann aptly puts it, "not found but purpose-built, planned as small cities of terror, with rows of barracks and roads, commando posts and guard towers, sewers and electricity, workshops and SS quarters."[4] Designed according to Himmler's plan as "new concentration camp[s] for the modern age, which can be extended at any time . . . [and] can guarantee the full security of the Reich against enemies of the state," concentration camps like Sachsenhausen (opened in September 1936) and Buchenwald (opened in July 1937) had very little in common organizationally with the improvised camp sites of the early phase.[5]

The formation and expansion of the SS concentration camp system did not proceed in as smooth and linear a fashion as it might seem in hindsight. In 1934–1935, senior officials of the Nazi party and the state opposed Himmler's plans and argued for the abolition of the camps. With prisoner numbers declining to about 3,000 by the end of 1934, the camps seemed to be relics from the time of "revolutionary struggle."[6] In the meantime the regime had become well established. The state legal system had been furnished with repressive instruments capable of harshly prosecuting political offenders. Himmler was under acute pressure when Interior Minister Wilhelm Frick demanded a reduction of the high numbers of "protective custody" prisoners in Bavaria, while Justice Minister Franz Gürtner worried about untrammelled violence at these extralegal sites of detention, increasingly shielded from the investigation of state prosecutors. Several crucial interventions made by Hitler in 1935, however, secured the survival of the camp system. In February Hitler supported Himmler's refusal to release prisoners and, with this decision, strengthened Himmler's authority against Frick. Later in the year, Hitler agreed to the expansion of the SS guard units, and ordered that beginning in April 1, 1936, the concentration camps should be financed from the Reich budget. Finally, he pardoned some camp guards convicted of prisoner abuse and prohibited consultation with lawyers in cases of protective custody, thereby further limiting the judiciary's influence on the camps.[7]

In his attempt to establish the concentration camp as a permanent instrument of terror for the protection of the "people's community," Himmler was not merely driven by power politics. For him the concentration camps played a vital role in what he perceived as an apocalyptic struggle, "a fundamental world-conflict with . . . forces of organized subhumanity" represented chiefly by Jewry and Bolshevism.[8] When lecturing representatives of the German Army, the Wehrmacht, about the system of the concentration camps in January 1937, Himmler emphasized that in the future, in the case of war, there would be an "inner-German theater of war" in which one would have to fight an "ideological enemy" (namely Bolshevism), "the absolute fortification of Jewry's domination, the exact opposite of everything dear, valuable and precious to the Aryan people." What would be at stake was not just "some external conflict," but an existential "struggle of annihilation" touching upon the very "being or not being" of Germany as the "core people" of the Germanic race and humanity's "bearer of culture." Harsh treatment and punishment of concentration camp prisoners, as well as the establishment of a tough fighting unit of SS Death's Head divisions, were "necessary" to win this struggle.[9]

This Weltanschauung (world view) appealed to Hitler, who facilitated Himmler's rise to the top of the German police and with it the merger of state and party institutions into a powerful SS police apparatus. When Himmler was appointed Inspector of the Prussian Secret State Police on April 20, 1934, he was effectively put in charge of all state political police forces and was thereby responsible for protective custody matters all over the Reich. On June 17, 1936, he received the title Reich Leader SS and Chief of the German Police in the Reich Ministry of the Interior, a position that allowed him to remove the police forces from ministerial control and integrate them into a centralized and quasi-independent system of state terror.[10] Just as he installed Eicke as the head of the IKL, the institution in charge of managing the concentration camps, Himmler subordinated the Gestapo, the agency responsible for the arrest and release of most camp prisoners, to another loyal lieutenant: Reinhard Heydrich. As Chief of the Security Police (Sipo), Heydrich headed both the political police (Gestapo) and the criminal police (Kripo). A key figure in the identification and persecution of state enemies, he also oversaw the SD, the Nazi party's intelligence service.[11]

Becoming more and more powerful, the Gestapo continued to undermine juridical authority. Whenever the political police saw juridical decisions as not being in line with the higher political and ideological aims of the Nazi state, it tightened or "corrected" legal sanctions by implementing protective custody as a form of police justice. As a result of the Gestapo's "correctional" practice, a number of political activists were taken to the concentration camps in the mid-1930s after they were either acquitted by the courts or had served their sentences in prison. Among them were also Jewish resistance fighters like Werner Scholem, who was tried for "preparing for high treason" in front of the People's Court in March 1935. Immediately after the court had established that nothing incriminating could be held against him, the Gestapo "corrected" this verdict and deported Scholem to Lichtenburg concentration camp.[12]

As a leading activist of the KPD, Rudolf "Rudi" Arndt had been sentenced to three years of penitentiary in October 1934. Three years later, when his spell in the Brandenburg prison officially came to an end, Arndt fell back into the hands of the Gestapo. He was sent first to Sachsenhausen, and on November 27, 1937, he arrived in Dachau concentration camp.[13] Other Jewish Communists had similar fates. Emil Carlebach arrived in Dachau in April 1937 after a three-year detention in various prisons. Carlebach was a member of the Young Communist League of Germany (KJVD) and had been sentenced for distributing antifascist union papers.[14] The brothers August and Erwin Cohn from Oberkaufungen near Kassel each spent two years in prison following sentences for preparing for high treason. Erwin, the younger brother, was interned in Breitenau concentration camp from December 1933 to February 1934 before he was handed over to the legal authorities. August Cohn had already been sent to prison by the Kassel Higher District Court in July 1933. In July 1935 he was handed back to the Gestapo and brought to Esterwegen. In early 1937 the brothers met again in Dachau's Jew company.[15] Communist Herbert Mindus from Hamburg, too, was eventually imprisoned in Dachau after four years of detention in various prisons and concentration camps. Arrested in June 1933 for his involvement in the illegal distribution of the banned *Hamburger Volkszeitung*, Mindus was initially held in the protective custody wing of the Fuhlsbüttel prison; from there the Gestapo sent him to Esterwegen.[16] In Dachau and later also in Buchenwald, Arndt, Carlebach, Mindus, and the Cohn brothers belonged to a circle of Jewish Communists, some of whom as prisoner functionaries played an important role in the organization of the group of Jewish prisoners as a whole. As I shall elaborate below, their personalities also influenced the distinct dynamics of cohesion and conflict prevailing in the Jew blocks.

To be sure, the legal system also increasingly discriminated against Jewish prisoners after 1933. Although their treatment was by no means as brutal as in the camps, Jewish inmates of prisons and penitentiaries experienced antisemitic measures such as the curtailing of their traditional religious rights and, most importantly, their isolation from other prisoners.[17] A transfer from the prison to the concentration camp, however, constituted a radical break in their persecution, as can be learned, for example, from Ernesto Kroch's memoir. The Communist was transferred from the Breslau youth prison and arrived in Lichtenburg in May 1936, together with comrades Heinz Isaac and Lothar Müller. "We realized straight away that a different wind was blowing here than in the prison. We had entered the realm of arbitrariness and unpredictability . . . In contrast to the prison, here they made a distinction between 'Aryans' and 'Jews.'"[18] In Lichtenburg, Jews were spatially separated from other prisoners. Kroch reported that he had to share a small cell of about 16 square meters with eight other inmates. A diverse assembly of personalities, thrown together under the racial stigma, had to get along and manage the uncertainties of camp imprisonment and its day-to-day adversities. Kroch remembered another Communist who functioned as the cell elder, as well as a "very old and frail grandpa" (denounced for having told jokes about Göring), a homosexual man, a Jew from Russia, and two lawyers of middle-class backgrounds—one of whom can be identified as Ludwig Bendix.[19]

Taking this snapshot of the Lichtenburg cell as the point of departure for an investigation of the arrest and imprisonment of Jewish men during the years 1935 to early 1938, this chapter deals with the following questions: For what reasons were Jewish men imprisoned in the concentration camps of the mid-1930s? What were the conditions inside the camps, and to what extent did the treatment of Jews differ from location to location? And how did the victims respond to their persecution?

Arrests of Jews in the mid-1930s

When in the summer of 1935 the country witnessed an aggressive campaign of antisemitic defamation and attacks, some German Jews protested fiercely. One of them was Ludwig Bendix, the Berlin lawyer who had been held in protective custody for four months in 1933. After his forced exclusion from the bar, he had obtained the formal permission of the Gestapo to work as a legal counselor. When one day he found affixed to his nameplate at the entrance of the house an antisemitic sticker with a caricature of a Jew and the inscription "He who buys from the Jew is a traitor to the people," Bendix was outraged. Not only did he alert the police and have the sticker removed, he filed a petition to the local police chief demanding the removal of further discriminatory signs—in particular, a large white cloth panel carrying the inscription "We no longer want the Jews" that covered the whole front of a nearby Nazi party building.[20] The police forwarded Bendix's petition to the Gestapo. Two weeks later, by the end of July 1935, he was arrested. Testifying to his ordeal in the late 1930s, Bendix remembered a Gestapo official yelling at him during the interrogation: "'We don't understand why you are still here in Germany! Emigration is the only way for people like you! But you don't want to go, do you? You'll get protective custody! I'll see to it that you won't get out [of the camp] soon.'"[21] Indeed, his imprisonment in the early concentration camps of Spandau and Brandenburg had not forced the lawyer into emigration. His son recalled that Bendix had lost 30 pounds of weight, "but his spirit was undaunted."[22] A patriot deeply rooted in German culture, the Jewish lawyer had no intention of leaving his fatherland: "Germany is my homeland; leaving her I would commit desertion."[23]

Bendix was deported to Lichtenburg in early August 1935. As a recidivist *(Rückfälliger)*—a person taken to a concentration camp for a second time—he was initially kept in a special section for political prisoners, accommodated separately from the Jew Company.[24] Bendix was punished with almost two years of concentration camp imprisonment for his persistent protest against anti-Jewish measures. Discharged from Dachau in May 1937 on the condition that he emigrate from Nazi Germany, this time he had no choice but to leave his country. However insulted and violated, the Jewish lawyer's strong sense of justice and his inveterate belief in the law remained unbroken. His son Reinhard reported the shock he and his sister suffered when they discovered that their father was preparing a legal brief against former Lichtenburg commandant Hermann Baranowski, whom Bendix held responsible for the death of fellow prisoner Ignatz Manasse.[25] The lawyer objected that, although the camp leadership was aware of the dressmaker's cardiac problems, it did not exempt Manasse from the excruciating "camp sport" with which SS company leader Edmund Bräuning used to torture the Jewish prisoners in particular. Manasse suffered two heart attacks while in Lichtenburg, and a week before he died he told his wife that he feared he would not see her again: "[My] heart is weak and I cannot take [the hardships of camp imprisonment] any longer."[26] On July 21, 1936, the prisoner collapsed and died during the punitive drill. Manasse's death seriously affected the mood of the camp. Fellow prisoners were seized by grief and an agonizing powerlessness in the face of SS violence. They were disgusted by the grotesque burial ceremony at which Bräuning, the SS man who tormented Manasse to death, offered his insincere condolences to the late prisoner's widow and daughter.[27]

An eyewitness to the crime, Bendix must have been haunted by the experience of the gruesome event to such an extent that, as soon as he had escaped the realm of camp terror, he considered it his most urgent concern to bring to justice those responsible for the death of his fellow prisoner. What Reinhard Bendix later called "my father's stubborn legalism" constituted an immense risk not only to the released prisoner himself but also to his whole family, which already suffered from increasing social isolation: "Whoever had been friendly with us before withdrew on one pretext or another because, with my father in a concentration camp, we were a source of political contamination." Finally, in order to intercept any possible trouble, the Bendix children took turns standing guard over their father until their parents had safely left the country for Palestine.[28]

German Jews' defiant protests against ever-growing antisemitic discrimination were more common than hindsight might suggest. As the Bendix case shows, fear of persecution and terror would not necessarily deter those who felt the urgent need to rectify injustice and insist on respectful treatment. The regime, on the other hand, often saw no other way of dealing with dissent than by taking the protesters into protective custody. Apart from the persecution of individual acts of resistance, the Gestapo used the concentration camp to quell official protest by organizations like the National Representation of the German Jews, the Reichsvertretung, (an umbrella organization for Jewish groups in Germany) and the Confessional Church, a Protestant secession of the church in Nazi Germany that arose in opposition to the regime.

The Reichsvertretung's Leo Baeck and Otto Hirsch, in an attempt to counteract a growing demoralization that caught hold of large parts of German Jewry during the antiemitic campaigns of summer 1935, composed several spiritual addresses to buoy up the Jewish communities. On August 11, 1935, the uplifting memorandum "Sabbath of Solace" was read out in Jewish prayer houses all over Germany. As a Kol Nidre prayer to be heard in the synagogues on Yom Kippur, the Reichsvertretung distributed an address that called on German Jews to "regard with indignation and abhorrence the lies against us and the defamation of our religion and its testimonies." However, on October 4, 1935, shortly before the holiday, the National Representation of the German Jews informed the communities via cable that the Gestapo had prohibited the reading out of the appeal and had ordered its destruction. Baeck and Hirsch were soon arrested. Baeck was deported to Columbia-Haus concentration camp. The fact that his imprisonment lasted for only a couple of days was not unusual for this particular camp, where prisoners were generally kept only for short periods of time. Regarded as political opponents of the regime, prisoners in Columbia-Haus were held available for questioning at the nearby Gestapo headquarters in Prinz-Albrecht-Strasse, with decisions still pending about possible long-term detention at other camp locations.[29]

In the example of Max Dienemann, interned in the early concentration camp of Osthofen in late 1933, we saw how rabbis could be persecuted as political enemies. Their speeches and writings, which were meant to encourage the Jewish community in times of crisis, were perceived by the Gestapo as slanderous criticism of the regime. Apart from Baeck, we know of at least two other rabbis detained in Columbia-Haus in 1935–1936. Rabbi Emil Bernhard Cohn of Berlin-Grunewald was arrested while addressing a Jewish meeting on December 20, 1935. He was accused of "ridiculing the section of the Nuremberg Laws that prohibit[s] employment by Jews of 'Aryan' women." Taken into protective custody, he was detained for about three weeks. His colleague Rabbi Ignaz Maybaum, the spiritual leader of the Jewish community in Frankfurt/Oder, was held in the same concentration camp for about six weeks.[30]

The arrest and imprisonment of religious dignitaries frequently prompted international protest that threatened to undermine the public image of Nazi Germany. The murder of the head of the Chancellery of the Confessional Church, Friedrich Weissler, on February 19, 1937, in Sachsenhausen concentration camp caused one such scandal. The case is noteworthy because it demonstrates in an extreme way the lethal power of the concentration camp to brand as "a Jew" a person whose own identity as a practicing Christian could not have diverged more starkly from the antisemitic categorization of the Nazis. Born to baptized parents of Jewish origin, Weissler was raised a devoted Protestant. However, his SS tormenters abused and killed him as a Jew. On October 3, 1936, the Gestapo arrested Weissler and accused him of having placed into the hands of foreign media the Confessional Church's secret memorandum to Hitler, which condemned antisemitism, state terrorism, and the concentration camp. After its publication in newspapers abroad, the memorandum caused a sensation and was read out from pulpits throughout Germany on August 23, 1936.[31] Together with pastor Werner Koch and vicar Ernst Tillich, Weissler was brought to Sachsenhausen on February 13, 1937. A note on the transport list identified him as a Jew, and upon entry into the camp, Weissler was separated from the other two, "Aryan" new arrivals.[32] Incarcerated in Sachsenhausen's newly built cell block, he was tortured to death. In a legal investigation carried out by the Berlin public prosecutor's office, twenty-six-year-old SS Scharführer Christian Guthardt openly confessed his participation in the abuse of Weissler. This SS man, who was in charge of the camp's cell block, described himself as a "fanatical Jew-hater," for whom "a Jew . . . was even less than cattle."[33] Under Guthardt's oversight, the cell block in Sachsenhausen became a notorious killing site for Jewish prisoners. At least five men imprisoned there as Jews were murdered in the two months between mid-December 1936 and mid-February 1937.[34]

Before turning to a more systematic analysis of the situation inside the concentration camps in the mid-1930, I will analyze one last category of arrest that affected a number of Jewish males: homosexuality. The Nazi persecution of gay men was significantly stepped up after the "Röhm purge" and the "discovery" of homosexuality among the SA leadership. The sharpening of article 175 of the Reich Criminal Code on June 28, 1935, tightened legal prosecution and widened the definition of the crime to include any act of male homosexuality. The number of concentration camp prisoners classified as homosexuals reached a high point during the years 1934 to 1936. In December 1934, some 200 homosexuals and transvestites were deported to Lichtenburg. The Prussian camp had by far the highest rate of homosexual prisoners. In June 1935 they were almost 50 percent of the prisoner population (325 out of 706). Most of the Jewish prisoners categorized as homosexuals were also to be found in Lichtenburg.[35]

As is the case with all perpetrator categorizations of concentration camp inmates, it is important to not assume that those imprisoned as homosexuals were indeed all gay. A telling example is the case of Günther Goldschmidt. From August until December 1935 he was detained in Columbia-Haus and Lichtenburg. Arrested without reasons given, the twenty-two-year-old learned only in his Gestapo interrogation that he was being persecuted as a homosexual. The incomprehension and the shock with which he reacted to this accusation still find their expression in an oral-history interview conducted more than half a century later: "To me that was a blow for I did not even know what homosexuality meant. It turned out that one of the young men with whom I was friendly was arrested, he was really a homosexual and because he had given the contacts of all the members [of the youth organization to the Gestapo], they arrested me, too."[36] By emphasizing that "of course, I was not homosexual," the former prisoner persistently distanced himself from his category of persecution.

Sociologist Rüdiger Lautmann points to the continuities in the discrimination and criminalization of homosexuals in Imperial Germany, the

Weimar Republic, and the Third Reich. Due to the existence of a broad antihomosexual consensus in large parts of society, Nazi policies against gay men assumed a kind of "normality" and "political self-evidence."[37] Hence, it comes as little surprise that the persecution of homosexual men by means of protective custody and camp terror was often triggered by denunciations. Wilhelm Tag, for example, was reported to the police by his landlord, who denounced the Jewish man as a pedophile. Summoned to the Munich police station, Tag admitted that he would let friends stay with him overnight but made it clear that he did not get intimate with them. "I prefer not to comment on my sexual orientation," he insisted. The incident, which occurred in 1932, had put Tag on the police records. In early 1936, when the persecution of homosexuals had radicalized, the Munich Gestapo followed up the case and took the thirty-one-year-old man into protective custody. Beginning in March 1936 Tag was imprisoned in Dachau, until, after more than half a year, the Munich District Court sentenced him to one year and five months in prison for offenses against article 175. After he had served his sentence, Tag was taken back to Dachau in January 1938. Attempts to free him were made by his lawyer, and although there were great difficulties in obtaining the necessary positive references for a man incriminated as a homosexual, the advocate managed to arrange for Tag's emigration to Shanghai in June 1939.[38]

On August 26, 1935, Louis Schild from Essen had approached a sixteen-year-old teenager at the train station and invited the boy into his home. After a neighbor had denounced the fifty-five-year-old salesman, he was taken into protective custody. Because ultimately a criminal act was not verifiable—otherwise Schild would have been persecuted by the legal system—he fell victim to police sanctions. On October 21 he arrived in Esterwegen concentration camp, where he died less than four weeks later, on November 18, 1935, allegedly of heart failure and pneumonia. In fact the notorious SS company leader Gustav Sorge had severely abused the frail man during work. Schild became delirious and passed away the same night. In his postwar trial, Sorge was found guilty of the murder of the Jewish prisoner. The former SS man sought exculpation by emphasizing that "according to the camp leader," Hans Loritz, the Jewish prisoner's life "was of no value."[39]

Comparable to the status of Jews in the camps, inmates categorized as homosexuals ranked at the bottom of the prisoner hierarchy. Raids conducted in gay bars, parks, and public toilets all over Bavaria on October

20–21, 1934, brought fifty-four men to Dachau. These homosexual prisoners were isolated from the rest of the inmates in a separate barrack, in which the lights were kept on all night and guards were positioned to deter them from "getting close to each other." The only other prisoner group that suffered from similar measures of isolation and heightened surveillance during Dachau's early phase were the Jews.[40] In the Lichtenburg camp, homosexual and Jewish prisoners were temporarily put together in the punishment company. The two prisoner groups were also grouped into the same work details that had to perform particularly heavy or filthy labor, like the cleaning of cesspits and sewers in Lichtenburg, or the gravel pit and the road roller in Dachau.[41] In enduring these harsh conditions, homosexual prisoners could expect little or no solidarity from other prisoners. What is more, other prisoners, and here the Jews were no exception, reproduced the stereotypes ascribed to them and often saw homosexuals as gossipy, mendacious, and enslaved to their uncontrollable sex drives. Some heterosexual prisoners later stated that they had been sexually harassed by homosexuals.[42] Both categories of inmates were selected for maltreatment by the camp guards; Jewish homosexual prisoners, carrying the double stigma, fared among the worst.

Leopold Obermayer, whose remarkable case has been documented by the literature, left a meticulous account of the torture he suffered for nine months in a darkened cell of the Dachau *Bunker*. The chief of the Würzburg Gestapo, Josef Gerum, who had made the case his own personal affair, quickly realized that the prisoner's report—composed during a short break from camp detention in the remand prison in October 1935—was "but a sole indictment of the National Socialist state." Instead of handing him over to the legal authorities for proper pretrial confinement, Gerum had Obermayer shipped back to Dachau. His second imprisonment lasted from mid-October 1935 to September 1936.[43] In the political police's zealous effort to criminalize the Jewish wine merchant, a collection of nude photographs of young men discovered in Obermayer's bank safe served as prime evidence. A public smear campaign branded the homosexual man an "enemy of the people," a "Jewish poisoner of the youth," a "sexual offender," and "devil incarnate."[44] But Obermayer resisted attacks and discrimination with admirable courage and astute legal expertise. He claimed that the nature of his relations with the young men constituted no offense to the law. He even appealed to the Reich Justice Minister himself and, in the face of all the injustice done to him, asked Gürtner provocatively whether the justice department was "still master in its own house or whether it became a compliant instrument of the Gestapo"—a question that undoubtedly touched on a sore point.[45] On December 13, 1936, Obermayer was sentenced to ten years of penitentiary to be followed by security confinement. As an "incorrigible" criminal offender, he was handed over to the SS in 1942 for "annihilation through labor" in a concentration camp—an extermination program launched by Himmler and the newly-appointed Minister of Justice Otto-Georg Thierack. Obermayer was deported to Mauthausen, where he died on February 22, 1943, under unknown circumstances.[46]

In the mid-1930s, too, Jewish prisoners' paths into the camps were diverse. They were interned for political opposition, open protest against antisemitic discrimination, defiance, and self-confident insistence on their rights. Others fell into the hands of the persecuting authorities for their nonconformist behavior and their homosexuality. It is rare to find men categorized as "criminals" among the Jewish prisoners of the mid-1930s. Taken into preventive police custody, "professional criminals" had been imprisoned in the camps since 1933. However, it was only with the first nationwide raid of March 1937 that the persecution of "criminals" and "asocials" became centralized and resulted in a systematic policy of arrest and imprisonment.[47] Administrative records register four Jewish preventive custody prisoners in Sachsenhausen in early 1937—a vanishingly small number in comparison to the approximately 540 non-Jewish preventive custody inmates held in the camp at that time.[48] In the month of March 1937, twenty-one new arrivals to the Dachau concentration camp were labeled as "P.S.V.-J."—Jewish prisoners held in "police security confinement" (*Polizeiliche Sicherungsverwahrung*), the camp administration's term for criminals with several previous convictions.[49] Former prisoner Alfred Eduard Laurence (formerly Alfred Lomnitz), himself not free of prejudice, described these men as "mostly stateless or foreign Jews." Some were owners of small businesses convicted for "fraud or the counterfeit of a bill," others pickpockets, cardsharpers, or smugglers.[50] Also documented is the killing of a Jewish "professional criminal" in Esterwegen on May 31, 1935. Forty-six-year-old Julius Agranoff, a Russian Jew, was "shot while trying to escape" from the camp. Apparently he had threatened the SS that he would make public the atrocities experienced in Esterwegen in his upcoming trial.[51]

In comparison with the arrest practice of the early years 1933–1934, in which the institution of protective custody was stretched beyond its official political remit to also bring to the camps other unwanted enemies of the regime, we can observe a further expansion of arrest categories in the period between the Röhm purge and the annexation of Austria. Inside the camps, the special treatment of Jewish prisoners ignored all of the individual "reasons," as well as personal backgrounds, that had led to an arrest, and violently turned the persecuted into "Jews." In the process of their exclusion from German society, in which the disfranchising articles of the Nuremberg Laws constitute a benchmark, the concentration camp worked to cement the enemy category of "the Jew."

Inside the SS Concentration Camps

During the period under scrutiny, the branding of "Jews" as a distinct prisoner group and their being set apart from other inmates, which had been unevenly practiced in the early concentration camps, was enforced in all SS camps. By and large, three main strategies of segregation emerged, some of which also affected other groups of prisoners. First, there was spatial separation into different housing units that generally reordered camp accommodations to resemble the grouping of inmates into different categories of imprisonment. In the case of Jewish prisoners, spatial separation took on an extreme form with periods of complete isolation. Second, various kinds of external markers of prisoners were developed to visually represent categories of imprisonment. Attached to their clothes, inmates bore color-coded signs in the shape of stripes, dots, or triangles. In some camps they were marked with their prisoner number or a combination of letters such as "BV" for professional criminal *(Berufsverbrecher)*.[52] Finally, there were various forms of humiliation and violence to brand Jewish prisoners, especially, as an enemy group. Their special treatment ranged from antisemitic verbal abuse to outright murder. The deployment of Jews into special work details set up to torment them also belongs to this third type of identification strategy.

Strategies of identification were enacted differently in each concentration camp. In February 1937 they were ultimately standardized with the centralization of all Jewish prisoners in Dachau—a key event in the history of Jewish camp detention, to which due attention will be devoted below. Before this, however, the conditions prevailing at different locations—Sachsenburg, Lichtenburg, Esterwegen, Sachsenhausen, and Dachau—will be outlined through a comparative analysis. To gain an overview over the numbers of Jewish prisoners during the period in question, it is necessary to undertake another statistical evaluation of the sources. As is the case for the early period, official documentation of inmate numbers in the mid-1930s remains fragmentary. Only for Sachsenhausen and Dachau have remnants of the camps' administrative records survived.[53] For the most part one has to rely on witness statements to reconstruct the numerical dimensions of Jewish prisoners.

It seems safe to say that before February 1937 the groups of Jewish prisoners in the various individual camps are to be measured in two-digit numbers. Judging from different statements, figures peaked in the summer/autumn of 1935 when, with the buildup of pressure for the promulgation of racial laws, Jewish men accused of race defilement were deported to the camps in larger numbers. In Sachsenburg, the arrival of dozens of Jewish race defilers led to the setting up of a separate Jew company in the camp. This newly founded Jew company was soon added to the camp's penal detachment, whose inmates were deployed to the excruciating task of breaking rocks in quarries along the Zschopau River. The Sachsenburg camp had been set up in May 1933 in an abandoned textile mill situated directly at the riverfront. Before this largest of the Saxon camps could be used, prisoners had to renovate the four-story building.

According to the testimony of Paul Wolff, the Jew company of Sachsenburg housed over 40 prisoners by the end of the summer of 1935. Earlier, upon his arrival in the camp in May, Jewish prisoners are said to have numbered only 16 men.[54] The development coincided with a general increase of prisoner numbers in Sachsenburg in 1935, which nearly tripled between July (528 men) and October (1,537 men).[55] Although, in general, prisoner numbers steadily declined to a total of about 700 held in the camp by the time of its dissolution in September 1937, the number of Jews at first remained relatively high. As indicated by an account published by the exile organization of the SPD (Sopade), there were still about 50 Jewish race defilers in Sachsenburg in early autumn 1936—a figure to which Jewish emigrants and politicals must be added. In February 1937, a final cohort of 14 Jews was transferred to Dachau.[56]

A similar situation prevailed in Lichtenburg. In the Prussian camp, too, the number of Jewish prisoners was at its height in 1935, when 50 to 60 inmates classified as race defilers were detained in a separate Jew company, which, strictly speaking, was a Jewish race defilers' company. According to Bendix's contemporary testimony, political Jews and so-called recidivists were not at that time housed together with the race defilers. It was only after the majority of those counted among the latter group had left the camp that all Jews were put together in "Jew cells" (*Judenzellen*) of four to six,

Figure 4.1 The Sachsenburg concentration camp at Zschopau River, July 1933.
Deutsches Historisches Museum. Photographer: Rudi Seidel.

but sometimes as many as nine, men, located in the camp's prison building.[57] The number of Jewish prisoners in late 1935 and 1936 can be estimated to have ranged between 30 and 40.[58] As accommodation in Lichtenburg was rearranged a couple of times and the topography of the old castle with its attic dormitories and small cells further complicated clear spatial distinction, it is difficult to speak of a Jew company in terms of a separate housing unit, in the way it existed, in its clearest and most definite structure, in the barrack camp of Dachau. At some point Lichtenburg's Jews were grouped together with prisoners persecuted as homosexuals. Toward the end of the period, they were isolated in cells and barred from work so as to give them no chance to mingle with other prisoners.[59] The definition of who was to belong to the Jews' group was still somewhat fuzzy in Lichtenburg; this becomes apparent when one considers that a small number of "half-Jews," among them the prominent prisoner Hans Litten, remained in the camp while all other 23 prisoners of the Jew company were transferred to Dachau in February 1937.[60]

In the concentration camp of Esterwegen, overall prisoner numbers were at a low of about 300 after the "Führer amnesty" of August 1934, effected on the occasion of Hitler's taking office as Reich president after Hindenburg's death. Of the three Emsland camps, Esterwegen was the only one that continued to function as a concentration camp after 1934. Originally the site of two separate prisoner camps, the walled compound was rearranged, and from July 1934 onward it comprised a section to accommodate the SS and a fenced-off prisoner section. The "camp street" (*Lagerstrasse*) ran through the whole area, but to enter and exit the prisoners' barracks camp one had to pass through an inner gate building with a machine-gun post on its roof.

After Esterwegen had become part of the IKL, prisoner figures ranged between 300 and 500 until, in 1936, the prisoner population rose to approximately 1,000. Jewish former inmates who testified within months of their release gave a figure of about 30 to 35 Jews interned in Esterwegen in 1935.[61] Living conditions for Jews worsened when camp commander Loritz, ap-

Figure 4.2 View of the prisoner barracks and the inner gate building in the Esterwegen concentration camp, 1935.
bpk.

parently in response to the promulgation of the Nuremberg Laws, ordered Jews, Jehovah's Witnesses, the newly arrived, and those who had received a punishment in the camp to be grouped together in a separate barrack. Within the rooms of this punishment company, Jews were strictly separated from other inmates.[62] When in the summer of 1936 the camp was evacuated before the SS sold it to the Reich Justice Ministry, some 20 Jewish prisoners were transferred to Sachsenhausen in early September.[63] Among them were long-term political prisoners Ernst Heilmann, Herbert Mindus, Max Levinsson, Kurt Eisner Jr., and August Cohn.

Former Sachsenhausen prisoner Alfred Laurence, whose 1938 autobiographical novel as well as later testimony are key to understanding the imprisonment of Jews in the camp in 1936–1937, wrote that what had been a small contingent of Jewish prisoners who had arrived from Esterwegen "doubled or even almost tripled" between September 1936 and February 1937. Laurence's account of the composition of the group, made up mainly of politicals and emigrants, is supported by its resemblance to the camp's official "head count" reports. In early 1937 the camp administration classified some 20 Jewish prisoners as held in protective custody, some 25 in instructive custody, and four in preventive custody. The highest number of Jews in Sachsenhausen, 52, was reached in mid-January, by which time the total number of prisoners had climbed to slightly over 1,600. In 1936–1937 Sachsenhausen was still a camp under construction. Initially Jewish prisoners were housed in the second hall of block 14, located on the western side of the first ring of barracks. Later on they were moved to block 7, first hall, which lay in the eastern part of the prisoner camp. As they were too few to occupy a whole hall, they shared their accommodation with a "dozen or so Jehovah's Witnesses."[64] On February 12, 1937, a transport of 48 Jewish prisoners left Sachsenhausen for Dachau concentration camp.[65]

The number of Jewish prisoners in Dachau could also be counted in double digits before February 1937. A report sent to the British Quakers in July 1935 estimated the strength of the Jewish prisoner group at "still about 50." Former prisoner Heinz Feldheim also reported that there were about 50 Jews in the camp when he arrived in October 1936. Another contemporary account counted 60 Jewish prisoners.[66] Through the transfer of 85 inmates from Lichtenburg, Sachsenburg, and Sachsenhausen, the number of Jewish prisoners rose to approximately 150 before early spring of 1937. With a total prisoner population ranging between 2,000 and 2,300, Jews at

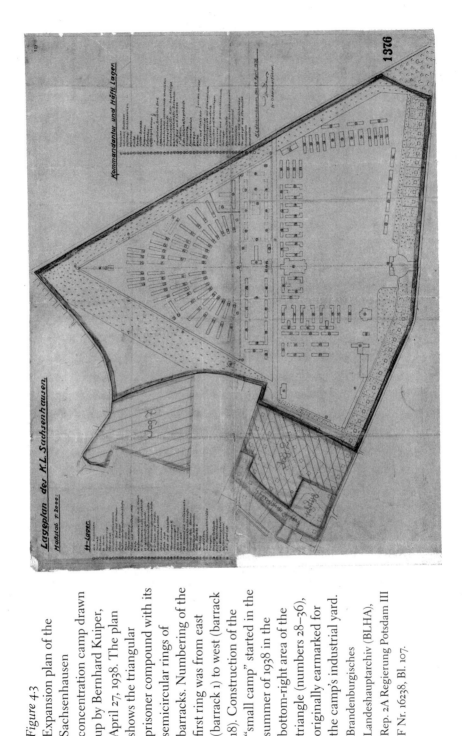

Figure 4.3
Expansion plan of the Sachsenhausen concentration camp drawn up by Bernhard Kuiper, April 27, 1938. The plan shows the triangular prisoner compound with its semicircular rings of barracks. Numbering of the first ring was from east (barrack 1) to west (barrack 18). Construction of the "small camp" started in the summer of 1938 in the bottom-right area of the triangle (numbers 28–36), originally earmarked for the camp's industrial yard. Brandenburgisches Landeshauptarchiv (BLHA), Rep. 2A Regierung Potsdam III F Nr. 1628, Bl. 107.

that point constituted around 7 percent of all inmates. Their absolute number rose to about 300 by the end of the year 1937 and to about 400 by the end of March 1938, just before the mass arrivals of Austrian prisoners began to fill up the camp.[67] Barrack number 6 was Dachau's Jew block. After the arrival of prisoners from other camps, Jews occupied three out of the five rooms; in the second half of 1937 a fourth room was filled.[68]

As was the case in Lichtenburg, in Dachau there existed a punishment company for those imprisoned in a concentration camp for a second time. Remarkably, Jewish recidivists were also quartered in the punishment company rather than in the Jew block. The racial stigma generally overruled all other categorization, but in this case it was secondary. The SS scorned recidivist prisoners as particularly obdurate enemies of Nazism. The order to accommodate them in separate sections was given by Himmler in March 1936.[69] The camp administrations imposed on the recidivists especially harsh conditions meant to deter other prisoners and to force them into giving up their resistance. "Second-timers" were isolated from other prisoners in Dachau's block number 1, which was enclosed by separate wire fencing. In 1937 the block was led by the SS man Albert Lütkemeyer. Prisoners under his oversight had to work longer and harder, had to bear constant humiliations, were forbidden to smoke, and were allowed to receive only 10 Reichsmarks (RM) once every three months instead of the regular 30 RM maximum every month. In spring 1937 there were a few Jewish prisoners among the estimated 180 recidivists of Dachau.[70]

In the mid-1930s, camp administrations used different signs to mark the different groups of prisoners. In Esterwegen, Jews bore yellow discs applied to the front and back of their grey uniforms, while in Sachsenburg it is said to have been a yellow Shield of David emblem. Jewish prisoners in Lichtenburg generally wore yellow bandages on a trouser leg as well as a longitudinal stripe on the back of their jackets. If they were classified as race defilers, the bandages were red. In Sachsenhausen, Jewish prisoners were marked with red or blue stripes and round yellow badges sewn onto their trousers and jackets. These colored stripes were also used in Dachau, where Jewish politicals were given red stripes with yellow dots, Jewish emigrants red stripes with blue dots, and Jewish race defilers yellow stripes with red dots.[71]

The color yellow, which gradually became the basic insignia of Jewish concentration camp prisoners, evoked the traditional stigma of the medieval yellow badge, a cloth patch sewn onto the outer garment to publicly mark and distinguish Jews from others. In Dachau, "half-Jews" like Hans Litten were also marked with the color yellow. When his mother was granted permission to visit him in the Bavarian camp shortly after his arrival from Lichtenburg in mid-October 1937, the change in designation immediately caught her eye. Her son appeared in a shabby, tattered, field-grey uniform marked with red stripes and yellow dots. Deeply concerned, Irmgard Litten brought up the issue in her next meeting with the Gestapo, pointing to the stigmatizing function of the yellow badge in history. "'The yellow spot,' I said, 'is the badge of the Jew . . . How is it that my son is suddenly wearing the yellow spot, which he has never had placed on his uniform before?'" When she announced that she would complain to Himmler personally about her son's placement in the Jew block, the official made it clear that such an appeal would have no prospect of success: "The Gestapo has decided that in the camps a man is a Jew if he has only 25 percent—indeed, if he has a single drop—of Jewish blood."[72]

The system of triangular badges, which standardized prisoner marking in all SS concentration camps from mid-1938 on, assigned to Jewish prisoners the Shield of David emblem comprising an upward-pointing yellow triangle and, sewed onto it, a second, downward-pointing triangle of the color that indicated the official reason for arrest.[73] The star-shaped signs used in the camps anticipated the identification markers introduced for Jews in occupied and annexed territories in the wake of the invasion of Poland in 1939 and for Jews of the Reich in September 1941. Their functions were similar. In the camps, the labels facilitated the identification of prisoners and visualized and encoded the official reasoning for their imprisonment. They created broadly defined groups of prisoners, thereby simplifying complex and heterogeneous individual backgrounds of persecution. Through the system of badges, prisoner groups were put into relation with one another and a hierarchy was thus most visibly consolidated.

In day-to-day situations—for example, at work—the signs easily flagged up Jewish prisoners. Marked with yellow symbols, the prisoners attracted attention and incurred abuse by the guards, especially when there were only few of them in a labor detachment. A former Sachsenhausen prisoner who was the only Jew in an earthwork detail reported that the SS immediately focused on him and tormented him with insults and particularly hard tasks.[74] Hence, to some extent, the markers solved the problems of identification that guards faced in the early concentration camps. To put it in the ironic words of the persecuted: "Fortunately, there were these yellow badges, so that one knew what the situation was and needed no longer worry about right and wrong: a Jew is a Jew, who belongs [to the category] is decided by the camp leadership."[75]

Still, some prisoners also came up with ways to sabotage the identification marks. In Sachsenhausen, Jewish inmates deliberately dirtied their clothes so that the signs became illegible: "We successfully hid our yellow Jewish spots whenever possible by taking off our coats, muddying our pants with cement dust to almost blot out the give-away yellow at work."[76] Harry Naujoks, former camp eldest in Sachsenhausen, reported that during the war years, Jewish inmates would secretly change their dress and wear uniforms without the Shield of David emblem, in order to overcome restrictive orders and to be able to enter the barracks of non-Jews.[77] Already during the mid-1930s the SS increasingly limited contacts between Jewish and non-Jewish prisoners. When in 1936, Naujoks met his friend and Communist comrade Herbert Mindus from Hamburg in the camp, he rejoiced in the unexpected reunion and invited Mindus into his barrack. Mindus, whom long years of imprisonment had made cautious, pointed to his Jewish mark and informed Naujoks that as a Jew he was forbidden to even speak to non-Jewish prisoners. The friends then agreed to meet secretly after dark.[78] Bendix observed that, even at a time when contacts were not officially forbidden between them, Jewish and non-Jewish prisoners in Lichtenburg tended to stick to their own groups during their free time: "The Jews sat together to play games or to converse. They stayed among themselves even when an 'Aryan' found his way to them." This staying-among-themselves was a kind of self-protection. In Lichtenburg the leader of the protective custody camp, SS Sturmbannführer Heinrich Remmert, threatened to punish those Jewish and non-Jewish prisoners he caught having contact with one another.[79]

Looking at camp labor more systematically, we see that in the early concentration camps the practice of assigning Jewish prisoners to heavy and dirty work continued in the mid-1930s. Often homosexuals, Jehovah's Witnesses, and so-called recidivists were also assigned these degrading tasks. All were regularly occupied with the emptying and cleaning of cesspits and sewers, and the hauling and breaking of heavy materials, such as stones.[80] In Sachsenhausen, Jewish prisoners were initially deployed in various details where they worked together with non-Jews on the construction of the camp complex. They toiled in building details, in the transport and unloading of construction materials, in excavations, in cleaning and rooting out trees, as well as on the wood yard. Naujoks recounted that the SS increasingly watched details with Jewish prisoners and, "through shrill orders and mistreatment, made work a torture" for them.[81] During the winter of 1936–1937, when their living conditions worsened, all Jewish prisoners of Sachsenhausen who were not already deployed to the punishment company were taken out of their various work details and put together to do earthworks. Laurence reported that some forty Jews dug, trenched, and leveled roads.[82]

Jewish prisoners who were transferred from Sachsenhausen to Dachau in early 1937 experienced labor in the new camp, in the main, as "completely useless," compared to the somewhat more productive tasks they had been forced to perform in the Prussian camp.[83] This is an interesting observation, as the two camps were in a comparable state of construction. The extensive rebuilding of the Bavarian camp commenced shortly after SS Oberführer Hans Loritz took office as commandant in 1936, and it was not finished until the summer of 1938. During the central building phase in 1937–1938, the prisoner camp was greatly expanded. Instead of ten barracks, it now came to comprise thirty-four barracks. Although productive prisoner labor assumed greater importance during the phase of construction, the camp SS forced Dachau prisoners to also perform entirely unproductive and tormenting tasks.[84] Jewish prisoners, in particular, suffered from senseless labor and mistreatment at work in the notorious gravel pit and pond-construction details.[85]

Jewish prisoners in Esterwegen, too, doubted that the labor they performed inside the camp and in the peat bog had any productive value. Those who were forced to dig trenches described the task as physically exhausting but not accompanied by any real progress. In the winter of 1935–1936, a construction detail mostly made up of Jewish prisoners was ordered to heap up a 5- to 10-meter-high mountain of sand. Esterwegen's commandant Loritz then forced the Jews into the lorries, which were pushed to roll downhill, and then crashed and injured the prisoners.[86] On the whole, the murder of prisoners also often took place in the context of work situations. By ordering them to step outside the cordon of sentries, sometimes by tossing caps some distance away, guards staged prisoners' attempts to break out of work details and then shot them "while trying to escape." In Esterwegen, Jewish prisoners Julius Agranoff, Bernhard Gerson, and Paul Lövy fell victim to this "method" of killing. Lövy, a fifty-seven-year-old painter from Königsberg, was commanded to work in a nearby forest, where he was then officially "found dead."[87]

Another pretext used to incite violence was the accusation that prisoners were lazy and thereby sabotaged the work effort. The killing of Breslau lawyer Kurt Riesenfeld, imprisoned in Dachau for race defilement, is described in many prisoner memoirs as particularly horrific. Riesenfeld, who arrived in Dachau on October 16, 1937, worked in an excavation detail under the oversight of SS man Wolfgang Seuss. One day commandant Loritz "caught" him supposedly pausing at work without permission. Riesenfeld was punished with one hour of hanging at the pole, one of the most dreaded disciplinary measures in Dachau, in which inmates were fastened to wooden poles with their hands tied behind their backs. After this torture, he could barely move but had to return to work. Seuss then forced the prisoner into a container that was used to transport building materials into a mixing machine. The container was lifted up and then released to crash to the ground. After this gruesome procedure was repeated a couple of times, Riesenfeld lost consciousness. He died of his injuries in the camp infirmary on November 14.[88]

Death rates are the ultimate indicator for judging living conditions in the concentration camps. As had been the case for the phase of the early concentration camps, the number of Jewish victims remained disproportionally high in the mid-1930s. In Esterwegen, where Jews made up 5 to 10 percent of the prisoner population, around a quarter of those who died were Jewish.[89] The number of deaths in Sachsenburg is unknown. Based on witness statements, there may have been more than twenty fatalities between August 1934 and the end of the year 1935.[90] Among them, three Jewish victims can be identified: the physician Curt Boas, who suffered from very harsh mistreatment; a forty-five-year-old merchant named Wertheim from Meerane, Saxony, imprisoned for race defilement; and the SPD politician and journalist Max Sachs from Dresden, who died on October 5, 1935.[91] The lowest number of Jews died in Lichtenburg. The memorial site counts twenty deaths for both the men's camp and the women's camp between 1933 and 1938. Apart from Ignatz Manasse, no other case has been found of a Jewish prisoner who lost his life in Lichtenburg.[92] At least twenty-eight deaths of Jewish prisoners in Dachau were documented between August 1934 and March 1938. Half of them, fourteen casualties, occurred in 1937, after Jewish prisoners from other concentration camps had been brought to Dachau. Within the total number of forty-one fatalities recorded in 1937, the fourteen Jewish deaths constitute 34 percent.[93] In contrast, the share of Jewish prisoners—between 200 and 300 men within a prisoner population that ranged from 2,000 to 2,500 in 1937—was significantly lower, at 8 to 12 percent. A similar overrepresentation of Jewish deaths can be observed in Sachsenhausen. Fifteen casualties were officially recorded by the end of February 1937; one-third were Jewish prisoners.[94]

The stark increase of Jewish deaths in Dachau coincided with SS Oberführer Hans Loritz taking office as commandant. His arrival in April 1936 was experienced as a caesura in the camp's history of violence. A Sopade report from the same year noted: "A new commandant has been installed in the Dachau concentration camp, Loritz from Augsburg. He reintroduced a system of brutal mistreatment."[95] Former prisoner Alfred Hübsch emphasized that it was mainly "Jews and 'second-timers'" who suffered from Loritz.[96] Under Loritz's command, the number of prisoners reported for punishments rose, and public beatings were frequently staged. Several survivors remembered that, in late March 1937, Loritz had the whole camp stand at attention in the roll call square to watch the whipping and pole-hanging of selected prisoners, among them Jews. In his speech that accompanied the gruesome spectacle, the commandant justified the torture as a necessary deterrent against the ongoing transgressions against the camp order. Bendix described this public enactment of violence as "the most horrible thing I ever saw."[97] Burkhard reported that Loritz, in contrast to other commandants, personally selected prisoners for punishment and himself participated in acts of violence. Burkhard had been imprisoned as a Jew in prewar Dachau for over five years, and he saw Loritz as "one of the most brutal rulers of the concentration camp."[98]

Another SS commandant who stood out through his pronounced anti-Jewish violence was SS Standartenführer Hermann Baranowski. Due to his hefty build and brutality, he assumed the name Vierkant (Foursquare). As commandant of Lichtenburg, he was responsible for the death of Jewish prisoner Ignatz Manasse. After Baranowski had repeatedly come into conflict with the guard units, Eicke transferred him to Dachau, where he became leader of the protective custody camp under Loritz. The two men collaborated closely, not least when it came to the maltreatment of prisoners. Former inmates characterized "the mighty Standartenführer" as "extremely brutal, particularly in his addresses," in which he often mocked and abused Jewish prisoners. On March 1, 1938, Baranowski took office as commandant of Sachsenhausen. On August 1, he made former Dachau Rapportführer (report leader) Rudolf Höss his adjutant.[99]

While prisoners came to know only too well the SS leaders and NCOs who served on the command staff inside the prisoner camp, most of the rank-and-file sentries from the guard troop who watched them every day during working hours remained nameless and unknown to them. Deployed in rotation at various posts, the members of the guard units were mostly young recruits. Survivors described how some of them mistreated prisoners when on duty in work details far removed from the oversight of their seniors.[100] Young sentries, not yet firmly consolidated in their ideology, sometimes showed their irritation when confronted with older men or with Jewish prisoners whose bodily features did not correspond with the propagated antisemitic stereotypes. Laurence reported that some of the younger guards "obviously in doubt . . . interrogated us at length and wanted to tie each one of us down in connection with some misdeed or crime to the German nation."[101] With *Der Stürmer* as one of the main influences on them—a display box of the antisemitic weekly was put up even inside the Dachau prisoner camp—rank-and-file SS men sought confirmation of Nazi racial lore in the living object. A Jewish prisoner from Esterwegen remembers the following conversation with a guard: "'You know the Talmud, don't you?' 'No. It is only those very learned men among us Jews who know it.' 'But that is a lie! You are acting upon it. The Talmud allows you to rape little girls.'"[102] Such humiliations of Jewish prisoners served also as reinforcements of antisemitic stereotypes.

Looking at manifestations of extreme violence against Jewish prisoners, it is noteworthy that external events, outside the concentration camps' day-to-day routines, often served as triggers or pretexts. Jewish prisoners were abused as hostages for the SS to retaliate against for incidents harmful to the Nazi regime. The reprisal pattern that had manifested itself for the first time in the "atrocity propaganda" affair of October 1933—staged as a brutal retaliation upon Dachau's Jewish prisoners for the publication of articles denouncing camp crimes—re-emerged, in aggravated form, in the mid-1930s.[103] The ill-treatment enacted in the camps in response to the assassination of Wilhelm Gustloff, leader of the NSDAP in Switzerland, is a remarkable example of this pattern. As an act of political resistance, the Jewish medical student David Frankfurter shot the Nazi functionary dead in his home in Davos on February 4, 1936. On February 12, the SS in Esterwegen flew flags at half-mast and took brutal "revenge" on the Jewish prisoners. Witnesses remembered their ordeal of excruciating punitive labor and "camp sport," which lasted from midday to evening, as having been "one of the worst days" in the camp.[104] In Lichtenburg, too, the Gustloff assassination was used as a pretext to tighten imprisonment conditions for Jewish detainees. According to Bendix's testimony, they were caged up in the small cells of the prison building.[105] A year after the event, when Esterwegen's prisoners and camp personnel had been transferred to Sachsenhausen, the SS enacted a gruesome "Gustloff memorial run." Block leaders attacked Jewish inmates and chased them through the camp until the victims fell in complete physical exhaustion.[106] In contrast to the nationwide pogrom of November 1938, the assassination of Gustloff did not entail any large-scale acts of public violence or mass arrests. The brutal retaliation was limited to outbursts of anti-Jewish aggression inside the concentration camps. Contemporaries understood that SA and SS rowdies were halted from openly attacking Jews in public spaces due to fears of international criticism and boycotts ill-timed for the regime's self-promotion at the 1936 Olympics. Indeed, the police and local authorities received secret orders to prevent attacks against Jews in public. After all, so the Nazi leadership might have calculated, the impending remilitarization of the Rhineland by German military forces would already strain diplomatic relations and provide enough reason for protest.[107]

Held collectively responsible for "shameless lies" about the camps "invented by the emigrant Jews" in exile, Jewish prisoners also suffered from periods of isolation imposed upon them in retaliation for "atrocity propaganda" published abroad.[108] In contrast to permanent segregation in special work commandos and housing units, these were periods of total seclusion from the rest of the camp, when Jews were locked into their barrack for weeks or months. They were deprived of even the basic rights of concentration camp inmates: buying additional food in the canteen, smoking, reading books or newspapers, and, most importantly, postal correspondence. It appears that such periods of total isolation of Jewish prisoners were enacted only in the Dachau concentration camp.[109] At least five periods occurred between early 1935 and late 1937. The earliest identifiable isolation seems to have been ordered by commandant Heinrich Deubel in the spring of 1935. It probably lasted for several months. Further isolations took place under Loritz's regime: Jews were shut into their barrack for months between the spring and autumn of 1936, then for about two weeks in the second half of March 1937, for a month in August 1937, and for five to six weeks from late November until the end of December 1937.[110] Each event proceeded in a similar fashion. First the SS openly blamed Jewish prisoners for the publication of "atrocity reports" by their "racial brethren" abroad. Then a total isolation was proclaimed: "After we were driven into our barrack like a herd of cattle, all the windows were painted from the outside with lime wash to block our view into the camp alleys, and to prevent other prisoners from contacting us."[111] Apart from short periods of punitive "camp sport" outdoors, prisoners were confined in the barrack all the time. Especially during the summer isolations, the air inside became nauseating. The atmosphere was tense, and with prisoners nervous and tetchy, "quarrels were constantly occurring on the slightest pretext."[112] The only positive side effect of the isolation was that Jewish prisoners were at least spared the degradation and torture they normally had to endure during work and roll call.[113]

The order to temporarily isolate Jewish prisoners from others was imposed on the Dachau camp leadership by Eicke's IKL. In the last instance Himmler himself seems to have been responsible. At least for the last two isolation periods, explicit documentation exists that they were ordered directly by the Reich Leader SS. Sources also show that at least the isolation of November/December 1937 was accompanied by a stop to releases.[114] As has been observed earlier, Himmler had decreed in August 1936 that the ultimate power of decision to release a Jew from the concentration camp would rest with him alone.

The isolation of Jewish prisoners in Dachau was made public through preformulated postcards and standardized letters that the prisoners had to send to their relatives. Initially the extent of the isolation was downplayed as a mere mail embargo, but the SS in 1937 chose more explicit wording to stress the fact that Jewish prisoners were held hostage under aggravated conditions. Families and friends were told that atrocity reports had been published in *Der Neue Vorwärts* (Karlsbad), *Deutsche Volkszeitung* (Paris), and *Die Stimme* (Vienna) and that therefore a punitive isolation had been imposed upon their loved ones: "We inform you hereby that for the duration of such isolation we are strictly segregated, lose all comforts, and can neither send nor receive letters. It is for you to persuade the emigrant Jews in Prague to tell no more such senseless lies about the concentration camps in the future, since the Jews in Dachau, as their racial brethren, will be made responsible for them."[115] Fighting relentlessly for the liberation of her son Hans, Irmgard Litten, on receipt of one such note written under coercion, decided to act. With her letters to the editors of the exile press she accomplished the almost impossible: she worded them in such a way that "the newspapers would be warned of the terrible conditions in Dachau and would therefore continue their campaign" while, on the other hand, the Gestapo gained "the impression that I was anxious to stop the reports of atrocities." Headlines like "Himmler's Blackmailing Letter to the D.V.Z." *(Deutsche Volkszeitung)* or "The Mother of the Rechtsanwalt Litten Compelled to Sign" proved that her coded writing had been understood correctly.[116]

The segregation of Jews from other prisoners, as radically practiced during the isolation periods, was implemented on a large scale when in February 1937 Jewish inmates from all other camps were brought together in Dachau. The directive for this action came from the highest office of the Gestapo. An order signed by Heydrich on February 17 decreed that "in the future, Jewish protective custody- and instructive custody prisoners are to be deported only to the Dachau concentration camp."[117] This order was a *post factum* decree. By the time it was issued, the transports with Jewish prisoners from other camps had already arrived in Dachau. Twenty-three inmates from Lichtenburg were brought to the Bavarian camp on February 4. Fourteen Jews transported from Sachsenburg joined the "Lichtenburgers" on February 8. On February 13, a larger transport of forty-eight Jewish prisoners from Sachsenhausen arrived in Dachau.[118]

As is the case with most of the perpetrator documentation, the rationale behind the decision to centralize Jewish prisoners in Dachau is not stated in Heydrich's decree. Hence, questions arise as to the reasons why Jews were interned together in one camp, and why exactly Dachau was chosen as the place of their concentration. To begin with, a centralization of prisoners of one particular category in one particular camp was not unprecedented in the history of the concentration camps. Attempts at a geographical distribution of prisoner categories to selected camps were made as early as 1934 when Prussia sent its preventive custody prisoners first to Lichtenburg and then to Esterwegen.[119] A systematic, nationwide practice, however, was never established, not least because this would have required extensive logistics and administrative efforts. Therefore, practical reasons cannot have been at the forefront of Heydrich's decision to deport Jewish captives from all over Germany to Dachau. Indeed, difficulties in implementing the order arose in particular from the prohibition against communicating it to the local and district police offices, which were largely responsible for executing the deportation of arrestees to concentration camps. In Sachsenhausen, for example, three Jewish prisoners were registered as having arrived after the ordinance had rendered the camp "free of Jews."[120]

As a search for practical reasons fails us, the rationale behind the order to centralize all Jews in Dachau might instead be found within the realm of Nazi racial ideology. The explanation suggested at the time by one of the Sachsenhausen Jews affected by the order is probably not too far-fetched: that the racial segregation between "Jews" and "Aryans" that the Nazis aimed for in society at large was also to be practiced in the prisoner society of the concentration camps. The "corrupting influence of the Jews" on the "German-blooded" prisoners should be prevented as far as possible by radically separating the two groups.[121] Indeed, the centralization of Jewish prisoners in one camp ultimately affirmed their position as outcasts among the outcasts. At a time when prisoner numbers were at a low, the concentration in one camp of the few Jews who had been scattered across various sites of detention maintained their special status and visibility as a selected minority group within the camp population. That Heydrich was preoccupied with enforcing racial segregation in German society at large becomes evident also from a letter sent around the same time to Rudolf Hess, the Deputy Führer and minister without portfolio. In this document Heydrich proposed to establish separate restaurants and pubs for Jews, and to label them as such. "Following the Nuremberg Laws this will offer another possibility to return the Jews to a ghetto, to prevent them from frequenting German restaurants, and to separate them more effectively than before from those of German blood."[122] In this early use by a leading policymaker of Nazi Germany, the term "ghetto" has, as Dan Michman has pointed out, "the sense of 'virtual ghetto': the social isolation of Jews from the Germans."[123]

The reason Dachau was chosen as the site of concentration for Jewish prisoners from all over Germany can be explained with reference to the fact that this camp, at the time of the centralization in February 1937, already held the largest group of Jewish inmates. Furthermore, Dachau had also served as the "model camp" with respect to the "special treatment" of Jews. Their segregation from other prisoners was practiced almost from the beginning of the camp's existence; the Dachau Jew company was set up in April/May 1933. A series of periods of total isolation reinforced this segregation and asserted most dramatically Jewish prisoners' status as a persecuted minority. Jews shipped to the Bavarian camp from Sachsenhausen immediately realized that Dachau was a much more violent camp: "Here we are in the headquarters of the adversary," in the national "school of violence," the "original home and permanent center of the SS."[124] The centralization of Jews in Dachau was in place for over a year. The practice was given up when the explosion of prisoner numbers in the wake of the mass arrests of 1938 made it impracticable.

Cohesion and Conflict in the Jew Blocks

The notorious "Dachau spirit" brutalized not only the guards but also the prisoners. Jews from Sachsenhausen were shocked when they realized that "the blows that fell upon us came from our fellow prisoners," and that "even Jews victimized their own comrades upon SS command."[125] The most prominent example for the high degree of brutalization of prisoners in Dachau is Heinz Eschen, the barrack elder of Dachau's Jew block. Eschen was the highest ranking and most influential Jewish prisoner functionary of the prewar concentration camps. Arrested in February 1933 in Munich, the twenty-three-year-old Communist and student of medicine had played a leading role in the resistance against the Nazi movement and its growing influence at the universities. He functioned as the chairperson of the Munich Red Students' League (Münchner Roter Studentenbund) and was a member of the Marxist Student Circle (Marxistischer Stundenkreis). At protest rallies and with numerous flyers Eschen and his comrades urgently warned of the dangers of "academic fascism" and often clashed with the SA and other Nazi radicals. When on February 2, 1933, Eschen led a demonstration through the Schwabing university quarter, he collided with the police. The wounded Jewish student was arrested, tried, and sentenced to prison. After a six-month spell in the prison of St. Georgen-Bayreuth, he was brought to Dachau on November 25, 1933. Apparently Eschen was appointed barrack elder of the Jew company sometime in 1936, after having temporarily served as the kapo of a work commando.[126]

Whereas some prisoners remembered Eschen with great respect and defended his conduct, others were disgusted by the violent behavior of "the juvenile potentate of our company" (Bendix). Those who respected him understood that the Jewish prisoner functionary was caught up in an impossible dual liability toward both prisoners and SS. As block elder, he virtually "had the duty of ill-treating fellow prisoners." Only by relentlessly executing the brutal "Dachau spirit" could he secure the trust of the SS, which in turn was crucial if he wanted to gain the influence necessary to protect Jewish inmates from worse abuse. Ultimately Eschen's ambiguous behavior is to be situated in that grey zone in which prisoner functionaries had to maneuver—described with all its dilemmas most strikingly by Primo Levi. In exchange for the risks they ran, prisoners functionaries enjoyed privileges like working inside the camp, mostly indoors, instead of in dangerous outside commandos. They were also allocated more food as well as the occasional free hour to rest. During the isolation period in August 1937, Eschen was the only one permitted to leave the Jew block for a few hours in the afternoon.[127]

Jewish prisoners who were transported to Dachau from Sachsenhausen compared and contrasted Eschen's extreme and ambiguous conduct with the behavior of August Cohn and Lothar Löwenberg, both of whom had assumed functionary positions in the Prussian camp. Löwenberg had served as the assistant of room elder Cohn. He, in particular, is remembered as a benign, fair, and responsible comrade; "our very best man, extremely clever and well-liked," as Laurence recalled.[128] Löwenberg's positive image was surely influenced by his tragic death less than three weeks after arrival in Dachau, a terrible shock for the Sachsenhausen Jews. The thirty-seven-year-old worker from Wiesbaden fell victim to humiliations and the aggravated conditions of the punishment company.[129] Like Löwenberg, the room elder Cohn belonged to the leading circle of political prisoners in Sachsenhausen who tried to resist SS terror and aid comrades in need. Cohn's connections were useful in his efforts to alleviate the living conditions of his fellow Jewish prisoners. He procured medicine for the sick and intervened on the behalf of the weak, for whom he secured easier work positions. He is also said to have initiated a patronage system, according to which every impoverished Jew was appointed a patron who was financially better off and with whom he could share money and food.[130] Although functionary prisoners, first and foremost, had to serve the interests of the SS, this example shows that they could sometimes also use their powers to help and support their fellow inmates.

Appointments of Jewish prisoners to functionary positions were very rare. Jews ranked too low in the camp hierarchy to assume tasks of influence in the kapo system. Positions that would have made them superior to non-Jews were entirely outside their reach and, at least in Sachsenhausen, forbidden as a matter of course.[131] The number of Jews in functionary positions who were able to exert at least a modest influence on the grave conditions of detention can be counted on one hand. Apart from Cohn, Löwenberg, and Eschen, we know of the block clerk Arno Isner from

Nuremberg, who arrived in Dachau in November 1935 and served as Eschen's right hand man, and of Emil Carlebach, whom Eschen made room elder of room number 4 in the Jew block in the second half of 1937.[132] All of these men were young Communists, and as such they were backed by the clandestine network of (non-Jewish) political prisoners operating in the camps.

It is noteworthy that Jewish political prisoners, although they dominated life in the Jew blocks through their functionary positions, made up only a small minority of the prisoner group. In Dachau, no more than twenty to thirty political activists were grouped around Heinz Eschen.[133] The imbalance caused by the power of a highly politicized minority over the majority of nonpolitical Jewish inmates provoked conflicts, and exacerbated the lack of unity within the heterogeneous prisoner group.[134] The political prisoners' sense of themselves as a close-knit community that consciously distanced itself from others outlived their period of imprisonment and led to an imbalance in remembrance, too. While historians long neglected the concentration camps, it was the former political prisoners who wrote the dominant narratives of the camps. In their writings, some politicals of Jewish descent made no effort to conceal their disdain for those "Jewish petit-bourgeois" who had lived in the illusion that they "could adapt to life under fascism."[135] Others went so far as to insist that the memory of fellow Jews who had "always stood outside of our community" should be blotted out of the history books. Equally conflicted are the memories of Werner Scholem and Ernst Heilmann, whom the Nazis imprisoned and killed for their political convictions but who diverted from the KPD party line and made no secret of their dissidence.[136]

One-sided memoirs by former political prisoners make it difficult to reconstruct the distinct dynamics of cohesion and conflict within the group of Jewish prisoners. The testimonies of Ludwig Bendix and Alfred Laurence, neither of whom belonged to the "Communist core," provide important counternarratives and are therefore all the more valuable to the historian. Both men acknowledged the rifts within the prisoner group caused by different political, social, and cultural backgrounds, but they also testified to a positive group identity and to acts of solidarity among the Jews. In Lichtenburg, as well as in Sachsenhausen and Dachau, men were helping each other where they could, and the young supported the old.[137] For some, these acts of solidarity were motivated by more than mere self-defense. Both Bendix and Laurence stated that "Jewishness" itself became a unifying bond, that the racial stigma was redefined as a badge of honor. The prisoner group of Jews, held together by "a common destiny created through a shared persecution by shared enemies," for some became a community rooted in a common tradition defined as "humanist, moral, intellectual, and including social justice and individual responsibility—even the most irreligious among us had a certain pride in our religious heritage."[138]

Bendix, who often clashed with fellow prisoners over various issues concerning money and property, reported that in Lichtenburg conflicts were settled in courtlike scenarios set up to discuss pro and contra and to give the defendant a serious chance to explain and justify his behavior. These court sessions were held mostly during the night. Both parties quietly argued for their respective interest, and a third prisoner, appointed judge or referee, decided the case.[139] The phenomenon of these quasi courts as a means of conflict resolution among Lichtenburg's Jewish prisoners can be attributed to the influence of Jewish lawyers like Bendix, Litten, and Scholem, who also provided legal counseling to fellow prisoners involved in proceedings outside the camp.[140]

Lichtenburg's "Jewish courts" remained rare exceptions though. The violent setting of the concentration camps left prisoners little possibility of negotiating conflicts peacefully. In Dachau, block elder Eschen and his assistants, like many other prisoner functionaries, meted out corporal punishment intended to discipline those Jews "who endangered all of us by their negligence, laziness or bad behavior."[141] These punishments were often executed in agreement with the SS, yet sometimes they were also a brutal form of political prisoners' self-administration of justice. Upon their arrival in Dachau, two Jewish Communists from Lichtenburg denounced prisoner Max Schier for his alleged antisocial behavior in the Prussian camp, and asked Eschen to "make an example and punish him for this." According to Bendix's testimony, the block elder did not hesitate and brutally assaulted the man, who was twenty to thirty years his senior.[142] Another incident of self-administration of justice reported by Laurence was Eschen's harsh action against the small group of religious Jews who regularly gathered in the first room of the Jew barrack to pray together. After he found some of them guilty of having stolen the bread of their fellow prisoners, Eschen had their prayer books burned. He made his point and ridiculed their religiosity in front of other prisoners.[143]

Functionary prisoners like Heinz Eschen lived dangerously. Maneuvering between the interests of the SS and the demands of the prisoner society in a system that was meant to inhibit solidarity, they had to constantly increase violence to hold on to their powers. For the SS, a kapo was just a cog in the machine of terror, replaceable at any time. The prisoners, on the other hand, feared their superiors. Some sought revenge after they had been put at a disadvantage by a kapo who favored and protected his own group of comrades.[144] As a result of his exposed and ambiguous position as a Jewish prisoner functionary, Eschen made enemies among both prisoners and SS men. Ultimately these enmities brought about his fall in late January 1938. Whether his death was a suicide or a murder can no longer be determined. Evaluating prisoner statements, three different narratives explaining Eschen's death can be reconstructed. The first and most widespread sees the block elder as a victim of a denunciation for alleged Communist resistance brought forward by his adversaries within the Jew block. Carlebach and Laurence both name the forty-five-year-old businessman Waldemar Millner, born in Vilnius, as the main denouncer. Millner had clashed with Eschen during the isolation period in August 1937 and sought revenge ever since. As Eschen had lost the favor of the SS after he had complained about some of the NCOs, the denunciation was readily taken up by the camp leadership as a welcome reason to get rid of him.[145] According to the second narrative, which is sometimes interwoven with the first, Eschen was denounced for an alleged homosexual relationship with the sixteen-year-old teenager Herbert Hirschfeld. According to the testimony of Fritz Rabinowitsch, Hirschfeld was sexually involved with various inmates in the Jew block. The nature of his relationship with Eschen, however, remains unclear. Laurence interpreted their connection as being for Eschen a kind of romanticized friendship, Mindus as "an all too close friendship," and Bendix as a "friendly-fatherly relation."[146] Finally, it is said that the SS wanted to extort from Eschen the names of the authors of a "revolutionary" song, which Jewish prisoners, in an act of defiance, had sung when they were released from their isolation and marched out of the barrack. Communist prisoner Gerhard Pinthus composed this first "Dachau song," with text by Kurt Wolfgang Isaac, brother of Heinz Isaac, mentioned above.[147]

Eschen's fall brought far-reaching investigations within the Jew block. Drawn into them were a number of political Jews. Hans Litten was interrogated by Baranowski while Eschen died. The lawyer's own suicide followed only days afterward.[148] Conditions for Jews in Dachau worsened as the SS purged Jewish Communists from functionary positions. August Cohn, who had initially succeeded Eschen as the block elder of the Jew company, was dismissed, as was Emil Carlebach, the room elder of barrack 6, room 4. Non-Jewish prisoners were installed in their place.[149] For the time being, the period in which Jewish prisoners held positions of influence and could intervene with the SS to avert some of the dangers that threatened them, had come to an end. In a sense Eschen's death marked a turning point in the history of Jewish prisoners in the prewar camps. What followed afterward, in the spring, summer, and autumn of 1938, were mass arrests that brought tens of thousands of Jews into the camps of Dachau, Sachsenhausen, and Buchenwald, which had a significant impact on camp life.

5

INSTRUMENTS OF MASS PERSECUTION

The Concentration Camps and Anti=Jewish Policy in 1938

S urvivors described the prisoner transports that carried off thousands of Austrian men to Dachau concentration camp in the spring and summer of 1938 as "a nightmare journey," "a hell on wheels," and "departure into Inferno."[1] The majority of the estimated 3,500 Austrian inmates held in the Bavarian camp during this period were deported from Vienna to Dachau by train. Captives classified as Jews were among the deportees on board virtually every transport. Among the very first batch of 150 "prominent" Austrians that arrived in Dachau on April 2, more than one-third of the prisoners—sixty-three men—were of Jewish origin. Several large transports arriving in late May and June consisted entirely of Jews. All in all, the camp administration registered some 2,000 of the 3,500 new arrivals from the recently annexed Alpine country as Jewish.[2]

The "Austrian invasion" of Dachau was the first of three waves of mass imprisonment.[3] The mass arrests after the Anschluss, whose victims made up the first large group of foreign camp inmates, together with the "Action Work-Shy Reich" (Aktion Arbeitsscheu Reich) of June 1938, and the mass imprisonment following the November Pogrom, in total brought over 30,000 Jewish men into the concentration camps. What reasons sent Jews into the camps in the late 1930s, and which new qualities were added to the enemy profile of "the Jew"? How were the thousands of new inmates absorbed into the camp system? How did the SS accommodate them and integrate them into the organization of labor? When, and under which circumstances, were Jews released from the camps in the period immediately preceding the outbreak of the war? And finally, what effects did the mass imprisonment of Jews have on the persecuted and on society at large?

Eyewitness testimonies show that the numerous Austrian transports to Dachau of spring and summer 1938 all proceeded in a similarly violent fashion. Prisoners were brought to Vienna's Western Station from their various jails across the city. Crammed into police vans, they did not know where they were heading. The escorting officers kept silent about the destination. When approaching the station, some policemen did, however, warn the prisoners to take off their glasses and "move as fast as you can out of the van and into the train."[4] As they disembarked, the captives were attacked by a rampaging horde of "dark figures" who, on closer inspection, were "young lads" in black uniforms and steel helmets. The prisoners panicked: "We ran toward the train. I stumbled; it was the foot of one of these dark figures. The next moment I felt a blow in the neck; I fell, picked myself up at once and was about to reach down for my hat and spectacles, which I had dropped in my fall, when I was seized under the shoulders and flung into the train."[5] The gruesome reception was accompanied by the sound of an "insane medley of curses, thuds, groans, and moans." It took place at the railroad yard of the freight train station, a section of the station seemingly protected from the public gaze.[6] While ordinary passengers who frequented the Western Station on the respective evenings of the transports might indeed have taken no notice of the unusual commotion, there were curious looks cast onto this "SS orgy" by local residents who could oversee the railroad yard from the windows of their nearby houses.[7]

During the overnight journeys, the prisoners were not granted a moment of respite. Terrified, they were shut into overcrowded compartments with the heating turned up high and a stifling atmosphere. The SS guards ordered them to sit perfectly still with their hands on their knees and their eyes fixed on the glaring ceiling lights. Leaning against the backrest was strictly prohibited. Whoever moved or dozed off was brutally beaten. The prisoners were forbidden to eat or drink. They were also not allowed to use the lavatories. SS men, some of them extremely drunk, took turns at illtreating the prisoners. They harassed, insulted, and ridiculed the men. Jewish prisoners were ordered to declaim mocking antisemitic verses. Again and again, the sentries clubbed their helpless victims with rifle butts. They did not even stop short of murder.[8] The Dachau memorial site has registered twelve deaths—nine of them Jews—that occurred on these Austrian transports en route to the camp.[9]

By way of a newly constructed siding track, the trains brought the Austrian captives directly into the Dachau camp complex, where they disembarked in yet another gruesome spectacle: "As the sliding door of the carriage opened we were ordered to 'hurry up,' and those of us who were unable to comply were dragged down by the SS men and beaten."[10] The guards hit, kicked, pushed, and chased their victims in the direction of the prisoner camp. Shots were fired. Yelling, shouting, and laughter filled the air. Off-duty SS men leaned out of the windows of their barracks, which flanked the narrow street leading from the station to the prisoner camp's gate building (*Jourhaus*), and cheered on the assaulters. Prisoners from transports that had suffered fatalities in transit were forced to carry the corpses into the camp.[11] The terror of the journey had shattered the nerves of many Austrian prisoners. When they arrived in the camp wounded, starving, and exhausted, to them "Dachau was just another word."[12]

Although prisoners had suffered on their way into the camps before, a new level of violence was reached in the handling of the Austrian transports in the early summer of 1938. Not only the high number of casualties attests to unprecedented outbreaks of brutality. The fact that SS men were sent out of the camp to receive the captives in their hometowns, and then guarded them throughout the journey, constitutes a startling new development. The "dark figures" whom prisoners encountered at Vienna's Western Station were members of the first SS Death's Head divisions Oberbayern, sent to Vienna from their base at Dachau.[13] On the transports the SS gave full vent to their hatred and cruelty. Camp violence thus extended far beyond the confines of the prisoners' barbed-wired enclosure. No previous prisoner transports in the history of the Nazi camps had such lethal effects, and it is crucial to note that this unparalleled outburst of violence occurred in the political context of the annexation of Austria. For the National Socialists, the aggressive act of crossing Germany's borders constituted an enormous gain in power that also strengthened the SS's "power to kill." War, the ultimate form of brutalization, became a much-anticipated scenario throughout the year 1938. In an atmosphere of conquest and victory, the SS treated Austrian captives like prisoners of war, as a contemporary source pointedly termed it.[14]

The mass arrests of Austrian Jews must be considered against the larger historical background of the *Anschluss* and its radicalizing impact on the persecution of Jews. Since autumn 1937, Nazi anti-Jewish policy had entered into a new qualitative phase closely entwined with the regime's expansionist foreign policy. After a reshuffling of key positions in the government and the army, Hitler could rely on broad support for his increasingly aggressive political course. As tension rose and Nazi propaganda prepared the public for an armed conflict, the enemy category of "the Jew" was prop-

agated with renewed vigor. The goals of anti-Jewish policy during this period were the complete isolation of the Jewish population, the deprivation of
their rights, and, more than ever before, their economic expropriation
through enforced "Aryanizations" as well as their expulsion from Nazi Germany. To be sure, the process of expropriation of Jewish economic assets and
their coerced transfer to non-Jewish ownership, often at throwaway prices,
had started long before 1938. From the early months of the Nazi regime,
Jews were confronted with boycotts of, as well as threats and obstructions to,
their professional activities, measures that aimed at isolating and excluding
them from economic life in Germany. As a result of this "creeping Aryanization," by early 1938 "around 60–70 per cent of Jewish businesses existing in 1933 were no longer in the hand of their former owners."[15] In 1938,
and explicitly after the November Pogrom, these factual expropriations
were increasingly sanctioned through corresponding acts of legalization.

The annexation of Austria, which instantly added another 190,000
people to the Jewish population of the new Greater German Reich, radicalized Nazi anti-Jewish policy in general and the regime's forced removal
of Jews from the economy in particular. Within a matter of months, thousands of Austrian Jews were dispossessed of their economic assets.[16] In Vienna, a Property Transfer Office, headed by Walter Rafelsberger, was set
up to centralize the rapid economic expropriation. Rafelsberger's proposal
to confront the increasing poverty among the dispossessed with the establishment of labor camps attests to the radical thinking of those in charge
of the persecution of Austria's Jewish population in 1938–1939.[17] Another
such radical thinker was SS Untersturmführer Adolf Eichmann, who was
appointed adviser on Jewish affairs to the Inspector of the Security Police
and the SD in Vienna. In practice Eichmann ran the Central Office for
Jewish Emigration, established in late August 1938. To accelerate the expulsion of Austria's Jews, he oversaw a "conveyor belt system" to speedily
process the complicated emigration formalities.[18]

The establishment of new organizational structures of oppression, together with the far-reaching initiatives thought up by radical and career-
minded "Jewish experts" in the Gestapo, SS, and SD, created a dynamic
of persecution that soon outpaced developments in the *Altreich*, that is pre-
annexation Germany. By the outbreak of the war, two-thirds of Austria's
Jews had fled the country. The rapid "success" of anti-Jewish methods advanced in Austria, as well as their later application in other occupied or
annexed countries, has prompted historians to speak of the "Viennese

model" as "a textbook example" of Jewish persecution.[19] Within the historiography of the concentration camps, however, the annexation of Austria usually marks nothing more than the first large influx of foreign prisoners.[20] The significance of the camp as an instrument of terror applied on a massive scale to intimidate Austrian Jews into giving up their businesses and leaving their homeland has not hitherto been fully elaborated. Neither has a systematic analysis been given of the considerable impact of the mass arrival of Austrian prisoners on the camp's—Dachau's, in this case—socioeconomic structure in general, and the dynamics within the Jewish prisoner group in particular.

Between 50,000 and 76,000 people were arrested within six weeks of the annexation.[21] The first wave of arrests targeted representatives of the fallen Schuschnigg regime, Communists, Socialists, prominent anti-Nazis active in culture, art, and the media, as well as unpolitical Jews. On March 18 the Nazis broke into the head office of the Vienna Jewish Community and arrested president Desider Friedmann, vice-president Jakob Ehrlich, and other functionaries. Friedmann and Ehrlich were sent to Dachau with the first Austrian prisoner transport of April 1–2, 1938, and their institution was closed down by the secret police.[22]

The Viennese Gestapo's protective custody department was responsible for compiling the first transport to Dachau. According to a police report, it consisted of "high-ranking officials of the former Chancellery, ministers, the mayor of Vienna, leading officials of the police department . . . and the gendarmerie," as well as other prominent representatives of the state. The report also lists "businessmen of the Jewish race" among the captives—an indication that economic motives played an important role in the selection of the deportees.[23] The police prison at Elisabethpromenade in Vienna's ninth district, the so-called "Liesl," served as the transport's point of departure. Prisoners spent long days between hope and fear there before their names were called up for the transport. Like many others, journalist Maximilian Reich was clueless as to why he had been arrested: "I had never engaged in political activities and sport was my main interest and field of work."[24] Similarly, Paul Kolisch, publisher of the popular *Der Montag*, represented a journal that dealt "with politics only as a side issue, and very cautiously." In search of a reason, his journalist colleague Bruno Heilig explained Kolisch's arrest with the fact that "he had not at once said 'Yes' when the Nazis demanded his paper."[25] Unlike Reich and Kolisch, Heilig knew he had "incriminated" himself with "hundreds of newspaper articles, signed with my full name" in which he "had severely attacked Hitler and his re-gime." Some of these articles also denounced the crimes committed by the SS in Dachau.[26] In the police prison, Heilig also met other captives classified as Jews. One of his cellmates was Robert Hecht, a high-ranking official of the authoritarian Ständestaat, in existence in Austria from 1934 to 1938 as a single-party state governed by the right-wing Fatherland Front (Vaterländische Front). Hecht had served as an influential legal advisor to Chancellor Engelbert Dollfuss. On the basis of the emergency laws which he had helped to formulate, many Austrian Nazis had been prosecuted and interned. Characterized as "the Jew Hecht," the Protestant convert was a prime target of Nazi propaganda. In Dachau, the short and rather corpulent man endured particularly violent treatment. When he was found hanged in the barrack on May 30, 1938, fellow prisoners had no doubt that the SS's constant maltreatment had driven Hecht to suicide.[27]

It lies beyond the scope of this study to introduce all sixty-three persons registered by the Dachau administration as newly arrived protective custody Jews on April 2, 1938. Besides those already mentioned, the politicians Robert Danneberg and Robert Stricker, the artists Fritz Beda-Löhner and Raoul Auernheimer, the jurists Alois Osio and Josef Gerö, the student Paul Martin Neurath and the associate professor Fritz Schreier, the boxer Wilhelm "Willy" Kurz and the journalist Mark Siegelberg, whose 1939 report is one of the earliest testimonies of the mass imprisonment of Austrians, may be named.[28] Among the "businessmen of Jewish race" on the transport were nine members of the well-known Viennese merchant families Schiffmann and Burstyn. Their arrest was intended to extort the "sale" of their wealthy enterprises. Ludwig Klausner, the general director of the family-owned DELKA shoe retail business was pressured to "negotiate" the "Aryanization" of his company while he was held in the police prison in Vienna. "They want my factory . . . 'Aryanizing' it, they call it," he is remembered as having told his cellmates. Instead of yielding to the pressure, Klausner demanded that he be released before settling the conditions of the confiscation. After all, this was a "question of property worth millions." His request was not granted and instead he found himself abducted to Dachau.[29] Finally, also among the Jewish prisoners on the April transport was Hans Kotanyi, proprietor of the biggest firm of spice importers in Austria. Kotanyi became the first Austrian prisoner to lose his life inside the Nazi concentration camp. A victim of severe ill-treatment by the Dachau SS, he committed suicide on April 28, 1938.[30]

The arrival of the first 150 Austrian prisoners in Dachau was an extraordinary event, disrupting the camp's daily routine. Fritz Schreier remembered: "We were the first group of Austrians brought to the camp and therefore we constituted a new sensation."[31] As the first foreigners, the men were received by the entire camp SS. Each individual prisoner was forced to "introduce" himself and then endure commandant Loritz's mockery and insults.[32] When Himmler visited the camp a couple of weeks after their arrival, he, too, was curious to inspect the 150 prominent Austrians and the degrading performance was repeated.[33]

Quartered in an unfurnished barrack, all the Austrians were initially separated from the rest of the prisoner population—a status that further increased the special attention devoted to them. A senior Dachau inmate explains this isolation in terms of the camp leadership's confusion as to whether the new arrivals were to be treated as Germans or as foreigners. The separation was apparently maintained until the plebiscite of April 10, in which, according to Nazi figures, the overwhelming majority of Austrians voted in favor of the *Anschluss*.[34] While questions of nationality might have puzzled the SS—in the Dachau arrival book the rubric "citizenship" is inconsistently filled out "D" (German), "D.Ö." (German-Austrian), or "Ö" (Austrian)—the new prisoners' racial classification was an indisputable issue. Although some of the Austrians refused to be grouped among Dachau's Jews, the SS, of course, were unmoved: "You're a Jew here!" was the harsh answer to those who dared to protest against their racial stigmatization.[35] When the initial isolation ended, the 150 Austrians were distributed among the other Dachau inmates. Jews were united with other Jewish prisoners in the Jew blocks.[36]

For as long as they were kept isolated in their arrival barrack, the Austrians were exempt from work. Afterward they were at once integrated into the routine of labor, which in April 1938 was still dominated by the extension and rebuilding of the camp complex.[37] Survivors remembered that the SS ordered the whole contingent of Austrians to demolish the old prison building: "A hundred and fifty men were dragging stones, hammering like madmen on concrete blocks, pushing heavily-laden tip-wags on a track beside the ditch."[38] Labor in Dachau became "hell let loose" through the yelling, pushing, and beating of SS sentries and prisoner foremen. This "Prussian pace" quickly drove the men to exhaustion.[39] Many of the Austrian prisoners were not used to physical labor and neither did they know how to handle the tools. Neurath recalled, "Unaccustomed to pickaxe, shovel, and wheelbarrow, our hands were covered with blisters within a few hours."[40]

Figure 5.1 Jewish prisoners in Dachau, bearing star-shaped badges of yellow and red triangles on their uniform trousers, are forced to shovel and dig in an area north of the new prisoner compound overlooking the barracks.
Bundesarchiv, Bild 152–27–15A / Friedrich Franz Bauer.

For nearly two months, the prominent prisoners from annexed Austria retained their exceptional status as the first foreigners of the camp. Only a few additional Austrians were brought to Dachau during this time, none of them Jews. The situation began to change in late May 1938. A second large transport of 165 captives from the Alpine country arrived in Dachau on May 24.[41] The camp administration classified 47 of the men as Jewish prisoners—among them the artists Paul Morgan, Fritz Grünbaum, and Kurt Fuss as well as Ernst Federn, a political activist of Trotskyite orientation who later wrote a pioneering, psychoanalytically informed theory of camp terror.[42] Exactly one week after their arrival, the first of the special trains loaded exclusively with Jewish captives brought 601 "round-up Jews" or "Action Jews" from Vienna to the camp. A second transport of 595 Viennese Jews followed shortly afterward on June 3; a third, with another 325 men, on June 25. Over 300 additional Jewish prisoners arrived together with non-Jews in various Austrian transports before the end of the month.[43] Before I discuss the considerable impact that this massive influx of prisoners had on the social and economic structure of the camp, it is necessary to analyze the arrest policy behind this action.

According to the postwar statement of Karl Ebner, an Austrian Nazi recruited into the Gestapo after the annexation, a so-called Jews action (*Judenaktion*) was ordered in May 1938 by the highest levels of the SS police apparatus.[44] A surviving directive of the Vienna Gestapo, dated May 24, 1938, reads: "It has been ordered that unwanted [*unliebsam*], previously convicted Jews are to be arrested immediately and transferred to the Dachau concentration camp."[45] In a secret SD memo, composed by Eichmann after the first special train with "Action Jews" had already left for Dachau, a similar characterization of the targeted group is given: "The Jews are mainly previously convicted or asocial elements." Eichmann quotes a target figure of 5,000 Jews to be arrested in the course of the action. Four thousand of them were to be captured in Vienna, the rest in the provinces.[46]

The adjectives "asocial" and "previously convicted," used here to stigmatize the Jewish captives from Austria, echo the enemy profiling applied in Action Work-Shy Reich, whose first wave had brought around 2,000 preventive police custody prisoners into the concentration camp in April 1938. Jews were officially targeted only by the second wave of arrests of "asocials" conducted by the criminal police all over the Reich in June 1938, very shortly after the round-up of Viennese Jews had begun. Due to the close temporal proximity, it is safe to assume that the two mass arrests had reciprocal effects on one another; hence the similar wording in the official enemy categorization. However, as we will see, official arrest orders for the nationwide "June-Action" adhered to a more narrowly defined Jewish enemy profile by listing specific criminological criteria regarding the captives' previous convictions. In contrast, the arrest criteria guiding the SD-ordered Viennese "Jews action" in May 1938 were more malleable and allowed for even broad interpretation. Similarly vague in definition were the instructions that the Vienna criminal police had received immediately after the annexation of Austria, namely to include the "names of Jewish lawbreakers" into a list of persons soon to be targeted as "professional criminals."[47]

Looking at the reality on the ground, the arbitrariness with which police, Gestapo, and SS proceeded in their arrests of thousands of Vienna's Jews is striking. Although the names of some of the victims, particularly doctors, lawyers, businessmen, and intellectuals, were inscribed on previously compiled "black lists," the overwhelming majority of the victims were kidnapped at random from streets and public places, cafés and restaurants, shops and warehouses, gardens and parks. A large number of the arrested also fell victim to denunciations by their neighbors.[48] Former Gestapo official Ebner admitted to this arbitrary procedure: "The Jews were captured randomly."[49] The official arrest criteria "unwanted," "asocial," and "previously convicted" were categories so vague and elastic that they could not serve as practical guidelines for the action in the first place. In practice, the police officers, Gestapo agents, and SA or SS men who executed the arrests decided on their own initiative who was to be regarded as an unwanted Jew. In this way, they practiced a form of previously unparalleled, open antisemitic exclusion. In the Vienna of early summer 1938, Jews were arrested as Jews. A nonracial pretext for their imprisonment was not needed. For the first time, the persecution of Jews by means of concentration camp terror was based solely on their racial status as alien to the Nazi "people's community."

A raid of enormous scale, the Viennese round-up of Jews confronted police and SS with extraordinary challenges. Overcrowded prisons and complicated transport logistics necessitated the establishment of improvised spaces of detention to hold the hundreds of captives. Many survivors remembered their detention in the provisional Gestapo prison, set up in a school building in Karajangasse in Vienna's 20th district. Hundreds of men were herded together there for days. They slept on straw mattresses and were "very badly treated" by police and SS. Information about the cruel scenes unfolding in this "assembly camp" soon spread to the public.[50]

Because of their visibility and their improvised character, sites of extra-legal detention established in Vienna in 1938 are reminiscent of the early concentration camps of 1933–1934 in Germany.

That Vienna's Jews experienced little to no solidarity from the general public can be discerned, for example, from the account of Emilie Reich, wife of Maximilian Reich. While her husband was still held in Vienna, she and hundreds of other women assembled outside the prison day after day, waiting to hear from their men. There they were harassed by a mocking crowd. The Reich's daughters, aged ten and eighteen, had to be taken out of school when "fingers were pointed at them and they were scorned because their father was imprisoned."[51] The criminalizing effects of concentration camp imprisonment, which also tainted the prisoner's family, manifest themselves most hauntingly in the discrimination suffered by children. We have noted this previously with the example of the young Reinhard Bendix, whose surroundings proved equally unwilling to regard his father as an innocent victim of political persecution. Instead the popular opinion was reproduced that imprisonment—whether in a jail or in a concentration camp—was the deserved punishment of a delinquent person.

The mass deportation of Viennese Jews to the concentration camp made its impression on the new "national comrades" of the *Ostmark*—the Nazi propaganda term for annexed Austria—in many ways. Graffiti reading "[He] is in Dachau!!!" written on deserted storefronts not only made the absence of the city's Jewish population all the more visible but also advertised the horror of the camp.[52] To passersby the name Dachau, at that time, had become synonymous with torture and death. A correspondent of the British newspaper *The Times* reported other such forms of antisemitic vandalism: "Shops were smeared with paint and tar, and such signs as, 'Pig of a Jew,' 'Go to Jerusalem' were painted on the windows. A café was renamed 'Café Dachau' by political decorators."[53]

The target figure of 5,000 deported Jews initially aimed at by the Gestapo and SD was never reached. According to Ebner, the round-up of Austrian Jews was discontinued after about 2,000 individuals had been shipped to Dachau. The order to stop the deportations, Ebner stated, had come from Göring via cable in the first instance, and was then reinforced by the SS and police leadership.[54] No clear reason for the cessation of the Viennese "Jews action" emerges from official documentation. On the basis of a larger survey of the sources, the historian may, however, provide the following possible explanations. First, the harsh persecution of Jews and other Austrians launched after the *Anschluss* had harmed Nazi Germany's foreign relations. Especially in Great Britain, where the *Times* reported on the aggressive "Nazi Treatment of Viennese Jews" and their deportation to Dachau in "special trains," leading diplomats, including Foreign Secretary Lord Halifax, expressed their concern about the events. On July 5, 1938, Ernst von Weizsäcker, state secretary at the Foreign Office, discussed the matter with Heydrich, who agreed that "the arrest action in Austria should not weigh as a continuous load" on the Reich's foreign relations. Only those "politically dangerous groups" whose cases could not be handed over to the courts should, in the long term, remain imprisoned.[55]

Secondly, the brutal excesses perpetrated against Austrian Jewish prisoners had provoked new investigations into camp violence by the public prosecutor's office. A secret order of the leader of the first SS Death's Head division Oberbayern, SS Obersturmbannführer Max Simon, to his subordinates reported that on the transport of June 2–3, 1938, "about 70 percent of the prisoners have been mistreated." With five officially registered casualties this was indeed the most lethal of all the transports. As a result, legal investigators visited the camp. Simon, in his order, did not forbid these assaults but stressed the need officially to declare them as "acts of self-defense against rebellious prisoners." Furthermore, he deemed it "unnecessary that SS men, as has recently happened, tell [people] in the town of Dachau or elsewhere, as well as their SS comrades, that they will apply even harsher measures on the next transport."[56]

During the month of June 1938, prisoner numbers in Dachau jumped from 3,410 to 6,116. Through the mass arrival of Austrian prisoners, the number of Jewish inmates in Dachau rose from about 400 to some 2,500 men.[57] The rapid and disproportionate growth of this prisoner group had noticeable impacts on the organizational structure of the camp. Starting with the mass arrivals of late May/June 1938, Dachau's camp administration requartered prisoners to the new barrack camp. This new camp consisted of thirty-four blocks, built one behind the other, in two large rows to the left and right of a broad street. Jewish prisoners occupied several barracks of the left-hand row. Instead of one Jew block, there were now at least eight. Spatial and social segregation was maintained, as "Aryan" prisoners were accommodated mainly in the right-hand row of barracks. Officially they were forbidden any contact with the Jews.[58] Around the same time, Dachau's prisoners also received new uniforms with blue and grey stripes, as well as triangular badges to signify their imprisonment category.[59]

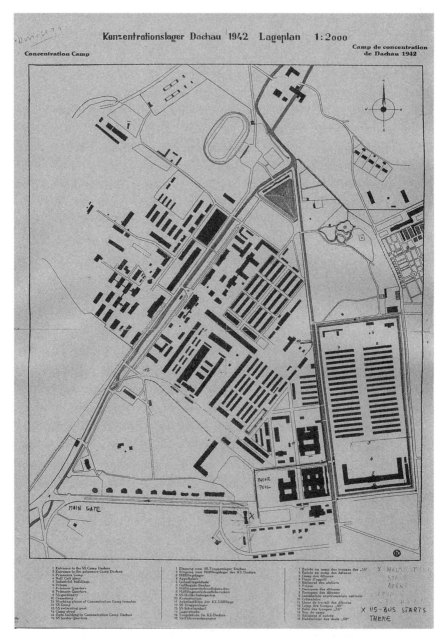

Figure 5.2 A site plan of Dachau concentration camp from 1942 shows the rectangular prisoner compound completed in 1938 on the right-hand side. The barracks of the SS troops, workshops, offices of the camp administration, garages, and other facilities are located left of the prisoner camp.
KZ-Gedenkstätte Dachau.

The first two transports of Austrians were absorbed into the Dachau system without major difficulties, but the camp administration was overwhelmed with the absorption of the more than 3,000 prisoners brought in within a short space of time in May and June 1938. The management of the overcrowded camp, and supervision of the thousands of new inmates, seriously challenged the command staff. The mailroom, for example, could not cope with the censoring of the flood of letters. As a result, the permitted correspondence was reduced from one letter per week to only two per month—a ruling that caused despair among the prisoners.[60] Generally, the SS had great difficulties controlling the unforeseen dynamics that affected the workings of the camp. The most palpable changes occurred in the daily routine of labor, and they were mainly caused by the fact that there was not enough work left to do in the nearly completed camp. With few reasonable tasks left to occupy the inmates, "unemployment," as one prisoner put it, threatened to "disintegrate the whole system."[61] The SS at first tried to avert this "danger" by keeping prisoners busy with senseless labor: "A frantic digging was begun here, there and everywhere. Earth was wheeled about aimlessly. Fresh gravel-pits were excavated."[62] Starting at the end of June, Saturday afternoons and Sundays were work-free.[63] Prisoners remembered as a radical break in the labor routine the morning roll call when, for the first time, only about a third of them were called up to form into work detachments and the rest were ordered to return to their accommodation to work inside the barracks (Stubendienst). From this remarkable day on, Dachau prisoners worked in shifts for only two or three days per week. Instead of labor, punitive drill was increasingly used to occupy them as in the early phase of the camp.[64]

The SS reacted to the threat of flagging camp discipline from "unemployment" with increased violence. In late June 1938, about 1,000 inmates were collectively punished with ten evenings of Torstehen—the arduous ritual of standing motionless at attention for hours on end by the gate building, "with hungry stomachs and thirsty throats after work."[65] On the whole, the nature of camp violence began to change as forms of indirect or structural violence—the suffering that resulted from prisoners' exposure to extreme climatic conditions, from chronic exhaustion and undernourishment, lack of hygiene, and insufficient medical treatment—were added to the more physical forms of abuse perpetrated directly by SS men against individual prisoners.

The "Austrian invasion" also led to considerable changes in the social structure and atmosphere of the camp. Before the summer of 1938, corruption had played an insignificant role in the workings of the Dachau camp. It became a serious problem only with the arrival of large numbers of nonpolitical prisoners, from a middle-class milieu, captured in the mass round-ups in Vienna. As many of them received regular payments from home, significantly more money was circulating in the camp than before. Corruption, which was seen as a Jewish phenomenon, swiftly assumed an enormous scale: "Everybody was open to bribery and everything was available for money."[66] A place in a different barrack where one could be with a friend could be bought, as could a better position in another work detachment. Although it was officially forbidden, every day large numbers of prisoners changed their places of work. Neurath reported that among the prisoner functionaries who worked as kapos and barrack elders, the prejudice quickly spread that it was easy "to make a Jew use his money for bribery." Rackets were organized, and whole barracks were made to pay in order to avoid being selected into a particularly dreaded work detail. A great deal of cash changed hands: "In the eight Jewish barracks, sub-cashiers were appointed and sub-sub cashiers for the rooms."[67]

The majority of the Austrian Jewish prisoners were released from the concentration camp before the outbreak of the Second World War. Their liberation, which was made conditional on leaving Nazi Germany, did not, however, occur as soon as they had hoped for.[68] In fact, only a tiny fraction— fewer than 50 Jewish inmates—were released during the months of June to September.[69] In mid-September 1938, the Dachau administration began to clear the camp of Jews by transferring them to Buchenwald. The first contingent of 70 Jewish prisoners was sent to the Thuringian camp on September 16. In the following week, all the remaining 2,310 of Dachau's Jews were shipped to Buchenwald in three additional transports: 30 prisoners left on September 21; 1,200 on September 22; and the last 1,080 on September 23, 1938.[70]

The transfer of Jewish prisoners of all categories from Dachau to Buchenwald had been ordered by Himmler.[71] It was part of a larger reorganization of the SS concentration camp system, its extension, and its integration in the regime's preparation for further territorial expansion and military conflict. Dachau's Jews were not the only prisoner group affected. On August 8, 1938, a first transport of 304 prisoners classified as criminals and asocials had already been sent from the Bavarian camp to the town of

Mauthausen near Linz in Upper Austria to establish and fill up a new concentration camp there. Further transports followed in the coming weeks.[72] Mauthausen was located at a granite quarry, at which the SS planned to exploit the prisoner workforce for the Reich's building projects. Similar economic factors had played a role in the choice of location for the Flossenbürg concentration camp, established in May 1938, in Bavaria's Upper Palatinate, an area with a number of quarries. "Criminal" prisoners sent from Dachau were forced to set up the camp. During the prewar years no Jews were imprisoned in Mauthausen or Flossenbürg.[73]

Through transports to Flossenbürg, Mauthausen, and Buchenwald, room was made in the overcrowded Dachau camp. In particular, the evacuation of almost 2,400 Jewish prisoners at the height of the "Sudeten crisis" attests to the high level of activity within the SS police apparatus in the general preparation for "Operation Green," the code name for the military's planned invasion of Czechoslovakia. The Munich Agreement of September 30, 1938, averted the danger of war through an arrangement that allowed Nazi Germany to annex the Sudentenland. Following the occupation, around 2,000 persons from this region mostly inhabited by ethnic Germans were deported to Dachau.[74] With the arrival of the transports from Dachau, the number of Jewish prisoners in Buchenwald rose from slightly more than 700 in mid-September 1938 to 3,124 in early October 1938. At that time, Jews made up more than 30 percent of the prisoner population.[75]

We can see that the annexation of Austria, which radicalized Nazi anti-Jewish policy in general, introduced a new dimension of violence into the persecution of Jews by virtue of camp terror. Of the total of 3,500 Austrians deported to Dachau in the spring and summer of 1938, the approximately 2,000 Jewish prisoners constituted by far the largest group. For the first time, a large-scale arrest raid, a "Jews action," aimed at mass detention was ordered from highest levels. The directive's vague enemy profiling led to a rather random selection of captives and, on the whole, Jews were arrested as Jews. Although the mass deportations of Austrian Jews to the concentration camp were eventually discontinued, the action nevertheless provided a learning process for future mass arrests. The interim accommodation of hundreds of arrestees in improvised detention centers across Vienna, and the organization of the complicated logistics for transporting them to the concentration camp, were repeated half a year later during the mass arrests of Jews in the wake of the November Pogrom. Through the public visibility of camp terror and the mass arrests, which interacted with other forms of direct and violent attacks on Austria's Jewish population, an enormous pressure was applied on the victims to leave Nazi Germany and surrender their economic assets. Inside the concentration camp, the first mass imprisonment of Jewish prisoners changed the social structure of the inmate population as well as the organization of camp labor.

The mass influx of Austrian Jews was not the only "invasion" that affected the organizational structure of the Nazi concentration camps and changed the social composition of the prisoner population in 1938. The arrival of about 12,000 "asocial" prisoners, deported mostly to Buchenwald and Sachsenhausen in April and June, also had decisive impacts on the day-to-day workings of the camps. Some 2,500 of the estimated 10,000 "asocials" who arrived in the camps in June were of Jewish origin.[76] I now turn to their arrest and imprisonment to determine whether and to what extent their persecution was different from the persecution of non-Jewish men classified as asocials.

Action Work-Shy Reich

The Nazis' social utopia of a strong, healthy, and productive people's community excluded all those who did not conform to Nazi ideological principles and behavioral norms. Apart from political opponents and "racial aliens," it was men and women on the margins of society who fell victim to discrimination and violent persecution. The police raids in the autumn of 1933 that targeted the poor and the homeless were early manifestations of Nazi social engineering. In a large-scale "beggars raid," many thousands were arrested off the streets or in homeless shelters and locked up in prisons, workhouses, and concentration camps.[77] At the same time, harsh police proceedings were launched against ex-convicts. Preventive detention for "professional criminals" was introduced. A secret order issued by Göring on November 13, 1933, empowered the criminal police in Prussia to arrest individuals on the flimsy grounds that "a criminal intent to commit murder, robbery, burglary, or arson reveals itself in their actions." As "a danger to public safety," these suspected criminals could now be taken into preventive police custody for an indefinite period of time.[78]

Until 1937, measures against social outsiders remained largely in the hands of traditional authorities, such as the welfare institutions, legal authorities, public health departments, and the labor exchange. Competences began to shift with the centralization of the police in 1936, when Gestapo and criminal police (Kripo) combined their forces in the newly founded Security Police (Sipo). Pursuing an agenda of "racial general prevention," the police in the mid-1930s increasingly also targeted nonpolitical enemies defined according to the principles of Nazi ideology.[79] This "cleansing," this removal of "community aliens" *(Gemeinschaftsfremde)* from the people's community, won the approval of wide sections of the German population. Deep-seated prejudices against social outcasts made many of the Nazis' radical practices of social engineering appear to be in accordance with popular sentiments. Exploring public perception of the regime's harsh policy of exclusion, Robert Gellately finds that "Germans generally turned out to be proud and pleased that Hitler and his henchmen were putting away certain kinds of people who did not fit in, or who were regarded as 'outsiders,' 'asocials,' 'useless eaters,' or 'criminals.'"[80] Besides prisons, provincial workhouses, and communal labor camps, concentration camps were filled up with larger numbers of social outsiders. In March 1937 the criminal police conducted the first nationwide mass arrest of "professional criminals." An estimated 2,000 ex-convicts and alleged offenders were sent to Dachau, Lichtenburg, Sachsenburg, and Sachsenhausen. Between twenty and thirty female captives were deported to Moringen.[81] Among the arrested were many minor offenders who had been repeatedly convicted for theft, burglary, receiving stolen goods, or forgery.[82]

The practice of preventive police custody was expanded with the Reich Decree on Preventive Crime Combat by the Police, issued by the Ministry of the Interior on December 14, 1937. The nationwide ruling standardized regionally differing practices of persecution. Apart from "professional criminals," the basic decree declared that anybody "who threatens the general public through his asocial behavior" should also be taken into preventive police custody.[83] A later ordinance of the Reich Criminal Police Office (RKPA) characterized as asocial any person "who through behavior opposed to the communal good, although not criminal in nature, demonstrates that he does not want to integrate into the community."[84] Vague in its official formulation, the label "asocial" became a catch-all term used to persecute persons who were considered alien, conspicuous, and nonconformist, including, as we shall soon see, Jews.

The Action Work-Shy Reich of 1938 was a massive coordinated assault on "community aliens" executed nationwide. Following Himmler's order to take into custody "work-shy" men, who "due to their demonstrable unwillingness to work must be counted among the asocials," a first wave of arrests was conducted by the Gestapo on April 21–30. Almost 2,000 men, many of whom had been denounced as work-shy by employment offices, were imprisoned in Buchenwald.[85] In mid-June, a second wave of arrests, this time carried out by the Kripo, by far exceeded the previous raid against social outsiders. Some 10,000 captives were taken to the camps of Buchenwald, Sachsenhausen, and Dachau.[86] By the summer of 1938, the mass influx of "criminals" and "asocials" had drastically raised the inmate population of the SS concentration camps to a total of 24,000 prisoners.[87]

Prior to June 1938 the persecution of Jews labeled as asocials was limited to a small number of individual cases.[88] Only in the second wave of coordinated arrests did Jews become a target group of those assaults. Thereupon, however, they were disproportionally affected, as prisoner numbers show. In Sachsenhausen, which absorbed more than half of the captives, 824 of the 6,224 men brought to the camp (13.24 percent) were classified as work-shy Jews.[89] In Buchenwald, Jews made up more than half of the prisoners taken in as so-called ASR-prisoners (*Arbeitsscheu Reich Häftlinge*). Of the 2,378 men carried off to Buchenwald, 1,256 (52.82 percent) were Jews.[90] Dachau absorbed 923 prisoners arrested in Action Work-Shy Reich in June; 179 of them were categorized as Jewish.[91] In total, 2,259 Jews were deported to the concentration camps as asocials in June 1938.

What were the official criteria applied to arrest and detain Jews as asocials? And what can be said about the motives and the wider aims behind this major assault? In the arrest order of June 1, 1938, issued by Heydrich in his capacity as the chief of the RKPA, the following categorization is given: "In the week from 13 to 18 June 1938, all male Jews . . . who are charged with at least one prison sentence of more than one month, are to be taken into police preventive custody."[92] Comparing these criteria with the instructions given half a year earlier in the Reich Decree on Preventive Crime Combat—in which Jews were not yet explicitly mentioned as a selected target group—we find some striking differences in the definition of the victims. In the earlier ordinance, persons to be taken into police preventive custody were described as "habitual or professional criminals" who "have been sentenced, at least three times, to at least three months of prison or penitentiary." Moreover, while originally those sentences were to date back no longer than five years, no such restriction of time was to be observed in the case of Jewish ex-convicts. A letter sent from the Munich Kripo to the municipal police in Rosenheim clarifies that for the arrests of Jews, it "does not matter when the sentence had been imposed."[93] Hence, Jewish former lawbreakers were judged according to much stricter criminological standards: they could be taken into preventive custody on the basis of fewer convictions and shorter periods behind bars, no matter how far back they dated.

It is important to note that with the "June action" of 1938 a critical stage in the expansion of the Jewish enemy category was reached. Jews who had become unemployed, poor, or delinquent, often as a result of ever-harsher persecution by the regime, were labeled as asocial and systematically punished with concentration camp detention. Such arrests magnified and reinforced the stereotypical equation of Jews with criminals. To be sure, the Nazis did not invent the topos of "Jewish criminality." As Michael Berkowitz has shown, this tenacious libel predates the rise of modern racism and belongs to the venerable arsenal of classic anti-Jewish prejudices. Precisely because the association of Jews with crimes such as smuggling, robbing, and begging was such an "important part of the mental landscape of European anti-Semitism," it was easy for the Nazis to play on and inflate this stereotype in order to legitimize their actions.[94] For Jews in Nazi Germany, on the other hand, breaking the law was sometimes unavoidable in a country where the law itself was gradually turned against them. In the sixth year of Nazi rule, an avalanche of antisemitic legislation, bans from professions, and open plundering of economic assets outlawed Jews and pushed them to the margins of society. The number of unemployed within the Jewish population rapidly doubled from 30,000 in late 1937 to approximately 60,000 in the spring of 1938.[95] A growing number of the persecuted sank into poverty, and the emergence of a Jewish proletariat began to threaten the overall aim of Nazi anti-Jewish policy, because most impoverished Jews without income were unable to emigrate.[96]

Historians have identified as one of the central motives of the mass raid against social outsiders the recruitment of workers for building up Germany's infrastructure, as envisaged in the Four-Year Plan. In the camps' brickworks and quarries, prisoner labor could be exploited to deliver construction materials for Hitler's imposing building projects. At the same time, the mass imprisonment of thousands of "work-shy" Germans had a disciplining effect on the nation's workforce at large.[97] Did these economic factors also play a role in the imprisonment of Jewish "asocials" and "criminals"? Can they explain why so many of them were suddenly included in the mass arrests of June 1938?

It has been suggested that the inclusion of Jews in the June raid on asocials is to be understood as the result of an order from Hitler.[98] In a series of memos exchanged between SD, the Gestapo, and RKPA in the early summer of 1938 there appears a reference to a meeting held on June 1, 1938—the very day that Heydrich gave the arrest order—in which "the confidential information has been presented that by order of the Führer, asocial and criminal Jews should be arrested across the Reich to perform important excavation work."[99] Does this source allow for the conclusion that the mass arrests of Jews in the course of Action Work-Shy Reich were primarily motivated by their recruitment for forced labor? Given that the prime solution to the "Jewish Question" at that time was seen as being forced emigration and not forced labor, this seems unlikely. Rather, the decision to incorporate a mass arrest of Jews into the criminal police's assault on asociality must be understood as an attempt to position the concentration camps as a radical means to drive Jews out of Nazi Germany.[100] Himmler and Heydrich seem to have seized on the opportunity of a vague Führer order and used it to include Jews in an arrest action officially targeting socially deviant persons labeled asocial. Using Ian Kershaw's by-now classic concept of "working towards the Führer," we can say that they translated a vague vision into a concrete and far-reaching discriminatory measure, not least in order to strengthen the role of the SS police apparatus among the various agencies competing for authority to solve the "Jewish Question."[101] That "the anti-social Jewish proletariat without means" ranked at the top of the list of those who should leave the country also becomes clear from an SD document setting out the principles of emigration policy. In early June 1938, this draft, which dealt with the threatening dilemma between the tightening exclusion of Jews from economic life and their growing impoverishment and resultant inability to emigrate, was returned to the SD's Jewish Department signed by both Heydrich and Himmler.[102]

Interpreting Action Work-Shy Reich, in the case of Jews, as a violent measure intended to enforce emigration and "Aryanization" rather than a means of recruitment of forced laborers, it becomes clear also why no importance was attached to the ability of the arrested Jewish men to work. While the arrest order, at least on paper, generally demanded that the captives be able-bodied workers, this condition did not officially apply to the Jews. The Coordinating Office of the Munich Criminal Police clarified that "by male persons fit for work are meant said asocials, whereas with male Jews the capacity to work is not required."[103] On the whole, the productivity of the thousands of "work-shy elements" deployed as laborers in the camps was very limited. Life-threatening conditions in the over-crowded camps thwarted the SS's effort to turn the concentration camps into efficiently working economic entities for the realization of the Four-Year Plan.[104]

The paradigmatic case study of "asocial" prisoner Josef Cahn further underscores the thesis that objectives different from the ones generally guiding the large-scale assault on social outsiders were at work in bringing to the camps Jews persecuted as asocials. Cahn's story, reconstructed mainly on the basis of his police file and postwar restitution case, is particularly illuminating with regard to the anti-Jewish thrust of the second wave ar-rests. On June 17, 1938, the criminal police in Munich arrested the fifty-five-year-old cattle dealer and merchant as an asocial. With reference to various misdemeanors and petty offenses, some dating back almost twenty years, the officials constructed his "life of crime." They emphasized that "Cahn is a Jew and has been sentenced to substantial fines for illicit trade with tobaccos, unauthorized cattle trade, and offenses of tax regulations for traveling salesmen in the years 1919, 1921 and 1927." Ultimately decisive for Cahn's being taken into preventive police custody was his having been sentenced to four months in prison for fraud and falsification of documents, convicted by the Munich District Court in 1931.[105]

The merchant's Jewish heritage had already figured prominently in his persecution before 1938. When the Munich police, in 1935–1936, tried to ban Cahn from plying his trade, the official in charge saw in "the cleansing of German cattle trade of Jews . . . an obligatory task of the German state."[106] In 1936 the Jewish cattle dealer indeed had to give up his business but could at least keep the tobacco shop he ran together with his wife. The police, however, did not forget about him, and he was deported to Sachsenhausen concentration camp as an asocial two-and-a-half years later. His arrest and detention were clearly motivated by the intention to destroy Jewish busi-nesses and banish their owners, and the concentration camp served as a powerful deterrent. A request for Cahn to surrender his business license was sent to Sachsenhausen by the responsible Trade Licensing Office.[107] While he was imprisoned in the camp, his wife, Betty, tried to secure his release by announcing to the authorities the family's intention finally to yield to pres-sure and give up their business. Her petition for release reads: "In order to prepare for emigration and especially for the liquidation of our business, the presence of my husband is absolutely necessary."[108]

Cahn was set free from Sachsenhausen on August 25, 1938. Analogous to the formal procedure for release of protective custody prisoners, which could be carried out only by the Gestapo headquarters in Berlin, the RKPA acted as the central authority deciding upon the release of concentration camp inmates held in preventive police custody. The RKPA's standard form for authorizing a release has survived in Cahn's police file. From this document, whose subject matter reads "preventive custody prisoners (Jew)," it becomes absolutely clear that the authorities' goals in imprisoning Jews were fundamentally different from their goals in the persecution of non-Jewish men arrested in Action Work-Shy Reich. The document reveals that the only acceptable reason to set free a Jewish asocial was proof of his already-planned emigration. Until they had left the country permanently, released Jewish prisoners were considered to be merely "suspended" from custody. In Cahn's case, a release was authorized because the prisoner had indicated that "he plans to emigrate to America."[109] This plan was thwarted, however, when less than two months later, in the wake of the nationwide November Pogrom, the Gestapo arrested Cahn yet again. This time he was sent to Dachau. Like thousands of other Jewish businesses, the family's tobacco shop was closed around that time. Cahn's second spell in a concentration camp lasted until November 25, when he was set free on the condition that he leave Germany within the next four weeks.[110] For reasons unknown, his planned emigration to the United States failed and Cahn fled to Italy in March 1939. Seven months later he arrived in Hungary, where he was arrested as an illegal immigrant and brought to the Garany internment camp near Kosice. As a last sign of life his son received a postcard in the summer of 1941 informing him that Cahn was on a transport to Poland. The date and place of his death are unknown.[111]

The case of Josef Cahn clearly reveals the authorities' deliberate exploitation of preventive custody measures for the two fundamental aims of Nazi anti-Jewish policy before the war: the removal of Jews from the German economy, often through "Aryanizations," and their forced emigration. The prisoners themselves were well aware of these Nazi motives at the time. According to a contemporary report, written by an anonymous author, the criminal police bluntly told arrested Jews that "only if they manage to arrange their emigration papers would they have a chance of being released again from the concentration camp."[112] The information that "no Jewish prisoner is ever released unless he can produce evidence that he is able to leave Germany" also reached the German Emergency Committee of the

British Quakers in late summer 1938.[113] The aim of pressuring Jews into emigration was thus made transparent from the beginning of the "action." However, in order to keep up a veneer of lawfulness the arrested were forced to affirm the official stereotypes of them as criminals or asocial Jews. Those who refused to incriminate themselves by "signing that I am a work-shy Jew," as Kurt Kohn (a construction worker from Berlin) did, were often subjected to mistreatment while still at the police station.[114] The examples demonstrate that beyond the rather "practical" aim of using the mass arrests as a large-scale means to pressure Jews into emigration, the raids, on an ideological level, were also meant to confirm and enforce the antisemitic image of the asocial Jew.

Jewish men arrested in Action Work-Shy Reich were brought to the camps, together with non-Jewish captives, on special trains. Some 600 Jews were among the prisoners who arrived in Buchenwald on June 15, 1938, with the largest transport of over 1,000 men deported from Berlin.[115] In contrast to the men on board the Austrian transports to Dachau, prisoners captured in the June action were guarded by policemen and did not suffer much abuse during the journey. Nonetheless, the SS gave them a violent reception as soon as they arrived at the station in Weimar. Attacked with insults and blows, Jews and non-Jews were driven onto trucks that took them to the Ettersberg, a mountain north of the town whose climatically harsh northern slope had been chosen as the location for the camp. Construction of the Buchenwald concentration camp had started in July 1937 and was still under way when the hundreds of captives classified as asocials arrived.[116]

The absorption of this mass influx of asocial prisoners severely challenged the camps' administrations. The new inmates were provisionally accommodated in half-finished barracks or other makeshift buildings. In Buchenwald, Jewish prisoners were housed in the cellar of the still-unfinished building of the camp kitchen and in a sheep pen located in the northwestern part of the camp. Some 500 men were packed into this sheep pen: "There was no room. No table, no chair, no bed was there for us. At night, we had to lie on the bare floor; we could not stretch out, it was way too crammed for that." Sanitary conditions were appalling.[117] In Sachsenhausen, too, the arrival of over 6,000 "asocials" constituted a radical upheaval in the camp's daily routine. Although the camp was in a more advanced state of construction than Buchenwald, living conditions worsened as a result of the mass influx of new prisoners. Designed for a standard occupancy of 146 men, some barracks became severely overcrowded and housed around 400 inmates. Each meal was accompanied by "a terrible pushing and shoving," one prisoner recalled, and there was never enough food to satisfy the hunger.[118]

The camp administrations assigned to "asocials" the black triangle to signify their category of imprisonment. "Work-shy" Jews arrested in June 1938 received a Shield of David emblem composed of a yellow triangle and an overlying black triangle to be attached to their uniform.[119] How did the persecuted react to this formal process of categorization? Dismayed by their criminalization, Jewish prisoners classified as asocials strove to clear themselves of the stigma forced upon them. In their memoirs, they refuted their labeling as work-shy by clarifying that they were not "bums and vagabonds": "The overwhelming majority of us are self-employed businessmen, or workers who have been pulled out of their jobs."[120] They stressed that it was often merely a transgression of the regime's antisemitic legislation that had turned Jews into "criminals." Discriminatory rules for reporting property and assets and for transferring funds as well as currency-exchange regulations sometimes *had* to be violated, knowingly or unknowingly, simply in order to survive. In his study of the Nazi fabrication of Jewish criminality, Berkowitz found that in some cases the victims' response to the regime's effort to criminalize Jewry was to invert Nazi allegations of Jewish criminality and instead to identify the persecutors as "thugs, robbers, and murders."[121] After all, Nazi Germany was, as one survivor put it, "ruled by criminals with criminal means."[122]

Among the Jewish prisoners taken during Action Work-Shy Reich, there were also elderly men, a few of them aged seventy and over. The medical officers who conducted routine examinations of the arrestees at the police departments had declared them fit to undergo detention.[123] Inside the camps, the elderly, the weak, and the sick among the prisoners easily fell victim to SS terror. Restricted in their movements, they at once attracted the attention of the guards. It is worth noting in this context that for guards in Buchenwald and Sachsenhausen the "June action" was their first real confrontation with large numbers of Jewish prisoners. Stirred up by antisemitic indoctrination and welcoming of a change in their monotonous daily routine, the SS lunged at the subjugated prisoners. Kurt Kohn remembered that the Buchenwald SS "greeted" him and other Berlin Jews with the threatening words: "'At last, we have you here, you Jew pigs. You shall all die a miserable death here.'"[124] An anonymous contemporary report about the mortality in the concentration camps of 1938 indicated that the high number of deaths among Jewish asocial prisoners was attributable in large part to a direct use of violence by the SS guards who appeared as "gun-toting" tormentors.[125]

Due to the abuse and killing of individual prisoners, combined with more indirect forms of mass violence, insufficient medical treatment, and adverse living conditions in the overcrowded camps, the number of casualties shot up to an unprecedented high during the summer of 1938. Prisoner deaths frequently occurred in the context of work situations where many fell victim to the abuse and humiliation through which kapos and SS supposedly wanted "to teach the Jews how to work"—here, the official arrest categories of work-shy and asocial aligned with traditional antisemitic stereotypes depicting Jews as shirking hard physical labor. Officially, the camp administrations in Sachsenhausen and Buchenwald registered over 120 deaths of Jewish asocial prisoners between June and September 1938; 24 Jewish prisoners are documented as having died in Dachau.[126] The actual number of victims is estimated to have been much higher. Contemporary reports give a figure of 110 Jewish fatalities for Buchenwald during the first five weeks alone.[127] The atmosphere among the desperate inmates was such that "now, we knew that we were all condemned to death."[128] Besides those who perished in the camps, an unknown number of men died after release as a consequence of their imprisonment. Dozens of urns with the ashes of the deceased were sent cash-on-delivery to the cemetery administrations of the Jewish communities for burial. As a result of the high rate of deaths in the summer of 1938, Eicke ordered the construction of Buchenwald's own crematorium.[129]

Releases of small numbers of Jewish asocial prisoners began a few weeks after their mass arrivals in mid-June. The fact that, in contrast to most other asocials arrested in June 1938, Jews were set free earlier further supports the argument that the authorities pursued different aims with the mass imprisonment of Jewish asocials. On the condition that he would leave Germany, a Jewish asocial prisoner could hope to be released from the concentration camp. In Sachsenhausen, the first releases of two asocial Jews are recorded for June 29, 1938. Just under thirty Jewish prisoners left the camp alive in the following month.[130] In Buchenwald, releases started in early July.[131] In mid-September 1938, just before the Dachau Jews were transported to the camp, the number of Jewish prisoners in Buchenwald sank to 720, which means that almost half of the 1,256 men who had arrived as asocials in June had been discharged from the camp. At the same time, in Sachsenhausen, there were still 510 of the original 824 Jewish asocials.[132]

Survivors of the regime's assault on social outsiders left the camps broken men. Many were physically injured and shocked by their experience of terror. CV representative Hans Reichmann, who met a number of Jewish prisoners after their release, stated that he found them emaciated and deeply disturbed: "Those of the released that were able to report all told the same almost word for word. The majority, however, were silent."[133] Another report based on talks with three former Buchenwald prisoners conducted a few days after their release attests to the fear that haunted them. "Men started to cry as soon as they were asked" about their imprisonment and the conditions in the camp. Nervous and in a delicate emotional state, they appeared utterly discouraged and, as the conclusion of the report puts it, "doubtlessly unable to emigrate. It is likely that a large number of them will perish later on in exile."[134] Hence in practice, the regime's official strategy of applying terror to pressure Jews into emigration was, to some extent, counterproductive: physically and mentally broken by the camp experience and increasingly pauperized through ongoing expropriation, Jews had great difficulties leaving Nazi Germany. For Jewish organizations that worked tirelessly to aid the persecuted in their attempts to leave the country, the mass arrests of 1938 destroyed all efforts to pursue a duly prepared "orderly emigration." Arthur Prinz who worked for the Aid Association for Jews in Germany (Hilfsverein der Juden in Deutschland), remembered "that the June Operation marked the beginning of the end of Jewish emigration policy."[135] Jewish organizations confronted the unresolvable conflict of how to act in the face of the regime's policy of increased pressure. Was it right to apply, beg, and even pay for visas to free the imprisoned from the concentration camps? Or would this not, in turn, confirm Heydrich's brutal measures and risk the confinement of even more Jewish hostages? As Beate Meyer stresses, mass suffering and rising death figures ultimately left Jewish organizations no other choice but to act for the release of the arrested with all means possible.[136] Furthermore, it was difficult to find countries willing to accept previously convicted emigrants branded as asocials. Sometimes this could only be "arranged by means of 'tailored' documents," which then "would render the emigration of other people much more difficult."[137] As Werner Rosenstock, active in the CV, later reported, Jewish organizations thus heatedly discussed whether "the limited emigration facilities [should] be used for them [the "asocial" prisoners] at the expense of other Jews?"[138]

Moreover, emigration possibilities were further limited when foreign countries refused to increase their immigration quotas. No solution to the problem of Jewish refugees was reached at the Evian conference. The meeting of delegates from 32 countries was held in France on July 6–14, 1938—exactly the time when mass violence against Jewish concentration camp prisoners captured in Action Work-Shy Reich was at its height and emigration became a matter of life and death for thousands. In historical perspective, the conference must be considered a failure: "No doors opened at Evian, and no hope was offered to the refugees."[139]

The mass imprisonment of "asocial" Jews in June 1938 contributed to the enforcement of the Nazi equation of Jews with criminals. By portraying Jews as lawbreakers and "work-shy asocial elements" and by allegedly waging a war on crime meant to protect German "national comrades," the perpetrators made it easier for the general public to accept the violent exclusion of Jews.[140] Readers of the newspapers in Berlin, where most of the arrests were conducted, were informed that "a number of Jewish criminals have been taken into preventive custody."[141] Propaganda and terror had their effects on the population at large. The arrest of Jewish preventive custody prisoners and their deportation to the concentration camps was accompanied by pogrom-like violence in the streets. In Berlin, these public assaults were orchestrated by Joseph Goebbels and his loyal aide, Police President Wolf Graf Heinrich von Helldorff. Anxious to secure their initiative in "solving the Jewish Question" against the competition of Heydrich's Gestapo, Kripo and SD, they aimed at a segregation of the city's Jews by means of vandalism and brutal antisemitic excesses from below.[142] In the afternoon of June 16, 1938, a rioting mob assembled on Berlin's Horst-Wessel-Platz (today Rosa-Luxemburg-Platz) and screamed "Jews, perish!" and "Kill the pig Jews!" while policemen were taking Jews into preventive custody.[143] Journalist Bella Fromm documented in her diary how the streets of the capital were smeared with antisemitic graffiti: "Everywhere were revolting and bloodthirsty pictures of Jews beheaded, hanged, tortured, and maimed, accompanied by obscene inscriptions." Shop windows were smashed, and loot from the stores lay scattered on the streets and in the gutter. The police, who were present during the riots, turned a blind eye to the riots.[144]

The June action of 1938 constitutes the first coordinated and nationwide arrest of Jews in the Reich. The mass imprisonments and the open pogrom-like violence came as a shock to German Jewry. As Reichmann observed, German Jews were "terrified and consumed with horror." Their trust in the state and in the rule of law was irretrievably shattered. The general "atmosphere of despair" that prevailed during these summer months also seized the CV representative himself. While until June 1938 he had somehow "got through the Hitler-time with its thousands of attacks on my nerves," his "strength was broken after these days." Reichmann realized, "It's over. It needed no such shattering documentation of my, of our, helplessness to make clear to me that this was the end of the Jews' fortunes in Germany. I knew it long before, but only now I felt that my capability to fight was lost."[145] These words, written in 1939 in close proximity to the events they describe and without any knowledge of the catastrophes still to come, testify very strikingly to the effects of camp terror, which not only broke the prisoners but terrified the Jewish population as a whole. For those living at the time, it was impossible to imagine that only a short time afterward, in November 1938, an antisemitic onslaught on a gigantic scale would dwarf the brutal excesses of the summer.

Mass Imprisonment after the November Pogrom

In the days following the 1938 November Pogrom a memorable reunion took place between Emil Carlebach and his father, Moritz Carlebach. Years had gone by since the young Communist left his parents' house in Frankfurt to go underground as a political resistance fighter. In 1934, at the age of nineteen, Emil Carlebach was arrested by the Gestapo. He was put on trial and convicted of "preparing for high treason." Throughout the years when he was detained in various prisons and concentration camps, his family feared for the young man's life. When father and son finally saw each other again, it was not at their home but in Buchenwald concentration camp. Emil Carlebach had been shipped to Buchenwald with the large transports of Dachau Jews in September 1938. Moritz Carlebach arrived in the camp on November 12 as part of a transport of hundreds of Jewish men from Frankfurt. His brother Emanuel, with whom he had run a thriving retail business, had been brought in the day before.[146] Together with some 10,000 other Jews deported to Buchenwald from towns and villages across Central Germany, the SS forced the brothers into the "special camp" (Sonderlager), a fenced-in zone with emergency shelters separated by barbed wire from the regular prisoner camp. To remove his father from the immediate dangers of the Jewish special camp, Emil Carlebach used his connections to the Communist underground of Buchenwald. Running great risks, he managed to get Moritz Carlebach transferred to the infirmary barrack inside the main camp. Here the following remarkable scene, as recalled by Emil, took place: "I stood facing him. His first words were not, 'Thank God, you are alive!' or 'How are you?' Instead his first words were, 'Was it necessary for you to come here? Can you believe how much Mother has already cried for you?' And my equally spontaneous answer was, 'You don't seem to notice that you are here yourself?' He didn't notice; he, of course, was innocent, [whereas] I, surely, was guilty."[147] To Moritz Carlebach his son, the political prisoner who was convicted and persecuted for his opposition to the Nazis, was "guilty." This notion, which might, in fact, have been more self-defense than accusation, attests strikingly to the criminalizing aura of camp imprisonment discussed previously in the context of the arrests of so-called asocials. The statement shows that even to a member of the persecuted minority, even to someone whose own son was imprisoned, the camps could still appear as "penal institutions for those who had committed crimes and therefore deserved punishment."[148]

The unusual meeting between father and son continued with the younger Carlebach explaining to his father that his admission to the infirmary was intended to secure his survival. This way, the near-sixty-year-old man could rest, eat, and drink—luxuries that other Jewish captives of November 1938 were denied. Moreover, in the infirmary he would be protected from the SS brutality that raged in the special camp. Not without pride, Emil told his father of the resistance work of the political prisoners and explained how they risked their lives to help their comrades. Moritz appeared unimpressed. He strongly objected to his preferential treatment and insisted on leaving the hospital barrack immediately. He was adamant: "'I don't want any help from Communists.'" On this discordant note, father and son parted. It would be their last encounter. Four weeks after his deportation to Buchenwald, Moritz Carlebach was released. He died in Frankfurt on March 29, 1939, from the consequences of his camp imprisonment. As Emil recalled, he "preferred to allow himself to be killed by the Nazis than to be helped by his Communist son."[149]

Powerful in numerous respects, the story of the Carlebachs provides important insights into the history of Jewish prisoners in the concentration camps after the November Pogrom. First, the fact that a father encountered his own son in a concentration camp illustrates the totality of the experience of camp terror at this particular point in the prewar Nazi persecution of the Jews. With an estimated 36,000 arrests and the deportation of more than 26,000 men to Buchenwald, Dachau, and Sachsenhausen, virtually every Jewish family in Nazi Germany was affected.[150] To capture the dimension of this onslaught, I will place this third wave of mass arrests in 1938 within the sequence of events unfolding after Herschel Grynszpan's assassination of the German diplomat Ernst vom Rath in Paris on November 7, 1938. The assassination followed the expulsion of Grynszpan's family from Hanover to Poland.[151] On October 27–29, German police arrested around 18,000 Polish Jews and drove them brutally over the border. Grynszpan's shooting act offered the Nazis a pretext to launch a large-scale pogrom in the course of which tens of thousands of German Jews were taken into camp custody. When were the orders for the "vom-Rath Action" given, and how were they implemented? How was the target group defined, and which new qualities were added to the Jewish enemy profile? And how did the camp administrations in Buchenwald, Dachau, and Sachsenhausen deal with the masses of captives? As the Carlebachs' experience shows, Jewish prisoners brought to Buchenwald in the wake of the 1938 November Pogrom were detained under life-threatening conditions. What drove their extreme treatment? How were the prisoners housed? How much nutrition and medical care did they receive? Were they kept strictly isolated from the rest of the prisoner population, as the testimony suggests? And what was their position in the camps? Wolfgang Benz emphasizes the "special status" of the Action Jews, whom he perceives as "short-term members of the prisoner society" who were not integrated into the day-to-day routine of the camps.[152] I will examine whether and how the "November Jews" were registered by the camp administrations and whether they were deployed for forced labor.[153] Differences between the three camps and policies of release also will be discussed. Moritz Carlebach's four-week spell in Buchenwald was by no means exceptionally short. Many prisoners were set free within a few weeks or months—a relatively short duration of imprisonment compared to those Jews arrested previously.

When the order to arrest 20,000 to 30,000 Jews was given to Gestapo offices all over the Reich in the night on November 9–10, a large-scale pogrom was unfolding in Germany. Nazi party activists set synagogues on fire and vandalized Jewish-owned shops by smashing windows and looting storerooms. In many towns and villages, SS and SA forced their way into houses and apartments, where they destroyed furniture, stole valuables, and humiliated and mistreated the Jewish inhabitants. Public physical violence was perpetrated against Jewish men, women, and children. According to official figures, 91 Jews were killed, 267 synagogues destroyed, and some

7,500 businesses demolished. In reality, the extent of destruction was even greater and the number of fatalities, including those who committed suicide, much higher.[154]

The Gestapo and SS were not initially involved in the large-scale anti-Jewish terror launched on the evening of November 9. Neither Himmler nor Heydrich was present when Goebbels gave his notorious antisemitic speech at the meeting of leading party representatives and "old fighters," which was traditionally held at Munich's Altes Rathaus in memory of the Nazi putsch of 1923. Fired up by the propaganda minister's words, senior party officials dashed to the telephones around 10:30 p.m. and instructed the headquarters of each Gau and the SA Group staffs to take violent action against the Jews.[155] Hitler himself maintained his customary aloofness from anti-Jewish actions, publicly commenting neither on the murder of vom Rath nor on the brutal rampage that ensued in Germany. Behind closed doors, however, he was closely involved. Goebbels's diary reveals that "the Führer has ordered that 2[5]–30,000 Jews should immediately be arrested."[156]

Although surprised by Goebbels's initiative, the Gestapo leadership took immediate action in the night of November 9–10. Telegrams sent by Gestapo Chief Heinrich Müller at 11:55 p.m. and by Heydrich at 1:20 a.m. alerted local Gestapo offices and instructed them not to interfere with the destruction of synagogues and Jewish businesses. Müller ordered the "arrest of 20–30,000 Jews in the Reich. Above all, wealthy Jews are to be selected."[157] Heydrich shortly afterward specified that the Jewish men should not only be "well off" but also "healthy and not too old." He decreed that all available spaces of detention were to be filled up and that the concentration camp responsible for the area was to be contacted immediately so as to arrange for the transport of the arrested.[158]

Comparing the arrest criteria guiding the "vom-Rath Action" with those of previous actions, we find that, for the first time, no other reason beyond a person's belonging to the "Jewish race" was officially needed to arrest him and take him to a concentration camp. Arrests based on racial grounds had, in practice, been made before, but on paper the authorities had always striven to give pseudo-legal pretexts for the imprisonment of Jews. With the mass arrests after the annexation of Austria and the raids conducted in the course of Action Work-Shy Reich, these officially nonracial categories were expanded further and further. Now, in the wake of the November Pogrom, the antisemitic motivation for arrest was openly and officially declared. The nationwide pogrom as well as the subsequent mass imprisonment were aimed at German Jewry in its entirety—a massive "degradation ritual," as Saul Friedländer puts it.[159] Groups hitherto largely spared persecution—such as war veterans and leading functionaries in Jewish organizations—were now also taken into custody. In principle, every Jewish man in Nazi Germany could be affected. Accordingly, any formal issuing of arrest orders was "unnecessary," as Himmler stated in a telegram to Gestapo offices.[160]

The Gestapo's vom-Rath Action lasted from November 10 to the evening of November 16, 1938, when Heydrich ordered a stop to arrests.[161] The action quickly developed its own momentum. Police and Gestapo proceeded in part from property and housing lists, but in general the arrests involved a good deal of arbitrariness. Despite Heydrich's instructions to take into custody primarily wealthy Jews who were not too old, men of all ages and all social strata were among the captives. In some of the smaller and rural towns, the police, Gestapo, and SA arrested almost the entire male Jewish population, from old men to teenagers.[162] The agricultural training farm for Jewish youth run by the National Representation of the German Jews (Reichsvertretung) in Gross-Breesen near Breslau, for example, was raided on November 10. The director, two members of staff, and some twenty boys were deported to Buchenwald.[163]

In the cities, temporary sites of detention were opened up to hold arrestees while the transports to the concentration camps were organized. In Vienna, the Gestapo again used the old school building in Karajangasse in which hundreds had been imprisoned during the mass arrests after the annexation of Austria. The Festhalle in Frankfurt became an improvised detention center for more than 3,000 Jews from that city. From Frankfurt, they were sent on several large transports to Buchenwald and Dachau. Survivor Julius Meyer described the mass imprisonment in the Festhalle. Guarded by police and SS men, Jewish prisoners were locked up in the large and cold hall. They had to turn in their money and valuables. The guards forced them to perform excruciating exercises that caused several to collapse, and one man to die of a stroke. When the Jews were driven out of the Festhalle and onto buses that were to take them to the train station, Meyer saw a large assembly of people "standing in front of the hall watching as we departed, all were silent and without protest or comment observed the spectacle."[164] His account shows that improvised short-term detention centers in the cities attracted the curiosity of the population; the violent exclusion of Jews was not done in secret.

Figure 5.3 Newly arrived Jewish prisoners stand at attention in their civilian clothes during a roll call in the Buchenwald concentration camp, November 1938.
United States Holocaust Memorial Museum, courtesy of Robert A. Schmuhl.

On November 10–13, 1938, 103 transports of Jewish prisoners arrived in Buchenwald. In total, 9,845 Jewish captives were brought to this concentration camp in the wake of the pogrom.[165] Veteran prisoners watched the endless stream of arrivals with bewilderment: "Jews were brought in. Jews, Jews, Jews, by the dozen, by the carload, by the hundred and by the thousand. In all stages of life—wounded, sick, crippled, with broken limbs, missing eyes, fractured skulls, half dead, and dead."[166]

No accommodation was ready to absorb the new prisoners. Upon arrival in the camp, thousands of November Jews were forced to stand or sit in the open. They watched prisoners fetching boards and planks from which makeshift huts were swiftly set up.[167] One of those ordered to build the emergency shelters was Max Rölz, a trained carpenter. He recalled that the work had to be done at an "indescribable speed." Although they had "gotten used to inhumanities" during their long imprisonment in the camp, Rölz and

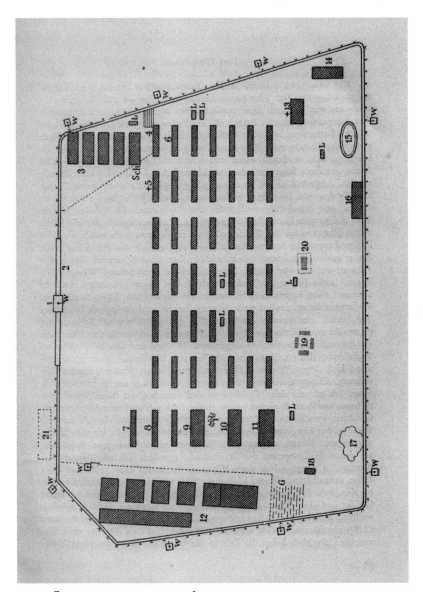

Figure 5.4
Site plan of the Buchenwald concentration camp in November 1938 showing the location of the Jewish "special camp" with its five barracks in the upper right-hand corner. Also shown: entry to the prisoner main camp and roll call area (1), "hospital" shack (4), infirmary barrack in the main camp (5), barrack for the typhoid infected (6), kitchen (9), workshops (12), latrines (L), and watchtowers (W). The plan was drawn by Buchenwald survivor Julius Freund and published in his book O *Buchenwald!* (Klagenfurt: Julius Freund, 1945), 28–29.

his fellow prisoner workers could not believe that the primitive huts were meant to house human beings until they saw Jewish prisoners driven into them.[168]

The construction of Buchenwald's Jewish special camp was undertaken while the transports were rolling in. It is possible to reconstruct an exact time line of the building of the five barracks. They were set up on November 10–13 on a fenced-off plot about one hectare in size and located next to the roll call area. This zone had been separated from the main camp in late September 1938 when 434 police prisoners, both Jews and non-Jews, were deported to Buchenwald from the Gestapo prison in Vienna. A barrack made of wood was established for them.[169] It was this barrack of the Austrian police prisoners that absorbed the first November Jews on November 10. In the following days, another four huts were built from "wooden boards provisionally nailed together which freely admitted the wind and weather through their many cracks and gaps."[170] Some 2,000 men were crammed together in each of the emergency shelters. Without a floor, the barracks stood directly on the clay soil, which turned to mud when it rained. In the beginning, prisoners slept on the floor; in time, bunkbeds as many as five bunks high were built into their huts. Washing facilities or toilets were not installed. There were only two open latrines for the thousands of prisoners in the special camp. A shack that had previously served as a laundry was now transformed into an improvised "hospital" for the sick. In the regular camp infirmary, SS doctor Werner Kirchert stopped treating Jewish prisoners.[171]

The November Jews endured constant violent excesses during the first days after their arrival in Buchenwald. Survivors remembered the "murder week" of November 10–14, when SS guards, mostly during the night, raided the barracks and beat up the helpless and terrified inmates. Their screams were heard by prisoners in the main camp. When, at the same time, diarrhea spread in the special camp, the SS did not permit free access to the latrines. Prisoners were forced to relieve themselves in the barracks. During the night, panic broke out in the overcrowded huts, which were always in danger of collapse. The SS suppressed the commotion with violence.[172] In this extreme situation, a number of prisoners suffered from nervous breakdowns. Because they attracted the attention of the guards, they constituted an acute danger for the whole group. Under the guidance of Austrian police prisoners, some of them medically trained, the mentally ill were taken to the laundry-shack-"hospital."[173]

The first epidemic in the history of the Nazi concentration camps was the typhoid that broke out in Buchenwald's special camp in December 1938. The disease quickly spread to the main camp as well as to villages located north of the Ettersberg. After the SS at first ignored the epidemic, the typhoid rapidly forced the camp administration to open-up a Jewish sick quarter (Judenrevier) in block 2 of the main camp. Doctors from the ranks of the Austrian prisoners risked their lives to provide medical care. In early 1939, anti-typhoid inoculations were administered in Buchenwald and the whole camp was quarantined.[174] As the typhoid raged, the number of deaths reached unprecedented heights. Julius Freund, one of the Viennese police prisoners, reported that the SS tried to lower the number of reported typhoid fatalities by making false statements about the causes of deaths. Officially only twelve inmate casualties from typhoid were registered. As a consequence of the unsanitary conditions that had sparked the epidemic, the barracks of the special camp were demolished in February 1939. About 250 remaining prisoners were transferred to the main camp.[175]

Of the three concentration camps that absorbed the captives of the vom-Rath Action, the most catastrophic living conditions prevailed in Buchenwald, where 227 Jewish prisoners died within the first six weeks in the special camp. Research by Harry Stein has identified the names of 255 November Jews who lost their lives in Buchenwald in 1938–1939.[176] Dachau absorbed the largest group of Jewish prisoners, a total of 10,911 men, 187 of whom were registered as dead by February 1939.[177] No official figures are available for Sachsenhausen. Historians estimate that around 6,000 Jews were deported to the Prussian camp in November 1938. Approximately 100 of them died within the first six weeks.[178] Taking into account the camp administrations' attempts, as witnessed in the case of Buchenwald, to dress up the statistics and disguise the atrocious mortality rates, the total number of Jews who lost their lives in the concentration camps after the November Pogrom must have been much higher than the documented minimum of about 600 casualties. Historians' recent estimates of about 1,000 deaths appear appropriate when taking into account also those November Jews who died, after release, from the consequences of their imprisonment.[179]

In Dachau and Sachsenhausen, too, the November Jews were spatially isolated from the rest of the camp. In Sachsenhausen they were quartered in the "small camp" (kleines Lager) on the lower right end of the roll call area, which the SS had forced prisoners to build during the summer of 1938. Originally this rectangular zone had been earmarked for the camp's own workshops and factories, but with prisoner numbers increasing in 1938, additional space was needed to accommodate them and the plans were changed. Eventually the small camp comprised of an extra eighteen barracks, of which in particular barracks 38 and 39 became known as the Jew blocks. In contrast to the Jewish special camp in Buchenwald, the small camp in Sachsenhausen was not completely closed off from the rest of the camp. Harry Naujoks reported that he and other non-Jewish politicals visited the barracks of the Jews and found political comrades among the November Jews.[180] In Dachau, too, the Jewish blocks were separated from the blocks of the non-Jews. Living conditions in the Bavarian camp were slightly better than in the other two camps. Barracks had sanitary facilities, dry solid floors, and apparently heating, too. They were, however, also turned into mass blocks, in which up to 800 instead of the regular 200 inhabitants had to fight for sleeping and eating spaces, for access to wash basins and toilets.[181]

Camp administrations struggled to keep up with the registration of the tens of thousands of new arrivals. Endless lists of names composed by the camp registries assigned individual prisoner numbers to the November Jews. Given that they were to remain in the camps only for relatively short periods of imprisonment, an enormous bureaucratic effort was made to register the November Jews. Hence, with regard to the official categorization, their status was actually less exceptional than Benz suggests when he writes that the Action Jews lacked any marking. In all three camps they received prisoner numbers, and in Dachau and Sachsenhausen some of the men were also clothed in uniforms complete with triangular badges.[182]

Benz's contention that the special status of the Jewish prisoners brought to the camps in November 1938 was also determined by their exemption from forced labor is true only for Dachau and Buchenwald. In these two camps, the November Jews were not deployed in work commandos. Instead they were forced to do punitive "sport" or to stand at attention for hours on end.[183] In Sachsenhausen, however, many of the Jewish prisoners captured in the vom-Rath Action were integrated in the camp's labor routine. Hans Reichmann was among those detailed to the notorious brickworks (*Klinkerwerk*) detachment. Always moving on the double, he had to tow sacks of cement and transport sand.[184] Other Jewish inmates had to work on the industrial yard next to the camp, where the SS had established their own workshops. Instead of at the originally planned space south of the prisoner camp—which became the site of the small camp—Sachsenhausen's industrial yard was established west of the triangular compound of the prisoner main camp. Here also the November Jews were forced to break stones, drag building materials, stack wood, and perform carpentry work. Many of them were also occupied with utterly senseless tasks.[185]

The mass influx of well-to-do Jewish prisoners in the aftermath of the November Pogrom intensified bribery and corruption in the camps. After the November Jews were brought in, a large-scale pilfering and extortion from Jewish prisoners took place in Dachau, Buchenwald, and Sachsenhausen. Paul Martin Neurath stated that now "there was so much more money that suddenly corruption passed beyond the barbed wire. SS men got involved, receiving big bribes."[186] A 1944 SS report of investigations against Karl Otto Koch, commandant of Buchenwald from 1937 until 1941, found that upon arrival, the November Jews had to "throw all their valuables into open boxes . . . A registration of these effects did not take place. This way, immeasurable sums of money and valuables whose whereabouts are unknown flowed into the personal-effects room." Koch not only tolerated the massive theft but also personally enriched himself.[187]

Many survivors reported that the November Jews could buy their way out of the camp if they agreed to the "Aryanization" of their businesses.[188] Release could indeed depend on the willingness to hand over economic assets. Leopold Engelmann from Weiden, for example, was forced to sign properties over to the municipality for prices far below their real value. Together with other Jews from his hometown he was brought from Dachau to the Gestapo's Wittelsbacher Palais in Munich. Fearing for his life, Engelmann was confronted there with Weiden's mayor, Hans Harbauer, who presented him with a preworded contract and threatened him, "'If you sign the sales agreement, I will seek to effect your release within eight days, and then you have to emigrate . . . If you do not sign, you will remain in Dachau.'" Engelmann had no doubts that "had I not agreed, I would have been sent back to Dachau with special instructions and Dachau would have meant martyrdom and death."[189] In his postwar trial, Harbauer sanctimoniously told the court that in order to walk free from custody, Jews would not have had to yield to this form of robbery by blackmailing. "But I cannot name any Jew from Weiden who was released from the concentration camp and had not sold [his property]."[190] Engelmann, who survived the Holocaust in exile, never received any money for the land that was expropriated from him.

Simultaneously with his order to stop the arrests, Heydrich on November 16 decreed that "negotiations for Aryanizations are not to be disturbed by the taking into protective custody of [business] owners or associates." Furthermore, it was ordered that Jews "who are in the possession of emigration papers or those whose date of departure is imminent" should also be set free from camp detention. Finally, no Jew older than sixty years, or sick or physically handicapped, should be imprisoned any longer.[191] In the following weeks and months, further decrees determining the criteria for the release of the November Jews were issued. They ordered the liberation of Jewish prisoners who had served as combat soldiers in the Great War (November 28, 1938), of those over the age of fifty (December 12, 1938), and of teenagers under the age of eighteen (January 21, 1939).[192]

Although Heydrich's instructions suggest an orderly procedure, the practice of release generally did not proceed systematically along the lines of official criteria. Political arbitrariness and administrative chaos resulting from the sheer dimension of the action influenced the Gestapo's decisions to set free Jewish prisoners. In his 1939 account, former Dachau prisoner Walter Solmitz told of the "big guessing game" of categories for release that constantly occupied the November Jews. A system was not discernible to them: "First the elderly over 70 and 60 as well as the youth under 18? Yes, but people in their 70s still remained imprisoned for weeks. Combat soldiers? Yes, but many people from the town of R. had been released to whom this [criterion] did not apply. People, who have all their emigration papers in order? Yes, but people still remained imprisoned who had everything ready—even those who possessed a shipping passage."[193] Releases of November Jews started around November 20, 1938.[194] Soon, 150 to 250 men were discharged daily from each camp. Administrators called out prisoners' names and numbers over loudspeakers. Inmates then received a superficial medical examination and sometimes their hair was shaved anew, in order to stigmatize them in public as concentration camp prisoners. They were forced to sign an oath not to talk about their experiences in the camps.[195] On their way out of the camp, the released were aided by representatives of the Jewish organizations who provided help and directions at train stations in Munich, Weimar, and Berlin. The general public reacted to them mostly with silence. Some survivors reported that they were given a free meal or experienced other small acts of solidarity. Ruth Abraham, a young Jewish woman who accompanied her future father-in-law back home when he was released from Dachau, however, recalled that people regarded with contempt the man "with the bald head and the terrified posture, who bore the external sign of a prisoner." Fellow passengers mocked him and "would have loved to throw him out of the train. They asked me what I, as a 'German woman,' had to do with this Jew."[196] All over Nazi Germany, Jewish men marked as concentration camp prisoners were publicly visible in the winter of 1938–1939. Their appearance documented their status as outlawed and unwanted "racial aliens" violently excluded from the Nazi people's community.

In the history of Jewish prisoners in the prewar Nazi concentration camps, the mass imprisonment in the aftermath of the 1938 November Pogrom was an exceptional event. The extraordinary release procedure gives striking evidence of this. Neither the Austrian Jews captured in the spring and early summer of 1938 nor the Jews deported to the camps as asocials in June were set free after such relatively short durations of imprisonment. On January 1, 1939, the number of "Action Jews" in Buchenwald had reduced from 9,845 to 1,605. In Sachsenhausen on that same date, only 958 of the over 6,000 Jews were still imprisoned.[197] In the following weeks the number of November Jews steadily diminished further. Sachsenhausen, for which we have detailed reports of the strength of prisoners detained in the camp, serves a well-documented example for this trend: On November 10, 1938, when the first captives of the vom-Rath Action were brought to Sachsenhausen, over 55 percent of the "asocial" Jewish prisoners deported to the camp five months previously, in June 1938, were still imprisoned—457 out of the original 824.[198] In early February 1939 the number of November Jews

Table 5.1 Numbers of Jewish Prisoners in Buchenwald on April 19, 1939, by Detention Categories

Politicals	1,143
Expulsion prisoners	35
Professional criminals	71
Emigrants	37
Bible student	1
Homosexuals	7
Race defilers	111
Work-shy Reich	494
Action Jews (November 1938)	28
Police prisoners	36
Total	1,963

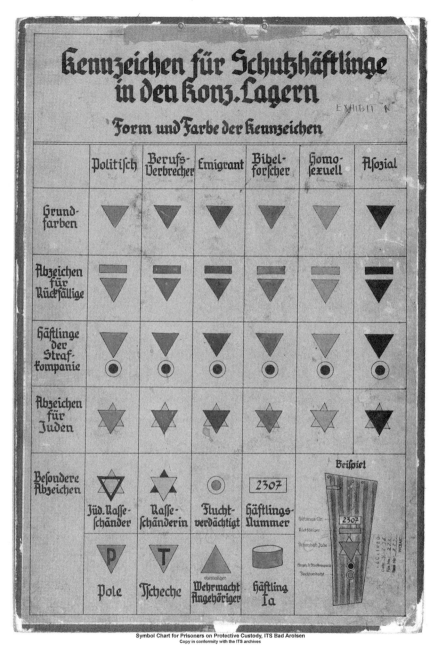

Figure 5.5 Black-and-white reproduction of the symbol chart indicating the various color-coded markings for concentration camp prisoners, ca. 1940. Categories across the top: political (red), professional criminal (green), emigrant (blue), Jehovah's Witness (purple), homosexual (pink), asocial (black). Categories reading down: basic color, badge for second-timers, prisoners in the punishment detail, badges for Jews (underlying yellow triangle), special badges. International Tracing Service.

still detained in Sachsenhausen (310 men) was, for the first time, lower than the number of "asocial" Jewish prisoners (321 men).[199] In the following months both categories were reduced in number, and from June 1939 to the outbreak of the war, figures remained static with around 180 asocial Jews and around 70 November Jews detained in the camp.[200] In Buchenwald, which held the largest group of Jewish inmates since the Dachau Jews were transferred to the camp in late September 1938, a report of April 19, 1939, details the number of Jewish prisoners (table 5.1).[201]

The small number of November Jews (28 men) present in the camp some five months after the vom-Rath Action is striking. In contrast, nearly 40 percent of the Jews brought to Buchenwald in the course of Action Work-Shy Reich—494 out of the original 1,256—were still held in custody. Of the total number of Buchenwald prisoners, which on that day amounted to 8,153 men, Jewish prisoners made up almost a quarter: they were no longer the majority of inmates.

Another important conclusion can be drawn. Jews were the only prisoners whose enemy profile incorporated virtually all offenses deemed harmful to the Nazi people's community. Less than five months before the outbreak of the war, camp administration identified Jews as a collection of subgroups branching off from every other existing prisoner category, be it political opposition, an alleged habitual inclination to criminality, the return from emigration, or a form of social deviance such as homosexuality or asocial behavior.

The infamous classification system of triangular color-coded markings strikingly epitomizes this uniqueness of the Jewish prisoner group. The column specifying the various star-shaped badges to be carried by Jewish camp inmates runs horizontally through all other categories. Jewish prisoners thus figured as the ultimate enemy category exposed to the stigma of every type of "community alien." Like the yellow triangle that formed the basis for the mark they were forced to bear on their prisoner clothes, "Jewishness" was understood to be the root of their essential hostility toward the German racial state. This "Jewishness," an attribute attached to the full range of offensive categories, intensified both the arrests of Jews and their violent special treatment inside the concentration camps. Over time the racial stigma had thus turned into a sufficient category of exclusion: "the Jew."

6

THE CALM AFTER THE STORM?

Jews in the Concentration Camps in 1939

The last months before the outbreak of the Second World War were a brief period of respite from the mass terror that had reigned in the concentration camps before and after the November Pogrom. In stark contrast to the over 30,000 Jews hauled to Dachau, Sachsenhausen, und Buchenwald over the course of the year 1938, the administrations of the three camps recorded the arrival of no more than 500 Jewish newcomers between January and August 1939.[1] In accordance with Himmler's order of January 31, 1939, which ruled that "Jewish protective custody prisoners who possess valid emigration papers should generally be set free," release became the characteristic feature of this period.[2] And in fact, large numbers of both Jewish and non-Jewish prisoners were liberated from camp custody in the months before the war. To Benedikt Kautsky, the Austrian-Jewish prisoner who witnessed the mass releases in Buchenwald without himself being among the fortunate ones, "the camp appeared to be on the way to self-liquidation." From a peak of nearly 20,000 inmates, reached in mid-November 1938, prisoner numbers in Buchenwald had declined to a mere 5,397 on August 31, 1939.[3]

Hundreds of prisoners returned home from the concentration camps in the days around April 20, 1939. Hitler's fiftieth birthday presented the regime with an opportunity to stage mercy, and give amnesty those it deemed worthy of reintegration into the "people's community." War veterans and married prisoners with young children are listed in Heydrich's order as those to be considered as primary candidates for release. Jews, on the other hand, were officially excluded. As the mass release of the November Jews was, however, still going on at that time, Jewish prisoners did, in fact, leave the camps on the Führer's birthday.[4] Contrary to the amnestied "Aryans," who were expected to align themselves to the regime as reformed "national comrades," liberated Jewish prisoners could not hope for a future in Nazi Germany and were forced into exile.

After the exceptional event of the November Pogrom, when Jews from all over the Reich were for the first time officially imprisoned in the concentration camps as Jews (that is, solely and explicitly on the basis of their "race"), the Gestapo returned to the status quo ante and arrested Jews for ostensibly nonracial reasons. The overarching and enduring rationale behind these new arrests was the regime's policy of enforcing Jewish emigration from Nazi Germany. A number of Jews brought to the concentration camps in 1939 were taken into "custody pending deportation" (*Ausweisungshaft*). With his decree of May 26, 1937, Himmler had ordered the Gestapo to send to the concentration camps "dangerous or bothersome" stateless persons and foreigners whose deportation from Germany could not be effected through other means. Their imprisonment was to "prepare them to leave the territory of the Reich as quickly as possible." If necessary, they were to be taken across the border illegally.[5] Jews are not mentioned in these regulations but nevertheless fell victim to arrests and custody pending deportation.

While the majority of the inmates held in custody pending deportation in Buchenwald were non-Jews, nineteen Jewish prisoners brought to the camp between January and August 1939 were also classified in this category.[6] One of them was Alfred Feinberg from Pirmasens, who arrived on February 3, 1939. His deportation from Germany as a "foreigner of alien race" (*fremdrassiger Ausländer*) followed a prison sentence of eighteen months for fraud. Suspected of having aided and abetted the abortion of his illegitimate child by a married "Aryan" woman, the ex-convict was judged "to have abused his right to hospitality in the German Reich."[7] On the basis of the 1938 Police Ordinance Regarding Foreign Nationals (*Ausländerpolizeiverordnung*), the Jewish merchant was prohibited from residing in Germany, and on January 5, 1939, the Berlin Gestapo ordered his custody pending deportation to be carried out in a concentration camp. Feinberg, who had been born in Germany and was naturalized in 1920, filed an official complaint against this decision. But by now the interplay of the various agencies and ordinances of persecution was well established, and his protest was easily "dismissed as unfounded." The authorities had simply to refer to the Denaturalization Law of July 14, 1933, to strip him of his German citizenship. Feinberg did not survive his imprisonment in Buchenwald; the thirty-eight-year-old died on October 27, 1939, almost ten months after his arrival at the camp. His parents, Abraham and Rosa Feinberg, were informed that an attack of cardiac asthma had caused their son's death.[8]

As we have seen, in 1938 the concentration camp functioned as a powerful weapon to pressure vast numbers of Jews into leaving Nazi Germany. The regime most effectively used it as a deterrent not only to speed up Jewish emigration but also to ensure that this mass expulsion proceeded in accordance with the rigid emigration regulations. Here, camp terror was situated in a complex interplay with other forceful methods deployed to drive Jews out of the country. In January 1939, Göring ordered the establishment of the Reich Central Office for Jewish Emigration; this was subordinated to Heydrich's authority and managed by Heinrich Müller, the head of the Gestapo. The bureaucratically organized expulsion of Jews pioneered by Adolf Eichmann in Vienna was now rolled out for the whole Reich. Applicants for emigration had to undergo a complicated and time-consuming process that aimed, first and foremost, at the near-complete confiscation of their remaining economic assets. Jews were thus forced to finance their own expulsion. The Reich Flight Tax, for example, which increasingly limited the possibility of transferring money abroad, became an important source of revenue for a state that was chronically lacking foreign exchange. After the November Pogrom, the Reich Flight Tax amounted to a record sum of 342.6 million RM.[9] In this large-scale theft of Jewish property, the Gestapo worked hand in hand with tax and customs offices as well as other agencies of extortion. From the end of 1938 onward, some Gestapo offices and police stations levied a special emigration tax on Jews leaving the Reich. In February 1939, Heydrich strove to standardize such "measures to promote the emigration" of Jews.[10]

In the aftermath of the November Pogrom, when tens of thousands of Jews tried frantically to get out of Germany, border police stations in the western regions of the Reich registered that the number of refugees was sharply increasing. Some escapees were caught by the German police, others were brought back to Germany by foreign authorities. Soon the political police took action against this "illegal emigration" and arrested those who attempted to cross the border without the required exit papers. Gestapo offices in border regions were ordered to take into protective custody and transfer to a concentration camp Jews who illegally emigrated from the Reich, as well as those "persons who aided the Jews in the interest of their personal benefit."[11] The arrests and camp imprisonments that followed such failed attempts to escape were often tantamount to a death sentence. For

Erwin Schwarz, for example, unsuccessful illegal emigration from Germany in the spring of 1939 had fatal consequences. Together with his wife, the twenty-nine-year-old Austrian bookbinder clandestinely crossed the German-Dutch border on May 30, 1939. By way of the Netherlands the couple hoped to reach Great Britain, to where their two young children had been evacuated by means of the Children's Transports (*Kindertransporte*) rescue mission a short while before. After the Dutch police had deported them back to Germany, Erwin Schwarz was arrested and brought to Dachau on June 24; his "Aryan" wife, who was six months pregnant, was released. All efforts to free Schwarz from the concentration camp failed. Transferred to Buchenwald, he died there in August 1940.[12]

Oskar Koch, arrested in May 1939 while attempting to escape to Switzerland, told the police that he had been unable to deal with the official emigration authorities because "he was completely finished with his nerves." As a result of severe injuries suffered during the November Pogrom, he had had to undergo medical treatment in three different hospitals and had finally reached the conclusion that "it was impossible for him to exist as a Jew in Germany."[13] After his arrest, Koch was sent to Dachau. At first he seemed to have been more fortunate than other captured refugees in that he was liberated from the camp after a few months. However, as emigration from Germany became more and more difficult once the war had begun, Koch found himself unable to leave the country. Attempts to find exile in Chile, Bolivia, and later in Shanghai all failed. After the end to legal emigration in October 1941, he was deported from his home in Düsseldorf to the Lodz ghetto. In December 1944 the Jewish merchant lost his life in Flossenbürg concentration camp.[14]

A rare case in which emigration succeeded in an orderly fashion after almost three months of imprisonment in Dachau is that of Josef Rosendahl. Arrested by the Aachen Gestapo in April 1939 while trying to escape to the Netherlands, he was held back in Germany against his will. On August 22, 1939, only days before the outbreak of the war, Rosendahl legally emigrated from Nazi Germany to Great Britain.[15]

On July 27, 1939, after the arrest and imprisonment of illegal Jewish emigrants had been practiced for more than half a year, the Gestapo modified and standardized its sanctions. A telegram sent to all Gestapo offices and border police stations ordered that each arrest case be carefully reviewed before a person was sent to a concentration camp. In order to grant them a better chance to properly organize their emigration, the arrested were, for the time being, to be kept in protective custody locally, pending transfer to a camp.[16] The reasons for this slight relaxation of sanctions are not documented, but the decree indirectly admits that the imprisonment of Jewish escapees in the concentration camps was counterproductive to the regime's overriding objective of driving Jews out of the country by all means necessary. Many Jews incarcerated for illegal emigration in 1939 never found their way out of the camps, let alone out of Germany.

After September 1938 Buchenwald held the largest group of Jewish prisoners, but most Jews arrested during the period immediately prior to the war were taken to Dachau. This is surely due to the fact that a general halt on the admission and release of all categories of prisoners was imposed over Buchenwald in the spring of 1939—most probably in reaction to the typhoid epidemic that had raged in the camp and its vicinity until February and had resulted in a quarantine. While the ban on releases was officially lifted a few days before the mass amnesty to mark Hitler's fiftieth birthday, new arrivals remained at a minimum until mid-June 1939. Among the 264 prisoners brought to Buchenwald between February and June there were "only" 36 Jews.[17] The Dachau arrival book for the year 1939 registered slightly more than 300 Jewish newcomers before the end of August. About 80 of them had been deported to the Bavarian camp from Czechoslovakia, the latest victim of Hitler's expansionist foreign policy.[18] After the annexation of the western border regions, which became the Reichsgau Sudetenland in October 1938, Germany aimed at conquering the remainder of Czechoslovakia. Following the German army's invasion on March 15, 1939, the country was divided into the semi-independent puppet state of the Slovak Republic in the east and the German-occupied Protectorate of Bohemia and Moravia in the west. Some 118,000 Jews now found themselves trapped in the newly created Protectorate; among them were refugees from Germany, Austria, and the Sudetenland. Brutal anti-Jewish violence, confiscation of property, and the rapid "Aryanization" of Jewish businesses accompanied the establishment of German rule in the region. In some places Jewish houses were vandalized and synagogues set on fire.[19]

In the immediate aftermath of the invasion, the Gestapo, SS, and SD launched Aktion Gitter (Operation Grid), the code name for mass arrests of the Reich's enemies in the Protectorate. Partly supported by the Czech police, the Germans rounded up thousands of political opponents, Communists, Social Democrats, antifascists, left-leaning intellectuals, and leading public figures, as well as emigrants from the Reich. Many Jews were among the captured. Within two months, 4,376 people had been arrested in Bohemia, according to official reports.[20] It has been estimated that in Moravia, for which no exact figures are known, more than 1,000 persons were imprisoned. For the most part, the captured were released after a relatively short-term confinement, once they had promised loyalty to the new regime. On May 13, 1939, the commander of the Security Police and SD in Prague reported that the number of those still held in custody in Bohemia had sunk to 1,125, among them 165 Jews.[21]

In contrast to the situation after the Anschluss of Austria the previous year, when some 3,500 captives from the annexed country were sent to Dachau, no similar mass deportations to the concentration camps followed the German occupation of the remainder of Czechoslovakia. Not only were the majority of those arrested in the Protectorate soon released again, but many spent their protective custody in local confinement. On March 15, 1939, the Czech philosopher and university professor Oskar Kraus, a Jewish convert to Protestantism, was arrested at his home in Prague. For more than two months he was detained in various jails in the city. In the infamous Pankrác prison, which the Gestapo quickly took over and later used as an execution site, he suffered a stroke. When his wife was finally allowed to visit him, she found him "emaciated like a skeleton and with red patches of skin on his face." She was told that a payment of 30,000 Czech koruna (Kč) had to be made, "otherwise Kraus will be deported to Dachau." Ultimately the professor was released from custody on May 26, 1939, without a bribe and managed to escape to London.[22] Two leading female representatives of the Jewish community in Czechoslovakia, Marie Schmolka and Hanna Steiner, were also temporarily detained in the Pankrác prison. All through the 1930s Schmolka had worked tirelessly to aid Jewish refugees. She functioned as the director of the Prague office of the HICEM, a composite of Jewish relief organizations, and was appointed president of the National Coordinating Committee for Refugees in Czechoslovakia in July 1936. Schmolka was released from Gestapo imprisonment after two months. After this she fled to London, where she took her own life in March 1940.[23]

The fact that the Gestapo refrained from deporting vast numbers of Czechs to German concentration camps in the spring and summer of 1939 must be understood within the wider context of the regime's attempt to appease international opinion, which had been outraged in the immediate aftermath of the occupation. The German invasion of the remainder of Czechoslovakia constituted a clear breach of the Munich Agreement. Unlike annexed Austria, the Protectorate formally retained the legal status of an autonomous territory. The Czech government officially continued to exist, and parts of the internal administration remained in the hands of Czech authorities.[24] For the time being, therefore, the Germans exercised a somewhat more moderate rule in the Protectorate. This situation would change rapidly with the outbreak of the war and the concomitant abandonment of all diplomatic considerations. At once, a new wave of terror and arrests, code-named Operation Albrecht I, swept through the region. On September 10, 1939, a transport of more than 550 prisoners from the Protectorate arrived in Dachau. The 113 men among them registered as Jewish prisoners more than doubled the number of Jews from Bohemia and Moravia imprisoned in the camp.[25] The outbreak of the war also affected the fate of Jewish political prisoners initially rounded up in Aktion Gitter who so far had been detained in local Czech prisons. The physician Walter Löbner, for example, was arrested in Prague on March 18, 1939, only days after the German invasion. His protective custody order gave "strong suspicion of high treason against the German people" as the reason for his capture. Due to his status as an active antifascist, the Nazis did not release him and after the outbreak of the war Löbner was transferred to Sachsenhausen concentration camp. An odyssey through various camps and subcamps followed, including Auschwitz, Gross-Rosen, and the Heinkel aircraft works in Oranienburg, until he finally regained his freedom in April 1945.[26]

Among the Protectorate's Jewish population, the SS terror and arrests in the spring and summer of 1939 caused panic and despair. As we learn from contemporary eyewitness accounts, many Jews did not spend the nights in their homes, out of fear of Gestapo raids. Some tried to escape the Germans by illegally crossing the border into Poland. Others were so desperate that they committed suicide. By the end of July 1939 approximately 20,000 Jews had left the country.[27] Reasons for the arrests of Jews in the aftermath of the invasion varied widely, and as we have seen in the analysis of previous such actions, often completely unpolitical people were arrested.[28] In May 1939 the Sopade published reports from a number of provincials towns and villages in Bohemia and Moravia about the arrests of Jews "who were released only on the condition that they give up their businesses and leave the place."[29]

Jews also fell victim to arrests conducted under the pretext of reprisals for casualties and damages suffered by the German occupiers. In all likelihood, the twenty-two Jewish prisoners from Pilsen (Plzeň) who arrived in Dachau on May 17, 1939, were captured in retaliation for the alleged taunting of German soldiers on the town's tram on April 24. To avenge this supposed humiliation, 150 "Marxists" and 150 Jews were rounded up in their homes as well as in public places such as cafés. As historian Livia Roth-kirchen stresses, Jews who lived in localities with large German populations, such as Pilsen, suffered especially from discrimination and anti-Jewish violence.[30] As part of an extensive reprisal action, the Gestapo deported 107 people to the concentration camp from the Kladno region in central Bohemia. The transport, which included leading public figures and five Jewish prisoners, reached Dachau on June 16, 1939, after a three-day detour via Mauthausen.[31] It was put together in retaliation for the killing of the German police sergeant Wilhelm Kniest in Kladno on June 8—an extraordinary event in the early months of the occupation, which the Germans interpreted as a political act, intended to provoke an uprising against them. The man who pulled the trigger was Jan Smudek, a student at Kladno's technical college and a member of the Czech resistance. Despite their intensive search, the Gestapo failed to apprehend him.[32]

Except for those prisoners aboard the Kladno transport, who briefly passed through Mauthausen, Jews from Czechoslovakia were exclusively brought to Dachau concentration camp before the outbreak of the war. Only from late September 1939 onward, when Dachau was temporarily vacated, were they deported to other camps, too. Before prisoners were again sent to the camp in February 1940, Dachau served as a training facility for the SS Death's Head Division. The first 182 Czech Jews arrived in Buchenwald on September 27, 1939, as part of a large clearance transport of over 2,000 men, which brought all of Dachau's 313 Jews to the Thuringian camp.[33] Inside Buchenwald, the Jews from Czechoslovakia were separated from the rest of the Protectorate inmates. The latter enjoyed a special status for a time, including exemption from work and from having their heads shorn, but the Jews were subjected to the same harsh conditions under which all Jewish inmates lived in the camp.[34]

By and large, little is known about the life and death of Jewish prisoners inside the concentration camps between January and August 1939. Testimonies, the main sources of information about the imprisonment conditions and experiences of the Jews, are scarce. As a relatively short period in the history of the concentration camps, sandwiched between two extraordinary events of extreme brutality—the November Pogrom and the outbreak of the war—survivors tended to skip over its comparatively run-of-the-mill, day-to-day violence in their recollections. The Communist Karl Röder, who spent ten years in the Dachau and Flossenbürg camps, wrote after the war that it was the breaks and turning points in camp life that remained in the memory. Events like the arrival of the Austrians in Dachau or the camp's temporary closure after the outbreak of the war "lifted the days on which they happened out of the sea of uniformity." The rest of the time, the prisoners "experienced death like the tides. It came and went, rose and fell, and then again threatened to swallow us all."[35] The experience of these tidal waves of violence, however, was not necessarily connected to clear-cut calendar dates.

Even if, in the bigger picture of camp history, the period immediately preceding the outbreak of the war appears like the calm after—and, at the same time, before—the storm, it must be understood that for the individual prisoner there was, of course, no respite from the everyday terror. Witnessing the mass release of the November Jews, those who stayed behind must have felt an ever-greater despair and a burning sense of injustice in the face of their continuing detention. Dachau inmate Alfred Hübsch described these Jews as an abandoned "remnant," in whose fate no one seemed to take any interest. In the eyes of the SS, "they might as well kick the bucket. Who gave a damn about them?" Estimating their number at about 1,000 in March 1939, Hübsch expressed his compassion when he depicted the Jews returning to their barracks at the end of a day filled with hard labor and abuse. "After the 'Dismiss!' order they dragged themselves back into their block, holding and supporting one another. Their faces and their hands were bloody, full of mud and dirt. Their clothes were wet and torn."[36]

Early 1939 saw an event of great significance for the lives of Jewish prisoners inside the camp take place in Buchenwald. For the first time in the history of this camp, Jews, who had been excluded in principle from positions of influence, were appointed as prisoner functionaries. This new, tiny share in the kapo system of power alleviated their situation slightly, as one of the survivors of Buchenwald's Jew blocks remembered.[37] The change was brought about as a result of a larger reshuffling of functionary positions by which the SS camp leadership reacted to the theft, corruption, and disciplinary infractions that had reached alarming proportions among the "green" ("criminal") kapos in the aftermath of the November Pogrom. Moreover, many of the prisoner functionaries now dismissed had become privy to the SS's own large-scale illegal enrichment via extorted Jewish valuables.[38] The changes in prisoner personnel in Buchenwald in 1939 are proof of the fact that the kapo system was never stable. As we have seen with the death of Dachau's Jewish block elder Heinz Eschen in January 1938, the SS liquidated and replaced functionary prisoners at will. Furthermore, the kapo system was recurrently eroded by shifting alliances, plots, and schemes fought out among the prisoners.[39]

The first Jewish block eldest was installed at the end of January 1939. Walter Rosenbaum from Berlin, who was made responsible for Jewish block 17, bore the green triangle of the "criminals," having been previously convicted for car theft. Soon Jewish political prisoners, and in particular those with a Communist orientation, dominated in functionary positions. Among them were the block eldest August Cohn (block 23), Stefan Heymann (block 3), the Austrian Gustav Herzog (block 16 and others), as well as Emil Carlebach and Rudolf Arndt (block 22).[40] Their appointment was backed and suggested to the SS by the new camp eldest Ernst Frommhold, a Communist prisoner who took office in the spring of 1939, thereby ending the reign of the "criminals" for the time being. In their recruitment of prisoner personnel, the SS often listened to the recommendations of senior functionary prisoners.

The participation of the Jewish inmates in the powers—however limited—bestowed upon functionary prisoners, involved the Buchenwald Jews in what Carlebach described as "the struggle between criminals and politicals." The scramble for power and privileges—in late 1938 over 500 prisoners held functionary posts in Buchenwald—fought out fiercely between "reds" and "greens" was thus carried into the Jews' blocks.[41] Tensions within this prisoner group, which in the late 1930s held a sizable number of inmates categorized as criminals, exploded with new vigor and were fueled by rivalry for the few, much-sought-after posts in the kapo system. Ultimately these conflicts and rifts brought about the fall of the most influential of Buchenwald's Jewish block elders, Rudolf Arndt, whom the SS nicknamed "emperor of the Jews" (*Judenkaiser*). His murder in the camp's quarry on May 3, 1940, was most probably triggered by a denunciation by the "greens," who sought revenge for their exclusion from functionary positions. Mirroring the conflicts that raged between the two groups at large, Jewish inmates with red and green triangles also instigated intrigues and denunciations to block the other side's access to key positions of power and influence. In addition to Arndt, the Buchenwald SS killed other influential or prominent Jewish political prisoners in the first half of 1940, among them Ernst Heilmann, Werner Scholem, and Max Wulkan, a Polish Jew who had functioned as a room eldest. Walter Rosenbaum, said to have been one of Arndt's denouncers, eventually was himself murdered; the SS listed him for a transport to the T4 "euthanasia" center in Bernburg (Saale), where he was killed in March 1942.[42]

Finally, the period immediately preceding the war saw the establishment of the first purpose-built women's concentration camp. Ravensbrück opened on May 15, 1939, with the arrival of almost 1,000 Lichtenburg inmates. On May 21, the first official "head count" numbered 137 female Jewish prisoners.[43] One of them was the Communist activist Ilse Rolfe (later Ilse Rolfe), who had been detained in the concentration camp since the spring of 1936. She remembered Ravensbrück as "a large camp with a capacity of about 2,000 prisoners. The conditions were far worse than in Lichtenburg."[44] Rolfe was released on May 26, 1939, so her memory of Ravensbrück remained sketchy in comparison with the details she provided on the other two women's camps she experienced. To the best of our knowledge, the only other testimony composed by a Jewish woman imprisoned in Ravensbrück before the outbreak of the war is the report of Marianne Wachstein, who arrived in the camp on July 27, 1939. Written in April 1940, while she was hospitalized in Vienna during a temporary absence from the camp, the account describes her brutal treatment in solitary confinement and the antisemitic abuse she suffered from the camp personnel. In contrast to Rolfe, Wachstein did not survive the Holocaust; she was murdered in February 1942 in Bernburg (Saale).[45] Almost thirty Jewish women were deported to Ravenbrück before the end of August 1939. Most of them were registered as race defilers.[46] But as in the men's camps, the number of released Jews outweighed the number of new arrivals during the period before the outbreak of the war. The "head counts" for August 7 and September 26, 1939, recorded 124 and 128 Jewish women, respectively, as being detained in Ravensbrück.[47]

On the eve of the war, the total number of Jews in the SS concentration camps amounted to no more than 1,500 men and women. For Sachsenhausen, the number of Jewish prisoners detained in the camp on August 31, 1939 is documented to have amounted to 247 men. In the cases of Buchenwald and Dachau, the records of the camp administration allow for a calculation of the respective numbers of Jews. While 761 Jews were imprisoned in Buchenwald on August 31, 1939, Dachau held 191. On the whole, the share of Jewish prisoners in the overall prisoner population of the camps,

Figure 6.1 View of the barracks in the Ravensbrück concentration camp,
1940–1941.
Sammlung der Mahn- und Gedenkstätte Ravensbrück/Stiftung Brandenburgische
Gedenkstätten.

which in August 1939 added up to some 21,400 inmates, had fallen back to
well under 10 percent—roughly the same proportion that Jewish prisoners
had made up before the mass imprisonments.[48]

A Glimpse into the Wartime Camps

"The war came, and with it the great turning point in the history of the
concentration camps. But who could then have foreseen the horrifying task
assigned to them as the war went on?" Thus wrote Rudolf Höss in 1947,
facing the gallows in a Polish prison. To him personally, the war had offered new career opportunities. In May 1940 he was appointed the commandant of Auschwitz—a new concentration camp in the German east
that before long became the largest and most notorious of them all—and
as such Höss became one of the top executioners of the wartime camps'
"horrifying tasks."[49] Looking back shortly after liberation to his imprison-

ment in Buchenwald, Benedikt Kautsky, too, found that "the outbreak of the war completely changed the face of the camp." Within weeks, large numbers of Jews began to arrive. Like no other prisoner group, they fell victim to the intensified terror and violence with which the SS marked the German invasion of Poland.[50] During the war, the camp system expanded into a vast network of twenty-three main camp complexes, from which hundreds of satellite camps branched off. Inmate numbers rose starkly. The arrivals from countries conquered by the Wehrmacht internationalized the prisoner populations and turned German nationals into a small minority. In the course of the war the importance of forced labor increased. Initially the SS stepped up the exploitation of prisoners for the production of building materials, and from 1942 it increasingly deployed them in the armament industry.

The outbreak of the war presents a natural cutoff point for this study. A systematic analysis of the history of Jewish prisoners in the wartime camps, which remains a desideratum, demands to be approached with different research questions and strategies than those that have guided my work. It will need to account for the fact that the overwhelming majority of Jews in the wartime camps did not come from German-speaking countries and as such could not have been stripped by the force of camp terror of their— however troubled—sense of belonging to the German people and adherence to German culture. Because the overarching goal of Nazi anti-Jewish policy shifted from expulsion to genocide, any future study of the fate of Jewish prisoners during the war must also investigate in detail the links between the SS concentration camp system and the "Final Solution." From 1942 onward, Jewish inmates confronted a reality of imprisonment that subjected them to systematic biological annihilation on an industrial scale.[51] The possibility of escaping camp terror through emigration from the German sphere of influence no longer existed. In the spring of 1940, Himmler ordered a "general stop to releases of Jewish concentration camp prisoners for the duration of the war." One final exception to this rule was granted to those "whose emigration has already been prepared and who can soon emigrate—Apr[il]—under the condition that they do not give rise to any political or other concerns."[52] Long-term prisoner Hugo Burkhard, held in camp custody ever since his arrival in Dachau in the summer of 1933, was one of the few fortunate ones set free after the outbreak of the war. Released from Buchenwald on March 19, 1940, he boarded the Italian ocean liner SS *Conte Rosso* soon afterward, and sailed to Shanghai—one of the last places where refugees from Nazi terror could still find exile and needed no immigration visa.[53]

As much as both the prisoners and the SS perpetrators may have experienced the outbreak of the Second World War as a qualitative turning point, historians of the concentration camps now mostly concur that developmental changes in the camp system did not constitute a complete break with the past. Astonishingly capable of adapting to changing realities and new situations, the concentration camps assumed new functions without giving up older ones.[54] Accordingly, the history of Jews in the camps, too, is characterized by continuities and discontinuities across its different phases.

Enthusiasm for war was low among the German populace, as the hard times they had endured during and after the Great War were by no means forgotten. In an attempt to mobilize the people, Nazi propaganda blamed the Jews as the instigators of the new military conflict. In general the regime now stepped up the persecution of the Jews. As Germany's internal enemies, Jews living in the Reich were to be punished for alleged provocations, which were perceived as ever more unbearable now that the nation was at war. Heydrich decreed that Jews should be "ruthlessly arrested and transferred to a concentration camp" for "violating orders or behaving in a way hostile to the state."[55] In a similar vein, the Nazi party leadership in Kitzingen-Gerolzhofen declared that "the time has now come to gather all Jews together, confined in a concentration camp, so that they really will no longer be able to have contact with German national comrades"[56] Several violent incidents and assaults against Jews had occurred in the region in early September. Inside the camps, the SS broadcasted speeches by Nazi leaders accusing the Jews of having started the war. This antisemitic propaganda provided the guards with a welcome excuse for severely mistreating the inhabitants of the Jew blocks.[57]

On September 1, 1939, the Sachsenhausen SS informed camp eldest Harry Naujoks that imprisonment conditions were to be tightened due to the outbreak of the war. Effective immediately, food rations were reduced significantly. Prisoners had to move on the double during working hours, and all new arrivals received low-quality wooden clogs instead of leather shoes.[58] In Buchenwald, Jewish inmates were especially disadvantaged by the tightening measures. On September 6, they were forbidden to buy additional food in the camp canteen. From this date onward, Jews received only 400 grams of bread and one liter of soup. Their mail allowance was reduced to one postcard per month.[59]

Figure 6.2 Jewish prisoners in Sachsenhausen stand at attention during a roll call in the "small camp," ca. 1939.
Yad Vashem Photo Archives 2688/9.

The first Jewish prisoners to be deported to the concentration camps in September and October 1939 were Polish Jews residing in the territory of the Reich. The German invasion of Poland had turned the estimated 40,000 Jews of (former) Polish citizenship that still lived in Nazi Germany into enemy aliens; the regime now openly aimed at their total expulsion. On September 7, Heydrich ordered the Gestapo to arrest all male Jews from Poland over the age of sixteen.[60] While a part of the captured men and teenagers were deported directly to the occupied territories, some 2,000 Polish or stateless Jews were sent to Sachsenhausen and Buchenwald.[61] Through the arrivals of further transports with Jews arrested in the Protectorate of Bohemia and Moravia and in Poland, the number of Jewish prisoners increased to about 2,500 in Buchenwald in late October, and to 1,335 in Sachsenhausen on December 30, 1939.[62] In both camps Polish Jews were detained under lethal conditions in an isolated zone secluded from the main camp.

While spatial separation can be seen as a continuity with the prewar period, the atrocities perpetrated in these "special camps" of autumn 1939 exceeded in brutality the mass violence endured by the November Jews in the winter of 1938–1939. In Sachsenhausen, the SS locked up Polish-Jewish prisoners in barracks 37 to 39 of the small camp. Doors and windows were sealed, food rations reduced at random or completely withheld, using the lavatory was strictly regimented, and no medical treatment was provided. SS men frequently stormed the barracks to severly abuse and even kill their helpless victims. During weeks of total isolation, which lasted for the duration of the Poland Campaign, 35 Jewish prisoners lost their lives in Sachsenhausen. By March 1940 the death toll had risen to over 300 Jews. Only a small minority of the Polish Jews of Sachsenhausen were released and survived the war.[63] One of them was Leon Szalet from Berlin, who was arrested on September 13, 1939, after an unsuccessful attempt to escape to Great Britain. He was sent to Sachsenhausen that same day, as one of 534 Polish Jews rounded up across the city. Szalet's detailed contemporary report of the atrocities they suffered constitutes one of the very few testimonies given by a member of this prisoner group.[64]

Like the Polish Jews of Sachsenhausen, those deported to Buchenwald were also imprisoned in a secluded special camp, made up of four large tents and a wooden barrack. It contained 438 Polish citizens as well as 1,991 Jews who arrived in Buchenwald during the months of September and October.[65] Among the latter were 1,035 Polish and stateless Jews arrested in Vienna. Prior to their transport to Buchenwald they had been kept in a police detention camp provisionally set up in the city's Prater Stadium. Here, 440 of them were subjected to a so-called race-anthropological examination conducted by the staff of Vienna's Museum of Natural History. In order to complete the Museum's exhibition on "The Spiritual and Racial Appearance of the Jews" the scientists photographed and measured the prisoners, and made plaster casts of some of their faces.[66]

The Buchenwald tent camp soon became overcrowded, and appalling living conditions led to mass fatalities; a dysentery epidemic broke out in late October. The SS sealed off the special camp and intentionally starved the prisoners. Eight hundred men had died by the end of 1939.[67] The extreme situation in Sachsenhausen and Buchenwald clearly shows how the outbreak of the war further aggravated the living conditions for Jewish prisoners. The escalation of anti-Jewish violence during the conquest and later occupation of Poland forms the backdrop for this. The ideology that accompanied this first of Nazi Germany's racial wars depicted the enemy population as "subhuman" Slavs.[68] Increased SS terror, illness, and starvation claimed the lives of hundreds of concentration camp inmates by the first months of the war—among them were many Jewish and non-Jewish Poles.

In continuity with prewar camp terror, events outside the concentration camps continued to serve the SS as pretexts to abuse Jewish prisoners. As Leon Szalet remembered, "The concentration camp's SS staff recorded every event somehow connected to the Eastern Campaign with the precision of a seismograph. Our bodies were the scrolls on which the SS seismograph wrote, our blood was the stylus."[69] Although no Jews participated in the killing of German civilians in the Polish town of Bydgoszcz on September 3, 1939, the "Bloody Sunday of Bromberg" sparked anti-Jewish violence in Sachsenhausen and Buchenwald. Szalet remembered that on the march from the Oranienburg train station to the camp, Jews "had to pose as the alleged murderers from Bromberg." Curious onlookers insulted and maltreated them.[70]

On November 9, 1939, Jewish concentration camp prisoners fell victim to the most brutal "revenge" for Georg Elser's failed attempt on Hitler's life in the Munich Bürgerbräukeller the previous evening. Despite the fact that the assassin was not Jewish and had acted alone, Jews were regarded as having been behind the attack. In Buchenwald, retaliatory violence took the form of a mass execution, the kind of which the concentration camp had never seen before. Without orders from above, commandant Karl Koch had twenty-one Jewish prisoners shot dead in the camp's quarry. The victims were mostly younger men in their twenties and thirties who had been randomly selected from the blocks of the German and Austrian Jews housed in the main camp. When reporting the incident to his superiors, Koch used a well-established cover story: The Jews "had attempted a mutiny" and were "shot while trying to escape." The SS imposed a period of isolation and hunger upon the remainder of Buchenwald's Jewish prisoners, which lasted for several days and claimed further casualties.[71]

In Ravensbrück, Jewish women also suffered for the failed assassination. They were isolated in their barrack, block 11, for almost a month. A mail embargo was imposed upon them, and the daily roll calls and inspections, which were now carried out inside the block, exposed them to increased violence. In her 1947 witness statement, former prisoner Ida Hirschkron accused Emma Zimmer, a particularly violent female guard, of both verbal and physical maltreatment throughout the isolation period: "When she entered the block our hearts beat quicker. There was a storm of the foulest abuse such as 'Jewish swine,' 'Jewish rabble,' and 'lazy lot of Jews.' At the same time, Zimmer beat us with all her force, indiscriminately, whoever was near her. This went on until 3 Dec. 39."[72] In Sachsenhausen, the SS assaulted the Jew blocks during the night of November 9, maltreating the prisoners so brutally that a number of them later died from their injuries. According to Szalet, "the block leaders were feeding on a blood frenzy . . . when they began trampling on us, jumping on our bodies with all force as if they wanted to stamp us to the grounds, we started to scream terribly."[73]

Finally, when reading Szalet's testimony as well as others, it becomes apparent that Polish-Jewish prisoners, in an attempt to restore their dignity and to cope with their traumatic experience of victimization in the concentration camp, rationalized SS terror in a slightly different way than their fellow sufferers from the Reich did. While antisemitic violence challenged German Jews not only as Jews but also as Germans, Jewish prisoners from other countries did not have to defend their national identity (however troubled) with the same urgency. In their condemnation of SS terror, they could thus more easily interpret the camp as "a German hell," to quote Sachsenhausen prisoner Yehoshuah Friedmann. Szalet, too, was full of disgust for the Germans when he tried to make sense of the horrors of the camp: "My conviction deepened that the inhuman cruelty that I had witnessed was neither instilled into [the SS men] nor ideologically motivated, as so many . . . believe. To me it rather appeared to be the outcome of an innate and a uniquely German instinct, as if this cruelty had not been created by the Nazi worldview but National Socialism had merely brought a preexisting national character to the forefront."[74] His denunciation of the German "national character" ultimately helped the author distance himself from the trauma he had lived through. Arguably, such methods of "othering" were not naturally available to German Jews, some of whom were fighting fiercely against their devaluation from "Germans" into "Jews," violently executed by the SS in the camps. Future research on Jewish prisoners' various responses to the concentration camp during wartime will need to probe and quantify this observation. Leon Szalet, for his part, survived the concentration camp. Thanks to his daughter's relentless efforts to organize his emigration, he was set free from Sachsenhausen on May 7, 1940. The two of them boarded a ship to Shanghai only days afterward.[75]

The great majority of Jewish prisoners detained in the concentration camps in 1938–1939 were released. Those who had the means emigrated from Nazi Germany and survived the war. After the November Pogrom, the SS, Security Police, and SD took the lead in enforcing the regime's anti-Jewish policy. The expulsion of Jews was enforced by the establishment of the Reich Central Office for Jewish Emigration in early 1939, while camp terror was used to deter Jews from fleeing the country without the necessary exit papers. After the outbreak of the Second World War, opportunities to escape camp terror through emigration were significantly limited for Jewish prisoners. On October 23, 1941, the Nazi state prohibited any further German-Jewish emigration. By that time the regime's Jewish policies had shifted from expulsion toward annihilation. Millions of European Jews fell into the hands of the Nazis with Hitler's ongoing military conquest of the Continent. The concentration camps became sites of forced labor and mass death for many hundreds of thousands of them.

CONCLUSION

The history of Jews in the concentration camps is usually told from a post-Holocaust perspective: Mass murder in the gas chambers, pictures of heaps of dead bodies or mass graves overshadow the comparatively prosaic prewar years. This study has reevaluated the arrest and imprisonment of Jewish camp inmates before the war and demonstrated that this period is much more than a prelude to the Holocaust. It is a crucial phase of transition, when discrimination still took place right in the midst of German society, its members responsible for working toward or preventing the cementation of the fateful enemy category of "the Jew."

We have seen how the Nazis, from early on, included Jews in their campaign of terror. The rationales for their arrests and imprisonment in early concentration camps were numerous. While those who actively fought the Nazi movement constituted the very first and most obvious targets, protective custody and camp terror were also used to persecute "ordinary" Jews. Extensively and seamlessly, Jews of various backgrounds were immediately drawn into the initial dragnet of targeted enemies. Hence, we find among the camp inmates of 1933–1934 not only left-wing activists, politicians, and political journalists with Jewish roots but also lawyers, merchants, cattle dealers, and other businessmen brutally excluded from their professions for being "non-Aryans." Furthermore, there were Jewish men—and later also women—defamed as race defilers for their relations with non-Jewish partners. Others ended up in camp custody after they had been denounced for their criticism of the regime or simply because they were considered "unwanted," like the teenagers from the Wolzig Youth Home. In later years, Jews were arrested after their return to Germany from longer stays abroad. As returning emigrants they endangered the Nazis' vision of a Third Reich "free of Jews." Some Jews persecuted as homosexuals were also deported to the camps. In 1938 large numbers of Jewish camp inmates were arrested as being asocials or work-shy.

By using the categories "protective custody," "instructive custody," and "preventive custody" the National Socialists punished nonconformist behavior and, at the same time, propagated the illusion that their repressive policies were a just measure to maintain law and order. Inherently nonracist political and criminological enemy conceptions were employed to legitimize the arrests of Jews in concentration camps. A pseudo-legal set of categories and orders, framed loosely enough for "the Jewish enemy" to be included, was expanded to a racist practice of persecution and a lasting criminalization of the arrestees. Over the years, the arrests of Jews and their deportations to concentration camps became more systematic and coordinated. From the wider range of motives and agencies responsible for the isolation of Jews in the early concentration camps—SA, SS, Gestapo, local NSDAP organizations, state authorities, police stations, welfare institutions, and individual members of the public—arrest and release was gradually centralized in the hands of the Gestapo and Kripo, acting with the objectives of pressuring Jews into emigration and of expropriating Jewish businesses. The concentration camps played an important role in driving the forced emigration of Jews from Nazi Germany. Starting in the spring of 1935, with the persecution of Jewish returning emigrants, a policy evolved that used the camp as a threat to forcibly remove the Jews from the Nazi "people's community." Gradually emigration became the only valid condition for release, and the only way out of the camps for Jewish prisoners led into exile.

Camp terror against Jews in the prewar years was embedded into a broader context of anti-Jewish measures. Although suffering in the camps was undoubtedly the most extreme in nature, Jews everywhere had to cope with many forms of discrimination, physical abuse, and hidden violence, all gradually leading toward "social death."[1] Before they even reached the camp gates, Jews had to endure a humiliating process of arrest, sometimes involving public pillory processions through their hometowns. Severe mistreatment could occur at police stations or on prisoner transports en route to the camp—here, the Austrian transports of spring 1938 stand out as particularly violent. After their release, Jewish camp inmates returned to a broken outside world, burdened with the stigma of criminality and pressured to leave their homeland. Precisely because camp terror was intertwined with other measures of persecution—we saw this, in particular, with the enforcement of professional bans against Jewish jurists as well as at the Gestapo's practice to "correct" legal sanctions—Jews in Nazi Germany always had to fear deportation to a concentration camp. Like other groups in so-ciety that found themselves in dangerous opposition to the Hitler regime, they were most likely to grasp the true nature of the camp early on. In his diary Victor Klemperer records the brutal murder of a Communist pris-oner in the Königstein concentration camp in April 1933, noting that it had been covered up as a deadly case of dysentery. His sardonic remarks clearly demonstrate that he did not buy into the regime's official image of the camp—and neither did those with whom he discussed this and other vio-lent incidents of camp terror.[2] As Paul Moore established in his study of German popular opinion of the concentration camps, "Everybody in Ger-many knew of the Nazi concentration camps." As visible and audible sites of terror, "they had permeated German consciousness, as early as 1933."[3]

Inside the camps the presence of Jewish prisoners quickly became con-stitutive for the "order of terror." From the beginning, Jews ranked at the bottom of the prisoner hierarchy. Together with Jehovah's Witnesses, pris-oners classified as homosexuals, and prominent representatives of the workers' movement, Jews were singled out for degrading punitive labor, public humiliation, and violent abuse. In contrast to some of the other groups of victims, their "racial otherness" precluded Jews from the "reeducation" propagated in the Nazi-controlled media as the main function of the camps. In order to downplay the crimes perpetrated at these sites of terror, the re-gime presented the camps as a necessary evil in its radical efforts to fight Bolshevism and reintegrate into the emergent "people's community" the "savaged Marxists" and "German brothers still standing aside."[4] Jews, on the other hand, were exempt from any such coercive "betterment." For them the camp functioned as a public affirmation of their outlawed status. As an extrajudicial space, it offered the opportunity to apply against them harsh measures—the execution of violence and murder.[5]

In the course of the prewar years, SA and SS guards developed strate-gies to forcefully turn Germans into Jews. Besides the segregation of Jews into special work commandos for filthy and heavy labor, the procedure of housing Jewish camp inmates in separate Jew blocks was gradually estab-lished. External markers affixed to clothes—standardized in the late 1930s with the system of color-coded triangular badges—were introduced. Through these measures Jews were rendered visible and forced together under the racial stigma. As an act of brutal collectivization, the creation of broadly defined groups of prisoners simplified complex and heterogeneous individual backgrounds of persecution and facilitated the identification of "the Jewish enemy." Time and again, however, camp guards confronted individual Jewish prisoners who because of their physical features or biographical characteristics manifestly contradicted antisemitic stereotypes. These situations expose the difficulties of establishing the Jewish enemy category even in the camp's context of violence.

The persecuted resisted their stigmatization as "Jew pigs" and "enemies of the German nation." The evaluation of a large body of testimonies has revealed Jewish prisoners' various strategies of self-assertion in the face of violent degradation. Many political prisoners with Jewish roots could connect to the camps' Communist underground established to alleviate conditions for comrades. Some of them were involved in smuggling out of the camps reports documenting the Nazis' crimes. Other Jewish prisoners responded on an individual level to preserve their identities as patriotic Germans and their dignity as sovereign actors. Many protested against the camp's criminalizing effects by inverting their defamation, highlighting the perpetrators as the real criminals. Fewer resorted to religion as a source of strength, as only a minority came from traditional religious backgrounds. Some Jews remained unbroken by their camp imprisonment, like young Eva Mamlok, who continued her resistance against the regime after her release. Older prisoners like Ludwig Bendix unwillingly escaped into exile, where they then often felt "unsettled and out of place."[6] Bendix reached Palestine in 1937 and immigrated to the United States a decade later. His frustration over his destroyed career never left this Jewish lawyer. As his son remembered, in Bendix's "later years, his hopes . . . were overshadowed by the profound failure of German-Jewish assimilation. That sense of failure stayed with him during the rest of his life."[7]

As a result of the sociopolitical diversity of Jewish prisoners, the inhabitants of the Jew blocks were not automatically bound to one another as a community with a shared destiny. As was the case with other prisoner groups forced together by Nazi ideology, different political worldviews and different social and cultural backgrounds in principle did not render feelings and acts of solidarity impossible, but they complicated the experience of living together. In the camps' context of violence, conflicts between Jewish prisoners seriously undermined their efforts to get along and manage collectively the uncertainties of imprisonment and its day-to-day adversities.

By using the concentration camps as murderous instruments of deterrence, humiliation, and expulsion, the Gestapo and the SS helped to transform German Jews from a heterogeneous minority group within society to outsiders perceived as a homogeneous group of enemies to be excluded from German communal life. Concentration camps, therefore, helped to shape an enemy category that was still in the making. While pursuing an overarching antisemitism, the National Socialists in these ways also strengthened the cohesion of the remaining "people's community." New allegiances, through complicity in criminality, could effectively be created. Those carrying out the arrests of Jews gradually became accustomed to isolating and treating them violently—as did those denouncing their Jewish neighbors, business partners, or former lovers to the authorities. Using camp terror against the Jews, the Nazis tested the limits of their extending power while seeking maximum influence over the German public. By exposing and violently discriminating Jews as a presumed common enemy, the regime sought to fortify its bond with all those whom it counted in the envisaged people's community.

With the definition of Jews as "not German," as alien and foreign, as opponents and enemies, the fight against them was legitimized and every anti-Jewish measure became a response to a perceived provocation.[8] When Hitler gave his infamous Reichstag speech to celebrate the sixth anniversary of the Nazi seizure of power on January 30, 1939, he drew heavily on the Jewish enemy type, the *Weltfeind* against whom war must be waged, a war at whose end he saw "not the Bolshevization of the earth and thereby a victory of Jewry but the annihilation of the Jewish race in Europe."[9] Concentration camp terror had helped to pave the way for this racial war. A society that had grown accustomed to police-state methods of arrest and the detention of Jews at extralegal sites of terror, depicted as necessary to protect and cleanse the people's community from the perceived Jewish threat, seemed more likely to follow into a war whose ultimate end lay in the elimination of that threat.

No straight lines exist between the systematic mass murder of Jews in the concentration camps of the war and the "special treatment" of the prewar period. The Holocaust, which profoundly changed the system of the concentration camps, was a product of ever-radicalizing violent dynamics of persecution unleashed in the course of Germany's war of annihilation against the Soviet Union.[10] In the 1930s the transformation of concentration camps into sites of mass extermination of Jews was unforeseeable. However, Jews' perilous status at the bottom of the prisoner hierarchy was built into the camp system from the very beginning. As outcasts among the outcast, Jewish prisoners were set apart from others and branded as enemies of the German people. From early on, Jews in the concentration camps had to fear for their lives. The percentage of Jews among the dozens, later hundreds, of deaths was always disproportionally high. All this cannot explain the Holocaust, but it helps to understand why, in the course of seven long prewar years of camp terror against Jewish prisoners, the perpetrators, from the rank-and-file camp guards to men holding the highest ranks in the SS police apparatus, grew accustomed to the notion that the life of a Jew in the camp was not worth much. As members of the *Waffen* SS, many were later involved in the mass killings of Jews outside the concentration camps. Without this habituation to the systematic discrimination, exploitation, and violation of Jewish concentration camp inmates, the transition to systematic mass murder, which only the war could enable, would probably not have happened so quickly. When Nazi Germany embarked on war in the autumn of 1939, the Jewish enemy category had been firmly established inside the camps.

For the majority of Jews interned during the whole period of the Nazi regime's twelve-year existence, the concentration camps were sites of murder and death. Most of the camps' 1.2 million Jewish victims were killed at Auschwitz. Around 400,000 were detained as prisoners of German concentration camps in the official sense.[11] Instead of being murdered upon arrival, they received prisoner numbers and color-coded markers, and were integrated into the camp system. The great majority of these "regular" Jewish inmates were deported to the concentration camps in wartime and did not survive. By contrast, probably about a tenth—about 40,000 Jews—were held in the prewar camps. While an estimated 2,000 to 3,000 of them died—either inside the camps or from the consequences of their imprisonment—most of the Jewish prisoners of the prewar period stayed alive and were able to escape Nazi persecution.

APPENDIX

SS Ranks and U.S. Army Equivalents

Schutzstaffel (SS)	U.S. Army
SS Generals	
Reichsführer SS	General of the Army
SS Oberstgruppenführer	General
SS Obergruppenführer	Lieutenant General
SS Gruppenführer	Major General
SS Brigadeführer	Brigadier General
SS Officers	
SS Oberführer	
SS Standartenführer	Colonel
SS Obersturmbannführer	Lieutenant Colonel
SS Sturmbannführer	Major
SS Hauptsturmführer	Captain
SS Obersturmführer	First Lieutenant
SS Untersturmführer	Second Lieutenant
SS Non-Commissioned Officers (NCOs)	
SS Hauptscharführer	Master Sergeant
SS Oberscharführer	Sergeant First Class
SS Scharführer	Staff Sergeant
SS Unterscharführer	Sergeant
SS Soldiers	
SS Rottenführer	Corporal
SS Sturmmann	Lance Corporal
SS Mann	Private
SS Anwärter	Recruit

ABBREVIATIONS

AO	Archiv des NS Dokumentationszentrums Rheinland-Pfalz / KZ Osthofen (Archives of Osthofen Memorial Site)
AS	Archiv Gedenkstätte und Museum Sachsenhausen (Memorial and Museum Sachsenhausen Archives)
BArch	Bundesarchiv Koblenz
BArchB	Bundesarchiv Berlin
BayHStA M	Bayerisches Hauptstaatsarchiv München
BayStA A	Bayerisches Staatsarchiv Amberg
BayStA M	Bayerisches Staatsarchiv München
BayStA W	Bayerisches Staatsarchiv Würzburg
BLHA	Brandenburgisches Landeshauptarchiv
bpk	Bildarchiv Preussischer Kulturbesitz
BPP	Bayerische Politische Polizei (Bavarian Political Police)
BwA	Archiv der Stiftung Gedenkstätten Buchenwald und Mittelbau-Dora
	(Buchenwald and Mittelbau-Dora Memorials Foundation Archives)
CJ	Archiv der Stiftung Neue Synagoge Berlin
CV	Centralverein deutscher Staatsbürger jüdischen Glaubens (Central Association of German Citizens of Jewish Faith)
CZA	Central Zionist Archives
DaA	Archiv der KZ-Gedenkstätte Dachau (Dachau Concentration Camp Memorial Site Archives)
DStP	Deutsche Staatspartei (German State Party)
GDALi	Archiv der KZ-Gedenkstätte Lichtenburg (Archives of the Lichtenburg Concentration Camp Memorial)
Gestapo	Geheime Staatspolizei (Secret State Police)
GStA PK	Geheimes Staatsarchiv Preussischer Kulturbesitz

HessStA D	Hessisches Staatsarchiv Darmstadt
IGNN	Informationsstelle zur Geschichte des Nationalsozialismus in Nordhessen
IfZ	Institut für Zeitgeschichte Archives
IKL	Inspektion der Konzentrationslager (Inspectorate of the Concentration Camps)
IMT	International Military Tribunal (Nuremberg)
ITS	International Tracing Service
KJVD	Kommunistischer Jugendverband Deutschlands (Young Communist League of Germany)
JFB	Jüdischer Frauenbund (Jewish Women's League)
KL / KZ	Konzentrationslager (Concentration Camp)
KPD	Kommuistische Partei Deutschlands (German Communist Party)
KPO	Kommunistische Partei (Opposition) (Communist Party Opposition)
Kripo	Kriminalpolizei (Criminal Police)
LArch Berlin	Landesarchiv Berlin
LArch NRW R	Landesarchiv Nordrhein-Westfalen Abteilung Rheinland
LArch Sp	Landesarchiv Speyer
LBIA	Leo Baeck Institute Archives
LBIYB	*Leo Baeck Institute Year Book*
NHStA H	Niedersächsisches Hauptstaatsarchiv Hannover
NSDAP	Nationalsozialistische Deutsche Arbeiter Partei (National Socialist German Workers' Party)
NSDStB	Nationalsozialistischer Deutscher Studentenbund (National Socialist German Students' League)
NSF	NS-Frauenschaft (National Socialist Women's Association)
NStA O	Niedersächsisches Landesarchiv—Staatsarchiv Osnabrück
RFSS	Reichsführer SS (Reich Leader SS) Heinrich Himmler
RGBl	*Reichsgesetzblatt*
RjF	Reichsbund jüdischer Frontsoldaten (Reich Federation of Jewish Front Soldiers)
RKPA	Reichskriminalpolizeiamt (Reich Criminal Police Office)
RM	Reichsmark
RMJ	Reichsjustizministerium (Reich Ministry of Justice)

RSHA	Reichssicherheitshauptamt (Reich Security Head Office)
RStGB	Reichsstrafgesetzbuch (Reich Criminal Code)
SA	Sturmabteilung (Storm Troopers)
SächsHStA D	Sächsisches Hauptstaatsarchiv Dresden
SAJ	Sozialistische Arbeiter-Jugend (Socialist Workers' Youth)
SAP	Sozialistische Arbeiterpartei (Socialist Workers' Party)
SD	Sicherheitsdienst (Security Service)
Sipo	Sicherheitspolizei (Security Police)
Sopade	Sozialdemokratische Partei Deutschlands (Social Democratic Party of Germany in exile)
SPD	Sozialdemokratische Partei Deutschlands (Social Democratic Party of Germany)
SS	Schutzstaffel (Protection Squad)
ThHStA W	Thüringisches Hauptstaatsarchiv Weimar
ULAP	Universum-Landesausstellungspark (Universal State Exhibition Park)
USHMMA	United States Holocaust Memorial Museum Archives
VEJ	Project Edition *Verfolgung und Ermordung der europäischen Juden durch das nationalsozialistische Deutschland, 1933–1945*
VfZ	*Vierteljahreshefte für Zeitgeschichte*
WL	Wiener Library
WVHA	Wirtschaftsverwaltungshauptamt (Business and Administration Main Office)
YVA	Yad Vashem Archives
ZfG	*Zeitschrift für Geschichtswissenschaft*

NOTES

Introduction

Epigraphs: Julius Meyer, *Buchenwald*, 1940, Wiener Library London (WL), P.II.d.No.77, 77–79. Translations throughout are mine, unless otherwise noted.

1. Transports from Frankfurt brought 2,621 Jewish men to Buchenwald in November 1938. See Harry Stein, "Das Sonderlager im Konzentrationslager Buchenwald nach den Pogromen 1938," in Monica Kingreen, ed., *Nach der Kristallnacht: Jüdisches Leben und antijüdische Politik in Frankfurt am Main, 1938–1945* (Frankfurt, 1999), 28–29.

2. SS: Schutzstaffel; Protection Squad. For acronyms and other abbreviations, see the Abbreviations in the endmatter. For English equivalents of SS rank titles, see the Appendix.

3. See Meyer, *Buchenwald*, 40, 61–62, 129. Alfred Siegfried Meyer died in Buchenwald on November 19, 1938. See also Stein, "Sonderlager," 49.

4. Meyer, *Buchenwald*, 128–129.

5. Of more than 50,000 Jewish emigrants from Germany and Austria who had reached Great Britain by 1940, "thousands had already been imprisoned in German concentration camps." See Miriam Kochan, *Britain's Internees in the Second World War* (London, 1983), 2; see also 18.

6. See Nikolaus Wachsmann, "The Dynamics of Destruction: The Development of the Concentration Camps, 1933–1945," in Jane Caplan and Nikolaus Wachsmann, eds., *Concentration Camps in Nazi Germany: The New Histories* (London, 2010), 17.

7. See Raul Hilberg, *The Destruction of the European Jews* (New York, 1985), 53–55.

8. See Karl A. Schleunes, *The Twisted Road to Auschwitz: Nazi Policy toward German Jews, 1933–39* (London, 1972).

9. In differentiating between these periods, the Holocaust is understood as the period of systematic mass murder of every Jewish woman, man, and child within the German sphere of influence, euphemistically referred to by the perpetrators as the "Final Solution" and launched in the months after the

attack on the Soviet Union in June 1941. The term itself, derived from the Greek *holokauston* ("burnt whole"), is problematic because it associates genocide with religious sacrifice. It is, however, used and given preference here over the terms "Shoah" and the more neutral "genocide of the Jews of Europe," because, as Walter Laqueur points out, "in the English speaking world the word is so deeply rooted that it is impractical to deviate from it." See Walter Laqueur, "In Place of a Preface," in *The Holocaust Encyclopedia*, ed. Walter Laqueur (New Haven, CT, 2001), xiii.

10. Fritz Stern, contribution to panel discussion, quoted in Martin Broszat et al., eds., *Deutschlands Weg in die Diktatur: Internationale Konferenz zur national-sozialistischen Machtübernahme im Reichstagsgebäude zu Berlin; Referate und Diskussionen; Ein Protokoll* (Berlin, 1983), 141.

11. For criticism on hindsight condemnations of Jewish reactions to Nazism, see Werner T. Angress, *Between Fear & Hope: Jewish Youth in the Third Reich* (New York, 1988), 3; Marion A. Kaplan, *Between Dignity and Despair: Jewish Life in Nazi Germany* (New York, 1998), 16; Moshe Zimmermann, *Deutsche gegen Deutsche* (Berlin, 2008), 15–16. For an example of a historian's use of moral judgment, see John V. H. Dippel, *Bound upon a Wheel of Fire: Why So Many German Jews Made the Tragic Decision to Remain in Nazi Germany* (London, 1996).

12. Kaplan, *Between Dignity and Despair*, 39. See also, 4, 9.

13. See Gershom Scholem, "Wider den Mythos vom deutsch-jüdischen Gespräch" (1964), in *Judaica II* (Frankfurt, 1970), 7–12, and Scholem, *Von Berlin nach Jerusalem: Jugenderinnerungen* (Frankfurt, 1994), 30–31. See also Samuel Moyn, "German Jewry and the Question of Identity: Historiography and Theory," *Leo Baeck Institute Year Book* 41 (1996): 291–308.

14. See Michael A. Meyer, ed., *German-Jewish History in Modern Times*, vol. 4: *Renewal and Destruction, 1918–1945* (New York, 1998), 30, 32, 91.

15. See Rainer Liedtke and David Rechter, eds., *Towards Normality? Acculturation and Modern German Jewry* (Tübingen, 2003).

16. See Shulamit Volkov, "Antisemitismus als kultureller Code," in *Antisemitismus als kultureller Code: Zehn Essays* (Munich, 2000), 13–36.

17. Foundation appeal of the CV, 1893, quoted in Eva G. Reichmann, "Der Centralverein deutscher Staatsbürger jüdischen Glaubens" (1930), in *Grösse und Verhängnis deutsch-jüdischer Existenz: Zeugnisse einer tragischen Begegnung* (Heidelberg, 1974), 23.

18. Eva G. Reichmann, "Vom Sinn deutsch-jüdischen Seins" (1934), in *Existenz*, 59.

19. See Hans Reichmann, *Deutscher Bürger und verfolgter Jude: Novemberpogrom und KZ Sachsenhausen, 1937 bis 1939*, edited by Michael Wildt (Munich, 1998).

20. See letter from Gershom Scholem to Walter Benjamin, March 29, 1935, in *Walter Benjamin, Gershom Scholem, Briefwechsel 1933–1940*, ed. Gershom Scholem (Frankfurt, 1980), 194.

21. Scholem, *Von Berlin nach Jerusalem*, 181.

22. See Falk Pingel, *Häftlinge unter SS-Herrschaft: Widerstand, Selbstbehauptung und Vernichtung im Konzentrationslager* (Hamburg, 1978), 95–96.

23. For an all-encompassing account of the history of Jews in modern Germany and Austria, see Meyer, *German-Jewish History*, vols. 3–4.

24. See Angelika Königseder, "Die Entwicklung des KZ-Systems," in Wolfgang Benz and Barbara Distel, eds., *Der Ort des Terrors: Geschichte der nationalsozialistischen Konzentrationslager*, vol. 1: *Die Organisation des Terrors* (Munich, 2005), 30–32. Historians discuss the terminology with which to signify the extralegal detention sites of the years 1933–1934. Whereas the somewhat exculpatory term "wild camps," coined by the former chief of the Prussian Gestapo Rudolf Diels, has generally been discarded, there is continued disagreement about whether the term "concentration camp" can be applied for this period. In her structural-organizational history of the camps, Karin Orth strongly urges a strict differentiation between the camps of the early period and the SS concentration camps subordinated under the SS Inspectorate of the Concentration Camps (IKL). To designate the first, she has coined the term "early camps," which has since been used by other scholars. Relativizations of this narrow typology are made by historians like Carina Baganz and Irene Mayer-von-Götz, who, in the decade after Orth's study, extensively researched the prewar history of the camps and found much continuity between the IKL camps and those never administered by the IKL. Signifying that many features of the "early camps" persisted under the IKL, they advanced the term "early concentration camps." To follow in their wake makes sense for a study like this, which puts great emphasis on analyzing the reality inside the camps and the experiences of the prisoners, for whom it was secondary which institution officially ran the regime of terror. Although I will therefore give preference to the term "early concentration camps," I will, in the interest of readability and style, sometimes also use "early camps." See Rudolf Diels, *Lucifer ante portas: Zwischen Severing und Heydrich* (Zurich, 1949), 190; Johannes Tuchel, *Konzentrationslager: Organisationsgeschichte und Funktion der "Inspektion der Konzentrationslager," 1934–1938* (Boppard, 1991), 38–43; Karin Orth, *Das System der nationalsozialistischen Konzentrationslager: Eine politische Organisationsgeschichte* (Hamburg, 1999), 26; Carina Baganz, *Erziehung zur "Volksgemeinschaft"? Die frühen Konzentrationslager in Sachsen, 1933/34–1937* (Berlin, 2005); Irene Mayer-von Götz, *Terror im Zentrum der Macht: Die frühen Konzentrationslager in Berlin, 1933/34–1936* (Berlin, 2008).

25. Of the forty-four early camps presented in greater detail in the first three volumes on the history of the concentration camps edited by Wolfgang Benz and Barbara Distel, the imprisonment of Jews can be documented for at least twenty-five sites, among them Breitenau, the Emsland camps, Heuberg, Kislau, Oranienburg, Osthofen, Sonnenburg, and Turenne-Kaserne. See Wolfgang Benz and Barbara Distel, eds., *Terror ohne System: Die ersten Konzentrationslager im Nationalsozialismus, 1933–1935* (Berlin, 2001); Benz and Distel, eds., *Herrschaft und Gewalt: Frühe Konzentrationslager, 1933–1939* (Berlin, 2002); and Benz and Distel, eds., *Instrumentarium der Macht: Frühe Konzentrationslager, 1933–1937* (Berlin, 2003).

26. Special camp order for the Esterwegen prisoner camp issued by Theodor Eicke, August 1, 1934, Archives of the United States Holocaust Memorial Museum (USHMMA), RG-11001 M.20, Reel 91, Fond 1367, Opis 2, Folder 19, 4, emphasis in the original. Research assumes that this order was issued as early as October 1, 1933, in Dachau. See Pingel, *Häftlinge unter SS-Herrschaft*, 40, 240.

27. Address by Heinrich Himmler to the *Staatsräte*, March 5, 1936, Bundesarchiv Berlin (BArchB), NS 19/4003, quoted in Tuchel, *Konzentrationslager*, 300. See also 298–299.

28. See Jane Caplan, "Gender and the Concentration Camps," in Caplan and Wachsmann, *Camps in Nazi Germany*, 83.

29. Ibid., 83, 85.

30. See Pingel, *Häftlinge unter SS-Herrschaft*, 91; Jürgen Matthäus, "Verfolgung, Ausbeutung, Vernichtung: Jüdische Häftlinge im System der Konzentrationslager," in Günter Morsch and Susanne zur Nieden, eds., *Jüdische Häftlinge im Konzentrationslager Sachsenhausen, 1936 bis 1945* (Berlin, 2004), 66.

31. The census of June 16, 1933, counted 499,700 Jews in Germany (0.77 percent of the population). In 1934 there were 190,492 Jews registered as living in Austria (2.8 percent of the population), 90 percent of them in Vienna. See Götz Aly and Karl Heinz Roth, *Die restlose Erfassung: Volkszählen, Identifizieren, Aussondern im Nationalsozialismus* (Berlin, 1984), 57; Meyer, *German-Jewish History*, 4:30, 32, 91.

32. See Wolfgang Sofsky, *The Order of Terror: The Concentration Camp* (Princeton, NJ, 1997).

33. See Hans Beimler, *Four Weeks in the Hands of Hitler's Hell-Hounds: The Nazi Murder Camp of Dachau* (London, 1933), 22, 27.

34. See Paul Moore, "German Popular Opinion on the Nazi Concentration Camps, 1933–1939" (PhD dissertation, Birkbeck, University of London, 2010), 146.

35. Walter Tausk, *Breslauer Tagebuch, 1933–1940* (Leipzig, 1995), 94–95.

36. See Orth, *Das System*, 343–348; Wachsmann, "Dynamics," 25.

37. See Detlef Garbe, "Absonderung, Strafkommandos und spezifischer Terror: Jüdische Gefangene in nationalsozialistischen Konzentrationslagern," in Arno Herzig and Ina Lorenz, eds., *Verdrängung und Vernichtung der Juden unter dem Nationalsozialismus* (Hamburg, 1992), 174; Franciszek Piper, "Die Rolle des Lagers Auschwitz bei der Verwirklichung der nationalsozialistischen Ausrottungspolitik: Die doppelte Funktion von Auschwitz als Konzentrationslager und als Zentrum der Judenvernichtung," in Ulrich Herbert et al., eds., *Die nationalsozialistischen Konzentrationslager: Entwicklung und Struktur* (Göttingen, 1998), 1:390–414.

38. See Hilberg, *Destruction*, 31.

39. Dieter Pohl, "The Holocaust and the Concentration Camps," in Caplan and Wachsmann, *Camps in Nazi Germany*, 149.

40. Ibid., 163.

41. Meyer, *Buchenwald*, 47.

42. For recent examples, see Armin Nolzen, "Inklusion und Exklusion im 'Dritten Reich': Das Beispiel NSDAP," in Frank Bajohr and Michael Wildt, eds., *Volksgemeinschaft: Neue Forschungen zur Gesellschaft des Nationalsozialismus* (Frankfurt, 2009), 60–77; Thomas Kühne, *Genocide and Belonging: Hitler's Community, 1918–1945* (New Haven, CT, 2010). See also Niklas Luhmann, "Inklusion und Exklusion," in *Soziologische Aufklärung*, vol. 6: *Die Soziologie und der Mensch* (Opladen, 2008), 237–264.

43. Harald Welzer, *Täter: Wie aus ganz normalen Menschen Massenmörder werden* (Frankfurt, 2005), 15.

44. See ibid., 37, 57.

45. See, for example, Max Weber, *Basic Concepts in Sociology* (London, 1962), 117.

46. Alf Lüdtke, "Einleitung: Herrschaft als soziale Praxis," in Lüdtke, ed., *Herrschaft als soziale Praxis: Historische und sozial-anthropologische Studien* (Göttingen, 1991), 12–13.

47. See ibid., 44. The term "power to kill" *(Macht zu töten, Todesmacht)* was coined and defined by Heinrich Popitz. See Popitz, *Phänomene der Macht: Autorität, Herrschaft, Gewalt, Technik* (Tübingen, 1986), 69–71.

48. See Sofksy, *Order*, 16–27.

49. This approach, developed mostly within German research on Nazi history, is currently debated. See Hans Mommsen, "Forschungskontroversen zum Nationalsozialismus," *Aus Politik und Zeitgeschichte* 14–15 (2007): 14–21; Ian Kershaw, "'Volksgemeinschaft': Potenzial und Grenzen eines neuen Forschungskonzepts," *Vierteljahreshefte für Zeitgeschichte (VfZ)* 58 (2011): 1–18; Michael Wildt, "Volksgemeinschaft: Eine Antwort auf Ian Kershaw," *Zeithistorische Forschungen/Studies in Contemporary History* 8:1 (2011), http://www.zeithistorische-forschungen.de/16126041-Wildt-1-2011; Detlef Schmiechen-Ackermann, ed., *Volksgemeinschaft: Mythos, wirkungsmächtige soziale*

Verheissung oder soziale Realität im Dritten Reich? (Paderborn, 2012); Martina Steber and Bernhard Gotto, eds., *Visions of Community in Nazi Germany: Social Engineering and Private Lives* (Oxford, 2014).

50. See Frank Bajohr and Michael Wildt, "Einleitung," in their *Volksgemeinschaft*, 8; Michael Wildt, "Die Ungleichheit des Volkes: 'Volksgemeinschaft' in der politischen Kommunikation der Weimarer Republik," in Bajohr and Wildt, *Volksgemeinschaft*, 24–40.

51. See Michael Wildt, *Volksgemeinschaft als Selbstermächtigung: Gewalt gegen Juden in der deutschen Provinz, 1919 bis 1939* (Hamburg, 2007); Wildt, "Ungleichheit," 6–7.

52. See David Schoenbaum, *Hitler's Social Revolution: Class and Status in Nazi Germany, 1933–1939* (New York, 1967); Timothy W. Mason, *Sozialpolitik im Dritten Reich: Arbeiterklasse und Volksgemeinschaft* (Opladen, 1977). See also Kershaw, " 'Volksgemeinschaft.' "

53. See Detlev J. K. Peukert, *Volksgenossen und Gemeinschaftsfremde: Anpassung, Ausmerze und Aufbegehren unter dem Nationalsozialismus* (Cologne, 1982).

54. See Robert Gellately, *The Gestapo and German Society: Enforcing Racial Policy, 1933–1945* (Oxford, 1990); Eric A. Johnson, *Nazi Terror: The Gestapo, Jews, and Ordinary Germans* (London, 2000).

55. See Bajohr and Wildt, "Einleitung," 8–9; Alf Lüdtke, "Funktionseliten: Täter, Mit-Täter, Opfer? Zu den Bedingungen des deutschen Faschismus," in *Herrschaft*, 559–590.

56. Polh, "Holocaust"; Leni Yahil, "Jews in Concentration Camps in Germany Prior to World War II," in Israel Gutman and Avital Saf, eds., *The Nazi Concentration Camps: Structure and Aims, the Image of the Prisoner, Jews in the Camps; Proceedings of the Fourth Yad Vashem International Historical Conference, Jerusalem, January 1980* (Jerusalem, 1984), 69–100.

57. Garbe, "Absonderung," 176–178.

58. See Matthäus, "Verfolgung," 65–66, 71–72.

59. See Detlef Garbe and Sabine Homann, "Jüdische Gefangene in Hamburger Konzentrationslagern," in Arno Herzig, ed., *Juden in Hamburg, 1590 bis 1990: Wissenschaftliche Beiträge der Universität Hamburg zur Ausstellung "Vierhundert Jahre Juden in Hamburg"* (Hamburg, 1991), 545–559.

60. See Harry Stein, *Juden in Buchenwald, 1937–1942* (Weimar, 1992).

61. See Linde Apel, *Jüdische Frauen im Konzentrationslager Ravensbrück, 1939–1945* (Berlin, 2003).

62. Morsch and zur Nieden, *Jüdische Häftlinge*.

63. See Kim Wünschmann, "Jüdische Häftlinge im KZ Osthofen: Das frühe Konzentrationslager als Terrorinstrument der nationalsozialistischen Judenpolitik," in *Vor 75 Jahren: "Am Anfang stand die Gewalt . . ." Dokumentation der Gedenkveranstaltung zur Erinnerung an die Errichtung des Konzentrations-*

lagers Osthofen, ed. Landeszentrale für politische Bildung Rheinland-Pfalz (Mainz, 2008), 18–33; Julia Pietsch, "Jüdische Häftlinge im frühen Konzentrationslager Oranienburg: 'Schutzhaft' im Spannungsfeld von Antisemitismus und 'Judenpolitik'" (Diploma thesis, Otto-Suhr-Institut für Politikwissenschaft, Freie Universität Berlin, 2010). See also Marco Esseling, "Juden als Häftlingsgruppe in Konzentrationslagern: Verhaftung von Juden und ihre Stellung im Lager bis 1942 unter besonderer Berücksichtigung des KZ Dachau" (MA dissertation, Institut für Neuere Geschichte, Ludwig-Maximilians-Universität München, 1995).

64. See Barbara Distel, "'Die letzte Warnung vor der Vernichtung.' Zur Verschleppung der Aktionsjuden in die Konzentrationslager nach dem 9. November 1938," *Zeitschrift für Geschichtswissenschaft (ZfG)* 48:11 (1998), 985–990; Wolfgang Benz, "Mitglieder der Häftlingsgesellschaft auf Zeit. Die 'Aktionsjuden 1938/39'" *Dachauer Hefte* 21 (2005), 179–196; Heiko Pollmeier, "Die Inhaftierung deutscher Juden im November 1938" (MA dissertation, Kommunikations- und Geschichtswissenschaft, Technische Universität Berlin, 1995).

65. See Christian Faludi, ed., *Die "Juni-Aktion" 1938: Eine Dokumentation zur Radikalisierung der Judenverfolgung* (Frankfurt, 2013).

66. See Knut Bergbauer et al., *Denkmalsfigur: Biographische Annäherung an Hans Litten* (Göttingen, 2008); Benjamin Carter Hett, *Crossing Hitler: The Man Who Put the Nazis on the Witness Stand* (Oxford, 2008); Linde Apel, "Olga Benario: Kommunistin, Jüdin, Heldin?," in Insa Eschebach et al., eds., *Die Sprache des Gedenkens: Zur Geschichte der Gedenkstätte Ravensbrück* (Berlin, 1999), 196–217; Jane Caplan, "Gabriele Herz: 'Schutzhaft' im Frauen-Konzentrationslager Moringen, 1936–1937," in Gisela Bock, ed., *Genozid und Geschlecht: Jüdische Frauen im nationalsozialistischen Lagersystem* (Frankfurt, 2005), 22–43; Karl-Heinz Jahnke, "Heinz Eschen: Kapo des Judenblocks im Konzentrationslager Dachau bis 1938," *Dachauer Hefte* 7 (1991): 24–33; Hans-Peter Klausch, *Jakob de Jonge: Aus deutschen Konzentrationslagern in den niederländischen Untergrund* (Bremen, 2002).

67. See Thomas Rahe, *"Höre Israel": Jüdische Religiosität in nationalsozialistischen Konzentrationslagern* (Göttingen, 1999).

68. See Bock, *Genozid*.

69. See Caplan, "Gender"; Kim Wünschmann, "Die Konzentrationslagererfahrungen deutsch-jüdischer Männer nach dem Novemberpogrom 1938: Geschlechtergeschichtliche Überlegungen zu männlichem Selbstverständnis und Rollenbild," in Susanne Heim et al., eds., *"Wer bleibt opfert seine Jahre, vielleicht sein Leben": Deutsche Juden, 1938–1941* (Göttingen, 2010), 52–57; Wünschmann, "Männlichkeitskonstruktionen jüdischer Häftlinge in NS-Konzentrationslager," in Anette Dietrich and Ljiljana Heise, eds.,

Männlichkeitskonstruktionen im Nationalsozialismus: Formen, Funktionen und Wirkungsmacht von Geschlechterkonstruktionen im Nationalsozialismus und ihre Reflexion in der pädagogischen Praxis (Frankfurt, 2013), 201–219; Christopher Dillon, "'Tolerance Means Weakness': The Dachau Concentration Camp S.S., Militarism and Masculinity," *Historical Research* 86:232 (2013): 373–389.

70. See Yosef Hayim Yerushalmi, *Zakhor: Jewish History and Jewish Memory* (New York, 1982); James E. Young, *Writing and Rewriting the Holocaust: Narrative and the Consequences of Interpretation* (Bloomington, IN, 1988), 16.

71. See Heiko Pollmeier, "Inhaftierung und Lagererfahrung deutscher Juden im November 1938," *Jahrbuch für Antisemitismusforschung* 8 (1999): 107–130; Kim Wünschmann, "'Natürlich weiss ich, wer mich ins KZ gebracht hat und warum . . .': Die Inhaftierung von Juden im Konzentrationslager Osthofen, 1933/34," in Andreas Ehresmann et al., eds., *Die Erinnerung an die nationalsozialistischen Konzentrationslager: Akteure, Inhalte, Strategien* (Berlin, 2011), 97–111.

72. See Martin Broszat, "The Concentration Camps, 1933–45," in Helmut Krausnick et al., eds., *Anatomy of the SS State* (London, 1968), 397–504; Pingel, *Häftlinge unter SS-Herrschaft.*

73. For a historiographical survey of the early phase of concentration camp research, see Horst Kuss, "Aussonderung, Konzentration, Vernichtung: Zur Geschichte der nationalsozialistischen Konzentrationslager und der Vernichtung des europäischen Judentums; Ergebnisse und Fragen der zeitgeschichtlichen Forschung seit 1981," *Neue Politische Literatur* 34:3 (1989): 380–381.

74. Gudrun Schwarz, *Die nationalsozialistischen Lager* (Frankfurt, 1990); Tuchel, *Konzentrationslager*; Klaus Drobisch and Günther Wieland, *System der NS-Konzentrationslager, 1933–1939* (Berlin, 1993); Orth, *Das System.* For recent surveys of the literature, see Nikolaus Wachsmann, "Looking into the Abyss: Historians and the Nazi Concentration Camps," *European History Quarterly* 36:2 (2006): 247–278; Karin Orth, "Die Historiografie der Konzentrationslager und die neuere KZ-Forschung," *Archiv für Sozialgeschichte* 47 (2007): 579–598.

75. Baganz, *Erziehung*; Mayer-von Götz, *Terror.* Both studies were published in the series *Geschichte der Konzentrationslager, 1933–1945.* See Wolfgang Benz and Barbara Distel, eds., *Geschichte der Konzentrationslager, 1933–1945*, 15 vols. (Berlin, 2001–2014). Parallel with this, Benz and Distel have published a more encyclopedic history of the Nazi concentration camps. See Benz and Distel, *Der Ort des Terrors.*

76. See Christian Goeschel and Nikolaus Wachsmann, eds., *Before Auschwitz: New Approaches to the Nazi Concentration Camps, 1933–1939*, special issue of the *Journal of Contemporary History* 45:3 (2010). On the project, see also http://www.camps.bbk.ac.uk/. Besides my own study, four additional monographs have been composed within the framework of the Birkbeck project. They are

forthcoming as Christopher Dillon, *Dachau and the SS: A Schooling in Violence*; Julia Hörath, *Experimente zur Kontrolle und Repression von Devianz und Delinquenz: Die Einweisung von "Asozialen" und "Berufsverbrechern" in die Konzentrationslager, 1933 bis 1937/38*; Paul Moore, *The View from Outside: The Nazi Concentration Camps and the German Public*; Nikolaus Wachsmann, *KL: A History of the Nazi Concentration Camps*.

77. Gestapo case-files were mostly destroyed during the war. Only fragmentary records of the three former Gestapo offices in Neustadt an der Weinstrasse, Würzburg, and Düsseldorf are accessible in Landesarchiv Speyer, Bayerisches Staatsarchiv Würzburg, and Landesarchiv Nordrhein-Westfalen—Abteilung Rheinland (Düsseldorf), respectively.

78. Felix Burger [alias Kurt Grossmann], *Juden in brauner Hölle: Augenzeugen berichten aus SA-Kasernen und Konzentrationslagern* (Prague, 1933); Anon., *Konzentrationslager: Ein Appell an das Gewissen der Welt; Ein Buch der Greuel; Die Opfer klagen an* (Karlsbad, 1934); *Das Schwarzbuch: Tatsachen und Dokumente; Die Lage der Juden in Deutschland, 1933*, ed. Comité des Délégations Juives (Paris: 1934).

79. See Max Abraham, *Juda verrecke: Ein Rabbiner im Konzentrationslager* (Teplitz-Schönau, 1934), reprinted in Irene Diekmann and Klaus Wettig, eds., *Konzentrationslager Oranienburg. Augenzeugenberichte aus dem Jahre 1933: Gehard Seger, Reichstagsabgeordneter der SPD, Max Abraham, Prediger aus Rathenow* (Potsdam, 2003), 117–167; Werner Hirsch, *Hinter Stacheldraht und Gitter: Erlebnisse und Erfahrungen in den Konzentrationslagern Hitler-Deutschlands* (Zurich, 1934); Hirsch, *Sozialdemokratische und kommunistische Arbeiter im Konzentrationslager* (Strasbourg, 1934).

80. See Thomas Rahe, "Die Bedeutung der Zeitzeugenberichte für die historische Forschung zur Geschichte der Konzentrations- und Vernichtungslager," *Kriegsende und Befreiung: Beiträge zur Geschichte der nationalsozialistischen Verfolgung in Norddeutschland* 2 (1995): 86–87.

81. See Saul Friedländer, *Nazi Germany and the Jews*, vol. 2: *The Years of Extermination, 1939–1945* (London, 2007), xv; Friedländer, "An Integrated History of the Holocaust: Possibilities and Challenges," in Christian Wiese and Paul Betts, eds., *Years of Persecution, Years of Extermination: Saul Friedländer and the Future of Holocaust Studies* (London, 2010), 21–29.

82. The most important collections of survivor testimonies are held in the Wiener Library, London; the Archives of the Leo Baeck Institute, New York; and the Yad Vashem Archives in Jerusalem. German memorial sites archives have also collected a significant number of memoirs.

1. In the Beginning There Was Violence

1. Testimony of Carl Mosse, autumn 1933, Yad Vashem Archives (YVA), O.1/195, published in Kurt Jakob Ball-Kaduri, *Das Leben der Juden in Deutschland im Jahre 1933* (Frankfurt, 1963), 171.

2. Testimony of Dora Mosse, December 1933, YVA, O.1/195, published in Ball-Kaduri, *Das Leben der Juden*, 169.

3. See Elisabeth Kraus, *Die Familie Mosse: Deutsch-jüdisches Bürgertum im 19. und 20. Jahrhundert* (Munich, 1999), 533.

4. See Rudolf S. Mosse, "Auf's Land!," in *Jüdische Bauernsiedlung in deutscher Heimat*, ed. Reichsbund jüdischer Frontsoldaten (Berlin, ca. 1920), 12–19.

5. See testimony of Dora Mosse, in Ball-Kaduri, *Das Leben der Juden*, 163–164; interview, Dora Mosse with L. J. Kahn, December 21, 1955, London, Leo Baeck Institute Archives (LBIA), AR 99, AR 25184-5/19, cited according to Kraus, *Die Familie Mosse*, 532, 723.

6. See testimony of Dora Mosse, in Ball-Kaduri, *Das Leben der Juden*, 164, 170; Kraus, *Die Familie Mosse*, 533.

7. Autopsy report for Rudolf S. Mosse, August 1933, Universitätsarchiv der Humboldt Universität zu Berlin, Universitätsinstitut für Rechtsmedizin der Charité, Sektionsprotokolle 1933, file no. 1506. For his help in interpreting this source, I am indebted to Thomas Müller.

8. See "Todesopfer des Konzentrationslagers Oranienburg," in Günter Morsch, ed., *Konzentrationslager Oranienburg* (Berlin, 1994), 220.

9. Testimony of Dora Mosse, in Ball-Kaduri, *Das Leben der Juden*, 168–169. On Hans Krüger's vita, see Bernward Dörner, "Ein KZ in der Mitte der Stadt: Oranienburg," in Wolfgang Benz and Barbara Distel, eds., *Terror ohne System: Die ersten Konzentrationslager im Nationalsozialismus* (Berlin, 2001), 127.

10. Günter Morsch, "Oranienburg—Sachsenhausen, Sachsenhausen—Oranienburg," in Ulrich Herbert et al., eds., *Die nationalsozialistischen Konzentrationslager: Entwicklung und Struktur* (Göttingen, 1998), 1:122.

11. On Oranienburg, see Dörner, "KZ." On Columbia-Haus, see Kurt Schilde and Johannes Tuchel, *Columbia-Haus: Berliner Konzentrationslager, 1933–1936* (Berlin, 1990); Kurt Schilde, "Vom Tempelhofer Feld-Gefängnis zum Schutzhaftlager: Das 'Columbia-Haus' in Berlin," in Wolfgang Benz and Barbara Distel, eds., *Herrschaft und Gewalt: Frühe Konzentrationslager, 1933–1939* (Berlin, 2002), 65–81; Kurt Schilde, "Columbia-Haus," in *The United States Holocaust Memorial Museum Encyclopedia of Camps and Ghettos, 1933–1945*, vol. 1, pt. 1 (Bloomington, IN, 2009) (hereafter *USHMM Encyclopedia I*), 59–61; Karoline Georg et al., eds., *"Warum schweigt die Welt?!" "Why is the world still silent?!": Häftlinge im Berliner Konzentrationslager Columbia-*

Haus, 1933 bis 1936; Prisoners in Berlin's Columbia-Haus Concentration Camp, 1933 to 1936 (Berlin, 2013).

12. See Dietfrid Krause-Vilmar, *Das Konzentrationslager Breitenau: Ein staatliches Schutzhaftlager, 1933/34* (Marburg, 1998), 80.

13. See Ball-Kaduri, *Das Leben der Juden*, 161; Fritz Ball, "Die SA Kaserne in der General-Pape-Strasse," in ibid., 58–59, and "Die Nacht in der General-Pape-Strasse," in ibid., 59–80.

14. Thomas Mann, *Tagebücher, 1933–1934*, ed. Peter de Mendelssohn (Frankfurt, 1977), 178.

15. Notes of Dr. Blumenthal, Institut für Zeitgeschichte Archives (IfZ), 54/16255, 7. See also the entry "Mosse, Rudolf S.," in Salomon Wininger, *Grosse Jüdische National-Biographie mit mehr als 8000 Lebensbeschreibungen namhafter jüdischer Männer und Frauen aller Zeiten und aller Länder: Ein Nachschlagewerk für das jüdische Volk und seine Freunde*, vol. 7 (Cernowitz, 1936), 334.

16. See Broszat et al., eds., *Deutschlands Weg in die Diktatur* (Berlin, 1983); David Welch, *The Third Reich: Politics and Propaganda* (London, 1993).

17. The auxiliary police (Hilfspolizei) was made up of 50 percent SA, 30 percent SS, and 20 percent Stahlhelm. See Johannes Tuchel, *Konzentrationslager: Organisationsgeschichte und Funktion der "Inspektion der Konzentrationslager," 1934–1938* (Boppard, 1991), 46.

18. See Wolfgang Benz and Barbara Distel, eds., *Der Ort des Terrors: Geschichte der nationalsozialistischen Konzentrationslager*, vol. 2: *Frühe Lager, Dachau* (Munich, 2005). In Berlin alone, there were over 170 SA and SS torture sites. See Irene Mayer-von Götz, *Terror im Zentrum der Macht: Die frühen Konzentrationslager in Berlin, 1933/34–1936* (Berlin, 2008), 19.

19. See Joseph Robert White, "Introduction to the Early Camps," in *USHMM Encyclopedia I*, 3–16.

20. See Karl A. Schleunes, *The Twisted Road to Auschwitz: Nazi Policy toward German Jews, 1933–39* (London, 1972), 71; Robert Gellately, *Backing Hitler: Consent and Coercion in Nazi Germany* (Oxford, 2001), 21; Markus Kienle, "Das Konzentrationslager Heuberg bei Stetten am kalten Markt," in Benz and Distel, *Terror ohne System*, 50. Laudable exceptions are Krause-Vilmar, *Breitenau*; Hans-Peter Klausch, *Jakob de Jonge: Aus deutschen Konzentrationslagern in den niederländischen Untergrund* (Bremen, 2002). See also Robert Gellately, "The Prerogatives of Confinement in Germany, 1933–1945: 'Protective Custody' and Other Police Strategies," in Norbert Finzsch and Robert Jütte, eds., *Institutions of Confinement: Hospitals, Asylums, and Prisons in Western Europe and North America, 1500–1950* (Cambridge, 1996), 205.

21. See Saul Friedländer, *Nazi Germany and the Jews*, vol. 1: *The Years of Persecution, 1933–1939* (New York, 1998), 17n36, 18; Marion A. Kaplan, *Between*

Dignity and Despair: Jewish Life in Nazi Germany (New York, 1998), 18–20; Peter Longerich, *Holocaust: The Nazi Persecution and Murder of the Jews* (Oxford, 2010), 32–38.

22. For an encompassing survey of the literature on the persecution of Jews in the prewar years, see Michael Wildt, *Volksgemeinschaft als Selbstermächtigung: Gewalt gegen Juden in der deutschen Provinz, 1919 bis 1939* (Hamburg, 2007), 9–25.

23. See Order of the Reich President for the Protection of People and State, February 28, 1933, *Reichsgesetzblatt (RGBl)* I (1933), 83. To enhance readability the quotation marks around ideologically-loaded terminology used in Nazi language that are frequently used throughout this book (such as protective custody, people's community, race defilement, or special treatment) are gradually omitted.

24. Martin Broszat, "The Concentration Camps, 1933–45," in Helmut Krausnick et al., eds., *Anatomy of the SS State* (London, 1968), 400.

25. See Michael P. Hensle, "Die Verrechtlichung des Unrechts: Der legalistische Rahmen der nationalsozialistischen Verfolgung," in Benz and Distel, *Der Ort des Terrors*, 1:79.

26. Jane Caplan, "Political Detention and the Origin of the Concentration Camps in Nazi Germany, 1933–1935/36," in Neil Gregor, ed., *Nazism, War and Genocide: Essays in Honour of Jeremy Noakes* (Exeter, 2005), 26.

27. See Broszat, "The Concentration Camps," 401; Klaus Drobisch and Günther Wieland, *System der NS-Konzentrationslager, 1933–1939* (Berlin, 1993), 16, 25.

28. See Drobisch and Wieland, *System*, 27–31.

29. See Hensle, "Verrechtlichung," 80.

30. See Hans Mommsen, "Der Reichstagsbrand und seine politischen Folgen," *VfZ* 12 (1964), 351–413; Benjamin Carter Hett, *Burning the Reichstag: An Investigation into the Third Reich's Enduring Mystery* (Oxford, 2014).

31. Circular by Hermann Göring, March 3, 1933, quoted in Hensle, "Verrechtlichung," 80.

32. According to official figures, 4,000 of the arrestees were Communists. See Hensle, "Verrechtlichung," 76, 79.

33. See Friedländer, *Nazi Germany*, 1:106.

34. See Martin Schumacher, ed., *M.d.R. Die Reichstagsabgeordneten der Weimarer Republik in der Zeit des Nationalsozialismus: Politische Verfolgung, Emigration und Ausbürgerung* (Düsseldorf, 1994), 437–440; Michael Buckmiller and Pascal Nafe, "Die Naherwartung des Kommunismus: Werner Scholem," in Michael Buckmiller et al., eds., *Judentum und politische Existenz: Siebzehn Porträts deutsch-jüdischer Intellektueller* (Hanover, 2000), 67; Mirjam Zadoff, *Der rote Hiob: Das Leben des Werner Scholem* (Munich, 2014).

35. Letter from Betty Scholem to Gershom Scholem, February 28, 1933, in *Betty Scholem, Gershom Scholem, Mutter und Sohn im Briefwechsel, 1917–1946* (Munich, 1989), 278–279, emphasis in the original.

36. A report of Scholem's arrest was published, for example, in *Vossische Zeitung*, February 28, 1933.

37. See Bernd Kaufmann et al., *Der Nachrichtendienst der KPD, 1919–1937* (Berlin, 1993), 142–148, 203; Buckmiller and Nafe, "Naherwartung," 75.

38. See *Buchenwald Concentration Camp, 1937–1945: A Guide to the Permanent Historical Exhibition*, ed. Gedenkstätte Buchenwald (Göttingen, 2004), 67, 119.

39. Letter from Gershom Scholem to Walter Benjamin, April 19, 1936, in *Walter Benjamin, Gershom Scholem, Briefwechsel, 1933–1940* (Frankfurt, 1980), 216.

40. Letter from Werner Scholem to Gershom Scholem, October 5, 1933, reproduced in Schumacher, *M.d.R.*, 439.

41. See clemency plea of Helene Hirsch-Lipa, addressed to State Secretary Ludwig Grauert, August 4, 1934, Geheimes Staatsarchiv Preussischer Kulturbesitz (GStA PK), I. HA Rep. 77, Preussisches Ministerium des Inneren, Tit. 4043, Nr. 484: Schutzhaft 1934, 133–136.

42. See Reinhard Müller, "Der Fall Werner Hirsch: Vom KZ Oranienburg in die Moskauer Lubjanka," *Internationale wissenschaftliche Korrespondenz zur Geschichte der Arbeiterbewegung* 36 (2000): 47–61.

43. Werner Hirsch, *Hinter Stacheldraht und Gitter: Erlebnisse und Erfahrungen in den Konzentrationslagern Hitler-Deutschlands* (Zurich, 1934); Hirsch, *Sozialdemokratische und kommunistische Arbeiter im Konzentrationslager* (Strasbourg, 1934).

44. Testimony of Heinz Altmann, ca. 1935, quoted in Müller, "Der Fall Werner Hirsch," 41–42.

45. Transcript of an interview with Rudolf Bernstein, conducted on March 22, 1962, by the Institut für Marxismus-Leninismus (GDR), quoted in Karin Hartewig, *Zurückgekehrt: Die Geschichte der jüdischen Kommunisten in der DDR* (Cologne, 2000), 67–68. See also Stefan Szende, *Zwischen Gewalt und Toleranz: Zeugnisse und Reflexionen eines Sozialisten* (Frankfurt, 1975).

46. See Hirsch, *Arbeiter*, 16; Hirsch, *Hinter Stacheldraht und Gitter*, 15.

47. See Kreszentia Mühsam, *Der Leidensweg Erich Mühsams* (Zurich, 1935); Lawrence Baron, "Erich Mühsam's Jewish Identity," *Leo Baeck Institute Year Book (LBIYB)* 25 (1980); Chris Hirte, *Erich Mühsam: "Ihr seht mich nicht feige"* (East Berlin, 1985).

48. Friedländer, *Nazi Germany* 1:92. See also Mühsam, *Leidensweg*, 9, 13; Baron, "Erich Mühsam," 275, 284.

49. See Mühsam, *Leidensweg*, 9.

50. See ibid., 15, 20, 22. See also Kurt Hiller, "Schutzhäftling 231," *Die neue Weltbühne: Wochenschrift für Politik, Kunst, Wirtschaft*, February 7, 1935, 175.

51. Mühsam, *Leidensweg*, 15.
52. See Johannes Tuchel, "Die Systematisierung der Gewalt: Vom KZ Oranienburg zum KZ Sachsenhausen," in Morsch, *Oranienburg*, 128; Dörner, "KZ," 137.
53. See Mühsam, *Leidensweg*, 28–30; Drobisch and Wieland, *System*, 211–212; Dörner, "KZ," 133.
54. Mühsam, *Leidensweg*, 28. On Hans Stahlkopf, see Dörner, "KZ," 127.
55. On Hans Litten, see Max Fürst, *Talisman Scheherezade: Die schwierigen Zwanziger Jahre* (Munich, 1976); Fürst, *Gefilte Fisch und wie es weiterging* (Munich, 2004); Knut Bergbauer et al., *Denkmalsfigur: Biographische Annäherung an Hans Litten* (Göttingen, 2008); Benjamin Carter Hett, *Crossing Hitler: The Man Who Put the Nazis on the Witness Stand* (Oxford, 2008).
56. Irmgard Litten, *A Mother Fights Hitler* (London, 1940), 63–66.
57. Hett, *Crossing Hitler*, 83.
58. See Bergbauer et al., *Denkmalsfigur*, 33–72; Hett, *Crossing Hitler*, 87–102.
59. Litten was interned in Sonnenburg, April 6–25, 1933. See Anon., *Folterhölle Sonnenburg: Tatsachen und Augenzeugenbericht eines ehemaligen Schutzhäftlings* (Zurich, 1934), 6; Hans Ullmann, "Das Konzentrationslager Sonnenburg, eingeleitet und kommentiert von Kaspar Nürnberg," *Dachauer Hefte* 13 (1997): 76–91; Bergbauer et al., *Denkmalsfigur*, 233–243; Hett, *Crossing Hitler*, 164. Rudolf Bernstein survived Nazi terror, but Georg Benjamin lost his life in Mauthausen in 1942. He was interned in Sonnenburg from April to December 1933. See Luise Kraushaar, *Deutsche Widerstandskämpfer, 1933–1945: Biographien und Briefe* (East Berlin, 1970), 1:112–115. On Sonnenburg, see also Kaspar Nürnberg, "Sonnenburg," in *USHMM Encyclopedia I*, 163–166.
60. See speech by Joseph Goebbels at Nuremberg party rally, September 13, 1935, printed in Hanns Kerrl, ed., *Reichstagung in Nürnberg, 1935: Der Parteitag der Freiheit* (Berlin, 1936), 190, 183. On the stereotype of the Jewish Bolshevist, see Daniel Gerson, "Der Jude als Bolschewist: Die Wiederbelebung eines Stereotyps," in Wolfgang Benz, ed., *Antisemitismus in Deutschland: Zur Aktualität eines Vorurteils* (Munich, 1995), 158–180; Kim Wünschmann, "Jüdische politische Häftlinge im frühen KZ Dachau: Widerstand, Verfolgung und antisemitisches Feindbild," in Sybille Steinbacher and Nikolaus Wachsmann, eds., *Die Linke im Visier: Zur Errichtung der Konzentrationslager, 1933* (forthcoming).
61. See Drobisch and Wieland, *System*, 38; Nikolaus Wachsmann, "The Dynamics of Destruction: The Development of the Concentration Camps, 1933–1945," in Jane Caplan and Nikolaus Wachsmann, eds., *Concentration Camps in Nazi Germany: The New Histories* (London, 2010), 18–19, 37.
62. See Wolfgang Röll, *Sozialdemokraten im Konzentrationslager Buchenwald, 1937–1945* (Göttingen, 2000), 17.

63. See Wolfgang Langhoff, *Die Moorsoldaten: 13 Monate Konzentrationslager* (Stuttgart, 1982), 220–222; Wolfgang Kirchhoff, "Alfred Kantorowicz," in *Zahnmedizin und Faschismus* (Marburg, 1988), 127–134; Klausch, *Jakob de Jonge*, 37.

64. See Barbara Danckwortt, "Jüdische 'Schutzhäftlinge' im KZ Sachsenhausen, 1936 bis 1938: Verfolgungsgeschichten von Kommunisten, Sozialdemokraten und Liberalen," in Günter Morsch and Susanne zur Nieden, eds., *Jüdische Häftlinge im Konzentrationslager Sachsenhausen, 1936 bis 1945* (Berlin, 2004), 149–150.

65. On Ludwig Marum, see Ludwig Marum, *Briefe aus dem Konzentrationslager Kislau*, ed. Elisabeth Marum-Lunau and Jörg Schadt (Karlsruhe, 1984); Schumacher, *M.d.R.*, 309–312; Monika Pohl, *Ludwig Marum: Ein Sozialdemokrat jüdischer Herkunft und sein Aufstieg in der badischen Arbeiterbewegung, 1882–1919* (Karlsruhe, 2003). On Ernst Heilmann, see Horst Möller, "Ernst Heilmann: Ein Sozialdemokrat in der Weimarer Republik," *Tel Aviver Jahrbuch des Instituts für Deutsche Geschichte* 9 (1982): 261–294; Schumacher, *M.d.R.*, 175–178; Röll, *Sozialdemokraten*, 89–102; Danckwortt, "'Schutzhäftlinge,'" 154–156; Meiko Keller, "Heilmann, Ernst," in the online exhibition *Die politischen Häftlinge des Konzentrationslagers Oranienburg*, produced by Museum Memorial Site Sachsenhausen, http://www.stiftung-bg .de/kz-oranienburg/index.php?id=345.

66. Paul Moore, "German Popular Opinion on the Nazi Concentration Camps, 1933–1939" (PhD dissertation, Birkbeck, University of London, 2010), 35–38.

67. Original press text glued to back of propaganda photo, quoted in Morsch, *Oranienburg*, 193.

68. Gerhart Seger, *Oranienburg: Erster authentischer Bericht eines aus dem Konzentrationslager Geflüchteten* (Karlsbad, 1934), 41.

69. Anon., *Als sozialdemokratischer Arbeiter im Lager Papenburg* (Moscow, 1935), 37.

70. See, for example, ibid., 43; Langhoff, *Moorsoldaten*, 234–243.

71. See Röll, *Sozialdemokraten*, 94–95; Keller, "Heilmann, Ernst." The observation that characteristics and events from the time before the camp imprisonment influenced the inmates' standing in and experience of the camp was made by Falk Pingel. See Falk Pingel, *Häftlinge unter SS-Herrschaft: Widerstand, Selbstbehauptung und Vernichtung im Konzentrationslager* (Hamburg, 1978), 10–11.

72. See *Die politischen Häftlinge des Konzentrationslagers Oranienburg* (online exhibition), http://www.stiftung-bg.de/kz-oranienburg/index.php?id=37.

73. See Drobisch and Wieland, *System*, 128; Angelika Borgstedt, "Das nordbadische Kislau: Konzentrationslager, Arbeitshaus und Durchgangslager für Fremdenlegionäre," in Benz and Distel, *Herrschaft und Gewalt*, 223.

74. *Der Stürmer*, no. 17 (April 1934), translated in Moore, *German Popular Opinion*, 90. See also Schumacher, *M.d.R.*, 309.

75. Reports of the event appeared also in the international press. See "Baden Ex-Premier Humiliated: Hooted on Way to Prison," *The Times*, May 17, 1933; "Empörende Vorfälle in Karlsruhe," *Prager Tageblatt*, May 17, 1933.

76. Testimony of Elisabeth Marum under pseudonym Margarete Leib, in Eric A. Johnson and Karl-Heinz Reuband, *What We Knew: Terror, Mass Murder, and Everyday Life in Nazi Germany; An Oral History* (London, 2005), 8.

77. Wildt, *Volksgemeinschaft*, 213–218.

78. See *Volkswacht*, March 4, 1933, and *Badischer Beobachter*, May 17, 1933, both reprinted in Marum, *Briefe*, 114–116, 122.

79. Report of Albert Nachmann, ca. 1945; letter from Ludwig Marum to his wife Johanna, May 21, 1933; both reprinted in Marum, *Briefe*, 141, 72.

80. *Der Führer*, May 17, 1933, reprinted in Marum, *Briefe*, 123.

81. See *Neue Zürcher Zeitung*, April 8, 1934, printed in Schumacher, *M.d.R*, 312; report of Albert Nachmann, 148.

82. See Felix Burger, *Juden in brauner Hölle: Augenzeugen berichten aus SA-Kasernen und Konzentrationslagern* (Prague, 1933), 38–39.

83. It remains unclear whether Ernst Eckstein had been detained in the Breslau-Dürrgoy camp. Most likely he died before he could be deported there. See ibid., 39; Walter Tausk, *Breslauer Tagebuch, 1933–1940* (Leipzig, 1995), 61; Andrea Rudorff, "'Privatlager' des Polizeipräsidenten mit prominenten Häftlingen: Das Konzentrationslager Breslau-Dürrgoy," in Wolfgang Benz and Barbara Distel, eds., *Instrumentarium der Macht: Frühe Konzentrationslager, 1933–1937* (Berlin, 2003), 150–152.

84. See Tausk, *Breslauer Tagebuch*, 96.

85. See Detlef Garbe and Sabine Homann, "Jüdische Gefangene in Hamburger Konzentrationslagern," in Arno Herzig, ed., *Juden in Hamburg, 1590 bis 1990: Wissenschaftliche Beiträge der Universität Hamburg zur Ausstellung "Vierhundert Jahre Juden in Hamburg"* (Hamburg, 1991), 546–547.

86. Letter from Mayor of Schmalkalden to Schmalkalden County Executive, August 7, 1933, in file 603, Municipality of Schmalkalden "Confiscation of property of SPD, SPD-newspaper, and Reichsbanner," closed October 13, 1937, Privatarchiv Ludwig Pappenheim, source accessed in Informationsstelle zur Geschichte des Nationalsozialismus in Nordhessen, Universität Kassel (IGNN). On Ludwig Pappenheim, see also Dietfrid Krause-Vilmar, "Über Ludwig Pappenheim," *DIZ Nachrichten. Aktionskomitee für ein Dokumentations- und Informationszentrum EMSLAND e.V.* 15 (1992): 24–29.

87. Letter from Ludwig Pappenheim to Governmental President Kassel, March 31, 1933, quoted in Krause-Vilmar, *Breitenau*, 73.

88. See witness testimony of Arnold Janz, July 30, 1964, Niedersächsisches Landesarchiv—Staatsarchiv Osnabrück (NStA O)., Rep 945 Akz. 2001/054 Nr. 123, 160; Krause-Vilmar, "Pappenheim," 26, 28.

89. See Hermann Schueler, *Auf der Flucht erschossen: Felix Fechenbach, 1894–1933; Eine Biographie* (Warburg, 1995), 247; Edith Raim, "Die Verfolgung und Vernichtung der fränkischen Juden in der NS-Zeit," in Michael Brenner and Daniela F. Eisenstein, eds., *Juden in Franken* (Munich, 2012), 202. Raim points to the files of the legal investigation into Fechenbach's death stored at Staatsarchiv Detmold, Paderborn 2 Ks 1/48, D 21 C, Zug. 118/93 Nr. 1; Paderborn 2 Ks 1/67, D 21 C, Zug. 24/84 Nr. 30.

90. See Peter Steinbach, ed., *"Das Schicksal hat bestimmt, dass ich hierbleibe": Zur Erinnerung an Felix Fechenbach (1894–1933); Mit der Zusammenstellung der Artikel von "Nazi-Jüsken"* (Berlin, 1983), 20–26; Schueler, *Flucht*, 244–248.

91. *Lippischer Kurier*, March 13, 1933, reprinted in Steinbach, *Schicksal*, 19.

92. See Schueler, *Flucht*, 229, 239.

93. Sixth Fire Slogan, quoted in Ulrich Walberer, ed., *10. Mai 1933: Bücherverbrennung in Deutschland und die Folgen* (Frankfurt, 1983), 115.

94. *Mainzer Volkszeitung*, March 6, 1933, quoted in Bundesrechtsanwaltskammer, ed., *Anwalt ohne Recht: Schicksale jüdischer Anwälte in Deutschland nach 1933* (Berlin, 2007), 381–382. See also Angelika Arenz-Morch, "Max Tschornicki: Der 'mutige Lausbub mit den kurzen Hosen,'" *Mainzer Zeitung*, August 9, 1990.

95. See Förderverein Projekt Osthofen, *Häftlingsbiographie Max Tschornicki*, http://www.projektosthofen-gedenkstaette.de/html/tschornicki.html.

96. My own database documents 64 cases of Jewish jurists who fell victim to early Nazi terror. Reinhard Weber, who has systematically researched the persecution of Jewish lawyers in Bavaria, detected 36 cases, which represent 7.8 percent of the 460 Jewish lawyers registered in Bavaria. If we assume a similar quota for Prussia, which can be compared to Bavaria in terms of the harsh antisemitic legal policies advanced by fanatic National Socialists who came to head the juridical authorities (Hans Frank in Bavaria and Hanns Kerrl in Prussia), around 250 of the total 3,500 Prussian Jewish lawyers would have been affected in Germany's largest state alone. See Reinhard Weber, *Das Schicksal der jüdischen Rechtsanwälte in Bayern nach 1933* (Munich, 2006), 2, 39–56; Bundesrechtsanwaltskammer, *Anwalt*, 10.

97. See Friedländer, *Nazi Germany*, 1:28–29; Simone Ladwig-Winters, *Anwalt ohne Recht: Das Schicksal jüdischer Rechtsanwälte in Berlin nach 1933* (Berlin, 1998), 32; Michael A. Meyer, ed., *German-Jewish History in Modern Times*, vol. 4: *Renewal and Destruction, 1918–1945* (New York, 1998), 201–202; Gellately, *Backing Hitler*, 24–31.

98. Jurists and political scientists Ernst Fraenkel and Franz Neumann produced contemporary analyses of the Nazi state. See Fraenkel, *The Dual State: A*

Contribution to the Theory of Dictatorship (New York, 1941); Neumann, *Behemoth: The Structure and Practice of National Socialism, 1933–1944* (London, 1942).

99. See *Das Schwarzbuch: Tatsachen und Dokumente; Die Lage der Juden in Deutschland 1933*, ed. Comité des Délégations Juives (Paris, 1934),493; Tillmann Krach, *Jüdische Rechtsanwälte in Preussen: Über die Bedeutung der freien Advokatur und ihre Zerstörung durch den Nationalsozialismus* (Munich, 1991), 138, 170–171. On the SA torture at ULAP, see Irene Mayer, "Berlin-Tiergarten (Universum-Landesausstellungspark)," in *USHMM Encyclopedia I*, 42–43.

100. Krach, *Rechtsanwälte*, 124–125.

101. Longerich, *Holocaust*, 33.

102. See Bundesrechtsanwaltskammer, *Anwalt*, 10; Weber, *Schicksal*, 1; Meyer, *German-Jewish History*, 4:34–35.

103. Ludwig Bendix, *Konzentrationslager Deutschland und andere Schutzhafter-fahrungen, 1933–1937, 1937–1938*, LBIA, ME 40, book 1:38; Reinhard Bendix, *From Berlin to Berkeley: German-Jewish Identities* (New Brunswick, NJ, 1986), 50.

104. See Bundesrechtsanwaltskammer, *Anwalt*, 320; Peter Pulzer, *Jews and the German State: The Political History of a Minority* (Oxford, 1992), 210.

105. See *RGBl* I (1933), 188. The law was promulgated on April 10, 1933, but backdated to April 7, the same day the Law for the Restoration of the Professional Civil Service came into force. See *RGBl* I (1933), 175. See also Simone Ladwig-Winters and Rechtsanwaltskammer Berlin, eds., *Anwalt ohne Recht: Das Schicksal jüdischer Rechtsanwälte in Berlin nach 1933* (Berlin, 2007), 99. A general professional ban of Jewish lawyers was decreed in September 1938.

106. In Prussia, 1,706—according to other sources, even 2,009—of the former 3,500 "non-Aryan" lawyers had to be readmitted. Outside Prussia, some 1,200 of the former 1,539 could continue their practice. See Bundesrechtsanwaltskammer, *Anwalt*, 12–13; Ladwig-Winters and Rechtsanwaltskammer Berlin, *Anwalt*, 99.

107. See Ladwig-Winters and Rechtsanwaltskammer Berlin, *Anwalt*, 55. Article 3 of the Ordinance decreed that the juridical authorities could request of "other departments that appear appropriate" a "notice in writing [informing the juridical authorities] which lawyers, in their view, had been active for the Communist cause."

108. See Weber, *Schicksal*, 46.

109. Report of Head of local Nazi Party Group sent to the President of the Berlin Supreme Court, June 15, 1933, Brandenburgisches Landeshauptarchiv (BLHA), Rep. 2A, Regierung Potsdam, I Pol. Nr. 1183, 236.

110. Protective custody order issued by Niederbarnim County Executive, July 4, 1933, reproduced in Philipp Rothe, "Martin Rosenthal," in *Die politischen*

Häftlinge des Konzentrationslagers Oranienburg (online exhibition), http://www
.stiftung-bg.de/kz-oranienburg/index.php?id=344.

111. Petition for release filed by Lilli Rosenthal to Altlandsberg Police Office, June
29, 1933, BLHA, Rep. 2A, Regierung Potsdam, I Pol. Nr. 1183, 248.

112. Letter from Altlandsberg Police Office to Niederbarnim County Executive,
June 29, 1933, ibid., 238.

113. See Appeal of Lilli Rosenthal to Altlandsberg Police Office, July 3, 1933,
ibid., 242.

114. Dismissal certificate for Martin Rosenthal issued by Reich Justice Ministry,
July 27, 1933, reproduced in Rothe, "Martin Rosenthal."

115. The account titled "Concentration Camp Germany" comprises over 500
tightly filled pages. It was composed in 1937–1938 after Bendix had arrived in
Palestinian exile.

116. L. Bendix, *Konzentrationslager*, bk. 1:3, 7.

117. R. Bendix, *From Berlin to Berkeley*, 129.

118. L. Bendix, *Konzentrationslager*, bk. 1:34, 57, bk. 5:108.

119. R. Bendix, *From Berlin to Berkeley*, 122.

120. Ibid., 159.

121. Ibid., 147.

122. Kalter had attempted to take his life while held in "protective custody" in
March 1933. After release, he left his hometown, deeply ashamed of the
imprisonment and his attempted suicide. When the Gestapo summoned him
again, he committed suicide by drowning in the river on October 29, 1934. See
Weber, *Schicksal*, 47–49.

123. See Michael Wildt, "Violence against Jews in Germany, 1933–1939," in David
Bankier, ed., *Probing the Depth of German Antisemitism: German Society and
the Persecution of Jews, 1933–1941* (Jerusalem, 2000), 181–209; Harald Welzer,
Täter: Wie aus ganz normalen Menschen Massenmörder werden (Frankfurt,
2005), 48–67; Frank Bajohr, "The 'Folk Community' and the Persecution of
Jews: German Society and National Socialist Dictatorship, 1933–1945," *Holocaust and Genocide Studies* 2:2 (2006): 183–206; Wildt, *Volksgemeinschaft*. For
an analysis of wartime antisemitic propaganda aimed at presenting "the Jew"
as the enemy of the German people, see Jeffrey Herf, *The Jewish Enemy: Nazi
Propaganda during World War II and the Holocaust* (Cambridge, MA, 2006).

124. See Peter Longerich, *Die braunen Bataillone: Geschichte der SA* (Munich,
1989), 170; Hans-Norbert Burkert et al., *"Machtergreifung" Berlin, 1933* (Berlin,
1982), 113–115.

125. Anon., *The Murder of Leo Krell by National Socialists in Berlin in the Year 1933*
(n.d.), Friends House Library and Archives, London, Friends Committee for
Refugees and Aliens, Political Prisoners, Correspondence 1933–1938,
FCRA/19/4.

126. Hannah Arendt, *The Origins of Totalitarianism* (New York, 1951), 438.

127. Eric A. Johnson, *Nazi Terror: The Gestapo, Jews, and Ordinary Germans* (London, 2000), 91. See also 92–96, 521.

128. This assumption can be found, for example, in Eberhard Jäckel, "Die Einzig-artigkeit des Mordes an den europäischen Juden," in Lea Rosh, ed., *"Die Juden, das sind doch die anderen": Der Streit um ein deutsches Denkmal* (Berlin, 1999), 156.

129. According to the 1933 census, 15.5 percent of German Jews lived in communities with fewer than 10,000 inhabitants; an additional 3.4 percent lived in communities with 10,000 to 20,000 inhabitants. See Werner J. Cahnman, "Village and Small-Town Jews in Germany: A Typological Study," *LBIYB* 19 (1974), 107; Monika Richarz and Reinhard Rürup, eds., *Jüdisches Leben auf dem Lande: Studien zur deutsch-jüdischen Geschichte* (Tübingen, 1997).

130. Register of protective custody prisoners in Bavaria interned longer than three months, Bayerisches Hauptstaatsarchiv Munich (BayHStA M), MInn 73690, 164.

131. Hermann Rothschild was brought to Dachau concentration camp on July 30, 1934. In his prisoner file, the Würzburg Gestapo gave "Jew" as the reason for his detention. See Bayerisches Staatsarchiv Würzburg (BayStA W), Gestapo 11308; Prisoner database of the Dachau Concentration Camp Memorial Site Archives (hereafter DaA prisoner database).

132. Letter from Reinhard Heydrich to Prime Minister of Bavaria, August 10, 1933, BayHStA M, StK 5482, n.p.; DaA prisoner database.

133. Register Protective Custody Prisoners in Bavaria, BayHStA M, MInn 73690, 157.

134. Ibid., 165. On this case, see also BayStA W, Gestapo 11082, and note the variations in the name spelling ("Normann Rosenbusch").

135. Sächsisches Hauptstaatsarchiv Dresden (SächsHStA D), AH Marienburg, Nr. 2196, reproduced in Carina Baganz, *Erziehung zur "Volksgemeinschaft"? Die frühen Konzentrationslager in Sachsen, 1933/34–1937* (Berlin, 2005), 125, emphasis in the original.

136. *Bayerischer Kurier*, April 21, 1933, quoted in Drobisch and Wieland, *System*, 33.

137. Letter from Franz von Papen to Hermann Göring, April 26, 1933, GStA PK, Rep. 77, Nr. 31, 75–76.

138. For a detailed study of the history of Jewish prisoners in Osthofen concentration camp, see Kim Wünschmann, "'Natürlich weiss ich, wer mich ins KZ gebracht hat und warum . . .': Die Inhaftierung von Juden im Konzentrationslager Osthofen, 1933/34," in Andreas Ehresmann et al., eds., *Die Erinnerung an die nationalsozialistischen Konzentrationslager: Akteure, Inhalte, Strategien* (Berlin, 2011), 97–111. In the context of this earlier research, I evaluated 117 case studies of Jewish prisoners. In 60 cases the background of the arrest can be

reconstructed. Applying the above-introduced distinction, an arrest because of political activism can be ascertained in 24 cases (40 percent).

139. See Angelika Arenz-Morch, "Das Konzentrationslager Osthofen, 1933/34," in Hans-Georg Meyer and Hans Berkessel, eds., *Die Zeit des Nationalsozialismus in Rheinland-Pfalz*, vol. 2: *"Für die Aussenwelt seid ihr tot!"* (Mainz, 2000), 43.

140. Decree on the Establishment of a Concentration Camp in Osthofen, May 1, 1933, Hessisches Staatsarchiv Darmstadt (HessStA D), G 24/360, 38–39, 92–94. On Best's vita, see Ulrich Herbert, *Best: Biographische Studien über Radikalismus, Weltanschauung und Vernunft* (Bonn, 1996).

141. Examination of Josef Wachenheimer by the Gernsheim Gendarmerie, July 15, 1933, Archives of Osthofen Memorial Site (AO), Häftlingsunterlagen Josef Wachenheimer.

142. Ibid.

143. Verdict in the trial of Josef Wachenheimer in front of the Gernsheim Municipal Court, March 15, 1934, ibid.

144. Report of Ernst Starthartinger (Biebesheim, 1997), ibid.

145. See testimony of Richard Hirsch, 1933, Wiener Library, P.II.c.No.980; Entry "Richard Hirsch," in *Gedenkbuch: Opfer der Verfolgung der Juden unter der nationalsozialistischen Gewaltherrschaft in Deutschland, 1933–1945*, ed. Bundesarchiv Koblenz (Koblenz, 1986) (hereafter *BArch Gedenkbuch*), http://www.bundesarchiv.de/gedenkbuch/index.html.de.

146. Announcement of Kreislandbund Weener, published in *Rheiderland*, August 3, 1933, quoted in Klausch, *Jakob de Jonge*, 29.

147. See "Eine Aufsehen erregende Verhaftung," in *Rheiderland*, July 28, 1933, quoted in Klausch, *Jakob de Jonge*, 28. See also *Historisches Handbuch der jüdischen Gemeinden in Niedersachsen und Bremen*, vol. 2, ed. Herbert Obenaus in collaboration with David Bankier and Daniel Fraenkel (Göttingen, 2005), 1540.

148. Letter from Leer County Executive to Wilhelmshaven Gestapo, December 12, 1933, quoted in Klausch, *Jakob de Jonge*, 30.

149. See Langhoff, *Moorsoldaten*, 167–172; Klausch, *Jakob de Jonge*, 40–44, 60. After another camp imprisonment in Sachsenhausen in the aftermath of the 1938 November Pogrom, de Jonge fled to the Netherlands, where he survived the war in hiding.

150. *Leipziger Neueste Nachrichten*, April 1, 1933, quoted in *Braunbuch über Reichstagsbrand und Hitler-Terror* (Basel, 1933), 248. See also Dietfrid Krause-Vilmar et al., "Das KZ Breitenau bei Kassel, 1933/34," in Ulrich Schneider, ed., *Hessen vor 50 Jahren: Naziterror und antifaschistischer Widerstand zwischen Kassel und Bergstrasse, 1932/33* (Frankfurt, 1983), 72; Drobisch and Wieland, *System*, 92–93.

151. See Krause-Vilmar, *Breitenau*, 232.

152. See ibid., 84. See also Falk Wiesemann, "Juden auf dem Lande: Die wirtschaftliche Ausgrenzung der jüdischen Viehhändler in Bayern," in Detlev Peukert and Jürgen Reulecke, eds., *Die Reihen fast geschlossen: Beiträge zur Geschichte des Alltags unterm Nationalsozialismus* (Wuppertal, 1981), 381–396; Robert Gellately, *The Gestapo and German Society: Enforcing Racial Policy, 1933–1945* (Oxford, 1990), 186; Stefanie Fischer, "Clashing Gears: Jewish Cattle Traders, Farmers, and Nazis in Conflict, 1926–35," *Holocaust Studies: A Journal for History and Culture*, 16:1–2 (2010): 15–38.

153. See Alexandra Przyrembel, *"Rassenschande": Reinheitsmythos und Vernichtungslegitimation im Nationalsozialismus* (Göttingen, 2003), 63–72, 185–227, 491; Wildt, *Volksgemeinschaft*, 223–249.

154. Przyrembel finds that in Berlin alone, 280 men were taken into "protective custody" during the months of July and August, 1935. The Breslau Gestapo arrested at least 60 people, both men and women, in the period from April to August, 1935. See Przyrembel, *"Rassenschande,"* 74, 76.

155. Bendix, *Konzentrationslager*, bk. 1:9–10.

156. See Transfers of protective custody prisoners to Dachau concentration camp, March 10–May 31, 1933, IfZ, Fa 315/1. As a separate category, "religion" appears, for example, on the listings kept by the Bayreuth District Court Prison (April 25, 1933) or the Rosenheim District Office (April 26, 1933).

157. Letter from SA leadership Kitzingen, May 13, 1933, ibid.

158. See Verdict of Jury Court at Munich District Court II against Hans Steinbrenner and Johann Unterhuber, March 10, 1952, BayStA M, Staatsanwaltschaften 34462/11, 69. See also Hans-Günter Richardi, *Schule der Gewalt: Das Konzentrationslager Dachau* (Munich, 1995), 97–99; Stansilav Zámečnik, *Das war Dachau* (Frankfurt, 2007), 33.

159. Verdict against Hans Steinbrenner, 69. See also Report of Chief Prosecutor Wintersberger and Coroner's Protocol, published as Dok. 644-PS, in *Der Prozess gegen die Hauptkriegsverbrecher vor dem Internationalen Militärgerichtshof, Nürnberg 14. November 1945–1. Oktober 1946* (hereafter IMT), vol. 26 (Nuremberg, 1947), 174–186.

160. See "Der Hebräer Louis Schloss—ein 'fainer' Jüdenvertreter," *Der Streiter: Kampfblatt der Nationalsozialistischen Freiheitsbewegung*, January 9, 1926; "Frauen- und Mädchenschänder Louis Schloss," ibid., January 16, 1926. Two additional case studies of Bavarian Jews Siegfried Reiter and Siegfried David, who were imprisoned as "race defilers" in the early Dachau camp, are documented in Raim, "Verfolgung," 202–203.

161. "Ein Rassenschänder in Schutzhaft," *Mainzer Warte*, May 26, 1934, reproduced in Bärbel Maul, "'Ihr müsst nicht glauben, dass das alles ist . . .' Diskriminiert, entrechtet, beraubt: Das Schicksal der Mainzer Juden bis zu ihrer Deportation," in Anton Maria Keim, ed., *Als die letzten Hoffnungen*

verbrannten: 9./10. November 1938; Mainzer Juden zwischen Integration und Vernichtung (Mainz, 1988), 48.

162. See Przyrembel, *"Rassenschande"*; Franco Ruault, *"Neuschöpfer des deutschen Volkes": Julius Streicher im Kampf gegen "Rassenschande"* (Frankfurt, 2006), 23, 35.

163. See Wildt, *Volksgemeinschaft,* 223–232.

164. See prisoner database of the Osthofen Concentration Camp Memorial Site Archives. Out of some sixty cases of Osthofen's Jewish prisoners, in which the background of the arrest could have been reconstructed, eight cases (13 percent) feature motivations commonly used to construct the "crime" of "race defilement." For example, "dancing" or "socializing with German girls," "paid intercourse with an Aryan woman," or "sexual assaults" on non-Jewish women.

165. Testimony of Isak Krieger (May 14, 1982), AO, Häftlingsunterlagen Isak Krieger, 2.

166. According to my own statistical evaluation of all 119 documented cases of Jews who were imprisoned in Osthofen concentration camp in 1933–1934, the average duration of detention was two to four weeks.

167. See testimony of Isak Krieger (May 14, 1982), AO, Häftlingsunterlagen Isak Krieger, 2.

168. Gellately, *Gestapo,* 160–161.

169. On the complexity of motives for denunciations, see Przyrembel, *"Rassenschande,"* 212, 492. My understanding of morality here follows Zygmunt Bauman's sociological theory. See Bauman, *Modernity and the Holocaust* (Cambridge, 1989), 170–175.

170. Report of Alzey District Office, March 28, 1934, HessStA D, G5 47.

171. Report of State Prosecutor's Office, Mainz, April 20, 1934, ibid.

172. See Przyrembel, *"Rassenschande,"* 212.

173. "Verordnung des Reichspräsidenten zur Abwehr heimtückischer Angriffe gegen die Regierung der nationalen Erhebung," *RGBl* I (1933), 135–136; "Gesetz gegen heimtückische Angriffe auf Staat und Partei und zum Schutz der Parteiuniformen," *RGBl* I (1934), 1269–1271.

174. See Bernward Dörner, "Gestapo und 'Heimtücke': Zur Praxis der Geheimen Staatspolizei bei der Verfolgung von Verstössen gegen das 'Heimtücke-Gesetz,'" in Gerhard Paul and Klaus-Michael Mallmann, eds., *Die Gestapo: Mythos und Realität* (Darmstadt, 1995), 325–342.

175. See Bernward Dörner, *"Heimtücke": Das Gesetz als Waffe; Kontrolle, Abschreckung und Verfolgung in Deutschland, 1933–1945* (Paderborn, 1998), 255, 275.

176. Trial against Alois Halbig in front of the Special Court at Berlin District Court, held on November 20 and 27, 1933, Landesarchiv Berlin (LArch Berlin), A Rep. 339 Nr. 702, 345. My thanks to Paul Moore for calling my attention to this as well as to the following two sources.

177. See Trial against Gerda Göhring in front the Special Court at Berlin District Court I, held on March 10 and 11, 1933, ibid., 81–85; Trial against Bruno Liebewirth in front of the Special Court at Berlin District Court, held on September 20, 1933, ibid., 220–222.

178. See Dörner, "Heimtücke," 313.

179. See Protective custody order issued by Hessian Police Department, Offenbach, against Max Dienemann, December 15, 1933, included in Mally Dienemann, *Aufzeichnungen*, ca. 1939, LBIA, ME112, 15. See also 12–14. The arrest of Rabbi Dienemann was reported in the local press as well as in the French paper *Le Temps*. See "Arrestation d'un Rabbin," *Le Temps*, December 19, 1933, transcribed in Dienemann, Aufzeichungen, 17.

180. See Hessian Kreisamt Alzey on the case of protective custody prisoner Eugen Kahn, September 13 and 16, 1933, in Landesarchiv Speyer, H 51 1533, 22–23, document consulted in AO.

181. See Klaus Drobisch, "Überfall auf jüdische Jungen im Juni 1933: Dokumente," in Dietrich Eichholtz, ed., *Brandenburg in der NS-Zeit: Studien und Dokumente* (Potsdam, 1993), 172.

182. Ibid., 169.

183. Letter from Hildegard Harnisch to Reich Commissar for the Provision of Employment, March 17, 1933, BLHA, Pr.Br.Rep. 2A, I Pol., Nr. 1913, 3–6.

184. See Report of SA-Sturmbann II/205, Untergruppe Brandenburg-Ost, June 7, 1933, cited according to Drobisch, "Überfall," 179–180.

185. Testimony of Fritz Hirsch, sport teacher in the Youth Home, quoted in Joseph Walk, "Das Ende des Jüdischen Jugend- und Lehrheims Wolzig (1933)," *Bulletin des Leo Baeck Instituts* 66 (1983): 10.

186. Drobisch, "Überfall," 174.

187. See Max Abraham, *Juda verrecke: Ein Rabbiner im Konzentrationslager* (Teplitz-Schönau, 1934), reprinted in Irene Diekmann and Klaus Wettig, eds., *Konzentrationslager Oranienburg: Augenzeugenberichte aus dem Jahre 1933; Gehart Seger, Reichstagsabgeordneter der SPD, Max Abraham, Prediger aus Rathenow* (Potsdam, 2003), 133.

188. Ibid., 124–128, 133.

2. Inside the Early Concentration Camps

1. See Johannes Tuchel, *Konzentrationslager: Organisationsgeschichte und Funktion der "Inspektion der Konzentrationslager," 1934–1938* (Boppard, 1991), 123–128; Sybille Steinbacher, *Dachau: Die Stadt und das Konzentrationslager in der NS-Zeit; Die Untersuchung einer Nachbarschaft* (Frankfurt, 1993), 84–87.

2. Kasimir Dittenheber, *Ich war Hitlers Gefangener: Der Weg in den Abgrund; Ein Erlebnisbericht, 1933–1939* (n.d.), 5–6, DaA, A 1316.

3. Karin Orth, "The Concentration Camp Personnel," in Jane Caplan and Nikolaus Wachsmann, eds., *Concentration Camps in Nazi Germany: The New Histories* (London, 2010), 51.

4. See ibid., 50. On the "power to kill," see Heinrich Popitz, *Phänomene der Macht: Autorität, Herrschaft, Gewalt, Technik* (Tübingen, 1986), 78–87.

5. Detlef Garbe, "Absonderung, Strafkommandos und spezifischer Terror: Jüdische Gefangene in nationalsozialistischen Konzentrationslagern," in Arno Herzig and Ina Lorenz, eds., *Verdrängung und Vernichtung der Juden unter dem Nationalsozialismus* (Hamburg, 1992), 176–177; Jürgen Matthäus, "Verfolgung, Ausbeutung, Vernichtung: Jüdische Häftlinge im System der Konzentrationslager," in Günter Morsch and Susanne zur Nieden, eds., *Jüdische Häftlinge im Konzentrationslager Sachsenhausen, 1936 bis 1945* (Berlin, 2004), 70; Orth, "Personnel," 54.

6. Orth states that camp personnel acted on the grounds of what she terms "healthy common sense" *(gesunder Menschenverstand)*, that is, "principles deemed 'normal' in their community, the validity of which was unquestioned." See Orth, "Personnel," 54. See also Harald Welzer, *Täter: Wie aus ganz normalen Menschen Massenmörder werden* (Frankfurt, 2005).

7. See Transfer lists of Communist protective custody prisoners, April 11, 1933, International Tracing Service of the Red Cross (ITS), KL Dachau GCC 3/68 I B 3, Ordner 93, 24–29. See also Günther Kimmel, "Das Konzentrationslager Dachau: Eine Studie zu den nationalsozialistischen Gewaltverbrechen," in Martin Broszat and Elke Fröhlich, eds., *Bayern in der NS-Zeit*, vol. 2: *Herrschaft und Gesellschaft im Konflikt* (Munich, 1979), 354–355; Günter Richardi, *Schule der Gewalt: Das Konzentrationslager Dachau* (Munich, 1995), 46–47, 55–56.

8. Willi Gesell, "Die ersten Transporte in das KZ Dachau," *Mitteilungsblatt der Lager-Gemeinschaft Dachau* (December 1972): 15.

9. "Ruhige Nacht in Fürth: Beginn der Generalsäuberung," *Fürther Anzeiger*, March 10, 1933. On Rudolf Benario, see Udo Sponsel and Helmut Steiner, "Erinnerung an Rudolf Benario, eines der ersten Opfer des nationalsozialistischen Terrors," *Fürther Heimatblätter* 2 (1997): 52–55; Manfred Lehner und die 9. Hauptschulklasse Soldnerstrasse, *Birken am Rednitzufer: Eine Dokumentation über Dr. Rudolf Benario am 12. April 1933 im KZ Dachau ermordet* (Fürth, 2005), http://www.der-landbote.de/Downloads/Benario_Hauptschule.pdf; Rolf Seubert, "'Mein lumpiges Vierteljahr Haft . . .': Alfred Anderschs KZ-Haft und die ersten Morde von Dachau; Versuch einer historiographischen Rekonstruktion," in Jörg Döring and Markus Joch, eds., *Alfred Andersch Revisited: Werkbiographische Studien im Zeichen der Sebald-Debatte* (Berlin, 2011), 82–85.

10. See Siegfried Imholz, "*Die Auswanderung des Siegfried 'Israel' Goldmann ist daher nicht mehr möglich . . .*" (Fürth, ca. 2008), 3, http://www.der-landbote.de/Downloads/Familie%20Goldmann%20gesamt.pdf.

11. See Seubert, "'Vierteljahr,'" 86–88.

12. The racial suffix "Jew" appears in two name entries only, those of Erich Gans and Karl Lehrburger. See Lists of Communist protective custody prisoners transferred to Dachau concentration camp, April 11, 1933, ITS, KL Dachau GCC 3/68 I B 3, Ordner 93, 25–26.

13. See Wenzel Rubner, "Dachau im Sommer 1933," in *Konzentrationslager: Ein Appell an das Gewissen der Welt; Ein Buch der Greuel; Die Opfer klagen an* (Karlsbad, 1934), 57; Richardi, *Schule*, 65–66; Stanislav Zámečník, "Dachau— Stammlager," in Wolfgang Benz and Barbara Distel, eds., *Der Ort des Terrors: Geschichte der nationalsozialistischen Konzentrationslager*, vol. 2 (Munich, 2005), 233.

14. See Christopher Dillon, "'We'll Meet Again in Dachau': The Early Dachau SS and the Narrative of Civil War," *Journal of Contemporary History* 45:3 (2010): 546.

15. See ibid., 546–547; Christopher Dillon, "The Dachau Concentration Camp SS, 1933–1939" (PhD dissertation, Birkbeck, University of London, 2010), 56–58, 234–236; Richardi, *Schule*, 253–254. See also Werdegang des Hans Steinbrenner, in Indictement of Hans Steinbrenner, August 7, 1951, DaA, 20.427/1.

16. See Gesell, "Transporte," 15.

17. A picture of the "JuBoWa" is published in *Konzentrationslager*, image opposite p. 80. See also Hugo Burkhard, *Tanz mal Jude! Von Dachau bis Shanghai: Meine Erlebnisse in den Konzentrationslagern Dachau—Buchenwald—Ghetto Shanghai, 1933–1948* (Nuremberg, 1967), 29; Richardi, *Schule*, 200.

18. See testimony of Anton Hirnickel, July 13, 1948, quoted in Richardi, *Schule*, 89.

19. Letters from Erwin Kahn to Evi Kahn, March 23, March 30, and April 5, 1933, Bayerisches Staatsarchiv München (BayStA M), Staatsanwaltschaften 34479/2, n.p. My thanks to Christopher Dillon, who brought these sources to my attention.

20. Ibid., April 5, 1933.

21. On Anton Vogel, see Dillon, "'Dachau,'" 548.

22. See testimony of Karl Procher, August 23, 1949, BayStA M, Staatsan-waltschaften 34832/1, n.p.; testimony of Johann Reiss, August 21, 1951, ibid., 34462/10, 23.

23. In his postwar testimony Reiss stated, "It was in the hours of late afternoon after the distribution of mail when Steinbrenner appeared and, from a small slip of paper that he held in his hand, read out the names Benario, Goldmann, and Kahn. Thereupon two Kahns came forward and Steinbrenner said to the second one: 'You will come along, too!'" Testimony Reiss, August 21, 1951, ibid., 34462/10, 23.

24. See letter from Carl Wintersberger to Attorney General of Munich Higher Regional Court II, April 24, 1933, USHMMA, 1995 A. 104 (Aviva Kempner Donation), Akten des Bay. Staatsministeriums der Justiz, 67–69.

25. See witness statement Emil Schuler, March 29, 1951, BayStA M, Staatsanwaltschaften 34465. See also Dillon, "Dachau," 64–65.

26. See Richardi, *Schule*, 286.

27. Hans Steinbrenner, *Hinter den Kulissen von Dachau*, Strafanstalt Landsberg am Lech, January 1962, DaA, 19.862, 2–3.

28. Witness statement Schuler, quoted in Dillon, "Dachau," 65.

29. See interrogation of Hans Steinbrenner, August 19–20, 1948, DaA, 6454.

30. See testimony of Fritz Hentrich, September 5, 1947, BayStA M, Staatsanwaltschaften 34461/3; testimony of Kaspar Schnitzler, August 9, 1949, ibid., 34832/1.

31. See interrogation of Anton Vogel, January 15, 1951, BayStA M, Staatsanwaltschaften 34461/3, 19. See also testimony Procher, ibid., 24832/1; Robert Eisinger, "Die ersten Judenmorde im KZ. Dachau 12. April 1933," *Mitteilungsblatt der Lager-Gemeinschaft Dachau* (August 1963): 8.

32. See Martin Grünwiedl, *Dachauer Gefangene erzählen . . .* , 1934, DaA 29.037, 5–6.

33. "Drei Kommunisten auf der Flucht getötet," *Münchner Neueste Nachrichten*, April 14, 1933; "Missglückter Fluchtversuch im Konzentrationslager Dachau," *Amper-Bote*, April 14/15, 1933; "Schreckliche Zustände im Konzentrationslager Dachau," leaflet quoted in *Dachauer Volksblatt*, April 15, 1933.

34. Steinbrenner, *Kulissen*, 4.

35. Ibid., 2–3.

36. See Dillon, "'Dachau,'" 545–546, also 536, 542–543.

37. Ibid., 553, also 544.

38. Address of SS Oberführer Johann Erasmus Freiherr von Malsen-Ponickau to the Dachau SS, April 11, 1933, quoted in Grünwiedl, *Gefangene*, 3. See also Dillon, "'Dachau,'" 547.

39. Interrogation Steinbrenner, August 19–20, 1948, DaA, 6454. See also Richardi, *Schule*, 104–114.

40. See testimony of Wilhelm Gesell, March 7, 1950, BayStA M, Staatsanwaltschaften 34462/4, 135; testimonies of Georg Bieber, August 5, 1948, and Fritz Schopper, July 27, 1948, quoted in Richardi, *Schule*, 105; Gesell, "Transporte." On Karl Lehrburger, see also Knut Bergbauer and Stefanie Schüler-Springorum, *"Wir sind jung, die Welt ist offen . . .": Eine jüdische Jugendgruppe im 20. Jahrhundert* (Berlin, 2002), 57–58.

41. Report on the deaths of protective custody prisoners in KZ Dachau, n.d., USHMMA, 1995 A. 104, 7. On Wintersberger, see Richardi, *Schule*, 309. See also Verdict of the Jury Court at Munich District Court II against Hans

Steinbrenner and Johann Unterhuber, March 10, 1952, BayStA M, Staatsanwaltschaften 34462/11, 64.

42. See Lothar Gruchmann, "Die bayerische Justiz im politischen Machtkampf
1933/34: Ihr Scheitern bei der Strafverfolgung von Mordfällen in Dachau," in
Broszat and Fröhlich, *Bayern II*, 420; Richardi, *Schule*, 109–113.

43. The eight Dachau prisoners of Jewish descent who died between April 12 and
May 26 are: Rudolf Benario (April 12), Ernst Goldmann (April 12), Arthur
Kahn (April 12), Erwin Kahn (April 16), Louis Schloss (May 16), Wilhelm Aron
(May 19), Alfred Strauss (May 24), and Karl Lehrburger (May 25). Wäckerle
and his staff were also responsible for the deaths of Friedrich Dressel (May 7),
Josef Anton Götz (May 8), Leonhard Hausmann (May 17), and Sebastian
Nefzger (May 26). See BayStA M, Staatsanwaltschaften 34462/11, 17–19, 61–77
(Aron, Lehrburger); Dok. PS-641, in *Der Prozess gegen die Hauptkriegsver-
brecher vor dem Internationalen Militärgerichtshof, Nürnberg 14. November
1945–1. Oktober 1946* (hereafter IMT), vol. 26 (Nuremberg, 1947), 171–172
(Alfred Strauss); Dok. PS-644, in IMT, 174–186 (Louis Schloss); Dok. PS-645,
in IMT, 187–189 (Schloss, Strauss); Gruchmann, "Justiz," 416–418; Richardi,
Schule, 88–115.

44. See Sonderbestimmungen, May 1933, published as Dok. 922-D, in IMT, vol.
36, 6–10; Disziplinar- und Strafordnung für das Gefangenenlager sowie
Dienstvorschriften für die Begleitposten und Gefangenenbewachung,
October 1, 1933, published as Dok. 778-PS, in IMT, vol. 21, 291–296. For
Eicke's biography, see Tuchel, *Konzentrationslager*, 128–143, 202–204; Günter
Morsch, "Organisation und Verwaltungsstruktur der Konzentrationslager," in
Benz and Distel, *Der Ort des Terrors*, 1:58; Dillon, "Dachau," 195–200.

45. Information on the number of deaths in Dachau in 1933 varies in the scholarly
literature. On the basis of a postwar memorial register, Günther Kimmel
counts 21 victims and identifies 9 as Jews. See Kimmel, "Konzentrationslager,"
360; *Die Toten von Dachau: Deutsche und Österreicher; Ein Gedenk- und
Nachschlagewerk* (Munich, 1947). Orth states that "at least 14 Jews" were
among the 21 fatalities but does not appropriately reference this. See Karin
Orth, *Das System der nationalsozialistischen Konzentrationslager: Eine
politische Organisationsgeschichte* (Hamburg, 1999), 54. The Dachau Concentration Camp Memorial Site, whose statistics are mainly based on the entries
of the registry offices, counts 22 deaths. See Deaths in the Dachau concentration camp, 1933 to February 17, 1940, statistics compiled by DaA, 2002 (hereafter DaA deaths statistics). Variations in the counts also stem from determining whether a victim died in Dachau, en route, or in external sites like
hospitals. Jewish victims who died under the commandership of Eicke in 1933:
Siegfried Schmitz (August 29, 1933), Delwin Theodor Katz (October 1933), and
Albert Rosenfelder (probably October 1933).

46. See "Todesopfer des Konzentrationslagers Oranienburg," in Günter Morsch, ed., *Konzentrationslager Oranienburg* (Berlin, 1994), 220. Jewish victims of Oranienburg: Erich Koh (August 5, 1933) and Erich Mühsam (July 10, 1934). See "Das Konzentrationslager Oranienburg," *Das neue Tage-Buch* 1:11 (September 9, 1933): 263.

47. See Klaus Drobisch and Günther Wieland, *System der NS-Konzentrationslager, 1933–1939* (Berlin, 1993), 128. One of the Jewish victims was Fritz Solmitz.

48. Hans Alexander (September 2, 1933), Isaak Baruch (October 20, 1933), and Ludwig Pappenheim (January 4, 1934). For a complete list of all 17 names, see Dirk Lüerssen, " 'Wir sind die Moorsoldaten': Die Insassen der frühen Konzentrationslager im Emsland, 1933 bis 1936; Biographische Untersuchungen zum Zusammenhang zwischen kategorialer Zuordnung der Verhafteten, deren jeweiligen Verhaltensformen im Lager und den Auswirkungen der Haft auf die weitere Lebensgeschichte" (doctoral thesis Universität Osnabrück, 2001), http://repositorium.uni-osnabrueck.de/bitstream/urn:nbn:de:gbv:700-2006033114/2/E-Diss529_thesis.pdf, 64–65.

49. Paul Martin Neurath, *The Society of Terror: Inside the Dachau and Buchenwald Concentration Camps*, ed. Christian Fleck and Nico Stehr (Boulder, CO, 2005), 115, 274. On Neurath's work, see also Kim Wünschmann, "The 'Scientification' of the Concentration Camp: Early Theories of Terror and Their Reception by American Academia," *Leo Baeck Institute Year Book* 58 (2013): 121–125.

50. See Tuchel, *Konzentrationslager,* 155.

51. Arrestees from the Bavarian region of Franconia, which had an above-average Jewish population, were brought to Dachau, some 270 kilometers southeast of Würzburg and some 160 kilometers south of Nuremberg.

52. See Nikolaus Wachsmann, "The Dynamics of Destruction: The Development of the Concentration Camps, 1933–1945," in Caplan and Wachsmann, *Concentration Camps in Nazi Germany,* 18–19, 37n6.

53. Falk Pingel, *Häftlinge unter SS-Herrschaft: Widerstand, Selbstbehauptung und Vernichtung im Konzentrationslager* (Hamburg, 1978), 91; Richardi, *Schule,* 231; Garbe, "Absonderung," 176–177; Matthäus, "Verfolgung," 67.

54. Numbers include those arrested on the basis of official "protective custody" orders as well as those without. They account for inmates of both camps and traditional institutions of confinement run by the legal system.

55. Marco Esseling detects a crucial inaccuracy in Pingel's calculations, on which all later estimates are based. Pingel's source is the memoir of Rudolf Höss. Höss, however, listed as the inhabitants of one of Dachau's ten prisoner barracks "Jews, emigrants, homosexuals, and Jehovah's Witnesses," who *all*

together made up 10 percent of the inmates. See Marco Esseling, "Juden als Häftlingsgruppe in Konzentrationslagern: Verhaftung von Juden und ihre Stellung im Lager bis 1942 unter besonderer Berücksichtigung des KZ Dachau" (MA dissertation, Institut für Neuere Geschichte, Ludwig-Maximilians-Universität München, 1995), 72–73; Pingel, *Häftlinge*, 91, 263; Rudolf Höss, *Commandant of Auschwitz: The Autobiography of Rudolf Höss* (London, 2000), 70.

56. Copies of the Oranienburg *Häftlingspersonalakten* are stored in Brandenburgisches Landeshauptarchiv (BLHA), Rep. 35 G KZ Oranienburg Nr. 3, and ITS, KL Oranienburg GCC 12/1, Ordner 1–68.

57. Alphabetical arrival books of prisoners from 1933 and 1934, A–Z, ITS, KL Dachau GCC 3/60, Ordner 1–3.

58. Reports detailing changes made in KL Dachau, March 24, 1936–June 30, 1937, ITS, KL Dachau GCC 3/70 I B, Ordner 98; for the following years, see Ordner 99–106.

59. The add-on "Jew" occasionally occurs in the transport lists, but mostly prisoners' religion or "race" is not indicated. In the Dachau arrival book of 1934 we sometimes find a hand-drawn star symbol as well as the letter "J" added to an entry. See, for example, ITS, KL Dachau GCC 3/60, Ordner 2, 30–32.

60. See, for example, BLHA, Rep. 2A Regierung Potsdam I Pol. Nr. 1182 "Schutzhäftlinge vom 1.1.1933 bis 1.10.1933"; GStA PK, Rep. 90 Annex P, Nr. 64/3: Geheime Staatspolizei Schutzhaft 1934 (Bd. 2).

61. See Lüerssen, "Moorsoldaten," 206, 227–464. The memorial sites of the former camps in Breitenau, Dachau, and Osthofen have each compiled biographies of Jewish prisoners. My thanks are due to Dietfrid Krause-Vilmar, Albert Knoll, and Angelika Arenz-Morch for making this data accessible to me.

62. See Ino Arndt and Heinz Boberach, "Deutsches Reich," in Wolfgang Benz, ed., *Dimension des Völkermords: Die Zahl der jüdischen Opfer des Nationalsozialismus* (Munich, 1991), 24, 26.

63. See Fritz Ecker, "Die Hölle von Dachau: Betrachtungen eines Gemarterten nach sieben Monaten Dachau," in *Konzentrationslager*, 28; Rubner, "Dachau," 66; Walter Hornung [alias Julius Zerfass], *Dachau: Eine Chronik* (Zurich, 1936), 54; Richardi, *Schule*, 231. According to DaA, the highest prisoner number given out until the end of June 1934 was 6150.

64. Erich Braun, *Dachau: The Life of a German Born Jewish Doctor*, 6, quoted in Richardi, *Schule*, 169; Burkhard, *Jude*, 29; Ferdinand Kapelner, *Nur ein kleiner Ausschnitt meiner Erlebnisse in Dachau*, 14.1.1934, Wiener Library (WL), P. II.h.No.985, 2; testimony Siegmund Herz, September 4, 1951, BayStA M, Staatsanwaltschaften 34462/10, 49; letter from Reichsvertretung of the German Jews to Reich Ministry of the Interior, November 20, 1934, Bayerisches

Hauptstaatsarchiv München (BayHStA M), StK 6300, 119; "Jews in the Dachau Camp: Long Confinement in the Cells," *Manchester Guardian Weekly*, November 2, 1934.

65. During its nine-month existence, Breitenau held 470 prisoners altogether; a proven 22 of them were of Jewish origin. See Frank-Matthias Mann, "Jüdische Häftlinge in Breitenau," in Helmut Burmeister and Michael Dorhs, eds., *Juden—Hessen—Deutsche: Beiträge zur Kultur- und Sozialgeschichte der Juden in Nordhessen* (Hofgeismar, 1991), 155; Dietfrid Krause-Vilmar, "Das Konzentrationslager im Arbeitshaus Breitenau 1933/1934," in Wolfgang Benz and Barbara Distel, eds., *Terror ohne System: Die ersten Konzentrationslager im Nationalsozialismus* (Berlin, 2001), 143; Krause-Vilmar, *Das Konzentrationslager Breitenau: Ein staatliches Schutzhaftlager 1933/34* (Marburg, 1998), 80.

66. For Oranienburg, my database registers 86 prisoners of Jewish descent. The literature estimates that some 3,000 prisoners were held in the camp throughout its existence from March 1933 to July 1934. Max Abraham remembered 55 Jews imprisoned in the summer of 1933. Stefan Szende counted 14 to 18 Jews during January to March 1934. One of the boys from the Wolzig Youth Home stated that 5 percent of the prisoners were Jews. See Max Abraham, *Juda verrecke: Ein Rabbiner im Konzentrationslager* (Teplitz-Schönau, 1934), reprinted in Irene Diekmann and Klaus Wettig, eds., *Konzentrationslager Oranienburg: Augenzeugenberichte aus dem Jahre 1933; Gehart Seger, Reichstagsabgeordneter der SPD, Max Abraham, Prediger aus Rathenow* (Potsdam, 2003), 133; Stefan Szende, *Zwischen Gewalt und Toleranz: Zeugnisse und Reflexionen eines Sozialisten* (Frankfurt, 1975), 38; "Life in a Nazi Camp: A Farm Student's Experience," *The Times*, September 19, 1933; Bernward Dörner, "Ein KZ in der Mitte der Stadt: Oranienburg," in Benz and Distel, *Terror ohne System*, 128.

67. The low figure for the Emsland camps is due to a lack of sources. Only around 15 percent of the 8,000 to 10,000 prisoners detained up until 1936 are known by name. Lüerssen found 30 Jewish prisoners; my own research has nearly doubled his figures to 58 cases. Thirty-four of them arrived in the years 1933–1934. Assuming an average total of some 4,000 men, this would make a minimum of 0.85 percent of Jews. See Lüerssen, "Moorsoldaten," 206, 465–466.

68. The Osthofen memorial site estimates that an exceptional 16 percent of the prisoners were of Jewish origin. Based on my own research, I have, however, decided to work with the moderate minimum estimate that was reached by putting the number of 119 known cases into relation with the assumed prisoner total of between 2,500 and 3,000 men. See Hans-Georg Meyer and Kerstin Roth, "Zentrale staatliche Einrichtung des Landes Hessen: Das Konzentrationslager Osthofen," in Wolfgang Benz and Barbara Distel, eds.,

Instrumentarium der Macht: Frühe Konzentrationslager, 1933–1937 (Berlin, 2003), 200, 202.

69. This result mirrors the general demographic trend of Germany's Jewish population. See Michael A. Meyer, ed., *German-Jewish History in Modern Times*, vol. 4: *Renewal and Destruction, 1918–1945* (New York, 1998), 31.

70. See Monika Richarz, "Ländliches Judentum als Problem der Forschung," in Monika Richarz and Reinhard Rürup, eds., *Jüdisches Leben auf dem Lande: Studien zur deutsch-jüdischen Geschichte* (Tübingen, 1997), 1–8.

71. Lüerssen has evaluated the age groups of 927 Emsland camp prisoners: 4.6 percent of the prisoners were born before 1881 (in relation to the 11.95 percent of my sample); 1881–1890: 4.78 percent (my sample: 18.33 percent); 1891–1900: 33.76 percent (my sample: 18.33 percent), 1901–1910: 39.16 percent (my sample: 28.33 percent); and after 1910: 7.66 percent. Although clearly in both samples most prisoners were between the ages of 22 and 33 when they arrived in the camps, Jewish prisoners are more strongly represented in the age groups born before 1890. See Lüerssen, "Moorsoldaten," 467.

72. See, for example, Ludwig Bendix, *Konzentrationslager Deutschland und andere Schutzhafterfahrungen, 1933–1937, 1937–1938*, 5 books, LBIA, ME 40, here bk. 1:37, 56; Rubner, "Dachau," 68.

73. See Dillon, "Dachau," 30, 146.

74. See Falk Pingel, "Social Life in an Unsocial Environment: The Inmates' Struggle for Survival," in Caplan and Wachsmann, *Camps*, 60.

75. See Braun, *Dachau*, 6, quoted in Richardi, *Schule*, 169.

76. Bendix, *Konzentrationslager*, bk. 1:32.

77. See testimony of Isak Krieger (May 14, 1982), Archives of Osthofen Memorial Site (AO), Häftlingsunterlagen Isak Krieger, 2.

78. Testimony of Fritz Schopper, n.d. (ca. late 1940s), Bayerisches Staatsarchiv Amberg (BayStA A), Staatsanwaltschaft Weiden Nr. 74, 4.

79. Michael Brenner and Daniela F. Eisenstein, eds., *Juden in Franken* (Munich, 2012).

80. See Dillon, "Dachau," 29–30. Dillon evaluated a list of SS personnel, compiled by the Bavarian State Police from May 30, 1933. He found that of the 192 men, 75 were drawn from SS Standarte Munich, 23 from Standarte Greater Munich, 60 from Standarte Augsburg, and 23 from Landshut.

81. See Meyer and Roth, "Osthofen," 209–210; Förderverein Projekt Osthofen, ed., *Das Konzentrationslager Osthofen, 1933/34* (Main, 2000), 16.

82. Of the 86 case studies, the place of residence is known in 80 cases. Subtracting from the sum the 41 Wolzig boys, we have a sample of 39 people. Twenty of them came from Berlin.

83. Werner Schäfer, *Konzentrationslager Oranienburg: Das Anti-Braunbuch über das erste deutsche Konzentrationslager* (Berlin, 1934), 21.

84. See Tuchel, *Konzentrationslager*, 60–78.

85. The statistics count 2 cases from the Ruhr, 9 from Rhineland, and 1 from Westphalia (a total of 12), and 2 cases from Silesia.

86. Avraham Barkai, "Population Decline and Economic Situation," in Meyer, *German-Jewish History*, 4:34–38.

87. See Dillon, "Dachau," 30; Detlef Mühlberger, *Hitler's Followers: Studies in the Sociology of the Nazi Movement* (London, 1991), 186–189.

88. Rubner, "Dachau," 68.

89. "Das Konzentrationslager Oranienburg," 263.

90. Bruno Bettelheim, *The Informed Heart: Autonomy in a Mass Age* (New York, 1960), 206.

91. Ibid.

92. See *Völkischer Beobachter*, March 10, 1920, quoted in Drobisch and Wieland, *System*, 13.

93. *Völkischer Beobachter*, March 13, 1921, translated and partly printed in Christian Goeschel and Nikolaus Wachsmann, eds., *The Nazi Concentration Camps, 1933–39: A Documentary History* (Lincoln, NE, 2012), 8–9.

94. See Special camp order for the prisoner camp Esterwegen issued by Theodor Eicke, August 1, 1934, USHMMA, RG-11001 M.20, Reel 91, Fond 1367, Opis 2, Folder 19, 4.

95. See the cases of Polish nationals Schneuer and Siegmund Resch, interned in 1933 in Dachau and Osthofen, respectively, who were discharged from the camp after the Polish state institutions imposed political pressure on the German Foreign Office. Politisches Archiv des Auswärtigen Amtes, Inland Referat Deutschland, Aktenzeichen Po 5N.E. adh 3 Polen, Bd. 1, source consulted in AO; Anon., "Als Jude in Dachau," in *Konzentrationslager*, 82, 87; Hornung, *Dachau*, 149.

96. Jewish prisoners, who arrived with the first transports after the SS takeover of the camp on April 11, were still housed in barracks together with non-Jews. Willi Gesell stated that Karl Lehrburger lived with non-Jewish prisoners while all the other Jews were eventually housed separately. A separation must have thus been implemented after April 11 and before Lehrburger was killed on May 25, 1933. See Gesell, "Transporte," 15.

97. Ecker, "Hölle," 32, 48; "Als Jude in Dachau," 78; Otto Marx, *Mein Leben in Deutschland vor und nach dem 30. Januar 1933*, 1940, DaA, 23.090, partly published as Dok. 38, in *Die Verfolgung und Ermordung der europäischen Juden durch das nationalsozialistische Deutschland 1933–1945* (hereafter *VEJ*), vol. 1: *Deutsches Reich, 1933–1937* (Munich, 2008), 148; Richardi, *Schule*, 65.

98. See Leni Yahil, "Jews in Concentration Camps in Germany Prior to World War II," in Israel Gutman and Avital Saf, eds., *The Nazi Concentration Camps: Structure and Aims, the Image of the Prisoner, Jews in the Camps; Proceedings*

of the Fourth Yad Vashem International Historical Conference, Jerusalem January 1980 (Jerusalem, 1984), 72; Záměčník, "Dachau," 238.

99. See "Als Jude in Dachau," 78. Former prisoners deported to Dachau in 1936–1937 stated that Jewish inmates were housed in barrack number 6. See Bendix, *Konzentrationslager*, bk. 5:3; Alfred Hübsch, *Die Insel des Standrechts*, ca. 1960, DaA, A 1436, 6; *Nazi-Bastille Dachau: Schicksal und Heldentum deutscher Freiheitskämpfer* (Paris, 1939), 36.

100. See Hornung, *Dachau*, 101, 109; letter from Max Bronner to Oskar Winter (Winterberger), March 10, 1947, DaA, 1159; Richardi, *Schule*, 65.

101. Burkhard, *Jude*, 26.

102. See witness testimony of Siegmund Herz, September 4, 1951, BayStA M, Staatsanwaltschaften 34462/10, 49. On the early camp in Neustadt/Haardt, see Hans-Georg Meyer and Kerstin Roth, "'Wühler,' 'Saboteure,' 'Doktrinäre': Das Schutzhaftlager in der Turenne-Kaserne in Neustadt an der Haardt," in Benz and Distel, *Instrumentarium*, 221–238.

103. See "Als Jude in Dachau," 77–78; Rubner, "Dachau," 60–61; Richardi, *Schule*, 70, 72.

104. See Julia Pietsch, "Jüdische Häftlinge im frühen Konzentrationslager Oranienburg: 'Schutzhaft' im Spannungsfeld von Antisemitismus und 'Judenpolitik'" (diploma thesis, Otto-Suhr-Institut für Politikwissenschaft, Freie Universität Berlin, 2010), 107.

105. See Klaus Drobisch, "Oranienburg: Eines der ersten nationalsozialistischen Konzentrationslager," in Morsch, *Oranienburg*, 13.

106. Gerhart Seger, *Oranienburg: Erster authentischer Bericht eines aus dem Konzentrationslager Geflüchteten* (Karlsbad, 1934), 16. An image of Oranienburg prisoners lying on straw-strewn quarters in the cellars is reproduced in Hans Biereigel, *Mit der S-Bahn in die Hölle: Wahrheiten und Lügen über das erste Nazi-KZ* (Berlin, 1994), 241.

107. See Schäfer, *Anti-Braunbuch*, 67, 73; Seger, *Oranienburg*, 16; Szende, *Gewalt*, 36.

108. Szende, *Gewalt*, 38.

109. Seger, *Oranienburg*, 31.

110. See transport list of Prominent, Intellectuals, and Jewish Prisoners to be deported from the Oranienburg camp, September 6, 1933, BLHA, Rep 2A. I Pol. Nr. 1183, 539.

111. See Schäfer, *Anti-Braunbuch*, 109; Abraham, *Juda*, 133, 145.

112. See Schäfer, *Anti-Braunbuch*, 109. See also Drobisch, "Oranienburg," 18; Diekmann and Wettig, *Konzentrationslager*, 177–178.

113. Szende remembered between 14 and 18, Fürst between 20 and 23, prisoners in the "Jew company." See Szende, *Gewalt*, 38; Max Fürst, *Talisman Scheherezade: Die schwierigen Zwanziger Jahre* (Munich, 1976), 404.

114. Fürst, *Talisman*, 408; "Life in a Nazi Camp"; Seger, *Oranienburg*, 40; "Konzentrationslager Oranienburg," 260; Pietsch, *Häftlinge*, 109.

115. Hugo Jacoby from Dessau was one of the Jewish prisoners who remained in Oranienburg after the rest of the "Jew company" were transported to the Emsland camps on September 7, 1933. See BLHA, Rep. 35G Oranienburg Nr. 3/16; Andreas Möller, "Jacoby, Hugo," in online exhibition *Die politischen Häftlinge des Konzentrationslagers Oranienburg*, http://www.stiftung-bg.de/kz -oranienburg/index.php?id=434.

116. Fritz Kleine, "Lichtenburg," in *Konzentrationslager*, 207. According to Klausch, 78 prisoners were transported from the Emsland camps to Lichtenburg on October 17–18, 1933. Max Abraham, who counted 75 deportees, stated that "more than half of them were Jews." Klausch, *Jakob de Jonge*, 52; Abraham, *Juda*, 158.

117. See Paul Wolff, *Bericht eines "Rückwanderers" über Sachsenburg*, Amsterdam 1936, WL, P.III.h. No. 689, 3.

118. Paul D., "Auf 'Schloss Osterstein,'" in Felix Burger, *Juden in brauner Hölle: Augenzeugen berichten aus SA-Kasernen und Konzentrationslagern* (Prague, 1933), 24.

119. See DaA deaths statistics.

120. See "Todesopfer Oranienburg."

121. Schäfer, *Anti-Braunbuch*, 53, 109, 146. See also Paul Moore, "'The Man Who Built the First Concentration Camp': The *Anti-Brown Book* of Concentration Camp Commandant Werner Schäfer; Fighting and Writing the Nazi 'Revolution,'" *German History* (forthcoming).

122. See testimony of Albert Lehmann, quoted in Förderverein Projekt Osthofen, *Konzentrationslager Osthofen*, 16, also 17. See also testimony of Mally Dienemann, wife of Osthofen prisoner Max Dienemann, who attributed the closure of the camp in July 1934 to "the humane attitude of its director." Mally Dienemann, *Aufzeichnungen, 1883–1939*, 1939, LBIA, MM 18, 18.

123. See Landeszentrale für politische Bildung Rheinland-Pfalz, ed., *Verfolgung und Widerstand in Rheinland-Pfalz*, vol. 1: *Gedenkstätte KZ Osthofen: Ausstellungskatalog* (Mainz, 2008), 64.

124. See Studienkreis Deutscher Widerstand, ed., *Heimatgeschichtlicher Wegweiser zu Stätten des Widerstands und der Verfolgung, 1933–1945*, vol. 1: *Hessen*, pt. 1: *Regierungsbezirk Darmstadt* (Frankfurt, 1995), 17.

125. Letter from Theodor Eicke to Personalchef RFSS, May 28, 1938, Bundesarchiv Berlin (BArchB), BDC SSO Karl d'Angelo (born September 9, 1890). See also Johannes Tuchel, "Die Kommandanten des Konzentrationslagers Dachau," *Dachauer Hefte* 10 (1994), 81–82; Volker Gallé, "Karl d'Angelo: Lagerleiter des Konzentrationslagers Osthofen," in Hans-Georg Meyer and Hans Berkessel, eds., *Die Zeit des Nationalsozialismus in Rheinland-Pfalz*, vol. 2: "*Für die*

Aussenwelt seid ihr tot!" (Mainz, 2000), 69–79; Förderverein Projekt Osthofen, *Konzentrationslager Osthofen*, 22; Landeszentrale, *Verfolgung*, 64.

126. Letter from Hans Loritz to Theodor Eicke, April 29, 1936, and letter from Alfred Driemel to Christian Guthardt, April 30, 1936, BArchB, BDC SSO Karl d'Angelo. See also Dirk Riedel, *Ordnungshüter und Massenmörder im Dienst der "Volksgemeinschaft": Der KZ-Kommandant Hans Loritz* (Berlin, 2010), 142–145.

127. See minutes of interrogation of SS Standartenführer Karl d'Angelo in Dachau, April 23, 1936, BArchB, BDC SSO Karl d'Angelo.

128. Dillon, *"Dachau,"* 214–215.

129. See Falk Pingel, "Die Konzentrationslagerhäftlinge im nationalsozialistischen Arbeitseinsatz," in Waclaw Długoborski, ed., *Zweiter Weltkrieg und sozialer Wandel: Achsenmächte und besetzte Länder* (Göttingen, 1981), 151–163; Hermann Kaienburg, *Die Wirtschaft der SS* (Berlin, 2003); Wachsmann, "Dynamics," 24–25.

130. Hornung, *Dachau*, 94.

131. Max Fürst, *Gefilte Fisch und wie es weiterging* (Munich, 2004), 236.

132. See Burkhard, *Jude*, 51. On the Dachau "craftsmen company," see also Ecker, "Hölle," 77; Hornung, *Dachau*, 35; *Nazi-Bastille*, 44, 56–57.

133. See Ecker, "Hölle," 33.

134. See Hornung, *Dachau*, 81–83. On Zäuner, see Richardi, *Schule*, 96, 158–161.

135. See Ecker, "Hölle," 33–34; Hornung, *Dachau*, 58–60; Burkhard, *Jude*, 51–52; Richardi, *Schule*, 197. For the location of the gravel pit, see the site map of early Dachau reproduced in this chapter, p. 63.

136. See Namentliches Verzeichnis des Strassenbaukommandos, September 1933, ITS, KL Dachau GCC 3/87 II C/1, Ordner 139, 22–27.

137. See Hornung, *Dachau*, 111; Burkhard, *Jude*, 37–40.

138. Fürst, *Talisman*, 404.

139. See Szende, *Gewalt*, 35.

140. See ibid.

141. See Tuchel, *Konzentrationslager*, 61–78; Drobisch and Wieland, *System*, 61, 65–66; Lüerssen, "'Moorsoldaten,'" 96–104; Lüerssen, "'Moorsoldaten' in Esterwegen, Börgermoor und Neusustrum: Die frühen Konzentrationslager im Emsland, 1933 bis 1936," in Wolfgang Benz and Barbara Distel, eds., *Herrschaft und Gewalt: Frühe Konzentrationslager, 1933–1939* (Berlin, 2002), 157–165, 188–189.

142. See Lüerssen "'Moorsoldaten' in Esterwegen," 190. On prisoner work in the peat bog, see also Pingel, *Häftlinge*, 38; Drobisch and Wieland, *System*, 120–121.

143. A rare exception is Egon Bieber, interned in Esterwegen in spring 1935. Bieber obtained work as a bookbinder, "which they were not happy to grant me

because I was a Jew, but allowed me nevertheless since I was trained in this profession." Egon Bieber, "*Schulungslager Papenburg*," Amsterdam 1935, WL, P.II.c. No. 608, 3.

144. See Lüerssen, "'Moorsoldaten' in Esterwegen," 191.

145. Testimony of Karl Schwengler, August 11, 1950, Niedersächsisches Landesarchiv—Staatsarchiv Osnabrück (NStA O), Rep. 945 Akz. 6/1983 Nr. 354, 58.

146. See testimony of Theodor Meier, August 8, 1950, ibid., 49–50; testimony Schwengler.

147. Testimony of Rudolf Münch, August 11, 1950, ibid., 59–60.

148. Emil Meier testified on April 25, 1950, that "the Jew Meyer" was beaten up by Vogel "five to six times a day." "Quite often, Meyer had blood running from his mouth. Repeatedly, he was beaten up so severely that he collapsed." See ibid., 9. According to Ernst Althoff's testimony, given on the same day, Vogel ordered Meyer to dig his own grave. See ibid., 10. See also testimony of Karl Josef Drepper, October 2, 1950, ibid., 155.

149. Testimony of former SS man Wilhelm Heitmann, August 8, 1950, ibid., 47.

150. See Lüerssen, "'Moorsoldaten,'" 107; Ludwig Bendix, *Tatsachenbericht über meine zweimalige Schutzhaft*, LBIA, ME 40, 3; Drobisch and Wieland, *System*, 112; Angelika Arenz-Morch, "Das Konzentrationslager Osthofen, 1933/34," in Hans-Georg Meyer and Hans Berkessel, eds., *Die Zeit des Nationalsozialismus in Rheinland-Pfalz*, vol. 2: *"Für die Aussenwelt seid ihr tot!"* (Mainz, 2000), 46.

151. See Hornung, *Dachau*, 82, 167.

152. Roman Praschker, "Brandenburg," in *Konzentrationslager*, 142.

153. See Veronika Springmann, "'Sport machen': Eine Praxis der Gewalt im Konzentrationslager," in Wojciech Lenarczyk et al., eds., *KZ-Verbrechen: Beiträge zur Geschichte der nationalsozialistischen Konzentrationslager und ihrer Erinnerung* (Berlin, 2007), 89–101; Springmann, "'Das ist die Moorolympiade': 'Lagersport' als Differenzproduktion in Konzentrationslagern,' in Falk Bretschneider et al., eds., *Personal und Insassen von "Totalen Institutionen": Zwischen Konfrontation und Verflechtung* (Leipzig, 2011), 381–394.

154. See Springmann, "'Moorolympiade.'" On the ideal of the soldier, see also Kim Wünschmann, "Die Konzentrationslagererfahrungen deutsch-jüdischer Männer nach dem Novemberpogrom 1938: Geschlechtergeschichtliche Überlegungen zu männlichem Selbstverständnis und Rollenbild," in Susanne Heim et al., eds., *"Wer bleibt opfert seine Jahre, vielleicht sein Leben": Deutsche Juden, 1938–1941* (Göttingen, 2010), 52–57.

155. See Springmann, "'Moorolympiade,'" 390.

156. See Karin Orth, "Gab es eine Lagergesellschaft? 'Kriminelle' und politische Häftlinge im Konzentrationslager," in Norbert Frei et al., eds., *Ausbeutung*,

Vernichtung, Öffentlichkeit: Neue Studien zur nationalsozialistischen Lager-politik (Munich, 2000), 110. The origins of the term *kapo*, which had already entered camp language in the prewar years, are uncertain. Eugen Kogon stated that it derived from the Italian *capo* (head) and the French *caporal* (corporal). According to Lutz Niethammer it was the abbreviation of *Kamerad-schaftspolizei* (police of comrades). See Eugen Kogon, *Der SS-Staat: Das System der deutschen Konzentrationslager* (Munich, 1996), 89; Lutz Niet-hammer, ed., *Der "gesäuberte" Antifaschismus: Die SED und die roten Kapos von Buchenwald; Dokumente* (Berlin, 1994), 15; Nikolaus Wachsmann, *KL: A History of the Nazi Concentration Camps* (unpublished manuscript), chap. 2, 114n276.

157. On the prisoner functionary system, see Pingel, *Häftlinge*, 56–58, 159–166; Wolfgang Sofsky, *The Order of Terror: The Concentration Camp* (Princeton, NJ, 1997), 130–144; *The Dachau Concentration Camp, 1933 to 1945: Text- and Photo Documents from the Exhibition, with CD*, ed. Barbara Distel (Munich, 2005), 92; Günter Morsch, "Formation and Construction of Sachsenhausen Concentration Camp," in Morsch, ed., *From Sachsenburg to Sachsenhausen: Pictures from the Photograph Album of a Camp Commandant* (Berlin, 2007), 182–186; Wachsmann, *KL*, chap. 2, 113–120.

158. See Kleine, "Lichtenburg," 200; Wolfgang Langhoff, *Die Moorsoldaten: 13 Monate Konzentrationslager* (Stuttgart, 1982), 219–222.

159. See Langhoff, *Moorsoldaten*, 220–222; Wolfgang Kirchhoff, "Alfred Kantoro-wicz," in *Zahnmedizin und Faschismus* (Marburg, 1988), 127–134; Drobisch and Wieland, *System*, 144.

160. See DaA prisoner database; Hermann Schirmer, *Das andere Nürnberg: Antifaschistischer Widerstand in der Stadt der Reichsparteitage* (Frankfurt, 1974), 195.

161. See Hornung, *Dachau*, 163. See also "Als Jude in Dachau," 86; Drobisch and Wieland, *System*, 144.

162. Hornung, *Dachau*, 163. See also Zámečnik, *Dachau*, 45.

163. Hornung, *Dachau*, 163. See also Burkhard, *Jude*, 25; Ecker, "Hölle," 37.

164. See Braun, *Dachau*, 10, in Richardi, *Schule*, 196; "Als Jude in Dachau," 78.

165. See Namentliches Verzeichnis des Strassenbaukommandos, Monat: Sep-tember 1933, ITS, KL Dachau GCC 3/87 II C/1, Ordner 139, 22–27; testimony of Johann Kaucic, September 8, 1949, BayStA M, Staatsanwaltschaften 34832/1; Hornung, *Dachau*, 164; Richardi, *Schule*, 198–199.

166. "Als Jude in Dachau," 85–89; Hornung, *Dachau*, 165–170; *Nazi-Bastille*, 85–86; Burkhard, *Jude*, 43–50; Richardi, *Schule*, 202–210; Zámečnik, *Dachau*, 43–46. The location of the "rondel" is marked (position no. 17) on the map of early Dachau reproduced in this chapter, p. 63.

167. See Kapelner, *Nur ein kleiner Ausschnitt*, 2.

168. See Zámečnik, *Dachau*, 44. The death date of Albert Rosenfelder is officially determined for April 1934. Apparently he was not killed instantly in October 1933 but kept in the *Bunker*. See DaA deaths statistics; "Als Jude in Dachau," 87.

169. See letter from Heinrich Himmler to Bavarian Minister President, October 19, 1933, BayHStA M, StK 5490.

170. *Nazi-Bastille*, 25, 48.

171. Burkhard, *Jude*, 42–44. See also Drobisch and Wieland, *System*, 161.

172. See Robert Rozett, "Jewish Resistance," in Dan Stone, ed., *The Historiography of the Holocaust* (New York, 2004), 341–342.

173. See Leon Poliakov, "Jewish Resistance in the West," in *Jewish Resistance during the Holocaust: Proceedings of the Conference on Manifestations of Jewish Resistance, Jerusalem, April 7–11, 1968* (Jerusalem, 1971), 284–291; Yehuda Bauer, *Rethinking the Holocaust* (New Haven, CT, 2001), 148–149; Michael R. Marrus, *The Holocaust in History* (Toronto, 2000), 133–155; Rozett, "Resistance."

174. See Meir Dworzecki, "The Day-to-Day Stands of the Jews," in *Jewish Resistance*, 152–181; Rozett, "Resistance," 345–347.

175. See Roger S. Gottlieb, "The Concept of Resistance: Jewish Resistance during the Holocaust," *Social Theory and Social Practice* 9:1 (1983): 34–35.

176. See Pingel, *Häftlinge*, 57; Johannes Tuchel, "Selbstbehauptung und Widerstand in nationalsozialistischen Konzentrationslagern," in Jürgen Schmädeke and Peter Steinbach, eds., *Der Widerstand gegen den Nationalsozialismus: Die deutsche Gesellschaft und der Widerstand gegen Hitler* (Munich, 1985), 938–953.

177. See Tuchel, "Selbstbehauptung," 944, 951; Konrad Kwiet, "Organisation, Protest, Flucht, Widerstand: Die Reaktion der europäischen Juden auf die nationalsozialistische Verfolgung," in Morsch and zur Nieden, *Häftlinge*, 110–111.

178. "Als Jude in Dachau," 89.

179. See Angelika Arenz-Morch, "Max Tschornicki: Der 'mutige Lausbub mit den kurzen Hosen,'" *Mainzer Zeitung*, August 9, 1990; Förderverein Projekt Osthofen, *Konzentrationslager Osthofen*, 20–21.

180. See Fürst, *Talisman*, 415.

181. See Kleine, "Lichtenburg," 209; Drobisch and Wieland, *System*, 144; Ramona Ehert, "Schutzhaft im Schloss Neu-Augustusburg: Das Gefangenensammellager in Weissenfels," in Benz and Distel, *Instrumentarium*, 250.

182. See Drobisch and Wieland, *System*, 144.

183. Kleine, "Lichtenburg," 199; Rubner, "Dachau," 61; Burkhard, *Jude*, 30.

184. See Bettelheim, *The Informed Heart*, 151–153, 178–187; Giorgio Agamben, *Remnants of Auschwitz: The Witness and the Archive* (New York, 2008), 41–86;

Kathrin Wittler, "'Muselmann': Anmerkungen zur Geschichte einer Bezeichnung," *Zeitschrift für Geschichtswissenschaft* 61:12 (2013): 1045–1056.

185. See Ernst P. Katz, "Die Geschichte eines Juden aus Hungen," in Arbeitsgemeinschaft "Spurensuche" Hungen, ed., *Juden in Hungen* (Giessen, 1990), 50–51.

186. Abraham, *Juda*, 154. See also testimony Busse, June 6, 1950, NStA O, Rep 945 Akz. 6/1983 Nr. 362, 140; testimony of Heinrich Katzmann, former commandant of Esterwegen II, June 9, 1950, ibid., 154.

187. See Abraham, *Juda*, 155.

188. See Burkhard, *Jude*, 42; Christopher Dillon, "The Dachau SS and the Locality, 1933–1939," in Christiane Hess et al., eds., *Kontinuitäten und Brüche: Neue Perspektiven auf die Geschichte der NS-Konzentrationslager* (Berlin, 2011), 57.

189. Letter from Reichsvertretung der Deutschen Juden to Reich Ministry of the Interior, November 20, 1934, BayHStA M, StK 6300, 119–121. On the "Röhm purge" murders at Dachau, see Richardi, *Schule*, 234–239.

190. See Friedrich Schütz, "'Ihr weint Tränen der treuen Erinnerung . . .': Zum 100. Geburtstag von Dr. Sali Levi, dem letzten Mainzer Rabbiner," *Mainzer Vierteljahreshefte für Kultur, Politik, Wirtschaft, Geschichte* 3:4 (1983): 111; Heinz Leiwig, *Leidensstätten in Mainz, 1933 bis 1945: Eine Spurensicherung— Daten—Fakten—Namen* (Mainz, 1987), 28, 137–138.

191. Letter from Max Dienemann to his family, December 21, 1933, in Mally Dienemann, *Aufzeichnungen*, 18.

192. Abraham, *Juda*, 144.

193. Burkhard, *Jude*, 26.

194. See Kim Wünschmann, "Männlichkeitskonstruktionen jüdischer Häftlinge in NS-Konzentrationslager," in Anette Dietrich and Ljiljana Heise, eds., *Männlichkeitskonstruktionen im Nationalsozialismus: Formen, Funktionen und Wirkungsmacht von Geschlechterkonstruktionen im Nationalsozialismus und ihre Refelxion in der pädagogischen Praxis* (Frankfurt, 2013), 205–209.

195. See George L. Mosse, *The Image of Man: The Creation of Modern Masculinity* (New York, 1996), 119–132.

196. See Werner Hirsch, *Hinter Stacheldraht und Gitter: Erlebnisse und Erfahrungen in den Konzentrationslagern Hitler-Deutschlands* (Zurich, 1934), 4.

197. Ibid., 17–18, 20.

198. Erich Drucker, *Mein letztes Kapitel zur Familien-Chronik meines Grossvaters* (ca.1969), LBIA, MM 18, 24, 26.

199. Hirsch, *Stacheldraht*, 12.

200. Szende, *Gewalt*, 52.

201. Neurath, *Society*, 247, 257–258.

3. Her Transport to the Concentration Camp Has Been Ordered

1. Letter from Hugo Krack to Berlin Gestapo, December 21, 1934, Niedersächsisches Hauptstaatsarchiv Hannover (NHStA H), Hann. 158 Moringen, Acc. 105/96 Nr. 232, n.p. Eva Mamlok was arrested on November 24, 1934.

2. See testimony of Inge Berner née Gerson, ca. 1970, printed in Arnold Paucker (with Lucien Steinberg), "Some Notes on Resistance," *Leo Baeck Institute Year Book* (hereafter *LBIYB*) 16 (1971): 242.

3. See Berlin Gestapo, protective custody order Eva Mamlok, December 11, 1934, NHStA H, Hann. 158 Moringen, Acc. 105/96 Nr. 232.

4. Letter from Hilde Mamlok to Hugo Krack, April 6, 1935; letter from Martha Mamlok to Hugo Krack, April 6, 1935, ibid.

5. Letter from Martha Mamlok to Hugo Krack, April 6, 1935, ibid.

6. Letter from Hugo Krack to Martha Mamlok, April 8, 1935, ibid.

7. See entry "Eva Mamlok," *Gedenkbuch: Opfer der Verfolgung der Juden unter der nationalsozialistischen Gewaltherrschaft in Deutschland, 1933–1945*, ed. Bundesarchiv Koblenz (Koblenz, 1986) (hereafter *BArch Gedenkbuch*), http://www.bundesarchiv.de/gedenkbuch/index.html.de. See also testimony Inge Berger, in Paucker, "Notes"; Helmut Eschwege, "Resistance of German Jews against the Nazi Regime," *LBIYB* 15 (1970): 143–180; Arnold Paucker, *Deutsche Juden im Widerstand, 1933–1945: Tatsachen und Probleme* (Berlin, 2003), 33.

8. See Simone Erpel, "Struggle and Survival: Jewish Women in the Anti-Fascist Resistance in Germany," *LBIYB* 37 (1992): 402; Paucker, *Juden*, 14–15.

9. See Eric Brothers, "Profile of a German-Jewish Resistance Fighter: Marianne Prager-Joachim," *Jewish Quarterly* 34:1 (1987): 31–36; Len Crome, *Unbroken: Resistance and Survival in the Concentration Camps* (London, 1988), 165–167; Erpel, "Struggle," 406; Paucker, *Juden*, 30.

10. See Klaus-Michael Mallmann, *Kommunisten in der Weimarer Republik: Sozialgeschichte einer revolutionären Bewegung* (Darmstadt, 1996), 131–132.

11. See Konrad Kwiet and Helmut Eschwege, *Selbstbehauptung und Widerstand: Deutsche Juden im Kampf um Existenz und Menschenwürde, 1933–1945* (Hamburg, 1984), 113–114, 116; Erpel, "Struggle," 404–405.

12. See Brothers, "Profile," 33; Erpel, "Struggle," 406.

13. See Marion A. Kaplan, *Between Dignity and Despair: Jewish Life in Nazi Germany* (New York, 1998), 7, 17, 28–30, 35–36.

14. Michael Burleigh and Wolfgang Wippermann, *The Racial State: Germany, 1933–1945* (Cambridge, 2006), 242.

15. Antje Dertinger, *Weisse Möwe, gelber Stern: Das kurze Leben der Helga Beyer; Ein Bericht* (Berlin, Bonn, 1987), 62, 82. Helga Beyer did not survive the Holocaust. She was murdered in the T4 "euthanasia" center in Bernburg in March 1942.

16. Crome, *Unbroken*, 141, also 138–143. Helene's brother Jonny Hüttner was sentenced to three and a half years in prison and deported to the camp afterward. See ibid., 12–13.

17. See Knut Bergbauer and Stefanie Schüler-Springorum, *"Wir sind jung, die Welt ist offen . . .": Eine jüdische Jugendgruppe im 20. Jahrhundert* (Berlin, 2002), 60, 126.

18. *Erlebnisbericht der Käthe Baronowitz, 1933–1945,* recorded by Kurt Lewin, January 1955, Wiener Library (WL), P.II.c.No.383, trans. Marion A. Kaplan, in Kaplan, *Between Dignity and Despair,* 19–20.

19. Gisela Konopka, *Mit Mut und Liebe: Eine Jugend im Kampf gegen Ungerechtigkeit und Terror* (Weinheim, 1996), 119, 140–141.

20. See Herbert Diercks, "Fuhlsbüttel," in *The United States Holocaust Memorial Museum Encyclopedia of Camps and Ghettos, 1933–1945,* vol. 1, pt. 1 (Bloomington, IN, 2009) (hereafter *USHMM Encyclopedia I*), 77–79.

21. See Sybil Milton, "Deutsche und deutsch-jüdische Frauen als Verfolgte des NS-Staates," *Dachauer Hefte* 3 (1987): 5. See also Ino Arndt, "Das Frauenkonzentrationslager Ravensbrück," in Martin Broszat, ed., *Studien zur Geschichte der Konzentrationslager* (Stuttgart, 1970), 93. The following early camps had separate sections for women: Hohnstein, Bad Sulza, Bergkamen-Schönhausen, Brauweiler, and Moringen. See Renate Riebe, "Frauen in Konzentrationslagern, 1933–1939," *Dachauer Hefte* 14 (1998): 125.

22. See Max Fürst, *Gefilte Fisch und wie es weiterging* (Munich, 2004), 683–686, 692, 709; Knut Bergbauer et al., *Denkmalsfigur: Biographische Annäherung an Hans Litten* (Göttingen, 2008), 249–250.

23. See Klaus Drobisch and Günther Wieland, *System der NS-Konzentrationslager, 1933–1939* (Berlin, 1993), 38; Riebe, "Frauen," 126.

24. See respective entries in *USHMM Encyclopedia I.*

25. See Milton, "Frauen," 5. On numbers, see also Riebe, "Frauen," 129; Barbara Distel, "Frauen in nationalsozialistischen Konzentrationslagern: Opfer und Täterinnen," in Wolfgang Benz and Barbara Distel, eds., *Der Ort des Terrors: Geschichte der nationalsozialistischen Konzentrationslager,* vol. 1: *Die Organisation des Terrors* (Munich, 2005), 197; Jane Caplan, "Gender and the Concentration Camps," in Jane Caplan and Nikolaus Wachsmann, eds., *Concentration Camps in Nazi Germany: The New Histories* (London, 2010), 83.

26. See NHStA H, Hann. 158 Moringen, Acc. 105/96 Nr. 1–327, also available in International Tracing Service (ITS), KL Moringen, Ordner 1–12. These personal files constitute the most important source corpus for research on Moringen prisoners. The data, however, remains fragmentary; for instance, in the alphabetically ordered holding files of prisoners whose family names start with letters P, Q, and R are missing. Furthermore, the only cases documented are those with arrival dates from December 1934 to September 1937 and those

of prisoners who were released or transferred to institutions other than camps, such as police and court prisons or hospitals.

27. For the history of Jewish women in Ravensbrück, see Linde Apel, *Jüdische Frauen im Konzentrationslager Ravensbrück ,1939–1945* (Berlin, 2003).

28. See Johannes Tuchel, *Konzentrationslager: Organisationsgeschichte und Funktion der "Inspektion der Konzentrationslager," 1934–1938* (Boppard, 1991), 173.

29. See Circular of the Prussian Ministry of the Interior, October 14, 1933, Institut für Zeitgeschichte (IfZ,) Fa 183/1, 285–287, quoted in Arndt, "Frauenkonzentrationslager," 94.

30. Arndt in her 1970 study of women's camps called Lichtenburg "the first real women's concentration camp." See Arndt, "Frauenkonzentrationslager," 100. Hesse, however, reaches the conclusion that Moringen must be regarded as a concentration camp. See Hans Hesse, *Das Frauen-KZ Moringen, 1933–1938* (Göttingen, 2000), 10, 167–174. For general information, see also Joseph Robert White, "Morigen-Solling (Women)," in *USHMM Encyclopedia I*, 128–131.

31. See reports detailing monthly strength of prisoners sent by Hugo Krack to Berlin Gestapo, 1933–1937 (not consecutive), NHStA H, Hann. 158 Moringen, Acc. 84/82 Nr. 2. For a detailed evaluation of the strength of female prisoners in Moringen, see Hesse, *Frauen-KZ*, 38–41.

32. See Hesse, *Frauen-KZ*, 105, 107–111. His statistics, based on official reasons for arrest, further determine that among the prisoners there were Communists (21.4 percent), Social Democrats (1.5 percent), prostitutes (4.1 percent), "criminals" (3.3 percent), female "race defilers" (3.8 percent), "returning emigrants" (5.8 percent), and women arrested for criticism of the regime (13.8 percent).

33. See NHStA H, Hann. 158 Moringen, Acc. 105/96 Nr. 1–327.

34. See lists with names of prisoners transported from Moringen to Lichtenburg concentration camp on December 15, 1937, and February 21 and March 21, 1938, NHStA H, Hann. 158 Moringen, Acc. 84/82 Nr. 9, documents consulted in the Archives of the Lichtenburg Concentration Camp Memorial (GDALi), 904G, 905G, 906G, 907G, 908G, 909G. The names documented in the 327 prisoner dossiers are not identical with the names on the transport lists.

35. Most revealing is Krack's correspondence with various agencies of persecution, stored in NHStA H, Hann. 158 Moringen, Acc. Nr. 1 and Nr. 2. The most important memoir by a Jewish woman interned in Moringen has recently been published as Gabriele Herz, *The Women's Camp in Moringen: A Memoir of Imprisonment in Germany, 1936–1937*, trans. Hildegard Herz and Howard Hartig, ed. and intro. by Jane Caplan (New York, 2006).

36. See list of protective custody prisoners detained in Moringen, March 16, 1934, in NHStA H, Hann. 158 Moringen, Acc. 84/82 Nr. 2, 15. Lizzy Hirsch died in Auschwitz on May 15, 1944. See entry "Lizzy Hirsch" in *BArch Gedenkbuch* (online version).

37. See NHStA H, Hann. 158 Moringen, Acc. 105/96 Nr. 139; entry "Herta Kronheim," in Reiner Strätz, ed., *Biographisches Handbuch Würzburger Juden, 1900–1945* (Würzburg, 1989), 319–320.

38. See NHStA H, Hann. 158 Moringen, Acc. 105/96 Nr. 28; Ilse Rolfe née Gostynski, *Report*, 1955, WL, P.III.h.No.159.

39. Berlin Gestapo, protective custody order H. Berlowitz, August 2, 1935, NHStA H, Hann. 158 Moringen, Acc. 105/96 Nr. 19, unpaginated file.

40. See, for example, "Rassenschänder durch Staatspolizei verhaftet: Artvergessene Frauenpersonen und Juden im Konzentrationslager," *Schlesische Tageszeitung*, July 14, 1935, BArchB, R. 80.34 II/ 1495, 149, quoted in Przyrembel, *"Rassenschande,"* 281. As an example of the public defamation of non-Jewish women, see "Judenliebchen sehen Dich an!," *Hakenkreuzbanner* (Mannheim), August 27, 1933, quoted in Przyrembel, *"Rassenschande,"* 148.

41. See article 5.2 of the Law for the Protection of German Blood and German Honour, *Reichsgesetzblatt (RGBl)* 1 (1935): 1146, translation in Jeremy Noakes and Geoffrey Pridham, eds., *Nazism, 1919–1945: A Documentary Reader*, vol. 2: *State, Economy and Society, 1933–39* (Exeter, 1984), 535–536.

42. See Lothar Gruchmann, "'Blutschutzgesetz' und Justiz: Zur Entstehung und Auswirkung der Nürnberger Gesetze," *Vierteljahreshefte für Zeitgeschichte (VfZ)* 31 (1983): 437–440; Przyrembel, *"Rassenschande,"* 172–182.

43. See Przyrembel, *"Rassenschande,"* 263; Nikolaus Wachsmann, *Hitler's Prisons: Legal Terror in Nazi Germany* (New Haven, CT, 2004), 158.

44. Circular Berlin Gestapo to all Coordinating Offices of the Secret State Police, September 18, 1935, BArchB, R 58/264, 161.

45. Secret circular of the Head of Security Police to all Coordinating Offices of the Secret State Police and the Criminal Police, June 12, 1937, in BArchB, R 3001/20050 Reichsjustizministerium, 95.

46. See Przyrembel, *"Rassenschande,"* 284.

47. See Lotti Huber, *Diese Zitrone hat noch viel Saft: Ein Leben* (Munich, 1993), 27–34.

48. Ibid., 30. Huber chose the name "Marianne" for Annemarie Münzer, whereas Herz used the pseudonym "Anni Reiner." See Herz, *Women's Camp*, 83, 89.

49. See entry "Annemarie Münzer," ITS, Central Name Index.

50. See Patrick Wagner, *Volksgemeinschaft ohne Verbrecher: Konzeption und Praxis der Kriminalpolizei in der Zeit der Weimarer Republik und des Nationalsozialismus* (Hamburg, 1996), 367–369; Riebe, "Frauen," 133–134; Przyrembel, *"Rassenschande,"* 291.

51. Police preventive custody order issued by Hamburg Kripo, September 9, 1937, NHStA H, Hann. 158 Moringen, Acc. 105/96 Nr. 198, n.p. For a systematic treatment of the arrest category of "preventive police custody," see Chapter 5.

52. See Report Hugo Krack to Gestapo Hamburg, January 13, 1938, in ibid.; Hesse, *Frauen-KZ*, 151–152; Apel, *Frauen*, 369.

53. Letter from Hedwig Hirschel to Hugo Krack, August 14, 1937, NHStA H, Hann. 158 Moringen, Acc. 105/96 Nr. 140, n.p.

54. See prisoner dossier Charlotte Cohn, NHStA H, Hann. 158 Moringen, Acc. 105/96 Nr. 43, including information on Charlotte Droste, whose own file has not survived.

55. "Judendirnen: Welches Unglück jüdische Weiber über deutsche Männer bringen können," *Der Stürmer* 15:22 (May 1937).

56. Gestapo decree regarding dissemination of information to the Stürmer, April 24, 1937, USHMMA, RG-11001 M.01, Reel 4, Fond 500, Opis 1, Folder 261, 13–14.

57. Letter from Hedwig Hirschel to Hugo Krack, August 14, 1937, NHStA H, Hann. 158 Moringen, Acc. 105/96 Nr. 140.

58. Letters from Hugo Krack to Breslau Gestapo, October 20, 1937, and to Berlin Gestapo, February 2, 1938, in NHStA H, Hann. 158 Moringen, Acc. 105/96 Nr. 140.

59. See entry "Hedwig Hirschel," in *BArch Gedenkbuch* (online version). In seven of the eleven cases of Jewish female prisoners interned in Moringen for "race defilement," their further fate is known; two (Münzer and Huber) emigrated, five perished in the Holocaust.

60. See NHStA H, Hann. 158 Moringen Acc. 105/96 Nr. 47; Claudia Schoppmann, *Nationalsozialistische Sexualpolitik und weibliche Homosexualität* (Pfaffenweiler, 1997), 235–237.

61. See letters from Hugo Krack to Berlin Gestapo, July 22 and September 18, 1937, in NHStA H, Hann. 158 Moringen Acc. 105/96 Nr. 47; Gestapo report, undated, quoted in Schoppmann, *Sexualpolitik*, 236.

62. Stefanie Zweig, *Nowhere in Africa: An Autobiographical Novel* (Madison, WI, 2004), 50. See also Annemarie Hühne, "Fluchtziel Ostafrika: Die Verfolgungsgeschichte von Elsa Conrad," *Dokumente: Rundbrief der Lagergemeinschaft und Gedenkstätte KZ Moringen e.V.* 25 (2008), 22–23.

63. See Kaplan, *Between Dignity and Despair*, 62–73; Gudrun Maierhof, *Selbstbehauptung im Chaos: Frauen in der jüdischen Selbsthilfe, 1933–1943* (Frankfurt, 2002), 35–38.

64. Kurt Hiller, "Schutzhäftling 231," VI., *Die neue Weltbühne* 31:1 (January 3, 1935), 16.

65. Kurt Hiller, "Schutzhäftlinge 231," V., *Die neue Weltbühne* 30:50 (December 27, 1934), 1646–1647.

66. Hiller, "Schutzhäftling 231," VI., 16. On questions of emigration, see also David Jünger, "Vor dem Entscheidungsjahr: Jüdische Emigrationsfragen im nationalsozialistischen Deutschland, 1933 bis 1938" (doctoral thesis, Fakultät für Geschichte, Kunst- und Orientwissenschaften, Universität Leipzig, 2012).

67. See Juliane Wetzel, "Auswanderung aus Deutschland," in Wolfgang Benz, ed., *Die Juden in Deutschland, 1933–1945: Leben unter nationalsozialistischer Herrschaft* (Munich, 1988), 498.

68. See Herbert E. Tutas, *Nationalsozialismus und Exil: Die Politik des Dritten Reiches gegenüber der deutschen politischen Emigration* (Munich, 1975), 8, 11–3, 19–20.

69. Memorandum of SD Office IV/2, May 24, 1934, printed in *Die Judenpolitik des SD 1935 bis 1938: Eine Dokumentation,* ed. and intro. by Michael Wildt (Munich, 1995), 66.

70. Gestapo circular regarding measures against returning emigrants, January 28, 1935, BArchB, R 58/269, 167–170.

71. Ibid.

72. See ibid.; Gestapo circular, March 9, 1935, BArchB, R 58/269, 171–172.

73. Gestapo circular regarding measures against returning emigrants, January 18, 1937, in Brandenburgisches Landeshauptarchiv (BLHA), Rep. 2 A I Pol Nr. 1204, 61–62.

74. See Gestapo circular regarding measures against returning emigrants, June 13, 1935, IfZ, Fb 201. See also Tutas, *Nationalsozialismus,* 115; Jane Caplan, "Introduction," in Herz, *Women's Camp,* 1, 9.

75. Letter from Reich Leader SS and Chief of German Police to Reich Minister of Finance, August 31, 1937, BLHA, Rep. 2 A I Pol Nr. 1204, 72.

76. See Wetzel, "Auswanderung," 414, 497.

77. Letter from Theodor Eicke to Darmstadt Gestapo, April 30, 1936, and minutes of interrogation of Gottfried Fischer by Darmstadt Gestapo, May 19, 1936, BArchB, BDC SSO Karl d'Angelo (born September 9, 1890).

78. Report of SS Scharführer Christian Guthardt, May 2, 1936, ibid.

79. Minutes of Fischer interrogation, May 19, 1936, ibid.

80. Letter from Theodor Eicke to Personalchef RFSS, May 28, 1938, ibid. See also Dirk Riedel, *Ordnungshüter und Massenmörder im Dienst der "Volksgemeinschaft": Der KZ-Kommandant Hans Loritz* (Berlin, 2010), 143. On Fischer, see entry "Gottfried Fischer" in *BArch Gedenkbuch* (online version).

81. Letter from Getrud Glogowski to Hugo Krack, August 26, 1937, in NHStA H, Hann. 158 Moringen, Acc. 105/96 Nr. 104, file only partly paginated. For other further cases of imprisoned couples, see ibid., Nr. 39, Nr. 215, Nr. 220, Nr. 223, Nr. 229.

82. Identifiable cases of Jewish inmates in 1935: 20 "emigrants," 5 "race defilers"/prostitutes, 4 regime critics, 3 political activists, and 1 case of fraud. For 1936:

11 "emigrants," 2 political activists, 1 regime critic, and 1 "race defiler"/ prostitute.

83. See Frieda Sherwood (Schweitzer), *Bericht über meine Gefängnis- und Konzentrationslagerhaft*, 1955, WL, P.III.h.No.117, addendum.

84. See NHStA H, Hann. 158 Moringen, Acc. 105/96 Nr. 39, Nr. 223.

85. Ibid., Nr. 299. See also Wetzel, "Auswanderung," 497.

86. See NHStA H, Hann. 158 Moringen, Acc. 105/96, Nr. 16, Nr. 249.

87. See ibid., Nr. 52

88. See ibid., Nr. 156, Nr. 225.

89. See ibid., Nr. 67.

90. See ibid., Nr. 130; Herz, *Women's Camp*. For details on Herz's biography, see Caplan, "Introduction," 1–2, 5–10.

91. See "Centa Herker-Beimler berichtet über das KZ Moringen," in Jutta von Freyberg and Ursula Krause-Schmitt, *Moringen, Lichtenburg, Ravensbrück: Frauen im Konzentrationslager, 1933–1945* (Frankfurt, 1997), 17.

92. See Herz, *Women's Camp*, 82–83. Herz used the pseudonyms "Herta Kronau" for Herta Kronheim, "Ilse Lipinski" for Ilse Gostynski (Rolfe), and "Anni Reiner" for Annemarie Münzer. Ursula Krause-Schmitt has identified a great part of the pseudonyms Herz used in her memoir. See Ursula Krause-Schmitt, "Im 'Judensaal' des Frauenkonzentrationslagers Moringen," *Dokumente* 19 (2000): 6–12. See also the biographical appendix complied by Jane Caplan in Herz, *Women's Camp*, 166–168.

93. See Hesse, *Frauen-KZ*, 141, 144.

94. Herz, *Women's Camp*, 82. See also Hesse, *Frauen-KZ*, 49–54. Ilse Rolfe née Gostynksi, who arrived in Moringen in May 1936, counted 25 women from Bavaria and 12 Jewish prisoners. See Rolfe, *Report*, 1. The Sopade Report of August 1936 also counted "some 12 Jewish women" accommodated in a separate room. See *Deutschland-Berichte der Sozialdemokratischen Partei Deutschlands (Sopade Report)* 3 (1936) (Frankfurt, 1982), 1013.

95. See Herz, *Women's Camp*, 88–89.

96. Ibid., 100–103.

97. Service and house regulations for the women's protective custody camp Moringen, n.d., NHStA H, Hann. 158 Moringen Acc. 84/82 Nr. 2, 145.

98. Herz, *Women's Camp*, 116.

99. See letter from Dr. Guttmann to Centralverein deutscher Staatsbürger jüdischen Glaubens (CV), November 3, 1933, Archiv der Stiftung Neue Synagoge Berlin—Centrum Judaicum (CJ), CJA, 1, 75 C Ra 1, Allgemeiner Rabbinerverband in Deutschland, Nr. 19, # 12529, 254. My thanks are due to David Jünger, who brought this and the following sources to my attention.

100. Letter from CV to Allgemeiner Rabbinerverband, December 4, 1933, CJ, CJA, 1, 75 C, Ra 1, Allgemeiner Rabbinerverband in Deutschland Nr. 19, # 12529,

261. See also ibid., 256–257, for letter from CV to Allgemeiner Rabbinerverband, November 16, 1933.

101. See letter from Landesrabbinat Hildesheim to Director of the Women's Protective Custody Camp Moringen, November 11, 1937, NHStA H, Hann. 158 Moringen Acc. 84/82 Nr. 2, 151.

102. Letter from Hugo Krack to Landesrabbinat Hildesheim, November 13, 1937, ibid., 152. See also Hesse, *Frauen-KZ*, 96.

103. Rolfe, *Report*, attachment of an undated letter.

104. Herz, *Women's Camp*, 105.

105. See Sherwood, *Bericht*, 2.

106. See Herz, *Women's Camp*, 140–141.

107. See Sherwood, *Bericht*, 2.

108. See conduct report about Anni Krümmel sent by Hugo Krack to Hamburg Gestapo, March 11, 1938, NHStA H, Hann. 158 Moringen Acc. 105/96 Nr. 198, 18.

109. See Bayerisches Staatsarchiv Würzburg (BayStA W), Gestapo 717; Hartmut Mehringer, "Die KPD in Bayern, 1919–1945: Vorgeschichte, Verfolgung und Widerstand," in Martin Broszat and Hartmut Mehringer, eds., *Bayern in der NS-Zeit*, vol. 5: *Die Parteien KPD, SPD, BVP in Verfolgung und Widerstand* (Munich, 1983), 226; Strätz, *Handbuch*, 319–320.

110. See interview Hedwig Regnart, n.d., GDALi, AN 3471, quoted in Hesse, *Frauen-KZ*, 59.

111. See Herz, *Women's Camp*, 149; Krause-Schmitt, "'Judensaal,'" 6.

112. See list of women transported to Lichtenburg concentration camp on March 21, 1938, NHStA H, Hann. 158 Moringen Acc. 84/82 Nr. 9 (consulted in GDALi, 906G); entry "Herta Kronheim," ITS, Central Name Index; Strätz, *Handbuch*, 327–328.

113. See von Freyberg and Krause-Schmitt, *Moringen*, 34–35. Hans Beimler fell in the Spanish Civil War on December 1, 1936.

114. See service and house regulations, article 4, 145. See also Matthias Kuse, "Die Entlassung von Häftlingen aus dem Frauenkonzentrationslager Moringen, 1934–1938," *Dokumente* 19 (2000), 14–15.

115. Conduct report Margarete Sander, sent by Hugo Krack to Aachen Gestapo, August 7, 1935, NHStA H, Hann. 158 Moringen Acc. 105/96 Nr. 256, n.p.

116. Salomon Adler-Rudel, *Die Situation der deutschen Juden im Januar 1936*, n.d. (1936) and *The Situation of the Jews in Germany in January 1937*, n.d. (1937), Central Zionist Archives (CZA), A140–439, 2; A140–148, 8; Arthur Prinz, "The Role of the Gestapo in Obstructing and Promoting Jewish Emigration," *Yad Vashem Studies* 2 (1958): 216. My thanks are due to David Jünger for pointing me to these sources.

117. See Drobisch and Wieland, *System*, 280; Kuse, "Entlassung," 15.

118. See, for example, NHStA H, Hann. 158 Moringen Acc. 105/96 Nr. 22, Nr. 67.

119. Circular of the Political Police Commander, the Prussian Secret State Police Office, August 18, 1936, BArchB, R 58/264, 263.

120. Letter from Bavarian Ministry of the Interior, the Political Police Commander of Bavaria to Bavarian State Chancellery, May 14, 1936, BayStA W, Gestapo 8958 (Benno Oppenheimer), 73. On Oppenheimer, who lost his life in Sachsenhausen concentration camp on May 10, 1940, see also Elke Fröhlich, "Ein 'Volksschädling,' " in Martin Broszat and Elke Fröhlich, eds., *Bayern in der NS-Zeit*, vol. 6: *Die Herausforderung des Einzelnen: Geschichten über Widerstand und Verfolgung* (Munich, 1983), 112.

121. See Hesse, *Frauen-KZ*, 146–147, 164; Riebe, "Frauen," 134.

122. See letter from Krack to Breslau Gestapo, May 23, 1936, NHStA H, Hann. 158 Moringen Acc. 105/96 Nr. 320.

123. NHStA H, Hann. 158 Moringen Acc. 105/96 Nr. 43. Charlotte Cohn was deported to the concentration camp for a second time in 1938. She was killed in Bernburg in the "Action 14f13" on April 23, 1942. See *BArch Gedenkbuch* (online version). Charlotte Droste survived Nazi persecution and immigrated to Palestine in 1947. See ITS, Central Name Index.

124. Minutes of Himmler's visit to Moringen on May 28, 1937, NHStA H, Hann. 158 Moringen Acc. 84/82 Nr. 2, 119.

125. Adler-Rudel, *Situation*, 8.

126. Circular from Berlin Gestapo to all Gestapo desks and to the Leader of the SS Death's Head Divisions and Concentration Camps, January 31, 1939, BArchB, R 58/276, 203–204.

127. Circular of Reich Security Head Office (RSHA), April 10, 1940, BArchB, R 58/276, 252.

128. Prinz, "Role," 205–209.

129. See Jünger, "Entscheidungsjahr," 257–258. Apart from the Hilfsverein and the Palästinaamt the Reichsvertretung's own Hauptstelle für jüdische Wanderfürsorge (Central Office for Jewish Migration Welfare) was active in organizing emigration.

130. See letters from JFB (Hannah Karminski) to Hugo Krack, August 16 and December 22, 1937, January 18 and February 1 and 8, 1938, NHStA H, Hann. 158 Moringen Acc. 84/82 Nr. 2, 136, 168, 178, 179, 180; letter from Hugo Krack to Berlin Gestapo, August 17, 1937, and letter from Berlin Gestapo to Hugo Krack, September 8, 1937, in ibid. See also Maierhof, *Selbstbehauptung*, 48, 71–77, 110–114, 193–194. On the JFB, see Marion A. Kaplan, *The Jewish Feminist Movement in Germany: The Campaigns of the Jüdische Frauenbund, 1904–1938* (Westport, CT, 1979). On Rittel, interned from 1937 until her escape from Germany in 1939, see entry "Erna Rittel," ITS, Central Name Index.

131. Hesse, *Frauen-KZ*, 93; Hesse, "Von der 'Erziehung' zur 'Ausmerzung': Das Konzentrationslager Moringen, 1933–1945," in Wolfgang Benz and Barbara Distel, eds., *Instrumentarium der Macht: Frühe Konzentrationslager, 1933–1937* (Berlin, 2003), 134. On Krack, see also Matthias Kuse, "Hugo Krack: Ein 'Zivilist' als KZ-Direktor?," *Dokumente* 20 (2001): 8–11; Caplan, "Introduction," 20–25.

132. Letter from Hugo Krack to Hamburg Gestapo, March 11, 1938, NHStA H, Hann. 158 Moringen Acc. 105/96 Nr. 198, 18.

133. See letters from Hugo Krack to Berlin Gestapo, August, 10, and October 14 and 1935, NHStA H, Hann. 158 Moringen Acc. 105/96 Nr. 22, unpaginated file.

134. Letter from Milli Beermann to British Friends' German Emergency Committee, November 1, 1935, Friends House Library and Archives, London, Friends Committee for Refugees and Aliens, Political Prisoners, Correspondence 1933–1938, FCRA/19/1. See also Caplan, "Introduction," 24, 51.

135. Sherwood, *Bericht*, addendum. Krack is remembered by the name "Drake."

136. Huber, *Zitrone*, 28.

137. See Hesse, "'Erziehung,'" 133–135.

138. Rolfe, *Report*, 2.

139. See Kuse, "Krack," 10–11.

140. Mary Fulbrook, *A Small Town near Auschwitz: Ordinary Nazis and the Holocaust* (Oxford, 2012), 8.

141. See Joseph Robert White, "Morigen-Solling (Men)," in *USHMM Encyclopedia I*, 125, 127.

142. Fulbrook, *Town*, 356.

143. See report of Hugo Krack to Provincial Governor Hanover, December 20, 1937, NHStA H, Hann. 158 Moringen Acc. 84/82 Nr. 2, 160. See also Caplan, "Introduction," 24–25.

144. Fulbrook, *Town*, 343, 356.

145. See quote in Hesse, *Frauen-KZ*, 94.

146. This divergence lasted well into the war, as a recent study demonstrates. See Marc Buggeln, *Arbeit & Gewalt: Das Aussenlagersystem des KZ Neuengamme* (Göttingen, 2009), 508–518.

147. The term *Scharnier* (hinge) for Lichtenburg was coined by Günter Morsch. See Stefanie Endlich, "Die Lichtenburg, 1933–1939: Haftort politischer Prominenz und Frauen-KZ," in Wolfgang Benz and Barbara Distel, eds., *Herrschaft und Gewalt: Frühe Konzentrationslager, 1933–1939* (Berlin, 2002), 17.

148. See Endlich, "Lichtenburg," 12–15; Stefanie Endlich, "Lichtenburg," in *USHMM Encyclopedia I*, 120–123; Stefan Hördler, "Before the Holocaust: Concentration Camp Lichtenburg and the Evolution of the Nazi Camp System," *Holocaust and Genocide Studies*, 25:1 (2011): 101.

149. See Rolfe, *Report*, 2, 4–5; Huber, *Zitrone*, 28. See also Henning Fahrenberg and Nicole Hördler, "Das Frauenkonzentrationslager Lichtenburg: Einblicke, Funktion, Tendenzen," in Stefan Hördler and Sigrid Jacobeit, eds., *Lichtenburg: Ein deutsches Konzentrationslager* (Berlin, 2009), 170–171.

150. See lists of names for transport from Moringen to Lichtenburg, March 21, 1938, GDALi, 906G, 907G, 908G, 909G. These lists contain 164 names. However, according to a note by the Lichtenburg camp administration from June 9, 1938, 168 personal record cards of prisoners transported to Lichtenburg on March 21, 1938, were sent back to Moringen, which means that, in reality, 168 prisoners had been aboard the transport. See NHStA H, Hann. 158 Moringen Acc. 84/82 Nr. 8, 124. See also Fahrenberg and Hördler, "Frauen-Konzentrationslager," 168. Previously, 200 female prisoners were sent to Lichtenburg on December 15, 1937, and another 150 on February 21, 1938.

151. See GDALi, 908G.

152. There are 349 personal record cards of prisoners of the first two transports stored in NHStA H, Hann. 158 Moringen Acc. 84/82 Nr. 6, Nr. 7.

153. The only female Jewish prisoner whose arrival in the Lichtenburg can be ascertained to have predated the transport of March 21, 1938, is Olga Benario-Prestes, who was brought to the camp on February 15, 1938. See Ruth Werner, *Olga Benario: Die Geschichte eines tapferen Lebens* (East Berlin, 1961), 345; Barbara Bromberger et al., *Schwestern, vergesst uns nicht: Frauen im Konzentrationslager; Moringen, Lichtenburg, Ravensbrück, 1933–1945* (Frankfurt, 1988), 44.

154. Rolfe, *Report*, 2.

155. See Riebe, "Frauen," 136; Endlich, "Lichtenburg," 46; Fahrenberg and Hördler, "Frauen-Konzentrationslager," 185–186.

156. See Werner, *Olga Benario*, 368; Riebe, "Frauen," 137.

157. Testimony of former Lichtenburg prisoner Fini Gleixner, quoted in Klaus Drobisch, "Frauenkonzentrationslager im Schloss Lichtenburg," *Dachauer Hefte* 3 (1987): 106.

158. See Endlich, "Lichtenburg," 22; Fahrenberg and Hördler, "Frauen-Konzentrationslager," 169.

159. My own research builds upon the comprehensive biographical research on Lichtenburg prisoners conducted by Sven Langhammer and Katja Seybold for the Lichtenburg Memorial Site. I thank Sven Langhammer for sharing the results with me.

160. See Huber, *Zitrone*, 28; Werner, *Olga Benario*, 368; Drobisch, "Frauenkonzentrationslager," 111; Endlich, "Lichtenburg," 47; Fahrenberg and Hördler, "Frauen-Konzentrationslager," 171, 178.

161. See Drobisch, "Frauenkonzentrationslager," 111.

162. My research found that of the 123 identified Jewish women imprisoned in Moringen between 1934 and 1938, 21 died violent deaths in the Holocaust. Eleven of them were gassed in Bernburg in the spring of 1942. On "Action 14f13," see also Apel, *Frauen*, 296–316, in particular 314–315.

4. Cementing the Enemy Category

1. See Johannes Tuchel, *Konzentrationslager: Organisationsgeschichte und Funktion der "Inspektion der Konzentrationslager," 1934–1938* (Boppard, 1991), 159–204; Klaus Drobisch and Günther Wieland, *System der NS-Konzentrationslager, 1933–1939* (Berlin, 1993), 186–191.

2. See Joseph Robert White, "Introduction to the Early Camps," in *The United States Holocaust Memorial Museum Encyclopedia of Camps and Ghettos, 1933–1945*, vol. 1, pt. 1 (Bloomington, IN, 2009) (hereafter *USHMM Encyclopedia I*), 8; Angelika Borgstedt, "Das nordbadische Kislau: Konzentrationslager, Arbeitshaus und Durchgangslager für Fremdenlegionäre," in Wolfgang Benz and Barbara Distel, eds., *Herrschaft und Gewalt: Frühe Konzentrationslager, 1933–1939* (Berlin, 2002), 218, 227. The camps of Vechta in the state of Oldenburg and Kuhberg in Württemberg also continued to exist beyond the summer of 1934 and were closed in April and July 1935, respectively.

3. Bad Sulza was taken over by the SS on April 1, 1936, but only officially subordinated under the IKL a year later. See Udo Wohlfeld, "Bad Sulza," in *USHMM Encyclopedia I*, 22.

4. Nikolaus Wachsmann, "The Dynamics of Destruction: The Development of the Concentration Camps, 1933–1945," in Jane Caplan and Nikolaus Wachsmann, eds., *Concentration Camps in Nazi Germany: The New Histories* (London, 2010), 22.

5. Letter from RFSS and Chief of the German Police to Reich Ministry of Justice, February 8, 1937, quoted in Günter Morsch, "Formation and Construction of Sachsenhausen Concentration Camp," in Morsch, ed., *From Sachsenburg to Sachsenhausen: Pictures from the Photograph Album of a Camp Commandant* (Berlin, 2007), 89.

6. See Tuchel, *Konzentrationslager*, 308; Drobisch and Wieland, *System*, 203.

7. See Tuchel, *Konzentrationslager*, 307–317; Lothar Gruchmann, *Justiz im Dritten Reich, 1933–1940: Anpassung und Unterwerfung in der Ära Gürtner* (Munich, 2001), 632–658; Christian Goeschel and Nikolaus Wachsmann, eds., *The Nazi Concentration Camps, 1933–39: A Documentary History* (Lincoln, NE, 2012), 71–75.

8. Address by Heinrich Himmler to the Staatsräte, March 5, 1936, BArchB, NS 19/4003; parts of this are translated in Goeschel and Wachsmann, *Concentration Camps*, 81–83.

9. Lecture by Heinrich Himmler to the Wehrmacht, January 1937, published as document 1992(A)-PS in *Der Prozess gegen die Hauptkriegsverbrecher vor dem Internationalen Militärgerichtshof, Nürnberg 14. November 1945–1. Oktober 1946* (hereafter IMT), vol. 29 (Nuremberg, 1947), 222, 228–229, 233–234.

10. See Peter Longerich, *Heinrich Himmler: Eine Biographie* (Munich, 2008), 209, see also 187–210; Jane Caplan, "Introduction," in Gabriele Herz, *The Women's Camp in Moringen: A Memoir of Imprisonment in Germany, 1936–1937* (New York, 2006), 10–18.

11. See Robert Gerwarth, *Hitler's Hangman: The Life of Heydrich* (New Haven, CT, 2011), 50–109.

12. See letter from Betty Scholem to Gershom Scholem, March 12, 1935, in *Betty Scholem, Gershom Scholem, Mutter und Sohn im Briefwechsel, 1917–1946*, ed. Itta Shedletzky (Munich, 1989), 380; Michael Buckmiller and Pascal Nafe, "Die Naherwartung des Kommunismus: Werner Scholem," in Michael Buckmiller et al., eds., *Judentum und politische Existenz: Siebzehn Porträts deutsch-jüdischer Intellektueller* (Hanover, 2000), 74–78.

13. See Dachau Concentration Camp Memorial Site Archives (DaA), prisoner database; Knut Bergbauer, "'Der eben an uns vorüberging . . .': Rudi Arndt—ein jüdischer Kommunist im Widerstand," *transversal* 11:2 (2010): 32–36.

14. See Ephraim Carlebach Stiftung in collaboration with Sabine Niemann, *Die Carlebachs: Eine Rabbinerfamilie aus Deutschland* (Hamburg, 1995), 136–137.

15. See Jörg Kammler and Dietfrid Krause-Vilmar, *Volksgemeinschaft und Volksfeinde: Kassel, 1933–1945; Eine Dokumentation* (Fuldabrück, 1984), 206–207; Dietfrid Krause-Vilmar, *Das Konzentrationslager Breitenau: Ein staatliches Schutzhaftlager, 1933/34* (Marburg, 1998), 234; DaA prisoner database.

16. See Nachlass Herbert Mindus NL 5, in Memorial and Museum Sachsenhausen Archives (AS); Barbara Danckwortt, "Jüdische 'Schutzhäftlinge' im KZ Sachsenhausen, 1936 bis 1938: Verfolgungsgeschichten von Kommunisten, Sozialdemokraten und Liberalen," in Günter Morsch and Susanne zur Nieden, eds., *Jüdische Häftlinge im Konzentrationslager Sachsenhausen, 1936 bis 1945* (Berlin, 2004), 144–146.

17. See Nikolaus Wachsmann, *Hitler's Prisons: Legal Terror in Nazi Germany* (New Haven, CT, 2004), 159–164.

18. Ernesto Kroch, *Exil in der Heimat—Heim ins Exil: Erinnerungen aus Europa und Lateinamerika* (Frankfurt, 1990), 70–71. Kroch used the names "Käschen" for Heinz Isaac and "Lothar" for Lothar Müller. See also transcript of oral history interview with Lothar Müller, August 23, 2004, conducted by Anja Schmidt, Andrea Sorgenfrei, and Denny Kunze, Archives of the Lichtenburg Concentration Camp Memorial (GDALi).

19. See Kroch, *Exil*, 70–71, 75–76.

20. See letter from Ludwig Bendix to Chief of Police District 174, July 14, 1935, printed and trans. in Reinhard Bendix, *From Berlin to Berkeley: German-Jewish Identities* (New Brunswick, NJ, 1986), 163. See also Ludwig Bendix, *Tatsachenbericht über meine zweimalige Schutzhaft*, LBIA, ME 40, 7–8.

21. Ludwig Bendix, *Konzentrationslager Deutschland und andere Schutzhafter-fahrungen, 1933–1937, 1937–1938*, 5 books, LBIA, ME 40, bk. 3:20–21, trans. Reinhard Bendix in R. Bendix, *Berlin*, 165.

22. R. Bendix, *Berlin*, 119.

23. L. Bendix, *Konzentrationslager*, bk. 1:96.

24. See L. Bendix, *Tatsachenbericht*, 9–10; L. Bendix, *Konzentrationslager*, bk. 4:65–66, 87–88, 100, 107, 113; *Deutschland-Berichte der Sozialdemokratischen Partei Deutschlands (Sopade Report)* 3 (1936) (Frankfurt, 1982): 1624. See also Sandra Mette, "Schloss Lichtenburg: Konzentrationslager für Männer, 1933–1937," in Stefan Hördler and Sigrid Jacobeit, eds., *Lichtenburg: Ein deutsches Konzentrationslager* (Berlin, 2009), 161–163.

25. See R. Bendix, *Berlin*, 171–172, 176.

26. Letter from Ignatz Manasse to Irmgard Manasse, July 14, 1936, GDALi 808 G/1.

27. Officially a "half-Jew," Ignatz Manasse was buried at Prettin's Christian cemetery. See L. Bendix, *Konzentrationslager*, bk. 4:107–110.

28. R. Bendix, *Berlin*, 171–178.

29. See Leo Baeck, *Kol Nidre Address*, September 25, 1935, reprinted in *Deutsches Judentum unter dem Nationalsozialismus*, vol. 1: *Dokumente zur Geschichte der Reichsvertretung der deutschen Juden, 1933–1939*, ed. Otto Dov Kulka (Tübingen, 1997), 245–246. See also Hans Reichmann, *Memorandum*, August 31, 1956, Wiener Library (WL), P.II.c.No.340; Esriel Hildesheimer, *Jüdische Selbstverwaltung unter dem NS-Regime: Der Existenzkampf der Reichsvertretung und Reichsvereinigung der Juden in Deutschland* (Tübingen, 1994), 36; Johannes Tuchel, "Columbia Concentration Camp," in Morsch, *Sachsenburg*, 74.

30. See "2 Rabbis Held by Gestapo in Columbia House," *Jewish Telegraphic Agency*, December 25, 1935, Bayerisches Staatsarchiv München (BayStA M), Polizeidirektion München, Personal File No. 11680 (Emil Cohn).

31. See secret memorandum of Confessional Church Leadership to Adolf Hitler, June 4, 1936, partly quoted in Werner Koch, *Der Kampf der Bekennenden Kirche im Dritten Reich* (Berlin, 1988), 18–19; "Reich Clergy Warn Hitler: He Does Not Outrank God," *New York Herald Tribune*, July 28, 1936; "Political Resistance: Friedrich Weissler, February 19, 1937," in Günter Morsch, ed., *Murder and Mass Murder in Sachsenhausen Concentration Camp, 1936–1945* (Berlin, 2005), 70–78.

32. See Werner Koch, *"Sollen wir K. weiter beobachten?" Ein Leben im Widerstand* (Argenbühl-Christazhofen, 1993), 174, see also 184–187; Danckwortt, "'Schutzhäftlinge,'" 157–159.

33. Letter from Prosecutor General of Berlin District Court, June 3, 1937, quoted in Morsch, "Formation," 174, see also 144, 148, 162.

34. The dead Jewish prisoners are Franz Reyersbach (December 14, 1936), Kurt Zeckendorf January 21, 1937), Julius Burg (January 22, 1937), Bernhard Bischburg (January 22, 1937), and Friedrich Weissler (February 19, 1937). See reports detailing changes made in KL Sachsenhausen, International Tracing Service (ITS), KL Sachsenhausen GCC 10/87, Ordner 102, 23, 58, 59, 91.

35. So far, four cases of Jewish prisoners could be identified in which homosexuality figured as the reason for imprisonment in Lichtenburg. They can be contextualized with further cases from Esterwegen and Dachau. On homosexual camp inmates more generally, see Albert Knoll, "Totgeschlagen— totgeschwiegen: Die homosexuellen Häftlinge im KZ Dachau," *Dachauer Hefte* 14 (1998): 77–101; Rüdiger Lautmann, "The Pink Triangle: Homosexuals as 'Enemies of the State,'" in Michael Berenbaum and Abraham J. Peck, eds., *The Holocaust and History: The Known, the Unknown, the Disputed, and the Reexamined* (Bloomington, IN, 1998), 345–357; Joachim Müller, "Homosexuelle in den Konzentrationslagern Lichtenburg und Sachsenhausen: Werkstattberichte," in *Homosexuelle in Konzentrationslagern. Vorträge* (Bad Münstereifel, 2000), 74.

36. Transcript of oral-history interview with Gershom Ben-David (formerly Günther Goldschmidt), conducted by Shira Karmon, August 31, 1994, Yad Vashem Archives (YVA), O.3/7941, 8. See also entry "Günther Goldschmidt," ITS, Central Name Index.

37. Rüdiger Lautmann, "Homosexuelle in den Konzentrationslagern: Zum Stand der Forschung," in *Homosexuelle*, 35–36.

38. BayStA M, Polizeidirektion München, Personal File No. 15140 (Wilhelm Tag).

39. Verdict against Sorge and Schubert, Bonn District Court, February 6, 1959, quoted in Dirk Riedel, *Ordnungshüter und Massenmörder im Dienst der "Volksgemeinschaft": Der KZ-Kommandant Hans Loritz* (Berlin, 2010), 123. See also Rainer Hoffschildt, *Die Verfolgung der Homosexuellen in der NS-Zeit: Zahlen und Schicksale aus Norddeutschland* (Berlin, 1999), 42–44; Dirk Lüerssen, *"Wir sind die Moorsoldaten": Die Insassen der frühen Konzentrationslager im Emsland 1933 bis 1936; Biographische Untersuchungen zum Zusammenhang zwischen kategorialer Zuordnung der Verhafteten, deren jeweiligen Verhaltensformen im Lager und den Auswirkungen der Haft auf die weitere Lebensgeschichte* (doctoral thesis, Universität Osnabrück, 2001, online publication), 218–219, 415. On Gustav Sorge, see Andrea Riedle, *Die Angehörigen des*

Kommandanturstabs im KZ Sachsenhausen: Sozialstruktur, Dienstwege und biografische Studien (Berlin, 2011), 163–203.

40. See Knoll, "Totgeschlagen," 79, 89.

41. See ibid., 90–91; Müller, "Homosexuelle," 76.

42. See, for example, Hugo Burkhard, *Tanz mal Jude! Von Dachau bis Shanghai: Meine Erlebnisse in den Konzentrationslagern Dachau—Buchenwald—Ghetto Shanghai* (Nuremberg, 1967), 68–71; Kroch, *Exil*, 75. See also Albert Knoll, "Homosexuelle Häftlinge im KZ Dachau," in *Homosexuelle*, 69.

43. Report on Leopold Obermayer, October 2, 1935, and telex from Josef Gerum to BPP, November 11, 1935, both Bayerisches Staatsarchiv Würzburg (BayStA W), Gestapo 8873, reprinted in Elke Fröhlich, "Ein 'Volksschädling,'" in Martin Broszat and Elke Fröhlich, eds., *Bayern in der NS-Zeit*, vol. 6: *Die Herausforderung des Einzelnen: Geschichten über Widerstand und Verfolgung* (Munich, 1983), 81–88. On Leopold Obermayer, see ibid.; Robert Gellately, *The Gestapo and German Society: Enforcing Racial Policy, 1933–1945* (Oxford, 1990), 202–203; Saul Friedländer, *Nazi Germany and the Jews*, vol. 1: *The Years of Persecution, 1933–1939* (New York, 1998), 113–114; Knoll, "Totgeschlagen," 95–99.

44. *Würzburger Generalanzeiger*, December 14, 1936; "Jüdischer Jugendvergifter," *Der Stürmer* 27 (July 1937). See also "Satan vor Gericht: Der Prozess gegen den jüdischen Männerverderber Obermayer; Schauerliche Schandtanten eines echten Talmudjuden," *Der Stürmer* 52 (December 1936); Fröhlich, "'Volksschädling,'" 79, 109.

45. Appeal Leopold Obermayer to Reich Minister of Justice Franz Gürtner, October 20, 1936, quoted in Fröhlich, "'Volksschädling,'" 99.

46. See ibid., 110; Wachsmann, *Hitler's Prisons*, 284–318.

47. See Chapter 5 for a systematic treatment.

48. See daily strength reports of the Sachsenhausen concentration camp, January 4, 1937–February 12, 1937, AS, D 1 A 1017, 1–41. The total number of Jewish prisoners at that time was about 50, subdivided into three categories: "protective custody" (ca. 20), "instructive custody" (ca. 25), and "preventive custody" (4).

49. See reports detailing changes made in the Dachau concentration camp, March 1937, ITS, KL Dachau GCC 3/70 I B, Ordner 98, 72–79.

50. Alfred E. Laurence (formerly Alfred Lomnitz), *Leben für morgen: Autobiographischer Bericht*, n.d., ca. 1938, DaA, 30.357, 170. As a "returning emigrant," Laurence was arrested in Hamburg on September 21, 1936, and brought to Sachsenhausen shortly afterward. Originally from Breslau, he had studied in France and visited England and Spain, too. After his release from Dachau in October 1937, he escaped from Nazi Germany. Remarkably, Laurence returned to Dachau after the camp's liberation as a member of the American War Crimes Investigation Team and as such he took part in the Dachau Trials.

See notes about the call of Geoffrey West to the British Friends' German Emergency Committee, n.d., ca. autumn 1936, Friends House Library and Archives, London, FCRA/19/5, n.p.; DaA prisoner database.

51. See Lüerssen, " 'Moorsoldaten,' " 114–115.

52. See Burkhard, *Jude*, 56; Drobisch and Wieland, *System*, 206. Pictures of Esterwegen prisoners bearing the letters "BV" on their clothing can be seen in Morsch, *Sachsenburg*, 256, 259.

53. For Sachsenhausen, documentation begins on November 20, 1936, with daily reports detailing changes made in the prisoner population. Beginning on January 3, 1937, there are also strength reports, which indicate the total numbers of prisoners held in the camp. See reports detailing changes made in KL Sachsenhausen, November 20, 1936, to April 2, 1937, ITS, KL Sachsenhausen GCC 10/87, Ordner 102; daily strength reports of Sachsenhausen concentration camp, January 3 to December 30, 1937, AS, D 1 A 1017. For Dachau, there are daily reports detailing changes made through new arrivals, dismissals, transfers, and returns starting from March 24, 1936. The arrival book—that is, the camp register—consecutively lists new arrivals according to their prisoner number. See Reports detailing changes made in KL Dachau, March 24, 1936–June 30, 1937, and July 1, 1937–August 22, 1938, ITS, KL Dachau GCC 3/70, Ordner 98–99; arrival book Dachau concentration camp, ITS, KL Dachau GCC 3/61, Ordner 4–10.

54. See Paul Wolff, *Bericht eines "Rückwanderers" über Sachsenburg*, Amsterdam 1936, WL, P.III.h. No. 689, 2–3. On Sachsenburg, see also Joseph Robert White, "Sachsenburg (and Subcams)," in *USHMM Encyclopedia I*, 158–160.

55. See Heinz Pol, "Konzentrationslager," *Die neue Weltbühne*, December 19, 1935, 1615; *Sopade Report* (May 1937): 705–706; Carina Baganz, *Erziehung zur "Volksgemeinschaft?" Die frühen Konzentrationslager in Sachsen, 1933/34–1937* (Berlin, 2005), 253–254.

56. See *Sopade Report* (December 1936): 1622; report detailing changes made in Dachau concentration camp on February 8, 1937, ITS, KL Dachau GCC 3/70, Ordner 98, 66.

57. See *Tatsachenbericht*, 9–10; L. Bendix, *Konzentrationslager*, bk. 4:72; Kroch, *Exil*, 71.

58. See L. Bendix, *Tatsachenbericht*, 10; L. Bendix, *Konzentrationslager*, bk. 4:87; *Sopade Report* (December 1936): 1632; testimony of Bruno Günther, n.d., GDALi, 837 G, quoted in Müller, "Homosexuelle," 77.

59. See L. Bendix, *Konzentrationslager*, bk. 4:87–88. See also *Sopade Report* (December 1936): 1632.

60. See L. Bendix, *Tatsachenbericht*, 10; report detailing changes made in Dachau concentration camp on February 4, 1937, ITS, KL Dachau GCC 3/70, Ordner 98, 65.

61. See Egon Bieber, "*Schulungslager Papenburg*," Amsterdam 1935, WL, P.II.c. No. 608, 3; Anon., *Ein Rückkehrer erzählt seine Erlebnisse im Konzentrationslager (August 1936)*, WL, P.III.h.No.684, 5. For total numbers, see Lüerssen, "'Moorsoldaten,'" 163–164; Joseph Robert White, "Esterwegen, IKL," in *USHMM Encyclopedia I*, 65.

62. See Riedel, *Ordnungshüter*, 110.

63. See Herbert Mindus, Max Levinsson, *Kurze Geschichte der jüdischen Häftlinge in Sachsenhausen*, n.d., AS, NL 6/18 Archiv Harry Naujoks Hamburg, Briefwechsel u. a. 1945–1983, Ordner M–N, 93; Harry Naujoks, *Mein Leben im KZ-Sachsenhausen, 1936–1942: Erinnerungen des ehemaligen Lagerältesten* (Berlin, 1989), 39. See also Morsch, "Formation," 123–124, 126–127.

64. See Laurence, *Leben*, 35, 78, 93; Morsch, "Formation," 150.

65. See Alfred E. Laurence, "*Dachau Overcome*": *The Story of a Concentration Camp Survivor*, ca. 1970, DaA, 40 and *Leben*, 24, 45–47, 91. For official numbers, see daily strength reports of Sachsenhausen concentration camp, January 3–February 12,1937, AS, D 1 A 1017, 1–40; report detailing changes made in Sachsenhausen on February 12, 1937, ibid., 83–84; report detailing changes made in Dachau on February 13, 1937, ibid., 67–68.

66. See extract from a letter sent from an unnamed correspondent in Paris, July 25, 1935, Friends House, Friends Committee for Refugees and Aliens, Political Prisoners, Correspondence 1933–1938, FCRA/19/1; Heinz Feldheim, *Erlebnisse und Erfahrungen des Dr. Heinz D. Feldheim im nationalsozialistischen Deutschland*, September 1956, WL, P.III.h.No.143, 2; *Nazi-Bastille Dachau: Schicksal und Heldentum deutscher Freiheitskämpfer* (Paris, 1939), 36; Riedel, *Ordnungshüter*, 138.

67. The Dachau arrival book registers 102 new arrivals classified as Jews between July 10 and December 31, 1937, and another 100 between January 1 and March 31, 1938. See also Laurence, *Leben*, 114; anonymous report about Dachau sent to Oskar Winter (formerly Oskar Winterberger), n.d., DaA, 1180, 7; Riedel, *Ordnungshüter*, 192.

68. See anonymous report about Dachau, 2; Emil Carlebach, *Tote auf Urlaub: Kommunist in Deutschland; Dachau und Buchenwald, 1937–1945* (Bonn, 1995), 58.

69. See Himmler's decree on the separate accommodation of recidivist prisoners, March 23, 1936, BarchAB, NS 31/372, 7, quoted in Mette, "Schloss," 161.

70. See L. Bendix, *Konzentrationslager*, bk. 5:8, 10, 34, 51; Laurence, *Leben*, 23, 113–114, 130, 133; anonymous report about Dachau, 2; Carlebach, *Tote*, 49; Drobisch and Wieland, *System*, 206.

71. See Drobisch and Wieland, *System*, 206–207; Annette Eberle, "Häftlingskategorien und Kennzeichnungen," in Wolfgang Benz and Barbara Distel, eds.,

Der Ort des Terrors: Geschichte der nationalsozialistischen Konzentrationslager, vol. 1 (Munich, 2005), 92–93. On Esterwegen, see also Carl J. Burckhardt, *Meine Danziger Mission. 1937–1939* (Munich, 1960), 59. On Lichtenburg, L. Bendix, *Konzentrationslager,* bk. 4:23. On Sachsenhausen, Laurence, *Leben,* 20–21; Morsch, "Formation," 278. On Dachau, *Sopade Report* (May 1937): 686; Carlebach, *Tote,* 16.

72. Irmgard Litten, *A Mother Fights Hitler* (London, 1940), 260, 267. On the history of the yellow badge, see entry "Badge, Jewish," in *Encyclopaedia Judaica,* vol. 4 (Jerusalem, 1971), 62–73.

73. See Eberle, "Häftlingskategorien," 94, 102–104. Naujoks dates the introduction of the system of triangular badges in Sachsenhausen to the time immediately preceding the mass arrest of "asocials" in June 1938. See Naujoks, *Leben,* 77. According to former prisoner Bruno Heilig, the system was introduced in Dachau in early summer of 1938, sometime after the arrival of the Austrian prisoners. See Bruno Heilig, *Men Crucified* (London, 1941), 101.

74. See Laurence, *Leben,* 38. Bendix reported the same situation for Dachau. See L. Bendix, *Konzentrationslager,* bk. 5:33–34.

75. Laurence, *Leben,* 74.

76. Laurence, "Dachau," 44.

77. See Naujoks, *Leben,* 150.

78. See ibid., 39.

79. See L. Bendix, *Konzentrationslager,* bk. 4:68–69. On Remmert, see Stefan Hördler, "SS-Kaderschmiede Lichtenburg: Zur Bedeutung des KZ Lichtenburg in der Vorkriegszeit," in Hördler und Jacobeit, *Lichtenburg,* 88–89.

80. See *Sopade Report* (August 1936): 1010–1011; L. Bendix, *Konzentrationslager,* bk. 4:26–29; Pol, "Konzentrationslager," 1615; Baganz, *Erziehung,* 272.

81. Naujoks, *Leben,* 40.

82. See Laurence, *Leben,* 96–97; on prisoner labor, see also 38, 41.

83. Laurence, "Dachau," 8.

84. See Riedel, *Ordnungshüter,* 191, see also 139, 188; Burkhard, *Jude,* 74–75.

85. See Laurence, *Leben,* 121, 127, 148; Laurence, "Dachau," 38; L. Bendix, *Konzentrationslager,* bk. 5:27–29, 33–35; Feldheim, *Erlebnisse,* 2; Carlebach, *Tote,* 52, 55–56.

86. See Riedel, *Ordnungshüter,* 112–113.

87. Agranoff died on May 31, 1935, Gerson on November 1, 1935, and Lövy on August 12, 1936. See Lüerssen, "'Moorsoldaten,'" 114–115, 288, 353; Hans-Peter Klausch, *Tätergeschichten: Die SS-Kommandanten der frühen Konzentrationslager im Emsland* (Bremen, 2005), 292–294. On Gerson, see also witness testimony of former Esterwegen prisoner Bernhard Vornhusen, May 5, 1951, NStA O, Rep 945 Akz. 6/1983 Nr. 347, 32. On Lövy, see also *Sopade Report* (December 1936): 1610.

88. See bill of indictment against Wolfgang Seuss, March 11, 1960, DaA, 20.426/1; verdict of Jury Court at Munich District Court II, June 22, 1960, ibid., 20.246/2; Burkhard, *Jude*, 77; anonymous report about Dachau, 7; Carlebach, *Tote*, 51; Riedel, *Ordnungshüter*, 190. On "Pfahlhängen" or "Baumhängen," (hanging at the pole) see Burkhard, *Jude*, 57.

89. Jewish prisoners who died in Esterwegen: Willi Baron (March 2, 1935), Julius Agranoff (May 31, 1935), Bernhard Gerson (November 1, 1935), Louis Schild (November 18, 1935), David Rosenbaum (June 5, 1936), Ewald Meyer (July 14, 1936), and Paul Lövy (August 12, 1936). In 1935 there were four Jewish casualties out of the officially registered seventeen; in 1936 there were three out of eleven. See list of registered deaths in Klausch, *Tätergeschichten*, 292–294.

90. See Baganz, *Erziehung*, 274.

91. See Wolff, *Bericht*, 4–5; "Ein Rassenschänder," *Die neue Weltbühne*, February 27, 1936, 263–264; Pol, "Konzentrationslager," 1615–1616; *Sopade Report* (December 1936): 1616; *Sopade Report* (May 1937), 706; *Geheimnisse einer Todesanzeige: Der Fall Sachs*, n.d., WL, P.III.h.No.572; Baganz, *Erziehung*, 274–275.

92. See Stefanie Endlich, "Die Lichtenburg, 1933–1939: Haftort politischer Prominenz und Frauen-KZ," in Wolfgang Benz and Barbara Distel, eds., *Herrschaft und Gewalt: Frühe Konzentrationslager, 1933–1939* (Berlin, 2002), 54.

93. See DaA deaths statistics. In 1935, one of the twelve deaths was a Jewish prisoner; in 1936 it was two Jewish deaths out of eleven. All figures are to be regarded as minimum numbers.

94. The dead Jewish prisoners are Franz Reyersbach (December 14, 1936), Kurt Zeckendorf (January 21, 1937), Julius Burg (January 22, 1937), Bernhard Bischburg (January 22, 1937), and Friedrich Weissler (February 19, 1937). See reports detailing changes made in KL Sachsenhausen, ITS, KL Sachsenhausen GCC 10/87, Ordner 102, 23, 58, 59, 91. See also Morsch, "Formation," 188.

95. *Sopade Report* (December 1936): 1608. See also *Sopade Report* (August 1936): 1008.

96. Alfred Hübsch, *Die Insel des Standrechts*, ca. 1960, 9, quoted in Riedel, *Ordnungshüter*, 178.

97. L. Bendix, *Konzentrationslager*, bk. 5:76, see also 75–78; see also L. Bendix, *Tatsachenbericht*, 14–5. According to Bendix, two of the publically punished prisoners were Jews; one can be identified as Max Fichtmann ("Max Ficht"). Laurence, too, reported that two Jewish prisoners were publically abused. See Laurence, *Leben*, 165–166. See also *Sopade Report* (November 1937): 1542–1543. Here, the event is said to have taken place on March 27, 1937.

98. Burkhard, *Jude*, 55–56, 90.

99. Laurence, "*Dachau*," 33; L. Bendix, *Konzentrationslager*, bk. 5:73. See also Karin Orth, *Die Konzentrationslager SS: Sozialstrukturelle Analysen und biographische Studien* (Munich, 2004), 146–148; Hördler, "SS-Kaderschmiede," 83–85; Riedel, *Ordnungshüter*, 151–152.

100. L. Bendix, *Konzentrationslager*, bk. 5:25; Laurence, "*Dachau*," 34.

101. Laurence, "*Dachau*," 120.

102. See *Rückkehrer erzählt seine Erlebnisse*, 6.

103. On the "atrocity propaganda" affair of October 1933 in Dachau, see Chapter 2, 91–92.

104. See *Sopade Report* (August 1936): 1011. On the Gustloff murder, see also Jürgen Matthäus, "Verfolgung, Ausbeutung, Vernichtung: Jüdische Häftlinge im System der Konzentrationslager," in Günter Morsch and Susanne zur Nieden, eds., *Jüdische Häftlinge im Konzentrationslager Sachsenhausen, 1936 bis 1945* (Berlin, 2004), 71.

105. See L. Bendix, *Konzentrationslager*, bk. 4:10.

106. See Mindus and Levinsson, *Geschichte*; Naujoks, *Leben*, 50.

107. See *Sopade Report* (February 1936): 161; Alan E. Steinweis, *Kristallnacht 1938* (Cambridge, MA, 2009), 18.

108. Quotes taken from a preformulated letter, which Hans Litten had to send to his mother on December 6, 1937, quoted in Litten, *Mother*, 262.

109. See Marco Esseling, "Juden als Häftlingsgruppe in Konzentrationslagern: Verhaftung von Juden und ihre Stellung im Lager bis 1942 unter besonderer Berücksichtigung des KZ Dachau" (MA dissertation, Institut für Neuere Geschichte, Ludwig-Maximilians-Universität München, 1995), 92. Bendix reported an "isolation" of Jews in Lichtenburg in late 1936, which was apparently ordered in response to the opening of the trial against David Frankfurter. See L. Bendix, *Konzentrationslager*, bk. 4:100, 111. For descriptions of the various deprivations accompanying the Dachau isolations, see Laurence, *Leben*, 164; Burkhard, *Jude*, 89.

110. For the isolation in 1935, see *Dachau, 1933–1935, by Otto Marx, Prisoner 346*, 32–34, quoted in Esseling, *Juden*, 93; Burkhard, *Jude*, 89–91. For 1936, see *Nazi-Bastille*, 36–37. For March 1937, see *Sopade Report* (November 1937): 1542, and (March 16–30, 1937); L. Bendix, *Konzentrationslager*, bk. 5:66–77. For August 1937, see Alfred E. Laurence, *Heinz Eschen zum Gedenken*, July 3, 1939, DaA, 9394, 5; Hübsch, *Insel*, DaA, A1436, 6–7. For November/December 1937, see anonymous report about Dachau, 5; Knut Bergbauer et al., *Denkmalsfigur: Biographische Annäherung an Hans Litten* (Göttingen, 2008), 284.

111. Burkhard, *Jude*, 92.

112. See anonymous report by a former Dachau prisoner, 1930s, reprinted in Litten, *Mother*, 272.

113. See Laurance, *Leben*, 164; Carlebach, *Tote*, 24.

114. See letter from Dachau Kommandantur to Director of Moringen concentration camp, September 2, 1937, NHStA H, Hann. 158 Moringen, Acc. 105/96 Nr. 104, 11; conduct report on Herbert Hirschfeld, March 15, 1938, DaA, A 977; Burkhard, *Jude*, 90; Riedel, *Ordnungshüter*, 186. According to Laurence's testimony, releases were not automatically suspended during isolation periods. See Laurence, *Leben*, 164.

115. Preformulated letter sent by Hans Litten to Irmgard Litten, December 6, 1937, quoted in Litten, *Mother*, 262.

116. Litten, *Mother*, 262–263, 267.

117. Gestapo ordinance on the concentration of Jewish protective custody and instructive custody prisoners in Dachau, February 17, 1937, BArchB, R 58/264, 285.

118. See reports detailing changes made in the Dachau concentration camp on February 4, 8, and 13, 1937, ITS, KL Dachau GCC 3/70 I B, Ordner 98, 65–68. Although the Bad Sulza camp is also explicitly listed in Heydrich's order, evidence for a transport of Jews from Bad Sulza to Dachau cannot be found in the sources.

119. See Riedel, *Ordnungshüter*, 108; Hermann Kaienburg, "KZ-System und Häftlingsgruppen: Gab es eine Zuordnung von Häftlingskategorien zu bestimmten Konzentrationslagern?," in Wolfgang Benz et al., eds., *Nationalsozialistische Zwangslager: Strukturen und Regionen—Täter und Opfer* (Dachau, 2011), 163–174.

120. See reports detailing changes made in KL Sachsenhausen on February 12, 13, 18, 19, and 20, and on March 13, 1937, ITS, KL Sachsenhausen GCC 10/87, Ordner 102, 85, 91–92, 113; Morsch, "Formation," 152.

121. Laurence, *Leben*, 71, 78–79, 95.

122. Letter from Reinhard Heydrich to the Deputy Führer, February 1, 1937, published as Dok. 264 in *Die Verfolgung und Ermordung der europäischen Juden durch das nationalsozialistische Deutschland 1933–1945 (VEJ)*, vol. 1: *Deutsches Reich, 1933–1937* (Munich, 2008), 635.

123. Dan Michman, *The Emergence of Jewish Ghettos during the Holocaust* (Cambridge, 2011), 40. Mistakenly, Michman translates *Gastwirtschaften* as "holiday resorts" and not as "restaurants."

124. Laurence, *Leben*, 109; Laurence, "*Dachau*," 18.

125. Laurence, *Leben*, 111–112; Laurence, "*Dachau*," 11–12.

126. See Karl Heinz Jahnke, "Heinz Eschen: Kapo des Judenblocks im Konzentrationslager Dachau bis 1938," *Dachauer Hefte* 7 (1991): 24–26; Marion Ebner, "Heinz Eschen: Jüdischer Widerstand im KZ Dachau," in *Deckname "Betti": Jugendlicher Widerstand gegen die Nationalsozialisten in München oder; Ein Plädoyer für "Junge Demokratie"; Ein Projekt des Kreisjugendring München-Stadt und der DGB-Jugend München; In Zusammenarbeit mit dem Kulturre-*

ferat der Landeshauptstadt München (Munich, 1997), 50–51; Deutsche Kommunistische Partei München, ed., *Die wiedergefundene Liste: Porträts von Münchner Kommunistinnen und Kommunisten, die im antifaschistischen Widerstandskampf ihr Leben liessen; Entdeckt von Resi Huber* (Munich, 1998), 48–51.

127. L. Bendix, *Konzentrationslager*, bk. 5:69; anonymous report about Dachau, 5; Laurence, "Dachau," 13; Burkhard, *Jude*, 94; Jahnke, "Heinz Eschen," 28; Primo Levi, "The Grey Zone," in *The Drowned and the Saved* (London, 1996), 22–51.

128. Laurence, "Dachau," 42.

129. See ibid.; Laurence, *Leben*, 91–92.

130. See report of former prisoner Max Levinsson, printed in Naujoks, *Leben*, 41; Laurence, "Dachau," 41. In Levinsson's report August Cohn is falsely named "Max Cohn." On this mistake, see also Morsch, "Formation," 149–150. Morsch's assumption that August Cohn served as block senior in Sachsenhausen, however, is incorrect. For contrary evidence, see Laurence, *Leben*, 26, 29–30, 83, 91, 103; Laurence, "Dachau," 41.

131. See Morsch, "Formation," 149, 182–186.

132. See Laurence, *Leben*, 113, 115; Laurence, "Dachau," 48–49; DaA prisoner database. In *Leben*, Laurence used the pseudonym "Otto Wasser" for Isner. See also Carlebach, *Tote*, 30–31, 58; Bergbauer et al., *Denkmalsfigur*, 280.

133. See Litten, *Mother*, 268; Laurence, *Leben*, 167; Laurence, "Dachau," 91–93; Carlebach, *Tote*, 18; Bergbauer et al., *Denkmalsfigur*, 279–281.

134. See Morsch, "Formation," 150.

135. Carlebach, *Tote*, 19–22, 24, 65.

136. See letter from Werner Neukircher to Oskar Winter, July 13, 1946, DaA, 2237; Bergbauer, *Denkmalsfigur*, 279–280.

137. See L. Bendix, *Konzentrationslager*, bk. 5:71; Laurence, "Dachau," 90.

138. L. Bendix, *Konzentrationslager*, bk. 5:68; Laurence, "Dachau," 90.

139. See L. Bendix, *Konzentrationslager*, bk. 4:70–78.

140. See ibid., 80–81.

141. Laurence, "Dachau," 55.

142. L. Bendix, *Konzentrationslager*, bk. 5:69. According to Bendix, the two denouncers were Max Fichtmann ("Ficht") and Walter Czollek ("Anton").

143. See Laurence, *Leben*, 170–171; Laurence, *Heinz Eschen*, 3.

144. See Wolfgang Sofsky, *The Order of Terror: The Concentration Camp* (Princeton, NJ, 1997), 138–140.

145. See Laurence, *Heinz Eschen*, 5–6; anonymous report of a former Jewish prisoner, n.d., DaA, 28.309; Carlebach, *Tote*, 27–31; Jahnke "Heinz Eschen," 32; Bergbauer et al., *Denkmalsfigur*, 284–290; Benjamin Carter Hett, *Crossing Hitler: The Man Who Put the Nazis on the Witness Stand* (Oxford, 2008), 238–239.

146. Testimony of Fritz Rabinowitsch, ca. 1939, BArchB, SAPMO, Nachlass Hans Litten NY 4011/6, 48; Bergbauer et al., *Denkmalsfigur*, 288; Laurence, *Heinz*

Eschen, 6; L. Bendix, *Konzentrationslager*, bk. 5:72; Herbert Mindus, untitled report, ca. 1947, in AS, Nachlass Herbert Mindus.

147. See Bergbauer et al., *Denkmalsfigur*, 290–291, including the complete text of the song.

148. See Hett, *Hitler*, 239–240.

149. See Carlebach, *Tote*, 29–31, 60. Carlebach remembered that a non–Jewish prisoner called Mewes temporarily served as the block elder of block 6.

5. Instruments of Mass Persecution

1. Peter Wallner, *By Order of the Gestapo: A Record of Life in Dachau and Buchenwald* (London, 1941), 25; Ernst Stein, *Report on the Experiences of Ernst Stein in Dachau and Buchenwald*, May 1956, Wiener Library (WL), P.III.h.No.234, 1; Maximilian Reich, *Mörder-Schule Konzentrations-Lager*, 1939, WL, P.III.h.No.1058, 13.

2. See reports detailing changes made in KL Dachau, April 2–June 25, 1938, International Tracing Service (ITS), KL Dachau GCC 3/70, Ordner 99, 45–104; arrival book KL Dachau, ITS, KL Dachau GCC 3/61, Ordner 4–5. For numbers of Austrian prisoners in general, see also Jonny Moser, "Österreich," in Wolfgang Benz, ed., *Dimension des Völkermords: Die Zahl der jüdischen Opfer des Nationalsozialismus* (Munich, 1991), 88–91.

3. The term "Austrian invasion" was coined by Heilig and Neurath. See Bruno Heilig, *Men Crucified* (London, 1941), 113, 120; Paul Martin Neurath, *The Society of Terror: Inside the Dachau and Buchenwald Concentration Camps*, ed. Christian Fleck and Nico Stehr (Boulder, CO, 2005), 225.

4. Wallner, *Order*, 26. See also Reich, *Mörder-Lager*, 13.

5. Heilig, *Men*, 7.

6. Wallner, *Order*, 27.

7. See Reich, *Mörder-Lager*, 13–14.

8. See Heilig, *Men*, 8–15; Wallner, *Order*, 25–35; Rudolf Kalmar, *Zeit ohne Gnade* (Vienna, 1946), 41–43; Edgar Rhoden, *Dachau and Buchenwald*, December 1954, WL, P.III.h.No.51, 1–3; *Experiences of Ben Horowitz at Dachau and Buchenwald Concentration Camps, May 1938–May 1939*, December 1955, WL, P.III.h.No.170, 1–2; Fritz Schreier, *Von Wien nach Dachau und Buchenwald*, 1955, WL, P.III.h.No.482, 1; Hugo David, *Erlebnisse und Beobachtungen des Herrn Hugo David unter der Herrschaft der Nationalsozialisten*, November 1959, WL, P.III.h.No.1156, 2; Bruno Bettelheim, *The Informed Heart: Autonomy in a Mass Age* (New York, 1960), 121–126.

9. See Dachau Concentration Camp Memorial Site Archives (DaA), deaths statistics.

10. Wallner, *Order*, 35. See also Heilig, *Men*, 20; Karl Ludwig Schecher, *Rückblick auf Dachau*, DaA, 7566, 109–111.

11. See Alfred Hübsch, *Die Insel des Standrechts*, ca. 1960, DaA, A1436, 90–92; Stein, *Experiences*, 2.

12. Wallner, *Order*, 31. See also Heilig, *Men*, 20.

13. See Dirk Riedel, *Ordnungshüter und Massenmörder im Dienst der "Volksgemeinschaft": Der KZ-Kommandant Hans Loritz* (Berlin, 2010), 197.

14. See *Nazi-Bastille Dachau: Schicksal und Heldentum deutscher Freiheitskämpfer* (Paris, 1939), 18, 107. See also Heinrich Popitz, *Phänomene der Macht: Autorität, Herrschaft, Gewalt, Technik* (Tübingen, 1986), 69–71; Marco Esseling, "Juden als Häftlingsgruppe in Konzentrationslagern: Verhaftung von Juden und ihre Stellung im Lager bis 1942 unter besonderer Berücksichtigung des KZ Dachau" (MA dissertation, Institut für Neuere Geschichte, Ludwig-Maximilians-Universität München, 1995), 107.

15. Peter Longerich, *Holocaust: The Nazi Persecution and Murder of the Jews* (Oxford, 2010), 99, see also 65–66, 95–107; Avraham Barkai, *Vom Boykott zur "Entjudung": Der wirtschaftliche Existenzkampf der Juden im Dritten Reich, 1933–1943* (Frankfurt, 1988), 141–142.

16. See Herbert Rosenkranz, *Verfolgung und Selbstbehauptung: Die Juden in Österreich, 1938–1945* (Vienna, 1978), 26; Albert Lichtblau, "Österreich," in Wolf Gruner and Jürgen Osterloh, eds., *Das "Grossdeutsche Reich" und die Juden: Nationalsozialistische Verfolgung in den "angegliederten" Gebieten* (Frankfurt, 2010), 90; Longerich, *Holocaust*, 99.

17. See Walter Rafelsberger, *Vorschläge für eine wirkungsvolle Durchführung der Entjudung*, October 1938, partly printed in *Die Verfolgung und Ermordung der europäischen Juden durch das nationalsozialistische Deutschland, 1933–1945*, vol. 2: *Deutsches Reich, 1938–August 1939* (Munich, 2009) (*VEJ*), 325–326, see also 39; Saul Friedländer, *Nazi Germany and the Jews*, vol. 1: *The Years of Persecution, 1933–1939* (New York, 1998), 242–247; Götz Aly and Susanne Heim, *Architects of Annihilation: Auschwitz and the Logic of Destruction* (London, 2003), 20–23.

18. See David Cesarani, *Becoming Eichmann: Rethinking the Life, Crimes, and Trial of a "Desk Murderer"* (Cambridge, MA, 2006), 61–71.

19. See Friedländer, *Nazi Germany*, 1:243, 247; Aly and Heim, *Architects*, 16–27; Lichtblau, "Österreich," 91–93, 104.

20. See Martin Broszat, "The Concentration Camps, 1933–45," in Helmut Krausnick et al., eds., *Anatomy of the SS State* (London, 1968), 457; Klaus Drobisch and Günther Wieland, *System der NS-Konzentrationslager, 1933–1939* (Berlin, 1993), 261. No separate treatment of the mass imprisonment of Austrians can be found in Falk Pingel's groundbreaking study. See Falk Pingel,

Häftlinge unter SS-Herrschaft: Widerstand, Selbstbehauptung und Vernichtung im Konzentrationslager (Hamburg, 1978).

21. See Wolfgang Neugebauer and Peter Schwarz, *Stacheldraht mit Tod geladen . . . Der erste Österreichertransport in das KZ Dachau* (Vienna, 2008), 8.

22. See Rosenkranz, *Verfolgung*, 31; Cesarani, *Eichmann*, 63–64; Lichtblau, "Österreich," 87.

23. Report of Coordinating Office of the Vienna Criminal Police, April 1, 1938, reproduced in Neugebauer and Schwarz, *Stacheldraht*, 17, see also 20; see Rosenkranz, *Verfolgung*, 87.

24. Reich, *Mörder-Lager*, 9.

25. Heilig, *Men*, 34.

26. Ibid., 3, see also 13, 20.

27. See Heilig, *Men*, 4, 22–23, 89; Peter Huemer, *Sektionschef Robert Hecht und die Zerstörung der Demokratie in Österreich: Eine historisch-politische Studie* (Munich, 1975), 331–333.

28. See Mark Siegelberg, *Schutzhaftjude Nr. 13877* (Shanghai, 1939). For a complete list of names of Jewish prisoners, see report detailing changes made in KL Dachau, April 2, 1938, ITS, KL Dachau GCC 3/70, Ordner 99, 46–47 (starting with entry no. 118 "Auernheim, Raoul").

29. Heilig, *Men*, 4–6. See also Avraham Barkai, "Exclusion and Persecution: 1933–1938," in Michael A. Meyer, ed., *German-Jewish History in Modern Times*, vol. 4: *Renewal and Destruction, 1918–1945* (New York, 1998), 217.

30. See Heilig, *Men*, 96; Neugebauer and Schwarz, *Stacheldraht*, 38.

31. Schreier, *Wien*, 36.

32. See Reich, *Mörder-Lager*, 17.

33. See Schreier, *Wien*, 11; Reich, *Mörder-Lager*, 41; Heilig, *Men*, 97; Kalmar, *Zeit*, 41; Neurath, *Society*, 122.

34. See Emil Carlebach, *Tote auf Urlaub: Kommunist in Deutschland; Dachau und Buchenwald, 1937–1945* (Bonn, 1995), 69.

35. Heilig, *Men*, 15–16.

36. See ibid., 31, 46, 75; report detailing changes made in KL Dachau, April 2, 1938, ITS, KL Dachau GCC 3/70, Ordner 99, 46–47.

37. See Schreier, *Wien*, 9; Hugo Burkhard, *Tanz mal Jude! Von Dachau bis Shanghai: Meine Erlebnisse in den Konzentrationslagern Dachau— Buchenwald—Ghetto Shanghai* (Nuremberg, 1967), 102; Carlebach, *Tote*, 69.

38. Heilig, *Men*, 41. See also Neurath, *Society*, 26–27.

39. See Heilig, *Men*, 33, 38–39, 83; Schreier, *Wien*, 8.

40. Neurath, *Society*, 27.

41. The administrative records register the arrival of two Austrian prisoners on April 8, of ten Austrians on April 11, and of two Austrians on May 18, 1938. See arrival book KL Dachau, ITS, KL Dachau GCC 3/61, Ordner 4, 53–55, 60. See

also, arrival of 165 Austrian prisoners on April 24, ibid.; report detailing changes made in KL Dachau on May 24, 1938, ITS, KL Dachau GCC 3/70, Ordner 99, 57–59; Moser, "Österreich," 88–91.

42. See Ernst Federn, "The Terror as a System: The Concentration Camp (Buchenwald as It Was)," *Psychiatric Quarterly Supplement* 22 (1948): 52–68; Federn, "Essai sur la Psychologie de la Terreur," *Synthèses* 1 (1946): 81–108.

43. See arrivals of prisoners on May 31, June 3, 15, 17, 24, and 25, 1938, in arrival book KL Dachau, ITS, KL Dachau GCC 3/61, Ordner 4, 69–110, 113–124, and Ordner 5, 3–19, 21–53; Heilig, *Men*, 117. According the Neurath, the term "Action Jews" was used by both prisoners and the SS. See Neurath, *Society*, 227.

44. See testimony of Karl Ebner, July 19, 1947, printed in Rosenkranz, *Verfolgung*, 86–87.

45. See express letter from Vienna Gestapo to all District Police Departments in Vienna, May 24, 1938, printed in Jonny Moser, *Die Judenverfolgung in Österreich, 1938–1945* (Vienna, 1966), 6.

46. Secret memo of SD-Oberabschnitt Österreich, Department II 112, May 30, 1938, USHMMA, RG-11001 M.01, Reel 4, Fond 500, Opis 1, Folder 261, 33.

47. See Ordinance on "the Combat Against Professional Criminals" in Austria, issued by the Reich Criminal Police Office, March 31, 1938, reprinted in Christian Faludi, ed., *Die "Juni-Aktion" 1938: Eine Dokumentation zur Radikalisierung der Judenverfolgung* (Frankfurt, 2013), 139–140.

48. See Wallner, *Order*, 19, 42; Neurath, *Society*, 227; Schreier, *Wien*, 36; Josef Brukarz, *My Experience in the Concentration Camps Dachau and Buchenwald*, 1954, WL, P.III.h.No.67, 1; Rosenkranz, *Verfolgung*, 87.

49. Testimony Eber, in Moser, *Judenverfolgung*.

50. Stein, *Experiences*, 1. See also Rhoden, *Dachau*, 1; Horowitz, *Experiences*, 1; Rosenkranz, *Verfolgung*, 87.

51. Emilie Reich, *Die Rolle der Frau*, memoir attached to the report of Maximilian Reich, ca. 1939, WL, P.III.h.No.1058, 179

52. A picture of such a graffito is reproduced in Bernhard Kuschey, *Die Ausnahme des Überlebens: Ernst und Hilde Federn; Eine biographische Studie und eine Analyse der Binnenstruktur des Konzentrationslagers* (Giessen, 2003), 402.

53. "Jew-Baiting in Vienna: New Wave of Persecution," *The Times*, July 18, 1938.

54. See testimony Ebner, in Moser, *Judenverfolgung*, 87.

55. See cable from German Embassy, London, to Foreign Office, Berlin, June 28, 1938; notes of State Secretary Ernst von Weizsäcker on his meeting with Reinhard Heydrich, July 5, 1937, both printed in Dokumentationsarchiv des österreichischen Widerstands, ed., *"Anschluss" 1938: Eine Dokumentation* (Vienna, 1988), 529–532; "Nazi Treatment of Viennese Jews: 'Special Train' to Dachau," *The Times*, June 3, 1938. See also Neugebauer and Schwarz, *Stacheldraht*, 49–50.

56. Secret Order of the Leader of the first SS Death's Head division Oberbayern, June 10, 1938, DaA, 34.445; DaA deaths statistics.

57. See Stanislav Zámečník, "Dachau—Stammlager," in Wolfgang Benz and Barbara Distel, eds., *Der Ort des Terrors: Geschichte der nationalsozialistischen Konzentrationslager*, vol. 2 (Munich, 2005), 234, 246–248; Barbara Distel, "Dachau Main Camp," in *The United States Holocaust Memorial Museum Encyclopedia of Camps and Ghettos, 1933–1945*, vol. 1,pt. 1 (Bloomington, IN, 2009) (hereafter *USHMM Encyclopedia I*), 443.

58. See reports detailing changes made in KL Dachau, April 2 to June 25, 1938, ITS, KL Dachau GCC 3/70, Ordner 99, 45–104; Heilig, *Men*, 46; Wallner, *Order*, 44, 50, 79; Neurath, *Society*, 209; Zámečník, "Dachau," 246.

59. See Heilig, *Men*, 19, 101.

60. See Reich, *Mörder-Lager*, 33; Heilig, *Men*, 120; Schreier, *Wien*, 6.

61. Heilig, *Men*, 112.

62. Ibid.

63. See Reich, *Mörder-Lager*, 50; Wallner, *Order*, 85; Schreier, *Wien*, 9.

64. See Heilig, *Men*, 112, 126; Wallner, *Order*, 144; Schreier, *Wien*, 10; Rhoden, *Dachau*, 8.

65. Wallner, *Order*, 103, 197. See also Brukarz, *Experience*, 2–3; Hübsch, *Insel*, 103–104.

66. Schreier, *Wien*, 24. See also Neurath, *Society*, 204, 225; Kuschey, *Ausnahme*, 382.

67. Neurath, *Society*, 209, 229. See also Reich, *Mörder-Lager*, 62; Schreier, *Wien*, 29.

68. See Wallner, *Order*, 85.

69. See reports detailing changes made in KL Dachau, June 1 to September 23, 1938, ITS, KL Dachau GCC 3/70, Ordner 99, 68–127, Ordner 100, 1–12. See also Heilig, *Men*, 136.

70. See reports detailing changes made in KL Dachau, September 16–23, 1938, ITS, KL Dachau GCC 3/70, Ordner 100, 9–12; reports detailing changes made in KL Buchenwald, September 17–24, 1938, ITS, KL Buchenwald GCC 2/181 IB/2, Ordner 103, illegible pagination.

71. See letter from the Gestapo Office in Neustadt an der Weinstrasse, October 7, 1938, Landesarchiv Speyer (LArch Sp), Gestapostelle Neustadt an der Wein-strasse H 90, Sachakte 40.

72. See reports detailing changes made in KL Dachau, August 8–October 1, 1938, ITS, KL Dachau GCC 3/70, Ordner 99, 120–127, Ordner 100, 1–14.

73. The only exception are the five Jewish prisoners aboard a larger transport from Kladno, Bohemia, that stopped over in Mauthausen for three days before it reached its destination, Dachau, on June 16, 1939. See Chapter 6 (p. 218) for details. The first regular Jewish prisoner was registered in Mauthausen in September 1939. In Flossenbürg, the first eleven Jews arrived on May 24, 1940.

See Gordon J. Horwitz, *In the Shadow of Death: Living outside the Gates of Mauthausen* (New York, 1990), 13–14; Wolfgang Ayass, *"Asoziale" im National-sozialismus* (Stuttgart, 1995), 166, 168. Karin Orth, *Das System der nationalsozialistischen Konzentrationslager: Eine politische Organisationsgeschichte* (Hamburg, 1999), 51; Jörg Skribeleit, "Flossenbürg—Stammlager," in Benz and Distel, *Der Ort des Terrors*, 4, 31.

74. See arrival book KL Dachau, ITS, KL Dachau GCC 3/61, Ordner 5, 95–116; Harry Stein, *Juden in Buchenwald, 1937–1942* (Weimar, 1992), 31; *The Dachau Concentration Camp, 1933 to 1945: Text- and Photo Documents from the Exhibition, with CD*, ed. Barbara Distel (Munich, 2005), 81.

75. See Stein, *Juden*, 26, 33.

76. See Wolf Gruner, *Der geschlossene Arbeitseinsatz deutscher Juden: Zur Zwangsarbeit als Element der Verfolgung, 1938–1943* (Berlin, 1997), 44; Stefanie Schüler-Springorum, "Masseneinweisungen in Konzentrationslager: Aktion 'Arbeitsscheu Reich,' Novemberpogrom, Aktion 'Gewitter,'" in Benz and Distel, *Der Ort des Terrors*, 1:158–159.

77. See Ayass, *"Asoziale,"* 19–40; Nikolaus Wachsmann, "The Policy of Exclusion: Repression in the Nazi State, 1933–1939," in Jane Caplan, ed., *Short Oxford History of Germany: The Third Reich* (Oxford, 2009), 123, 128; Julia Hörath, "Experimente zur Kontrolle und Repression von Devianz und Delinquenz: Die Einweisung von 'Asozialen' und 'Berufsverbrechern' in die Konzentrationslager, 1933 bis 1937/38" (doctoral thesis, Otto-Suhr-Institut für Politikwissenschaft, Freie Universität Berlin, 2012), 261–386. For first published results, see "Terrorinstrumente der 'Volksgemeinschaft?' KZ-Haft für 'Asoziale' und 'Berufsverbrecher,' 1933 bis 1937/38," *ZfG* 60:6 (2012): 513–532

78. Secret ordinance of Prussian Minister of the Interior on the use of preventive police custody, November 13, 1933, cited in Lothar Gruchmann, *Justiz im Dritten Reich, 1933–1940: Anpassung und Unterwerfung in der Ära Gürtner* (Munich, 2001), 720. See also Karl-Leo Terhorst, *Polizeiliche planmässige Überwachung und polizeiliche Vorbeugungshaft im Dritten Reich: Ein Beitrag zur Rechtsgeschichte vorbeugender Verbrechensbekämpfung* (Heidelberg, 1985); Sven Langhammer, "Die reichsweite Verhaftungsaktion vom 9. März 1937: Eine Massnahme zur 'Säuberung des Volkskörpers,'" *Hallische Beiträge zur Zeitgeschichte* 17:1 (2007): 57.

79. See Ayass, *"Asoziale,"* 138, 158–159; Ulrich Herbert, "Von der Gegnerbekämpfung zur 'rassischen Generalprävention': 'Schutzhaft' und Konzentrationslager in der Konzeption der Gestapo-Führung, 1933–1939," in Ulrich Herbert et al., eds., *Die nationalsozialistischen Konzentrationslager: Entwicklung und Struktur*, vol. 1 (Göttingen, 1998), 78.

80. Robert Gellately, *Backing Hitler: Consent and Coercion in Nazi Germany* (Oxford, 2001), vii. See also Detlev J. K. Peukert, *Volksgenossen und Gemeinschaftsfremde:*

Anpassung, Ausmerze und Aufbegehren unter dem Nationalsozialismus (Cologne, 1982), 233–245; Wolfgang Benz, "Homosexuelle und 'Gemeinschaftsfremde': Zur Diskriminierung von Opfergruppen nach der nationalsozialistischen Verfolgung," *Dachauer Hefte* 14 (1998): 4–5; Wachsmann, "Policy," 133.

81. See Langhammer, "Verhaftungsaktion," 60–62; Nikolaus Wachsmann, "The Dynamics of Destruction: The Development of the Concentration Camps, 1933–1945," in Jane Caplan and Nikolaus Wachsmann, eds., *Concentration Camps in Nazi Germany: The New Histories* (London, 2010), 23.

82. See Ayass, "*Asoziale*," 170; Langhammer, "Verhaftungsaktion," 61–62.

83. Decree on preventive crime combat by the police, published in *Vorbeugende Verbrechensbekämpfung: Sammlung der auf dem Gebiete der vorbeugenden Verbrechensbekämpfung ergangenen Erlasse und sonstigen Bestimmungen; Schriftenreihe des Reichskriminalpolizeiamtes Berlin Nr. 15*, ed. Reichssicherheitshauptamt, Amt V (Berlin, 1941), IfZ, Dc. 17.02, 41–42.

84. Guidelines of RKPA for the execution of preventive crime combat, April 4, 1938, in *Verbrechensbekämpfung*, 65.

85. See Broszat, "Concentration Camps," 447–450; Ayass, "*Asoziale*," 140–143.

86. See Ayass, "*Asoziale*," 156; Schüler-Springorum, "Masseneinweisungen," 158.

87. See Detlef Garbe, "Absonderung, Strafkommandos und spezifischer Terror: Jüdische Gefangene in nationalsozialistischen Konzentrationslagern," in Arno Herzig and Ina Lorenz, eds., *Verdrängung und Vernichtung der Juden unter dem Nationalsozialismus* (Hamburg, 1992), 180; Wachsmann, "Dynamics," 23.

88. Isolated cases are documented in: List of professional and habitual criminals and sex offenders compiled by Coordinating Office of the Weimar Criminal Police, March 1937, Thüringisches Hauptstaatsarchiv Weimar (ThHStA W), Thüringisches Ministerium des Inneren, P. 110, Berufsverbrecherbekämpfung 1937, 17–18.

89. See report detailing changes made in KL Sachsenhausen, June 25, 1938, ITS, KL Sachsenhausen, GCC 10/87, Ordner 104, 291. The total number of prisoners detained in Sachsenhausen on that day was 9,139 men.

90. See Stein, *Juden*, 19–20.

91. See *Häftlinge nach Eintragungen im Zugangsbuch vom 10. Juli 1937–31. August 1938*, March 1, 2002, DaA.

92. Circular of RKPA on preventive crime combat by the police, June 1, 1938, in *Verbrechensbekämpfung*, 81.

93. Decree on preventive crime combat by the police, 41–42; letter from Coordinating Office of the Munich Criminal Police to Rosenheim Municipal Police, June 4, 1938, quoted in Ayass, "*Asoziale*," 150.

94. Michael Berkowitz, *The Crime of My Very Existence: Nazism and the Myth of Jewish Criminality* (Berkeley, CA, 2007), xiii.

95. See Avraham Barkai, "Der wirtschaftliche Existenzkampf der Juden im Dritten Reich, 1933–1938," in Arnold Paucker, ed., *Die Juden im nationalsozialistischen Deutschland, 1933–1945* (Tübingen, 1986), 156.

96. See Gruner, *Arbeitseinsatz*, 52–53.

97. See Ayass, "Asoziale," 150; Gruner, *Arbeitseinsatz*, 41–42; Orth, *System*, 47–49; Christian Dirks, "Die 'Juni-Aktion' 1938 in Berlin," in Beate Meyer and Hermann Simon, eds., *Juden in Berlin, 1938–1945* (Berlin, 2000), 34; Wachsmann, "Policy," 137; Wachsmann, "Dynamics," 24–25.

98. Wolf Gruner, *Jewish Forced Labor under the Nazis: Economic Needs and Racial Aims, 1938–1944* (Cambridge, 2006), 108–109. See also Gruner, *Arbeitseinsatz*, 43.

99. Memo Herbert Hagen, SD Jewish Desk, June 8, 1938, YVA, O.51/ OSOBI/88, 38.

100. See letter from SD Jewish Desk II 112, Herbert Hagen, to SD-Leader of SS-Regional District Munich, YVA, O.51/OSOBI/88, 47. In this letter, Hagen declared that "the idea of emigration is the guiding principle for all practical treatment of the Jewish Question. Every measure that might have negative effects on emigration . . . must be rejected."

101. Ian Kershaw, "'Working towards the Führer': Reflections on the Nature of the Hitler Dictatorship," *Contemporary European History* 2:2 (1993): 103–118.

102. Longerich, *Holocaust*, 101–102.

103. Letter from Coordinating Office of the Munich Criminal Police, June 4, 1938, quoted in Ayass, "Asoziale," 150.

104. See Wachsmann, "Policy," 137.

105. Bayerisches Staatsarchiv München (BayStA M), Polizeidirektion München, personal file 11807 (Cahn), microfilm frames 70–75.

106. Ruling on the interdiction of business by Munich Police Department from May 27, 1935, cited according to Wolfram Selig, *Leben unterm Rassenwahn: Vom Antisemitismus in der "Hauptstadt der Bewegung"* (Berlin, 2001), 96.

107. See ibid., 98.

108. Betty Cahn, petition for release, August 12, 1938, BayStA M, Polizeidirektion München 11807, frame 83.

109. Letter regarding the release of Josef Cahn sent from RKPA Berlin to Coordinating Office of the Munich Criminal Police, August 19, 1938, and Standard form for release of Jewish preventive custody prisoners, both ibid., frames 88–89.

110. See letter from Josef Cahn to Munich Police Headquarters, December 16, 1938, ibid., frame 69.

111. See Entschädigungsakte nach Josef Cahn geb. 06.07.1883 in Rülsheim, BEG 40.882, Bayerisches Landesamt für Finanzen/Landesentschädigungsamt München; *Biographisches Gedenkbuch der Münchner Juden, 1933–1945*, vol. 1.

ed. Stadtarchiv München (Munich, 2003), 227–229; entry "Josef Cahn," in *BArch Gedenkbuch* (online version).

112. Anon., "Buchenwald, das Vorzugsquartier," *Das Neue Tage-Buch* 6:47 (November 19, 1938): 1118. The report was transmitted to the British Foreign Office in February 1939. It is published as Dok. 52, in *VEJ* 2:187–196.

113. Statement by a Jewish ex-prisoner, August 1938, Friends House Library and Archives, London, Friends Committee for Refugees and Aliens, Political Prisoners, Correspondence 1933–1938, FCRA/19/1.

114. Kurt Kohn, *Mein Weg ins KZ*, n.d., Buchenwald Memorial Archives (BwA), 31/1065-65, 1. For a similar testimony, see (Anon.) *Nach Buchenwald im Zuge der "Asozialen-Aktion,"* 1957, WL, P.III.h.No.655, 1.

115. Camp administration registered 1,084 individuals on board this transport, which left Berlin by train from Anhalter Bahnhof on the evening of June 14. See report detailing changes made in KL Buchenwald, June 15, 1938, ITS, KL Buchenwald GCC 2/181 IB/2, Ordner 102, 25. See also Stein, *Juden*, 19.

116. See "Vorzugsquartier," 1119; Kohn, *Weg*, 1. On Buchenwald in general, see Harry Stein, "Buchenwald—Stammlager," in Benz and Distel, *Der Ort des Terrors*, 3:301–356.

117. "Vorzugsquartier," 1119. See also Kohn, *Weg*, 1; *Buchenwald im Zuge*, 1.

118. Harry Naujoks, *Mein Leben im KZ-Sachsenhausen, 1936–1942: Erinnerungen des ehemaligen Lagerältesten* (Berlin, 1989), 78–79.

119. See "Vorzugsquartier," 1119; Naujoks, *Leben*, 77; Eberle, "Häftlingskategorien," 97.

120. "Vorzugsquartier," 1119. See also Kohn, *Weg*, 1.

121. Berkowitz, *Crime*, 35, see also xviii, 29.

122. Harry Richard Loewenberg, *Homeless in Exile: Days of Persecution in Fall and Winter, 1938–1939*, USHMMA, RG-02.061, 11, quoted in Berkowitz, *Crime*, 27.

123. See "Vorzugsquartier," 1119; *Buchenwald im Zuge*, 1; Stein, *Juden*, 19.

124. Kohn, *Weg*, 1.

125. See Anon., *Todesfälle in den Konzentrationslagern (1938)*, ca. 1940s, WL, P.III.h.No.695, 1. See also *Sopade Report* (July 1937), 761.

126. My evaluation of the daily changes-reports *(Veränderungsmeldungen)* from the months June to September, 1938, found 88 deaths of Jewish prisoners in Buchenwald and 38 deaths in Sachsenhausen. See reports detailing changes made in KL Buchenwald, June 14–September 30, 1938, ITS, KL Buchenwald GCC 2/181 IB/2, Ordner 102–103; reports detailing changes made in KL Sachsenhausen, June 17–September 30, 1938, ITS, KL Sachsenhausen, GCC 10/87, Ordner 104–105. See also DaA deaths statistics, June 14–September 23, 1938; reports detailing changes made in KL Dachau, June14 to September 23, 1938, ITS, KL Dachau GCC 3/70, Ordner 99–100.

127. See *Todesfälle*, 1; "Vorzugsquartier," 1121.

128. Friedrich Weil, *Mein Leben in Deutschland vor und nach dem 30. Januar 1933*, New York, 1940, partly published in Monika Richarz, ed., *Jüdisches Leben in Deutschland*, vol. 3: *Selbstzeugnisse zur Sozialgeschichte, 1918–1945* (Stuttgart, 1982), 279.

129. See Hans Reichmann, *Deutscher Bürger und verfolgter Jude: Novemberpogrom und KZ Sachsenhausen, 1937 bis 1939* (Munich, 1998), 85, 87; Stein, *Juden,* 26–27.

130. See reports detailing changes made in KL Sachsenhausen, June 29–July 31, 1938, ITS, KL Sachsenhausen, GCC 10/87, Ordner 104, 295–294, Ordner 105, 1–33.

131. See Dismissals June 30–July 10, 1938, list attached to report detailing changes made in KL Buchenwald, July 12, 1938, ITS, KL Buchenwald GCC 2/181 IB/2, Ordner 102, 64.

132. Daily strength report of the Sachsenhausen concentration camp, September 16, 1938, AS, D 1 A 1020, 371; Stein, *Juden,* 26, 33.

133. Reichmann, *Bürger,* 86.

134. Anon., *Bericht über das Konzentrationslager Buchenwald nach der Asozialen-Aktion im Juni 1938*, received in 1957, WL, P.III.h.No. 654, 4.

135. Arthur Prinz, "The Role of the Gestapo in Obstructing and Promoting Jewish Emigration," *Yad Vashem Studies* 2 (1958): 211.

136. See Beate Meyer, *Tödliche Gratwanderung: Die Reichsvereinigung der Juden in Deutschland zwischen Hoffnung, Zwang, Selbstbehauptung und Verstrickung, (1939–1945)* (Göttingen, 2011), 30.

137. Prinz, "Role," 211.

138. Werner Rosenstock, "Exodus, 1933–1939: A Survey of Jewish Emigration from Germany," *Leo Baeck Institute Year Book* 1 (1956): 378, note 3.

139. Friedländer, *Nazi Germany,* 1:248. See also Frank Caestecker and Bob Moore, eds., *Refugees from Nazi Germany and the Liberal European States* (New York, 2010).

140. See Berkowitz, *Crime,* xiii–xiv, xxi.

141. "Vorzugsquartier," 1119.

142. See Patrick Wagner, *Volksgemeinschaft ohne Verbrecher: Konzeption und Praxis der Kriminalpolizei in der Zeit der Weimarer Republik und des Nationalsozialismus* (Hamburg, 1996), 280; Faludi, *Die "Juni-Aktion" 1938,* 56–57.

143. See Dirks, "'Juni-Aktion,'" 35. Anti-Jewish riots were not restricted to Berlin but took place also in Frankfurt, Cologne, Munich, Leipzig, Essen, Breslau, Königsberg, and in other cities across the Reich. See ibid., 37–38; Christoph Kreutzmüller et al., *Ein Pogrom im Juni: Fotos antisemitischer Schmierereien in Berlin, 1938* (Berlin, 2013), 12–23.

144. Bella Fromm, *Blood and Banquets: A Berlin Social Diary* (New York, 1944), 274. See also Reichmann, *Bürger,* 77.

145. Reichmann, *Bürger*, 92–93, see also 76, 84.

146. See report detailing changes made in KL Buchenwald, November 11, 1938, ITS, KL Buchenwald GCC 2/181 IB/2, Ordner 103, 198; *Die Carlebachs: Eine Rabbinerfamilie aus Deutschland*, ed. Ephraim Carlebach Stiftung (Hamburg, 1995), 136–137.

147. Transcript of Oral-History Interview with Emil Carlebach at Buchenwald Memorial in 1994, conducted by Hanno Brühl, printed in *Carlebachs*, 140. See also Carlebach, *Tote*, 93–97.

148. Berkowitz, *Crime*, xix.

149. Interview Carlebach, in *Carlebachs*, 140. See also entry "Moritz Carlebach" in BArch *Gedenkbuch* (online version).

150. For numbers, see Heiko Pollmeier, "Die Verhaftungen nach dem November-Pogrom 1938 und die Masseninhaftierung in den 'jüdischen Baracken' des KZ Sachsenhausen," in Günter Morsch and Susanne zur Nieden, eds., *Jüdische Häftlinge im Konzentrationslager Sachsenhausen, 1936 bis 1945* (Berlin, 2004), 164.

151. For a discussion of Grynszpan's motivation for the deed, including a critical assessment of his later statement that he had known vom Rath personally and that the two men had had a homosexual liaison, see Alan E. Steinweis, *Kristallnacht 1938* (Cambridge, MA, 2009), 142–147.

152. Wolfgang Benz, "Mitglieder der Häftlingsgesellschaft auf Zeit: Die 'Aktionsjuden 1938/39,'" *Dachauer Hefte* 21 (2005): 179–196.

153. The term "Action Jews" (*Aktionsjuden*) was used by the Nazi perpetrators for the Jewish men deported to the concentration camps after the 1938 November Pogrom—the "vom-Rath Action" —whereas the term "November Jews" (*Novemberjuden*) appears as a self-designation in many memoirs. See List of names of Action Jews to be released on November 21, 1938, ITS, KL Buchenwald GCC 2/181 IB/2, Ordner 104; 17; Julius Meyer, *Buchenwald*, 1940, Wiener Library London (WL), P.II.d.No.77, 98; Reichmann, *Bürger*, 236.

154. On the 1938 November Pogrom, see, most importantly, "Der Novemberpogrom 1938," in Wolfgang Benz, ed., *Die Juden in Deutschland, 1933–1945: Leben unter nationalsozialistischer Herrschaft* (Munich, 1988), 499–544; Hermann Graml, *Reichskristallnacht: Antisemitismus und Judenverfolgung im Dritten Reich* (Munich, 1988); Walter H. Pehle, ed., *Der Judenpogrom 1938: Von der "Reichskristallnacht" zum Völkermord* (Frankfurt, 1988); Dieter Obst, *"Reichskristallnacht": Ursachen und Verlauf des antisemitischen Pogroms vom November 1938* (Frankfurt, 1991); Steinweis, *Kristallnacht*.

155. See Joseph Goebbels, diary entry November 10, 1938, in *Die Tagebücher von Joseph Goebbels*, pt. 1: *Aufzeichnungen, 1923–1941*, vol. 6: *August 1938–Juni 1939*, ed. Elke Fröhlich (Munich, 1998), 180. See also Longerich, *Holocaust*, 110–111.

156. Ibid., 181. On an assessment of Hitler's role in the pogrom, see Friedländer, *Nazi Germany*, 1:270–278. On the exact sequence of events, see Uwe Dietrich Adam, "Wie spontan war der Pogrom?," in Pehle, *Judenpogrom*, 76–80.

157. Secret telegram from Heinrich Müller to all Gestapo Offices, November 9, 23:55 pm, BArchB, R 58/276.

158. Telegram from Reinhard Heydrich to all Gestapo Offices, November 10, 01:20 am, BArchB, R 58/276, 125–126.

159. See Friedländer, *Nazi Germany*, 1:277.

160. See Circular RFSS and Chief of the German Police to all Gestapo Offices, November 10, 1938, printed in Joseph Walk, *Das Sonderrecht für die Juden im NS-Staat: Eine Sammlung der gesetzlichen Massnahmen und Richtlinien— Inhalt und Bedeutung* (Heidelberg, 1981), 253–254.

161. See telegram from the Chief the Security Police to all Gestapo Offices, November 16, 1938 20:40 pm, BArchB, R 58/276, 149; Michael Wildt, "Einleitung," in Reichmann, *Bürger*, 23.

162. See Pollmeier, "Inhaftierung und Lagererfahrung deutscher Juden im November 1938," *Jahrbuch für Antisemitismusforschung* 8 (1999): 107–108; Pollmeier, "Verhaftungen," 167; Wildt, "Einleitung," 23; Wildt, *Volksgemeinschaft als Selbstermächtigung: Gewalt gegen Juden in der deutschen Provinz, 1919 bis 1939* (Hamburg, 2007), 319–335.

163. See Curt W. Bondy, "Problems of Internment Camps," *Journal of Abnormal and Social Psychology* 38:4 (1943): 453–475; Werner T. Angress, *Between Fear & Hope: Jewish Youth in the Third Reich* (New York, 1988), 61–71.

164. Meyer, *Buchenwald*, 26, see also 18–25; Harry Stein, "Das Sonderlager im Konzentrationslager Buchenwald nach den Pogromen 1938," in Monica Kingreen, ed., *Nach der Kristallnacht: Jüdisches Leben und antijüdische Politik in Frankfurt am Main, 1938–1945* (Frankfurt, 1999), 26; Benz, "Mitglieder," 183. A stop to deportations of Jewish prisoners to the overcrowded Buchenwald camp was ordered on November 12, 1938. See telegram from Gestapo Berlin to all Gestapo Offices, November 12, 1938, 14:30 p.m., BArchB, R 58/276, 141.

165. See Stein, "Sonderlager," 27–30; Pollmeier, "Inhaftierung," 109–110.

166. Neurath, *Society*, 124.

167. See Meyer, *Buchenwald*, 29; Stein, "Sonderlager," 33, 40–41.

168. Max Rölz, [untitled report], March 6, 1958, BwA, 5244-18.

169. See Julius Freund, *O Buchenwald!* (Klagenfurt, 1945), 36; Stein, *Juden*, 33, 43; Stein, "Sonderlager," 28–32.

170. Meyer, *Buchenwald*, 51.

171. See ibid., 33, 51–52; Freund, *Buchenwald*, 38, 78; Stein, *Juden*, 45.

172. See Meyer, *Buchenwald*, 34, 37, 51–52; Heilig, *Men*, 224–225; Stein, "Sonderlager," 32–33, 41–43.

173. See Freund, *Buchenwald*, 41; Meyer, *Buchenwald*, 45. On the Austrian "police prisoners," see Stein, "Sonderlager," 28–32.

174. See Stefan Heymann, *Das Judenrevier*, n.d., BwA, 52-44-15; Stein, *Juden*, 46, 51, 57, 65; Drobisch and Wieland, *System*, 321; *Buchenwald Concentration Camp, 1937–1945: A Guide to the Permanent Historical Exhibition*, ed. Gedenkstätte Buchenwald (Göttingen, 2004), 92. The Judenrevier was dissolved after most of the November Jews had been released in the spring of 1939.

175. See Freund, *Buchenwald*, 40, 95; Eugen Kogon, *Der SS-Staat: Das System der deutschen Konzentrationslager* (Munich, 1996), 232; Carlebach, *Tote*, 232; *Guide*, 92.

176. See Stein, "Sonderlager," 46.

177. See DaA deaths statistics.

178. Calculations of the number of Jewish prisoners sent to Sachsenhausen in the wake of the 1938 November Pogrom are complicated due to a crucial gap in the sources. Documentation of new arrivals in Sachsenhausen is missing for the period of November 10–20. For his estimates, Pollmeier used lists of dismissals and the strength reports of the personal-effects warehouse. See Pollmeier, "Verhaftungen," 171, 176–177. See also Reichmann, *Bürger*, 197; Benz, "Mitglieder," 180.

179. See Jürgen Matthäus, "Verfolgung, Ausbeutung, Vernichtung: Jüdische Häftlinge im System der Konzentrationslager," in Morsch and zur Nieden, *Häftlinge*, 76; Dieter Pohl, "The Holocaust and the Concentration Camps," in Caplan and Wachsmann, *Camps*, 150.

180. See Naujoks, *Leben*, 94. On Sachsenhausen's small camp, see also Rainer Potratz, "Die Geschichte des Ortes: Entstehung und Nutzung des 'kleinen Lagers' und der Baracken 38 und 39," in Morsch and zur Nieden, *Häftlinge*, 119–139. See also the Sachsenhausen expansion plan of April 1938 reproduced in Chapter 4 (p. 150) in which the area of the small camp is still earmarked for the workshops (numbers 28–39).

181. See various prisoner testimonies published in *Novemberpogrom 1938: Die Augenzeugenberichte der Wiener Library London*, ed. Ben Barkow, Raphael Gross, and Michael Lenarz (Frankfurt, 2008), 539, 548, 555, 561. See also Walter Solmitz, *Bericht über Dachau*, London, 1939, published in Joist Grolle, *Bericht von einem schwierigen Leben: Walter Solmitz (1905 bis 1962); Schüler von Aby Warburg und Ernst Cassierer* (Hamburg, 1994), 96; Pollmeier, "Inhaftierung," 113.

182. See Meyer, *Buchenwald*, 47; Pollmeier, "Inhaftierung," 111; Benz, "Mitglieder," 180; *Novemberpogrom 1938*, 538, 545, 548, 555–556; Riedel, *Ordnungshüter*, 200.

183. See Meyer, *Buchenwald*, 98; Barbara Distel, "'Die letzte Warnung vor der Vernichtung': Zur Verschleppung der Aktionsjuden in die Konzentrationslager

nach dem 9. November 1938," *ZfG* 48:11 (1998): 987; Riedel, *Ordnungshüter*, 200.

184. See Reichmann, *Bürger*, 165–169.

185. See Pollmeier, "Verhaftungen," 176.

186. Neurath, *Society*, 239. See also Heilig, *Men*, 226–227.

187. SS investigation report against Karl Otto Koch, 1944, quoted in Stein, "Sonderlager," 39.

188. See Naujoks, *Leben*, 92; Pollmeier, "Inhaftierung," 116.

189. Testimony of Leopold Engelmann, n.d. (late 1940s), Bayerisches Staatsarchiv Amberg (Bay StA A), Staatsanwaltschaft Weiden Nr. 80, 29.

190. Hearing of Hans Harbauer in front of the Weiden District Court, March 18, 1948, ibid., 52.

191. Telegram from Chief of Sipo to all Gestapo Offices, to the Leaders of the SS Death Head's Division and to the Concentration Camps Commandants, November 16, 1938, 20:40 pm, BArchB, R 58/276, 149–150.

192. See BArchB, R 58/276, 160, 172, 193. On December 8, Himmler lifted the stop to releases of Jewish prisoners. See letter from Chief of Sipo to Gestapo, December 8, 1938, ibid., 165.

193. Solmitz, *Bericht*, 122. See also Benz, "Mitglieder," 191; Riedel, *Ordnungshüter*, 202.

194. In the Dachau daily changes reports, a first larger group of "Action Jews" is registered as having been discharged on November 19. On November 21, 221 "Action Jews" were released from Buchenwald. See report detailing changes made in KL Dachau, November 19, 1938, ITS, KL Dachau GCC 3/70 I, Ordner 100, 175; report detailing changes made in KL Buchenwald, November 21, 1938, ITS, KL Buchenwald, GCC 2/181 IB/2, Ordner 105, 17. For Sachsenhausen, respective information is lacking due to the above-mentioned gap in the sources.

195. See Stein, *Juden*, 47–48; Pollmeier, "Inhaftierung," 116; Pollmeier, "Verhaftungen," 177–178.

196. Ruth Abraham, *Meine Erlebnisse während der nationalsozialistischen Zeit*, n.d., LBIA, ME 1, 5.

197. See report detailing daily strength of prisoners in KL Sachsenhausen, January 1, 1939, AS, D 1 A 1012, 2; Stein, "Sonderlager," 46.

198. See report detailing daily strength of prisoners in KL Sachsenhausen, November 10, 1938, AS, D 1 A 1020, 425.

199. See report detailing daily strength of prisoners in KL Sachsenhausen, February 6, 1939, AS, D 1 A 1012, 53.

200. Numbers in detail: March 6, 1939: 254 asocial Jews and 204 November Jews; April 3, 1939: 193 asocial Jews and 131 November Jews; May 2, 1939: 185 asocial Jews and 106 November Jews; June 7, 1939: 184 asocial Jews and 76 November

Jews. On September 1, 1939, the administration registered 172 asocial Jews and 66 November Jews. See reports detailing daily strength of prisoners in KL Sachsenhausen on the respective dates, AS, D 1 A 1012, 81, 108, 136, 170, 264.

201. ThHStA W, NS 4 Bu/137, 1, quoted in Stein, *Juden*, 70.

6. The Calm after the Storm?

1. The exact figures are: Dachau, 309; Sachsenhausen, 94; Buchenwald, 83. For the period January 1–August 31, 1939, see reports detailing changes made in KL Dachau, International Tracing Service (ITS), KL Dachau GCC 3/70, Ordner 101–102; reports detailing changes made in KL Sachsenhausen, ITS, KL Sachsenhausen GCC 10/87, Ordner 107–107; reports detailing changes made in KL Buchenwald, ITS, KL Buchenwald GCC 2/181 IB/3, Ordner 105–107.

2. Circular Berlin Gestapo to all Gestapo desks and to the Leader of the SS Death's Head Divisions and Concentration Camps, January 31, 1939, BArchB, R 58/276, 203.

3. Benedikt Kautsky, *Teufel und Verdammte: Erfahrungen und Erkenntnisse aus sieben Jahren in deutschen Konzentrationslagern* (Zurich, 1946), 30. The peak of 19,670 prisoners was reached on November 13, 1938. See reports detailing changes made in KL Buchenwald, January 1, 1939–August 31, 1939, ITS, KL Buchenwald GCC 2/181 IB/3, Ordner 107.

4. See Chief of Security Police, order for the release of protective custody prisoners on the occasion of the Führer's birthday, April 5, 1939, and telegram from Reinhard Heydrich to all Gestapo Offices and Coordinating Gestapo Offices, April 14, 1939, BArchB, R 58/1027, 79–84; Harry Naujoks, *Mein Leben im KZ-Sachsenhausen, 1936–1942: Erinnerungen des ehemaligen Lagerältesten* (Berlin, 1989), 116. In Buchenwald, Dachau, and Sachsenhausen combined, more than 3,000 concentration camp prisoners were released between April 18 and April 22, 1939.

5. Circular Berlin Gestapo, May 12, 1938, BArchB, R 58/1027, 37a–b; Klaus Drobisch and Günther Wieland, *System der NS-Konzentrationslager, 1933–1939* (Berlin, 1993), 281–282. On arrest practices after the November Pogrom, see also Marco Esseling, "Juden als Häftlingsgruppe in Konzentrationslagern: Verhaftung von Juden und ihre Stellung im Lager bis 1942 unter besonderer Berücksichtigung des KZ Dachau" (MA dissertation, Institut für Neuere Geschichte, Ludwig-Maximilians-Universität München, 1995), 53.

6. See reports detailing changes made in KL Buchenwald, January 1–August 31, 1939, ITS, KL Buchenwald GCC 2/181 IB/3, Ordner 105–107; *Buchenwald Concentration Camp, 1937–1945: A Guide to the Permanent Historical Exhibition*, ed. Gedenkstätte Buchenwald (Göttingen, 2004), 77.

7. Letter from the President of the Pfalz Government to the Mayor of Pirmasens, January 16, 1939, Landesarchiv Speyer (LArch Sp), Gestapostelle Neustadt an der Weinstrasse H 91, Nr. 7314 (Alfred Feinberg), 68.

8. See Ausländerpolizeiverordnung, August 22, 1938, *Reichsgesetzblatt* 1 (1938): 1053–1056; "Gesetz über den Widerruf von Einbürgerungen und die Aberkennung der deutschen Staatsangehörigkeit," July 14, 1933, ibid. (1933), 480; LArch Sp, H 91, Nr. 7314, 68–73; entries "Alfred Feinberg" and "Rosa Feinberg," in *Barch Gedenkbuch* (online version).

9. See Herbert A. Strauss, "Jewish Emigration from Germany: Nazi Policies and Jewish Responses (1)," *Leo Baeck Institute Year Book* 25 (1980): 344; Susanne Meinl and Jutta Zwilling, *Legalisierter Raub: Die Ausplünderung der Juden im Nationalsozialismus durch die Reichsfinanzverwaltung in Hessen* (Frankfurt, 2004), 40–42.

10. Letter from the Chief of the Security Police to all Gestapo Offices, February 9, 1939, Landesarchiv Nordrhein-Westfalen Abteilung Rheinland (LArch NRW R), Geheime Staatspolizei—Staatspolizeileitstelle Düsseldorf (hereafter Gestapo) RW 36, Nr. 19, 11–12. See also Meinl and Zwilling, *Raub*, 474–478; Peter Longerich, *Holocaust: The Nazi Persecution and Murder of the Jews* (Oxford, 2010), 120.

11. Letter from Berlin Gestapo regarding illegal emigration of Jews sent to Gestapo Offices in Karlsruhe, Münster, Aachen, Düsseldorf, Köln, Neustadt a.d. Weinstrasse, Osnabrück, Saarbrücken, Trier, Wilhelmshaven, December 23, 1938, LArch NRW R, Gestapo RW 36, Nr. 19, 2–3, and letter from Berlin Gestapo to the same addressees, March 15, 1939, BArchB, R 58/276, 215.

12. See LArch NRW R, Gestapo RW 58/45627; entry "Erwin Schwarz" in *BArch Gedenkbuch* (online version).

13. Letter from Karlsruhe Gestapo to Düsseldorf Gestapo, May 17, 1939, LArch NRW R, Gestapo RW 58/6305, frame 4.

14. See ibid., Gestapo RW 58/6305; entry "Oskar Koch" in *BArch Gedenkbuch* (online version).

15. See LArch NRW R, Gestapo RW 58/14521.

16. See telegram from Berlin Gestapo to all Gestapo Offices and Border Police Stations, July 27, 1939, BArchB, R 58/276, 227–228.

17. Telegrams from Berlin Gestapo to all Gestapo Offices with the exception of Bohemia and Moravia, April 14, 1939, and June 14, 1939, ITS, HIST Ordner 6–7a, 27–29; reports detailing changes made in KL Buchenwald, February 1–June 30, 1939, ITS, KL Buchenwald GCC 2 2/181 IB/2, Ordner 105–106; Harry Stein, *Juden in Buchenwald*, 1937–1942 (Weimar, 1992), 65.

18. According to the Dachau *Zugangsbuch*, a total of 309 Jewish prisoners were deported to the camp between January 1 and August 31, 1939. Depending on whether one considers "nationality" or "place of residence," the number of

Jews from Czechoslovakia varies between 74 and 79, respectively. This includes deportees from both the Sudetenland and the Protectorate. An additional 40 Jewish prisoners were brought to Dachau from the Sudeten region between October 1 and December 31, 1938. See arrival book Dachau concentration camp, ITS, KL Dachau GCC 3/61, Ordner 9–10.

19. See *Novemberpogrom 1938: Die Augenzeugenberichte der Wiener Library London*, ed. Ben Barkow, Raphael Gross, and Michael Lenarz (Frankfurt, 2008), 877–893.

20. See daily report of the Commander of the Security Police and the SD in Prague, May 13, 1939, published in Miroslav Kárný and Jaroslava Milotová, eds., *Anatomie okupační politiky hitlerovského Německa v "Protektorátu Čechy a Morava": Dokumenty z období říšského protektora Konstantina von Neuratha* (Prague, 1987), 84. My thanks are due to Zdenek Hrabec for helping me with the translation.

21. See ibid.; *Sopade Report* (July 1939): 899; Livia Rothkirchen, *The Jews of Bohemia and Moravia: Facing the Holocaust* (Jerusalem, 2005), 99–100; Chad Carl Bryant, *Prague in Black: Nazi Rule and Czech Nationalism* (Cambridge, MA, 2007), 34; *Die Verfolgung und Ermordung der europäischen Juden durch das nationalsozialistische Deutschland, 1933–1945*, vol 3: *Deutsches Reich und Protektorat, 1939–1941* (Munich, 2012), 23.

22. Midia Kraus, *Bericht über Prof. Dr. Oskar Kraus*, 1955, Wiener Library (WL), P.III.i.No.29.

23. See *Novemberpogrom 1938*, 879, 887; Rothkirchen, *Jews*, 53, 100. The HICEM was established in 1927 as a merger of the Hebrew Immigrant Aid Society (HIAS), the Jewish Colonization Association (ICA), and Emigdirect, a migration organization based in Berlin. The name HICEM is an acronym of HIAS, ICA, and Emigdirect.

24. See Detlef Brandes, *Die Tschechen unter deutschem Protektorat*, vol. 1: *Besatzungspolitik, Kollaboration und Widerstand im Protektorat Böhmen und Mähren bis Heydrichs Tod (1939–1942)* (Munich, 1969), 35; Rothkirchen, *Jews*, 98–99.

25. See arrival book Dachau concentration camp, ITS, KL Dachau GCC 3/61, Ordner 10, 34–38; Rothkirchen, *Jews*, 110.

26. See testimony of Walter Löbner, YVA O.33/182. My thanks are due to Sara Shor and Michael Tal for pointing me to this source. See also ITS, Central Name Index.

27. See *Novemberpogrom 1938*, 879–880, 887; Wolf Gruner, "Protektorat Böhmen und Mähren," in Wolf Gruner and Jürgen Osterloh, eds., *Das "Grossdeutsche Reich" und die Juden: Nationalsozialistische Verfolgung in den "angegliederten" Gebieten* (Frankfurt,2010), 155.

28. *Novemberpogrom 1938*, 887.

29. *Sopade Report* (May 1939): 576.

30. See arrival book Dachau concentration camp, ITS, KL Dachau GCC 3/61, Ordner 9, 88–89; Rothkirchen, *Jews*, 102.

31. In an alternative reading, Zámečník states that the Kladno transport consisted of 109 people. However, while the documentation of the Dachau administration remains unclear about the number of the transport—a total of 121 *Schutzhaft* prisoners arrived in the camp on that day—the Mauthausen administration unambiguously recorded only 107 *Schutzhäftlinge (Tschechen)*. See reports detailing changes made in KL Dachau on June 16, 1939, ITS, KL Dachau GCC 3/70, Ordner 102, 123–125; arrival and departure register for KL Mauthausen, ITS, KL Mauthausen OCC 15/4f IB/3, Ordner 50, 52–53; Zámečník, *Dachau*, 102.

32. See *Almanach Dachau: Kytice událostí a vzpomínek . . .* (Prague: Sopvp, 1946), 14–15; Stansilav Zámečník, *Das war Dachau* (Frankfurt, 2007), 102; Petr Koura, "Pozapomenutá legenda českého odboje: Případ Jana Smudka a nacistická okupační politika," *Soudobé dějiny* 11:1–2 (2004): 110–127.

33. See report detailing changes made in KL Dachau on September 26, 1939, ITS, KL Dachau GCC 3/70, Ordner 102, 170; reports detailing changes made in KL Buchenwald, September 27, 1939, ITS, GCC 2/181 I B/3 Ordner 107, 186; report by former Camp Prisoners Committee about the life of prisoners and crimes of fascists in the camps, 1945, USHMMA, RG-11001 M.20, Reel 91, Fond 1367, Opis 2, Folder 6, 10; Stein, *Juden*, 83.

34. See Kautsky, *Teufel*, 31; *Guide*, 83–85.

35. See Karl Röder, *Nachtwache: 10 Jahre KZ Dachau und Flossenbürg* (Vienna, 1985), 124, 129.

36. Alfred Hübsch, *Die Insel des Standrechts*, ca. 1960, DaA, A1436, 136.

37. See Emil Carlebach, *Zur Lage der jüdischen Häftlinge*, 1980, BwA, 31/574, 2.

38. See ibid., 2–3; Kautsky, *Teufel*, 30; Eugen Kogon, *Der SS-Staat: Das System der deutschen Konzentrationslager* (Munich, 1996), 86–87; Sofsky, *Order*, 134.

39. See Sofsky, *Order*, 136. On Heinz Eschen, see Chapter 4, 162–167.

40. See Carlebach, *Lage*, 3–4; Hugo Burkhard, *Tanz mal Jude! Von Dachau bis Shanghai: Meine Erlebnisse in den Konzentrationslagern Dachau—Buchenwald—Ghetto Shanghai* (Nuremberg, 1967), 124; Stein, *Juden*, 70–72.

41. For the numbers, see Nikolaus Wachsmann, *KL: A History of the Nazi Concentration Camps* (unpublished manuscript), chap. 2, 116. For the struggle between "criminals" and politicals, see Falk Pingel, *Häftlinge unter SS-Herrschaft: Widerstand, Selbstbehauptung und Vernichtung im Konzentrationslager* (Hamburg, 1978), 102–117; Karin Orth, "Gab es eine Lagergesellschaft? 'Kriminelle' und politische Häftlinge im Konzentrationslager," in Norbert Frei et al., eds, *Ausbeutung, Vernichtung, Öffentlichkeit: Neue Studien zur national-sozialistischen Lagerpolitik* (Munich, 2000), 109–133.

42. See Carlebach, *Lage*, 3–4; Carlebach, *Tote auf Urlaub: Kommunist in Deutschland; Dachau und Buchenwald, 1937–1945* (Bonn, 1995), 74, 111–115; Stein, *Juden*, 70–72; Bernhard Kuschey, *Die Ausnahme des Überlebens: Ernst und Hilde Federn; Eine biographische Studie und eine Analyse der Binnenstruktur des Konzentrationslagers* (Giessen, 2003), 456, 493–501; Knut Bergbauer, "'Der eben an uns vorüberging . . .': Rudi Arndt; Ein jüdischer Kommunist im Widerstand," *transversal* 11:2 (2010): 42–43; entry "Walter Rosenbaum" in *BArch Gendenkbuch* (online version).

43. Total strength of prisoners in Lichtenburg [*sic!*] concentration camp, May 21, 1939, Sammlungen Mahn- und Gedenkstätte Ravensbrück/Stiftung Brandenburgische Gedenkstätten (MGR/StBG), KL/14–18, n.p. My thanks are due to Johannes Schwartz, who helped locate this as well as the other two "head count" reports quoted below.

44. Ilse Rolfe née Gostynski, *Report*, 1955, WL, P.III.h.No.1595.

45. See letter from Marianne Wachstein to Hofrat Dr. Wilhelm, April 12, 1940, published in the original German as Dok. 68, in *VEJ* 3, 195–205, and in English translation in Irith Dublon-Knebel, *A Holocaust Crossroads: Jewish Women and Children in Ravensbrück* (London, 2010), 79–91. See also Linde Apel, *Jüdische Frauen im Konzentrationslager Ravensbrück, 1939–1945* (Berlin, 2003), 140–143.

46. See transport lists (women) arriving from various KLs, reports detailing changes made November 11, 1938–March 30, 1942, ITS, KL Ravensbrück GCC 9/ 32–33, Ordner 5a, 30–65.

47. Total strength of prisoners in the Ravensbrück concentration camp, August 7 and September 26, 1939, MGR/StBG, KL/14–18.

48. On the basis of the numbers of Jewish prisoners given, their precise overall share in the population of all SS concentration camps by the outbreak of the war was 6.2 percent. For the numbers, see report detailing daily strength of prisoners in KL Sachsenhausen, August 31, 1939, ITS, KL Sachsenhausen, GCC 10/87, Ordner 107. For Buchenwald we arrive at 761 when subtracting releases from, and adding new arrivals to, the number of 811 Jewish prisoners officially counted on August 11. See reports detailing changes made in KL Buchenwald between August 11 and August 31, 1939, ITS, KL Buchenwald GCC 2/181 IB/3, Ordner 107. For Dachau we arrive at 191 when subtracting those who arrived in the camp after September 1, 1939, from the total of 313 Jewish prisoners who were transported to Buchenwald on September 26. See reports detailing changes made in KL Dachau, ITS, KL Dachau GCC 3/70, Ordner 102. There were no Jews in Mauthausen or Flossenbürg at that time. For total prisoner numbers, see Drobisch and Wieland, *System*, 26.

49. Rudolf Höss, *Commandant of Auschwitz: The Autobiography of Rudolf Höss* (London, 2000), 81. On Höss's career, see Wachsmann, *KL*, chapter 2, 81–87.

50. Kautsky, *Teufel*, 31.

51. For pioneering studies of the concentration camps and the "Final Solution," see Dieter Pohl, "The Holocaust and the Concentration Camps," in Jane Caplan and Nikolaus Wachsmann, eds., *Concentration Camps in Nazi Germany: The New Histories* (London, 2010); Wachsmann, *KL*, chap. 6.

52. Telegram from RSHA to all Gestapo Offices and Coordinating Gestapo Offices, April 10, 1940, BArchB, R 58/276, 252. The order has been published as Dok. 67, in *VEJ* 3, 195. According to a later note of the RSHA's department IV C 2 for "'protective custody" matters, dated April 23, 1940, Himmler had already ordered the stop to releases of Jews from the camps on March 9, 1940. See BArchB, R 58/1027, 128.

53. See Burkhard, *Jude*, 135, 143–144.

54. See Günter Morsch, "Oranienburg–Sachsenhausen, Sachsenhausen–Oranienburg," in Ulrich Herbert et al., eds., *Die nationalsozialistischen Konzentrationslager: Entwicklung und Struktur* (Göttingen, 1998), 111–134; Falk Pingel, "Konzeption und Praxis der nationalsozialistischen Konzentrationslager, 1933 bis 1938: Kommentierende Bemerkungen," in ibid., 162; Wachsmann, *KL*, chap.4, 5–6.

55. Letter from Augsburg County Executive to Fischbach Gendarmerie, October 23, 1939, which refers to a respective order, BArchB, R 58/276, 242. See also Jeffrey Herf, *The Jewish Enemy: Nazi Propaganda during World War II and the Holocaust* (Cambridge, MA, 2006); *VEJ* 3, 26. 29.

56. Secret popular opinion report by the NSDAP District Direction Kitzingen-Gerolzhofen, September 11, 1939, printed in *The Jews in the Secret Nazi Reports on Popular Opinion in Germany, 1933–1945*, ed. Otto Dov Kulka and Eberhard Jäckel (New Haven, CT, 2010), 476.

57. See Leon Szalet, *Baracke 38: 237 Tage in den "Judenblocks" von Sachsenhausen* (Berlin, 2006), 288.

58. See Naujoks, *Leben*, 139.

59. See Kommandantur order no. 147 for the Buchenwald concentration camp, September 6, 1939, ThHStA W, NS 4 Bu/105, 12.

60. See secret telegram from the Chief of the Security Police and the SD, September 7, 1939, ThHStA W, Thüringisches Ministerium des Inneren, P. 94, 34, published as Dok. 6, in *VEJ* 3, 93–94. See also Yfaat Weiss, *Deutsche und polnische Juden vor dem Holocaust: Jüdische Identität zwischen Staatsbürgerschaft und Ethnizität, 1933–1940* (Munich, 2000), 212; Kathrin Külow, "Jüdische Häftlinge im KZ Sachsenhausen, 1939–1942," in Günter Morsch and Susanne zur Nieden, eds., *Jüdische Häftlinge im Konzentrationslager Sachsenhausen, 1936 bis 1945* (Berlin, 2004), 180–181.

61. See Stein, *Juden*, 85; Külow, "Häftlinge," 181; Jürgen Matthäus, "Verfolgung, Ausbeutung, Vernichtung: Jüdische Häftlinge im System der Konzentrationslager," in Morsch and zur Nieden, *Häftlinge*, 78.

62. See strength reports of the Sachsenhausen concentration camp, September 1 to December 30, 1939, AS, D 1 A 1012, 264–500; Stein, *Juden*, 83, 86, 129.

63. See Szalet, *Baracke*, 38–39; Naujoks, *Leben*, 146–150; Külow, "Häftlinge," 182–186, 191; Matthäus, "Verfolgung," 78–79.

64. See Szalet, *Baracke*. Written between 1942 and 1944, the testimony was first published in English translation as Leon Szalet, *Experiment "E": A Report from an Extermination Laboratory* (New York, 1945). For reports by other former prisoners, see Yehoshuah Friedmann, *Sachsenhausen: Die deutsche Hölle*, ca. 1944–1945, YVA, O.33/1098; Siegfried Halbreich, *Before—During—After: Surviving the Holocaust* (Los Angeles, CA, 2000).

65. 438 Polish citizens and 202 Jewish Polish citizens were separated from a transport of some 2,000 Poles that arrived in Buchenwald in mid-October 1939. See Stein, *Juden*, 83–86.

66. See Volkhard Knigge and Jürgen Seifert, eds., *Vom Antlitz zur Maske: Wien, Weimar, Buchenwald, 1939* (Weimar, 1999), 16–18; Claudia Spring, "Vermessen, deklassiert und deportiert: Dokumentation zur anthropologischen Untersuchung an 440 Juden im Wiener Stadion im September 1939 unter der Leitung von Josef Wastl vom Naturhistorischen Museum Wien," *zeitgeschichte* 32:2 (2005): 91–110.

67. See Stein, *Juden*, 88–92. Between January 12 and February 7, 1940, the Polish-Jewish special camp was dissolved and surviving prisoners were transferred to the main camp.

68. See Alexander B. Rossino, *Hitler Strikes Poland: Blitzkrieg, Ideology, and Atrocity* (Lawrence, KS, 2003); Jochen Böhler, *Auftakt zum Vernichtungskrieg: Die Wehrmacht in Polen 1939* (Frankfurt, 2006); Wachsmann, *KL*, chaps. 4, 6.

69. Szalet, *Baracke*, 88.

70. Ibid., 28.

71. See Kautsky, *Teufel*, 36–37; Nachtragsurteil Nr. 145d, Landgericht Frankfurt, February 27, 1970, in *Justiz und NS-Verbrechen. Sammlung deutscher Strafurteile wegen nationalsozialistischer Tötungsverbrechen 1945–1966* (Amsterdam, 1981), 22:784–788; Stein, *Juden*, 93–95; Carlebach, *Tote*, 110; Matthäus, "Verfolgung," 79.

72. Witness Testimony Ida Hirschkron, 1947, quoted in Apel, *Frauen*, 143–144, translated in Dublon-Knebel, *Holocaust*, 56–57.

73. Szalet, *Baracke*, 194. See also Külow, "Häftlinge," 182.

74. Szalet, *Baracke*, 211.

75. For Szalet's biograghy, see Winfried Meyer, "Nachwort," in Szalet, *Baracke*, 461–498.

Conclusion

1. See Marion A. Kaplan, *Between Dignity and Despair: Jewish Life in Nazi Germany* (New York,1998), 5. The idea of "social death" was originally conceptualized by Orlando Patterson to describe the slave condition. See Orlando Patterson, *Slavery and Social Death: A Comparative Study* (Cambridge, MA, 1982), 38–45.

2. See Victor Klemperer, *I Will Bear Witness: A Diary of the Nazi Years, 1933–1941* (New York, 1999), 17 (May 15, 1933); Carina Baganz, *Erziehung zur "Volksgemeinschaft"? Die frühen Konzentrationslager in Sachsen, 1933/34–1937* (Berlin, 2005), 195. See also the discussion of camp terror noted on August 10, 1933, in Klemperer, *Witness*, 28.

3. Paul Moore, "German Popular Opinion on the Nazi Concentration Camps, 1933–1939" (PhD dissertation, Birkbeck, University of London, 2010), 237.

4. "Erziehungs- und Besserungs-Anstalt in Osthofen," *Niersteiner Warte*, April 23/24, 1933; "Sie finden wieder zu ihrem Volke zurück! Besichtigung des Konzentrationslagers Osthofen durch die Vertreter der hessischen Presse," *Rheinische Warte*, May 6, 1933. See also Kim Wünschmann, "'Natürlich weiss ich, wer mich ins KZ gebracht hat und warum . . .': Die Inhaftierung von Juden im Konzentrationslager Osthofen, 1933/34," in Andreas Ehresmann et al., eds., *Die Erinnerung an die nationalsozialistischen Konzentrationslager: Akteure, Inhalte, Strategien* (Berlin, 2011), 105–106.

5. See "Warnung an die Juden," *Frankfurter Zeitung*, August 28, 1933. See also Thomas Kühne, *Genocide and Belonging: Hitler's Community, 1918–1945* (New York, 2010), 42.

6. Reinhard Bendix, *From Berlin to Berkeley: German-Jewish Identities* (New Brunswick, NJ, 1986), 191

7. Ibid., 288. See also Ludwig Bendix, *Konzentrationslager Deutschland und anderer Schutzhafterfahrungen, 1933–1937, 1937–1938*, LBIA, ME 40, bk. 5:107. Ludwig Bendix died on January 3, 1954, in Oakland, California.

8. See Moshe Zimmermann, *Deutsche gegen Deutsche* (Berlin, 2008), 14–15.

9. Max Domarus, *Hitler: Reden und Proklamationen, 1932–1945; Kommentiert von einem deutschen Zeitgenossen*, vol. 2: *Untergang*, pt. 1: *1939–1940* (Wiesbaden, 1973), 1058, see also 1055.

10. See Christopher R. Browning (with contributions by Jürgen Matthäus), *The Origins of the Final Solution: The Evolution of Nazi Jewish Policy, September 1939–March 1942* (Jerusalem, 2004).

11. See Dieter Pohl, "The Holocaust and the Concentration Camps," in Jane Caplan and Nikolaus Wachsmann, eds., *Concentration Camps in Nazi Germany: The New Histories* (London, 2010), 162.

BIBLIOGRAPHY

Archives

ARCHIV DES DOKUMENTATIONS- UND INFORMATIONSZENTRUMS EMSLANDLAGER

Erinnerungsberichte ehemaliger Häftlinge

ARCHIV GEDENKSTÄTTE UND MUSEUM SACHSENHAUSEN

D 1 A   Bestand Moskauer Sonderarchiv
NL   Nachlässe
P   Personalakten

ARCHIV DER KZ-GEDENKSTÄTTE DACHAU

Berichte ehemaliger Häftlinge
Häftlingsdatenbank
Dokumentensammlung
Ermittlungen und Prozesse

ARCHIV DER KZ-GEDENKSTÄTTE LICHTENBURG

Häftlingsunterlagen

ARCHIV DES NS DOKUMENTATIONSZENTRUMS RHEINLAND-PFALZ/ KZ OSTHOFEN

Häftlingsverzeichnis KZ Osthofen
Häftlingsunterlagen
Dokumentensammlung
Sammlung Zeitungsausschnitte

ARCHIV DER STIFTUNG GEDENKSTÄTTEN BUCHENWALD UND MITTELBAU-DORA

Berichtsammlung
Nachlässe

BIBLIOGRAPHY

ARCHIV DER STIFTUNG NEUE SYNAGOGE
BERLIN — CENTRUM JUDAICUM

Gesamtarchiv der deutsche Juden: 1, 75 C Organisationen

BAYERISCHES HAUPTSTAATSARCHIV MÜNCHEN

MJu	Bayerisches Staatsministerium der Justiz
MInn	Bayerisches Staatsministerium des Inneren
StK	Staatskanzlei

BAYERISCHES STAATSARCHIV AMBERG

Staatsanwaltschaften

BAYERISCHES STAATSARCHIV MÜNCHEN

Polizeidirektion München
Staatsanwaltschaften

BAYERISCHES STAATSARCHIV WÜRZBURG

Gestapostelle Würzburg

BRANDENBURGISCHES LANDESHAUPTARCHIV POTSDAM

Rep. 2A	Regierung Potsdam
Rep. 35G	KZ Oranienburg
Rep. 35H	KZ Sachsenhausen

BUNDESARCHIV BERLIN

NS 19	Reichsführer SS
R 58	Reichssicherheitshauptamt
R 3001	Reichsjustizministerium
NY 4011	Nachlass Hans Litten (SAPMO)

CENTRAL ZIONIST ARCHIVES, JERUSALEM

A140	Personal Papers Adler-Rudel, Shalom

FRIENDS HOUSE LIBRARY AND ARCHIVES, LONDON

FCRA	Friends Committee for Refugees and Aliens, Political Prisoners, Correspondence 1933–1938

BIBLIOGRAPHY

GEHEIMES STAATSARCHIV PREUSSISCHER KULTURBESITZ

I. HA Rep. 77   Preussisches Ministerium des Inneren
I. HA Rep. 90 P   Staatsministerium, Geheime Staatspolizei

HESSISCHES STAATSARCHIV DARMSTADT

G 5   Reichsstatthalter
G 24   Generalstaatsanwalt beim Oberlandesgericht Darmstadt

INFORMATIONSSTELLE ZUR GESCHICHTE DES NATIONALSOZIALISMUS IN NORDHESSEN, UNIVERSITÄT KASSEL

Privatarchiv Ludwig Pappenheim

INSTITUT FÜR ZEITGESCHICHTE

Dc. 17.02
Fa 183/1, Fa 315/1
Fb 201

INTERNATIONAL TRACING SERVICE ARCHIVES

Historical Documents
Detention and Persecution Documents
Central Name Index

LANDESAMT FÜR FINANZEN (FREISTAAT BAYERN) — LANDESENTSCHÄDIGUNGSAMT

Entschädigungsakten

LANDESARCHIV BERLIN

A Rep. 339   Landgericht Berlin

LANDESARCHIV NORDRHEIN-WESTFALEN ABTEILUNG RHEINLAND (DÜSSELDORF)

RW 36   Schutzhaft 1934–1944
RW 58   Geheime Staatspolizei—Staatspolizei(leit)stelle Düsseldorf

LANDESARCHIV SPEYER

H 90   Geheime Staatspolizei Neustadt—Verwaltung
H 91   Geheime Staatspolizei Neustadt—Ermittlungsakten

LEO BAECK INSTITUTE ARCHIVES

Memoir Collection

NIEDERSÄCHSISCHES LANDESARCHIV—
HAUPTSTAATSARCHIV HANNOVER

Hann. 158 Moringen, Acc. 84/82, Nr. 1–9
Hann. 158 Moringen, Acc. 105/96, Nr. 1–327

NIEDERSÄCHSISCHES LANDESARCHIV—STAATSARCHIV OSNABRÜCK

Rep. 945   Staatsanwaltschaft Osnabrück

THÜRINGISCHES HAUPTSTAATSARCHIV WEIMAR

NS 4 Bu   Konzentrationslager Buchenwald
Thüringisches Ministerium des Inneren

UNITED STATES HOLOCAUST MEMORIAL MUSEUM ARCHIVES

RG-11   Selected Record from the Former Special [Osobyi] Archive in the
           Russian State Military Archive (RGVA)
1995 A. 104 Aviva Kempner Donation

UNIVERSITÄTSARCHIV DER HUMBOLDT-UNIVERSITÄT ZU BERLIN

Universitätsinstitut für Rechtsmedizin der Charité

WIENER LIBRARY LONDON

Eyewitness Testimony Collection

YAD VASHEM ARCHIVES

O.1   K. J. Ball-Kaduri Testimonies and Reports of German Jewry
           Collection
O.3   Yad Vashem Collection of Testimonies
O.51 OSO   Copies from the OSOBI Archives in Moscow

Published Primary Sources

Abraham, Max. *Juda verrecke: Ein Rabbiner im Konzentrationslager.* Teplitz-Schönau,
    1934. Reprinted in Irene Diekmann and Klaus Wettig, eds., *Konzentrationslager
    Oranienburg: Augenzeugenberichte aus dem Jahre 1933; Gehart Seger, Reichstagsab-
    geordneter der SPD, Max Abraham, Prediger aus Rathenow*, 117–167. Potsdam, 2003.

Almanach Dachau: Kytice událostí a vzpomínek . . . [Almanach Dachau: A Bouquet
    of Events and Memories]. Prague, 1946.

Anon. *Als sozialdemokratischer Arbeiter im Lager Papenburg.* Moscow, 1935.

Anon. *Folterhölle Sonnenburg: Tatsachen und Augenzeugenbericht eines ehemaligen Schutzhäftlings.* Zurich, 1934.

Anon. *Konzentrationslager: Ein Appell an das Gewissen der Welt; Ein Buch der Greuel. Die Opfer klagen an. Dachau—Brandenburg—Papenburg—Königstein—Lichtenstein—Colditz—Sachsenburg—Moringen—Hohnstein—Reichenbach—Sonnenburg.* Karlsbad, 1934.

Ball, Fritz. "Die Nacht in der General-Pape-Strasse." In Kurt Jakob Ball-Kaduri, *Das Leben der Juden in Deutschland im Jahre 1933,* 59–80. Frankfurt, 1963.

———. "Die SA Kaserne in der General-Pape-Strasse." In Kurt Jakob Ball-Kaduri, *Das Leben der Juden in Deutschland im Jahre 1933,* 58–59. Frankfurt, 1963.

Ball-Kaduri, Kurt Jakob. *Das Leben der Juden in Deutschland im Jahre 1933.* Frankfurt, 1963.

Beimler, Hans, *Four Weeks in the Hands of Hitler's Hell-Hounds: The Nazi Murder Camp of Dachau.* London, 1933.

Bendix, Reinhard. *From Berlin to Berkeley: German-Jewish Identities.* New Brunswick, NJ, 1986.

Bettelheim, Bruno. *The Informed Heart: Autonomy in a Mass Age.* New York, 1960.

Betty Scholem, Gershom Scholem, Mutter und Sohn im Briefwechsel, 1917–1946. Edited by Itta Shedletzky. Munich, 1989.

Boberach, Heinz, ed. *Meldungen aus dem Reich: Die geheimen Lageberichte des Sicherheitsdienstes der SS, 1938–1945.* Hersching, 1984.

Bondy, Curt W. "Problems of Internment Camps." *Journal of Abnormal and Social Psychology* 38:4 (1943): 453–475.

Braunbuch über Reichstagsbrand und Hitler-Terror. Basel, 1933.

Burger, Felix [alias Kurt Grossmann]. *Juden in brauner Hölle: Augenzeugen berichten aus SA-Kasernen und Konzentrationslagern.* Prague, 1933.

Burckhardt, Carl J. *Meine Danziger Mission, 1937–1939.* Munich, 1960.

Burkhard, Hugo. *Tanz mal Jude! Von Dachau bis Shanghai: Meine Erlebnisse in den Konzentrationslagern Dachau—Buchenwald—Ghetto Shanghai, 1933–1948.* Nuremberg, 1967.

Carlebach, Emil. *Tote auf Urlaub: Kommunist in Deutschland; Dachau und Buchenwald, 1937–1945.* Bonn, 1995.

Collins, Margarethe. *Eric Collins, 1897–1993: Ein tapferes Leben im zwanzigsten Jahrhundert.* Oldenburg, 1995.

Czech, Danuta. *Auschwitz Chronicle, 1939–1945.* London, 1990.

Das Schwarzbuch: Tatsachen und Dokumente; Die Lage der Juden in Deutschland, 1933. Edited by Comité des Délégations Juives. Paris, 1934.

Der Prozess gegen die Hauptkriegsverbrecher vor dem Internationalen Militärgerichtshof, Nürnberg, 14. November 1945–1. Oktober 1946, vols. 1–42. Nuremberg, 1947–1949.

Deutsche Kommunistische Partei München, ed. *Die wiedergefundene Liste: Porträts von Münchner Kommunistinnen und Kommunisten, die im antifaschistischen Widerstandskampf ihr Leben liessen; Entdeckt von Resi Huber.* Munich, 1998.

Deutsches Judentum unter dem Nationalsozialismus, vol. 1: *Dokumente zur Geschichte der Reichsvertretung der deutschen Juden, 1933–1939.* Edited by Otto Dov Kulka. Tübingen, 1997.

Deutschland-Berichte der Sozialdemokratischen Partei Deutschlands (Sopade), vols. 1–6, 1934–1939. Salzhausen, 1982.

Die Judenpolitik des SD, 1935 bis 1938: Eine Dokumentation. Edited by Michael Wildt. Munich, 1995.

Die Tagebücher von Joseph Goebbels, part 1: *Aufzeichnungen, 1923–1941*, vols. 1–9. Edited by Elke Fröhlich. Munich, 1998–2006.

Die Toten von Dachau: Deutsche und Österreicher; Ein Gedenk- und Nachschlagewerk. Munich, 1947.

Diels, Rudolf. *Lucifer ante portas: Zwischen Severing und Heydrich.* Zurich, 1949.

Domarus, Max. *Hitler: Reden und Proklamationen, 1932–1945; Kommentiert von einem deutschen Zeitgenossen.* 2 vols. Wiesbaden, 1973.

Eisinger, Robert. "Die ersten Judenmorde im KZ Dachau, 12. April 1933." *Mitteilungsblatt der Lager-Gemeinschaft Dachau* (August 1963): 7–8.

Federn, Ernst. "Essai sur la Psychologie de la Terreur." *Synthéses* 1 (1946): 81–108.

———. "The Terror as a System: The Concentration Camp (Buchenwald as It Was)," *Psychiatric Quarterly Supplement* 22 (1948): 52–68.

Fraenkel, Ernst. *The Dual State: A Contribution to the Theory of Dictatorship.* New York, 1941.

Freund, Julius. *O Buchenwald!* Klagenfurt, 1945.

Fromm, Bella *Blood and Banquets: A Berlin Social Diary.* New York, 1944.

Fürst, Max *Gefilte Fisch und wie es weiterging.* Munich, 2004.

———. *Talisman Scheherezade: Die schwierigen Zwanziger Jahre.* Munich, 1976.

Gesell, Willi. "Die ersten Transporte in das KZ Dachau." *Mitteilungsblatt der Lager-Gemeinschaft Dachau* (December 1972).

Halbreich, Siegfried. *Before—During—After: Surviving the Holocaust.* Los Angeles, CA, 2000.

Heilig, Bruno. *Men Crucified.* London, 1941.

Herz, Gabriele. *The Women's Camp in Moringen: A Memoir of Imprisonment in Germany, 1936–1937.* Translated by Hildegard Herz and Howard Hartig. Edited by Jane Caplan. New York, 2006.

Hiller, Kurt. "Schutzhäftling 231." *Die neue Weltbühne: Wochenschrift für Politik, Kunst, Wirtschaft*, 12 parts, December 6, 1934–February 14, 1935.

Hirsch, Werner. *Hinter Stacheldraht und Gitter: Erlebnisse und Erfahrungen in den Konzentrationslagern Hitler-Deutschlands*. Zurich, 1934.

———. *Sozialdemokratische und kommunistische Arbeiter im Konzentrationslager*. Strasbourg, 1934.

Hornung, Walter [alias Julius Zerfass]. *Dachau: Eine Chronik*. Zurich, 1936.

Höss, Rudolf. *Commandant of Auschwitz: The Autobiography of Rudolf Höss* (1946). Translated by Constantine FitzGibbon. London, 2000.

Huber, Lotti. *Diese Zitrone hat noch viel Saft: Ein Leben*. Munich, 1993.

The Jews in the Secret Nazi Reports on Popular Opinion in Germany, 1933–1945. Edited by Otto Dov Kulka and Eberhard Jäckel. New Haven, CT, 2010.

Kalmar, Rudolf. *Zeit ohne Gnade*. Vienna, 1946.

Katz, Ernst P. "Die Geschichte eines Juden aus Hungen." In *Juden in Hungen*, ed. Arbeitsgemeinschaft "Spurensuche" Hungen. Giessen, 1990.

Kautsky, Benedikt. *Teufel und Verdammte: Erfahrungen und Erkenntnisse aus 7 Jahren in deutschen Konzentrationslagern*. Zurich, 1946.

Kerrl, Hanns, ed. *Reichstagung in Nürnberg 1935: Der Parteitag der Freiheit*. Berlin, 1936.

Klemperer, Victor. *I Will Bear Witness: A Diary of the Nazi Years, 1933–1941*. New York, 1999.

Koch, Werner. *Der Kampf der Bekennenden Kirche im Dritten Reich*. Berlin, 1988.

———. *"Sollen wir K. weiter beobachten?": Ein Leben im Widerstand*. Argenbühl-Christazhofen, 1993.

Kogon, Eugen. *Der SS-Staat: Das System der deutschen Konzentrationslager*. Munich, 1996.

Konopka, Gisela. *Mit Mut und Liebe: Eine Jugend im Kampf gegen Ungerechtigkeit und Terror*. Weinheim, 1996.

Kroch, Ernesto. *Exil in der Heimat—Heim ins Exil: Erinnerungen aus Europa und Lateinamerika*. Frankfurt, 1990.

Langhoff, Wolfgang. *Die Moorsoldaten: 13 Monate Konzentrationslager*. Stuttgart, 1982.

Levi, Primo. *The Drowned and the Saved*. London, 1996.

Litten, Irmgard. *A Mother Fights Hitler*. London, 1940.

Mann, Thomas. *Tagebücher, 1933–1934*. Edited by Peter de Mendelssohn. Frankfurt, 1977.

Marum, Ludwig. *Briefe aus dem Konzentrationslager Kislau*. Edited by Elisabeth Marum-Lunau and Jörg Schadt. Karlsruhe, 1984.

Mosse, Rudolf S. "Auf's Land!" In *Jüdische Bauernsiedlung in deutscher Heimat*, ed. Reichsbund jüdischer Frontsoldaten, 12–19. Berlin, ca. 1920.

Mühsam, Kreszentia. *Der Leidensweg Erich Mühsams.* Foreword by Werner Hirsch. Zurich, 1935.

Naujoks, Harry. *Mein Leben im KZ-Sachsenhausen, 1936–1942: Erinnerungen des ehemaligen Lagerältesten.* Berlin, 1989.

Nazi-Bastille Dachau: Schicksal und Heldentum deutscher Freiheitskämpfer. Paris, 1939.

Neumann, Franz. *Behemoth: The Structure and Practice of National Socialism, 1933–1944.* London, 1942.

Neurath, Paul Martin. *The Society of Terror: Inside the Dachau and Buchenwald Concentration Camps.* Edited by Christian Fleck and Nico Stehr. Afterword by Christian Fleck, Albert Müller, and Nico Stehr. Boulder, CO, 2005.

Novemberpogrom 1938: Die Augenzeugenberichte der Wiener Library London. Edited by Ben Barkow, Raphael Gross, and Michael Lenarz. Frankfurt, 2008.

Reichmann, Eva G. "Der Centralverein deutscher Staatsbürger jüdischen Glaubens" (1930). In *Grösse und Verhängnis deutsch-jüdischer Existenz: Zeugnisse einer tragischen Begegnung*, 22–32. Heidelberg, 1974.

———. "Vom Sinn deutsch-jüdischen Seins" (1934). In *Grösse und Verhängnis deutsch-jüdischer Existenz: Zeugnisse einer tragischen Begegnung*, 48–62. Heidelberg, 1974.

Reichmann, Hans. *Deutscher Bürger und verfolgter Jude: Novemberpogrom und KZ Sachsenhausen 1937 bis 1939.* Edited by Michael Wildt. Munich, 1998.

Röder, Karl. *Nachtwache: 10 Jahre KZ Dachau und Flossenbürg.* Vienna, 1985.

Schäfer, Werner. *Konzentrationslager Oranienburg: Das Anti-Braunbuch über das erste deutsche Konzentrationslager.* Berlin, 1934.

Schirmer, Hermann. *Das andere Nürnberg: Antifaschistischer Widerstand in der Stadt der Reichsparteitage.* Frankfurt, 1974.

Scholem, Gershom. *Judaica II.* Frankfurt, 1970.

———. *Von Berlin nach Jerusalem: Jugenderinnerungen.* Extended edition, translated from the Hebrew by Michael Brocke and Andrea Schatz. Frankfurt, 1994.

———, ed. *Walter Benjamin, Gershom Scholem, Briefwechsel, 1933–1940.* Frankfurt, 1980.

———. "Wider den Mythos vom deutsch-jüdischen Gespräch" (1964). In *Judaica II.* Frankfurt, 1970.

Seger, Gerhart. *Oranienburg: Erster authentischer Bericht eines aus dem Konzentrationslager Geflüchteten.* Karlsbad, 1934.

Siegelberg, Mark. *Schutzhaftjude Nr. 13877.* Shanghai, 1939.

Solmitz, Walter. *Bericht über Dachau* (London, 1939). In Joist Grolle, *Bericht von einem schwierigen Leben: Walter Solmitz (1905 bis 1962); Schüler von Aby Warburg und Ernst Cassierer*, 89–126. Hamburg, 1994.

Szalet, Leon. *Baracke 38: 237 Tage in den "Judenblocks" von Sachsenhausen*. Berlin, 2006.

———. *Experiment "E": A Report from an Extermination Laboratory*. New York, 1945.

Szende, Stefan. *Zwischen Gewalt und Toleranz: Zeugnisse und Reflexionen eines Sozialisten*. Frankfurt, 1975.

Tausk, Walter. *Breslauer Tagebuch, 1933–1940*. Leipzig, 1995.

Ullmann, Hans. "Das Konzentrationslager Sonnenburg, eingeleitet und kommentiert von Kaspar Nürnberg." *Dachauer Hefte* 13 (1997): 76–91.

Vorbeugende Verbrechensbekämpfung: Sammlung der auf dem Gebiete der vorbeugenden Verbrechensbekämpfung ergangenen Erlasse und sonstigen Bestimmungen; Schriftenreihe des Reichskriminalpolizeiamtes Berlin Nr. 15. Edited by Reichssicherheitshauptamt, Amt V. Berlin, 1941.

Wallner, Peter. *By Order of the Gestapo: A Record of Life in Dachau and Buchenwald*. London, 1941.

Weil, Friedrich. *Mein Leben in Deutschland vor und nach dem 30. Januar 1933* (New York, 1940). In Monika Richarz, ed., *Jüdisches Leben in Deutschland: Selbstzeugnisse zur Sozialgeschichte, 1918–1945*, 269–280. Stuttgart, 1982.

Wininger, Salomon. *Grosse Jüdische National-Biographie mit mehr als 8000 Lebensbeschreibungen namhafter jüdischer Männer und Frauen aller Zeiten und aller Länder: Ein Nachschlagewerk für das jüdische Volk und seine Freunde*. Vol. 7. (Cernowitz, 1936).

Zweig, Stefanie. *Nowhere in Africa: An Autobiographical Novel*. Madison, WI, 2004.

Selected Secondary Sources

Apel, Linde. *Jüdische Frauen im Konzentrationslager Ravensbrück, 1939–1945*. Berlin, 2003.

Arenz-Morch, Angelika. "Das Konzentrationslager Osthofen, 1933/34." In Hans-Georg Meyer and Hans Berkessel, eds., *Die Zeit des Nationalsozialismus in Rheinland-Pfalz*, vol. 2: *"Für die Aussenwelt seid ihr tot!,"* 32–51. Mainz, 2000.

Arndt, Ino. "Das Frauenkonzentrationslager Ravensbrück." In Martin Broszat, ed., *Studien zur Geschichte der Konzentrationslager*, 93–129. Stuttgart, 1970.

Ayass, Wolfgang. *"Asoziale" im Nationalsozialismus*. Stuttgart, 1995.

Baganz, Carina. *Erziehung zur "Volksgemeinschaft"? Die frühen Konzentrationslager in Sachsen, 1933/34–1937*. Berlin, 2005.

Bajohr, Frank, and Michael Wildt. *Volksgemeinschaft: Neue Forschungen zur Gesellschaft des Nationalsozialismus*. Frankfurt, 2009.

Benz, Wolfgang. "Der Novemberpogrom 1938." In Wolfgang Benz, ed., *Die Juden in Deutschland, 1933–1945: Leben unter nationalsozialistischer Herrschaft*, 499–544. Munich, 1988.

———. "Mitglieder der Häftlingsgesellschaft auf Zeit: Die 'Aktionsjuden 1938/39.'" *Dachauer Hefte* 21 (2005): 179–196.

Benz, Wolfgang, and Barbara Distel, eds. *Der Ort des Terrors: Geschichte der natio-nalsozialistischen Konzentrationslager.* 9 vols. Munich, 2005–2009.

——, eds. *Geschichte der Konzentrationslager, 1933–1945.* 15 vols. Berlin, 2001–2014.

Benz, Wolfgang, Barbara Distel, and Angelika Königseder, eds. *Nationalsozialistische Zwangslager: Strukturen und Regionen—Täter und Opfer.* Dachau, 2011.

Bergbauer, Knut. "'Der eben an uns vorüberging . . .': Rudi Arndt, ein jüdischer Kommunist im Widerstand." *transversal* 11:2 (2010): 27–49.

Bergbauer, Knut, Sabine Fröhlich, and Stefanie Schüler-Springorum. *Denkmalsfigur: Biographische Annäherung an Hans Litten.* Göttingen, 2008.

Berkowitz, Michael. *The Crime of My Very Existence: Nazism and the Myth of Jewish Criminality.* Berkeley, CA, 2007.

Borgstedt, Angelika. "Das nordbadische Kislau: Konzentrationslager, Arbeitshaus und Durchgangslager für Fremdenlegionäre." In Wolfgang Benz and Barbara Distel, eds., *Herrschaft und Gewalt: Frühe Konzentrationslager, 1933–1939,* 217–229. Berlin, 2002.

Bromberger, Barbara, Hanna Elling, Jutta von Freyberg, and Ursula Krause-Schmitt. *Schwestern, vergesst uns nicht: Frauen im Konzentrationslager; Moringen, Lichten-burg, Ravensbrück, 1933–1945.* Frankfurt, 1988.

Broszat, Martin. "The Concentration Camps, 1933–45." In Helmut Krausnick, Hans Buchheim, Martin Broszat, and Hans-Adolf Jacobsen, eds., *Anatomy of the SS State,* 397–504. London, 1968.

Broszat, Martin, et al., eds. *Bayern in der NS-Zeit.* 6 vols. Munich, 1977–1983.

Buchenwald Concentration Camp, 1937–1945: A Guide to the Permanent Historical Ex-hibition. Edited by Gedenkstätte Buchenwald. Göttingen, 2004.

Caplan, Jane. "Gabriele Herz: 'Schutzhaft' im Frauen-Konzentrationslager Moringen, 1936–1937." In Gisela Bock, ed., *Genozid und Geschlecht: Jüdische Frauen im na-tionalsozialistischen Lagersystem,* 22–43. Frankfurt, 2005.

——. "Gender and the Concentration Camps." In Jane Caplan and Nikolaus Wachs-mann, eds., *Concentration Camps in Nazi Germany: The New Histories,* 82–107. London, 2010.

——. "Political Detention and the Origin of the Concentration Camps in Nazi Ger-many, 1933–1935/36." In Neil Gregor, ed., *Nazism, War and Genocide: Essays in Honour of Jeremy Noakes,* 22–41. Exeter, 2005.

Caplan, Jane, and Nikolaus Wachsmann, eds. *Concentration Camps in Nazi Germany: The New Histories.* London, 2010.

The Dachau Concentration Camp, 1933 to 1945: Text- and Photo Documents from the Exhibition, with CD. Edited by Barbara Distel. Munich, 2005.

Danckwortt, Barbara. "Jüdische 'Schutzhäftlinge' im KZ Sachsenhausen, 1936 bis 1938: Verfolgungsgeschichten von Kommunisten, Sozialdemokraten und Liberalen." In Günter Morsch and Susanne zur Nieden, eds., *Jüdische Häftlinge im Konzentra-tionslager Sachsenhausen, 1936 bis 1945,* 141–163. Berlin, 2004.

Die Verfolgung und Ermordung der europäischen Juden durch das nationalsozialistische Deutschland, 1933–1945. Vols. 1–3. Edited on behalf of the German Federal Archives by Wolf Gruner, Susanne Heim, and Andrea Löw. Munich, 2008–2012.

Dillon, Christopher. "The Dachau Concentration Camp SS, 1933–1939." PhD dissertation, Birkbeck, University of London, 2010, unpublished.

———. "The Dachau SS and the Locality, 1933–1939." In Christiane Hess, Julia Hörath, Dominique Schröder, and Kim Wünschmann, eds., *Kontinuitäten und Brüche: Neue Perspektiven auf die Geschichte der NS-Konzentrationslager*, 47–63. Berlin, 2011.

———. "'Tolerance Means Weakness': The Dachau Concentration Camp S.S., Militarism and Masculinity." *Historical Research* 86:232 (2013): 373–389.

———. "'We'll Meet Again in Dachau': The Early Dachau SS and the Narrative of Civil War." *Journal of Contemporary History* 45:3 (2010): 535–554.

Dirks, Christian. "Die 'Juni-Aktion' 1938 in Berlin." In Beate Meyer and Hermann Simon, eds., *Juden in Berlin, 1938–1945*, 33–43. Berlin, 2000.

Distel, Barbara. "'Die letzte Warnung vor der Vernichtung': Zur Verschleppung der Aktionsjuden in die Konzentrationslager nach dem 9. November 1938." *Zeitschrift für Geschichtswissenschaft* 48:11 (1998): 985–990.

———. "Frauen in nationalsozialistischen Konzentrationslagern: Opfer und Täterinnen." In Wolfgang Benz and Barbara Distel, eds., *Der Ort des Terrors: Geschichte der nationalsozialistischen Konzentrationslager*, vol. 1: *Die Organisation des Terrors*, 195–209. Munich, 2005.

Dörner, Bernward. "Ein KZ in der Mitte der Stadt: Oranienburg." In Wolfgang Benz and Barbara Distel, eds., *Terror ohne System: Die ersten Konzentrationslager im Nationalsozialismus, 1933–1935*, 123–138. Berlin, 2001.

Drobisch, Klaus. "Frauenkonzentrationslager im Schloss Lichtenburg." *Dachauer Hefte* 3 (1987): 101–115.

———. "Überfall auf jüdische Jungen im Juni 1933: Dokumente." In Dietrich Eichholtz, ed., *Brandenburg in der NS-Zeit: Studien und Dokumente*, 168–206. Potsdam, 1993.

Drobisch, Klaus, and Günther Wieland. *System der NS-Konzentrationslager, 1933–1939.* Berlin, 1993.

Eberle, Annette. "Häftlingskategorien und Kennzeichnungen." In Wolfgang Benz and Barbara Distel, eds., *Der Ort des Terrors: Geschichte der nationalsozialistischen Konzentrationslager*, vol. 1: *Die Organisation des Terrors*, 91–109. Munich, 2005.

Endlich, Stefanie. "Die Lichtenburg, 1933–1939: Haftort politischer Prominenz und Frauen-KZ." In Wolfgang Benz and Barbara Distel, eds., *Herrschaft und Gewalt: Frühe Konzentrationslager, 1933–1939*, 11–64. Berlin, 2002.

Esseling, Marco. "Juden als Häftlingsgruppe in Konzentrationslagern: Verhaftung von Juden und ihre Stellung im Lager bis 1942 unter besonderer Berücksichtigung des KZ Dachau." M.A. dissertation, Institut für Neuere Geschichte, Ludwig-Maximilians-Universität Munich, 1995, unpublished.

Faludi, Christian, ed., *Die "Juni-Aktion" 1938: Eine Dokumentation zur Radikalisierung der Judenverfolgung.* Frankfurt, 2013.

Fahrenberg, Henning, and Nicole Hördler. "Das Frauenkonzentrationslager Lichtenburg: Einblicke, Funktion, Tendenzen." In Stefan Hördler and Sigrid Jacobeit, eds., *Lichtenburg: Ein deutsches Konzentrationslager,* 166–189. Berlin, 2009.

Förderverein Projekt Osthofen, ed. *Das Konzentrationslager Osthofen, 1933/34.* Mainz, 2000.

Freyberg, Jutta von, and Ursula Krause-Schmitt. *Moringen, Lichtenburg, Ravensbrück: Frauen im Konzentrationslager, 1933–1945; Lesebuch zur Ausstellung "Frauen im Konzentrationslager, 1933–1945."* Frankfurt, 1997.

Gallé, Volker. "Karl d'Angelo: Lagerleiter des Konzentrationslagers Osthofen." In Hans-Georg Meyer and Hans Berkessel, eds., *Die Zeit des Nationalsozialismus in Rheinland-Pfalz,* vol. 2: *"Für die Aussenwelt seid ihr tot!,"* 69–79. Mainz, 2000.

Garbe, Detlef. "Absonderung, Strafkommandos und spezifischer Terror: Jüdische Gefangene in nationalsozialistischen Konzentrationslagern." In Arno Herzig and Ina Lorenz, eds., *Verdrängung und Vernichtung der Juden unter dem Nationalsozialismus,* 173–204. Hamburg, 1992.

Garbe, Detlef, and Sabine Homann. "Jüdische Gefangene in Hamburger Konzentrationslagern." In Arno Herzig, ed., *Juden in Hamburg, 1590 bis 1990: Wissenschaftliche Beiträge der Universität Hamburg zur Ausstellung "Vierhundert Jahre Juden in Hamburg,"* 545–559. Hamburg, 1991.

Gellately, Robert. *The Gestapo and German Society: Enforcing Racial Policy, 1933–1945.* Oxford, 1990.

———. "The Prerogatives of Confinement in Germany, 1933–1945: 'Protective Custody' and Other Police Strategies." In Norbert Finzsch and Robert Jütte, eds., *Institutions of Confinement: Hospitals, Asylums, and Prisons in Western Europe and North America, 1500–1950,* 191–211. Cambridge, 1996.

Georg, Karoline, Kurt Schilde, and Johannes Tuchel, "Warum schweigt die Welt?!" "Why is the world still silent?!": Häftlinge im Berliner Konzentrationslager Columbia-Haus, 1933 bis 1936; Prisoners in Berlin's Columbia-Haus Concentration Camp, 1933 to 1936 (Berlin, 2013).

Goeschel, Christian, and Nikolaus Wachsmann, eds. *Before Auschwitz: New Approaches to the Nazi Concentration Camps, 1933–1939, Journal of Contemporary History* 45:3 (2010), special issue.

———. *The Nazi Concentration Camps, 1933–39: A Documentary History.* Lincoln, NE, 2012.

Gutman, Israel, and Avital Saf, eds. *The Nazi Concentration Camps: Structure and Aims—The Image of the Prisoner, Jews in the Camps; Proceedings of the Fourth Yad Vashem International Historical Conference, Jerusalem, January 1980.* Jerusalem, 1984.

Hensle, Michael P. "Die Verrechtlichung des Unrechts: Der legalistische Rahmen der nationalsozialistischen Verfolgung." In Wolfgang Benz and Barbara Distel, eds.,

Der Ort des Terrors: Geschichte der nationalsozialistischen Konzentrationslager, vol. 1: *Die Organisation des Terrors*, 76–90. Munich, 2005.

Herbert, Ulrich, Karin Orth, and Christoph Dieckmann, eds. *Die nationalsozialistischen Konzentrationslager: Entwicklung und Struktur.* 2 vols. Göttingen, 1998.

Hesse, Hans. *Das Frauen-KZ Moringen, 1933–1938: ". . . und wir daher an diesen Frauen verhältnismässig gut verdienen. Es wäre uns daher erwünscht, möglichst viel weibliche Polizeigefangene aufzunehmen."* Göttingen, 2000.

——. "Von der 'Erziehung' zur 'Ausmerzung': Das Konzentrationslager Moringen, 1933–1945." In Wolfgang Benz and Barbara Distel, eds., *Instrumentarium der Macht: Frühe Konzentrationslager, 1933–1937*, 111–146. Berlin, 2003.

Hett, Benjamin Carter. *Crossing Hitler: The Man Who Put the Nazis on the Witness Stand.* Oxford, 2008.

Homosexuelle in Konzentrationslagern: Vorträge. Edited by Dr. Olaf Mussmann, wissenschaftliche Tagung 12./13. September 1997, KZ-Gedenkstätte Mittelbau-Dora, Nordhausen. Bad Münstereifel, 2000.

Hörath, Julia. "Terrorinstrumente der 'Volksgemeinschaft'? KZ-Haft für 'Asoziale' und 'Berufsverbrecher' 1933 bis 1937/38." *Zeitschrift für Geschichtswissenschaft* 60:6 (2012): 513–532.

Hördler, Stefan. "Before the Holocaust: Concentration Camp Lichtenburg and the Evolution of the Nazi Camp System." *Holocaust and Genocide Studies* 25:1 (2011): 100–126.

Hördler, Stefan, and Sigrid Jacobeit, eds. *Lichtenburg: Ein deutsches Konzentrationslager.* Berlin, 2009.

Horwitz, Gordon J. *In the Shadow of Death: Living outside the Gates of Mauthausen.* New York, 1990.

Jahnke, Karl-Heinz. "Heinz Eschen: Kapo des Judenblocks im Konzentrationslager Dachau bis 1938." *Dachauer Hefte* 7 (1991): 24–33.

Johnson, Eric A. *Nazi Terror: The Gestapo, Jews, and Ordinary Germans.* London, 2000.

Kaienburg, Hermann. "KZ-System und Häftlingsgruppen: Gab es eine Zuordnung von Häftlingskategorien zu bestimmten Konzentrationslagern?" In Wolfgang Benz et al., eds., *Nationalsozialistische Zwangslager: Strukturen und Regionen—Täter und Opfer*, 163–174. Dachau, 2011.

Kaplan, Marion A. *Between Dignity and Despair: Jewish Life in Nazi Germany.* New York, 1998.

Kershaw, Ian. "'Volksgemeinschaft': Potenzial und Grenzen eines neuen Forschungskonzepts." *Vierteljahreshefte für Zeitgeschichte* 58 (2011): 1–18.

Kienle, Markus. "Das Konzentrationslager Heuberg bei Stetten am kalten Markt." In Wolfgang Benz and Barbara Distel, eds., *Terror ohne System: Die ersten Konzentrationslager im Nationalsozialismus, 1933–1935*, 41–63. Berlin, 2001.

Kimmel, Günther. "Das Konzentrationslager Dachau: Eine Studie zu den national-sozialistischen Gewaltverbrechen." In Martin Broszat and Elke Fröhlich, eds., *Bayern in der NS-Zeit*, vol. 2: *Herrschaft und Gesellschaft im Konflikt*, 349–413. Munich, 1979.

Klausch, Hans-Peter. *Jakob de Jonge: Aus deutschen Konzentrationslagern in den niederländischen Untergrund*. Bremen, 2002.

———. *Tätergeschichten: Die SS-Kommandanten der frühen Konzentrationslager im Emsland*. Bremen, 2005.

Knoll, Albert. "Totgeschlagen—totgeschwiegen: Die homosexuellen Häftlinge im KZ Dachau." *Dachauer Hefte* 14 (1998): 77–101.

Königseder, Angelika. "Die Entwicklung des KZ-Systems." In Wolfgang Benz and Barbara Distel, eds., *Der Ort des Terrors: Geschichte der nationalsozialistischen Konzentrationslager*, vol. 1: *Die Organisation des Terrors*, 30–42. Munich, 2005.

Krause-Vilmar, Dietfrid. *Das Konzentrationslager Breitenau: Ein staatliches Schutzhaftlager, 1933/34*. Marburg, 1998.

———. "Das Konzentrationslager im Arbeitshaus Breitenau. 1933/1934." In Wolfgang Benz and Barbara Distel, eds., *Terror ohne System: Die ersten Konzentrationslager im Nationalsozialismus, 1933–1935*, 139–161. Berlin, 2001.

Krause-Vilmar, Dietfrid, Marie Rügheimer, and Christian Wicke. "Das KZ Breitenau bei Kassel 1933/34." In Ulrich Schneider, ed., *Hessen vor 50 Jahren: Naziterror und antifaschistischer Widerstand zwischen Kassel und Bergstrasse, 1932/33*, 68–78. Frankfurt, 1983.

Kuschey, Bernhard. *Die Ausnahme des Überlebens: Ernst und Hilde Federn; Eine biographische Studie und eine Analyse der Binnenstruktur des Konzentrationslagers*. 2 vols. Giessen, 2003.

Kuse, Matthias. "Die Entlassung von Häftlingen aus dem Frauenkonzentrationslager Moringen, 1934–1938." *Dokumente. Rundbrief der Lagergemeinschaft und Gedenkstätte KZ Moringen e.V.* 19 (2000): 14–15.

Kuss, Horst. "Aussonderung, Konzentration, Vernichtung: Zur Geschichte der nationalsozialistischen Konzentrationslager und der Vernichtung des europäischen Judentums; Ergebnisse und Fragen der zeitgeschichtlichen Forschung seit 1981." *Neue Politische Literatur* 34:3 (1989): 375–408.

Kwiet, Konrad, and Helmut Eschwege. *Selbstbehauptung und Widerstand: Deutsche Juden im Kampf um Existenz und Menschenwürde, 1933–1945*. Hamburg, 1984.

Landeszentrale für politische Bildung Rheinland-Pfalz, ed. *Verfolgung und Widerstand in Rheinland-Pfalz*, vol. 1: *Gedenkstätte KZ Osthofen: Ausstellungskatalog*. Mainz, 2008.

Langhammer, Sven. "Die reichsweite Verhaftungsaktion vom 9. März 1937: Eine Massnahme zur 'Säuberung des Volkskörpers.'" *Hallische Beiträge zur Zeitgeschichte* 17:1 (2007): 55–77.

Lautmann, Rüdiger. "The Pink Triangle: Homosexuals as 'Enemies of the State.'" In Michael Berenbaum and Abraham J. Peck, eds., *The Holocaust and History: The Known, the Unknown, the Disputed, and the Reexamined*, 345–357. Bloomington, IN, 1998.

Longerich, Peter. *Heinrich Himmler: Eine Biographie*. Munich, 2008.

———. *Holocaust: The Nazi Persecution and Murder of the Jews*. Oxford, 2010.

Lüerssen, Dirk. "'Moorsoldaten' in Esterwegen, Börgermoor und Neusustrum: Die frühen Konzentrationslager im Emsland, 1933 bis 1936." In Wolfgang Benz and Barbara Distel, eds., *Herrschaft und Gewalt: Frühe Konzentrationslager, 1933–1939*, 157–210. Berlin, 2002.

———. *"Wir sind die Moorsoldaten": Die Insassen der frühen Konzentrationslager im Emsland, 1933 bis 1936; Biographische Untersuchungen zum Zusammenhang zwischen kategorialer Zuordnung der Verhafteten, deren jeweiligen Verhaltensformen im Lager und den Auswirkungen der Haft auf die weitere Lebensgeschichte*. PhD thesis, Universität Osnabrück, 2001, http://repositorium.uni-osnabrueck.de /bitstream/urn:nbn:de:gbv:700-2006033114/2/E-Diss529_thesis.pdf.

Mann, Frank-Matthias. "Jüdische Häftlinge in Breitenau." In Helmut Burmeister and Michael Dorhs, eds., *Juden—Hessen—Deutsche: Beiträge zur Kultur- und Sozialgeschichte der Juden in Nordhessen*, 155–162. Hofgeismar, 1991.

Matthäus, Jürgen. "Verfolgung, Ausbeutung, Vernichtung: Jüdische Häftlinge im System der Konzentrationslager." In Günter Morsch and Susanne zur Nieden, eds., *Jüdische Häftlinge im Konzentrationslager Sachsenhausen, 1936 bis 1945*, 64–90. Berlin, 2004.

Mayer-von Götz, Irene. *Terror im Zentrum der Macht: Die frühen Konzentrationslager in Berlin, 1933/34–1936*. Berlin, 2008.

Mette, Sandra. "Schloss Lichtenburg: Konzentrationslager für Männer, 1933–1937." In Stefan Hördler and Sigrid Jacobeit, eds., *Lichtenburg: Ein deutsches Konzentrationslager*, 130–165. Berlin, 2009.

Meyer, Hans-Georg, and Kerstin Roth. "'Wühler,' 'Saboteure,' 'Doktrinäre': Das Schutzhaftlager in der Turenne-Kaserne in Neustadt an der Haardt." In Wolfgang Benz and Barbara Distel, eds., *Instrumentarium der Macht: Frühe Konzentrationslager, 1933–1937*, 221–238. Berlin, 2003.

———. "Zentrale staatliche Einrichtung des Landes Hessen: Das Konzentrationslager Osthofen." In Wolfgang Benz and Barbara Distel, eds., *Instrumentarium der Macht: Frühe Konzentrationslager, 1933–1937*, 189–219. Berlin, 2003.

Milton, Sybil. "Deutsche und deutsch-jüdische Frauen als Verfolgte des NS-Staates." *Dachauer Hefte* 3 (1987): 3–20.

Moore, Paul. "German Popular Opinion on the Nazi Concentration Camps, 1933–1939." PhD dissertation, Birkbeck, University of London, 2010, unpublished.

——— "'The Man Who Built the First Concentration Camp': The *Anti-Brown Book* of Concentration Camp Commandant Werner Schäfer—Fighting and Writing the Nazi 'Revolution.'" *German History* (forthcoming).

Morsch, Günter, ed. *From Sachsenburg to Sachsenhausen: Pictures from the Photograph Album of a Camp Commandant*. Berlin, 2007.

——. "Oranienburg–Sachsenhausen, Sachsenhausen–Oranienburg." In Ulrich Herbert, Karin Orth, and Christoph Dieckmann, eds., *Die nationalsozialistischen Konzentrationslager: Entwicklung und Struktur*, 1:111–134. Göttingen, 1998.

——. *Konzentrationslager Oranienburg*. Berlin, 1994.

Morsch, Günter, and Susanne zur Nieden, eds. *Jüdische Häftlinge im Konzentrationslager Sachsenhausen, 1936 bis 1945*. Berlin, 2004.

Müller, Reinhard. "Der Fall Werner Hirsch: Vom KZ Oranienburg in die Moskauer Lubjanka." *Internationale wissenschaftliche Korrespondenz zur Geschichte der Arbeiterbewegung* 36 (2000): 34–61.

Neugebauer, Wolfgang, and Peter Schwarz. *Stacheldraht mit Tod geladen . . . Der erste Österreichertransport in das KZ Dachau*. Vienna, 2008.

Orth, Karin. "The Concentration Camp Personnel." In Jane Caplan and Nikolaus Wachsmann, eds., *Concentration Camps in Nazi Germany: The New Histories*, 44–57. London, 2010.

——. *Das System der nationalsozialistischen Konzentrationslager: Eine politische Organisationsgeschichte*. Hamburg, 1999.

——. "Die Historiografie der Konzentrationslager und die neuere KZ-Forschung." *Archiv für Sozialgeschichte* 47 (2007): 579–598.

——. *Die Konzentrationslager SS: Sozialstrukturelle Analysen und biographische Studien*. Munich, 2004.

——. "Gab es eine Lagergesellschaft? 'Kriminelle' und politische Häftlinge im Konzentrationslager." In Norbert Frei et al., eds., *Ausbeutung, Vernichtung, Öffentlichkeit: Neue Studien zur nationalsozialistischen Lagerpolitik*, 109–133. Munich, 2000.

Pietsch, Julia. "Jüdische Häftlinge im frühen Konzentrationslager Oranienburg: 'Schutzhaft' im Spannungsfeld von Antisemitismus und 'Judenpolitik.'" Diploma thesis, Otto-Suhr-Institut für Politikwissenschaft, Freie Universität Berlin, 2010, unpublished.

Pingel, Falk. "Die Konzentrationslagerhäftlinge im nationalsozialistischen Arbeitseinsatz." In Waclaw Długoborski, ed., *Zweiter Weltkrieg und sozialer Wandel: Achsenmächte und besetze Länder*, 151–163. Göttingen, 1981.

——. *Häftlinge unter SS-Herrschaft: Widerstand, Selbstbehauptung und Vernichtung im Konzentrationslager*. Hamburg, 1978.

——. "Social Life in an Unsocial Environment: The Inmates' Struggle for Survival." In Jane Caplan and Nikolaus Wachsmann, eds., *Concentration Camps in Nazi Germany: The New Histories*, 58–81. London, 2010.

Pohl, Dieter. "The Holocaust and the Concentration Camps." In Jane Caplan and Nikolaus Wachsmann, eds., *Concentration Camps in Nazi Germany: The New Histories*, 149–166. London, 2010.

Pollmeier, Heiko "Die Inhaftierung deutscher Juden im November 1938." M.A. dissertation, Kommunikations- und Geschichtswissenschaft, Technische Universität Berlin, 1995, unpublished.

——. "Inhaftierung und Lagererfahrung deutscher Juden im November 1938." *Jahrbuch für Antisemitismusforschung* 8 (1999): 107–130.

——. "Die Verhaftungen nach dem November-Pogrom 1938 und die Masseninhaftierung in den 'jüdischen Baracken' des KZ Sachsenhausen." In Günter Morsch and Susanne zur Nieden, eds., *Jüdische Häftlinge im Konzentrationslager Sachsenhausen, 1936 bis 1945*, 164–179. Berlin, 2004.

Rahe, Thomas. "*Höre Israel*." In *Jüdische Religiosität in nationalsozialistischen Konzentrationslagern*. Göttingen, 1999.

Richardi, Hans-Günter. *Schule der Gewalt: Das Konzentrationslager Dachau*. Munich, 1995.

Riebe, Renate. "Frauen in Konzentrationslagern, 1933–1939." *Dachauer Hefte* 14 (1998): 125–140.

Riedel, Dirk. *Ordnungshüter und Massenmörder im Dienst der "Volksgemeinschaft": Der KZ-Kommandant Hans Loritz*. Berlin, 2010.

Riedle, Andrea. *Die Angehörigen des Kommandanturstabs im KZ Sachsenhausen: Sozialstruktur, Dienstwege und biografische Studien*. Berlin, 2011.

Röll, Wolfgang. *Sozialdemokraten im Konzentrationslager Buchenwald, 1937–1945*. Göttingen, 2000.

Rudorff, Andrea. "'Privatlager' des Polizeipräsidenten mit prominenten Häftlingen: Das Konzentrationslager Breslau-Dürrgoy." In Wolfgang Benz and Barbara Distel, eds., *Instrumentarium der Macht: Frühe Konzentrationslager, 1933–1937*, 147–170. Berlin, 2003.

Schilde, Kurt. "Vom Tempelhofer Feld-Gefängnis zum Schutzhaftlager: Das 'Columbia-Haus' in Berlin." In Wolfgang Benz and Barbara Distel, eds., *Herrschaft und Gewalt: Frühe Konzentrationslager, 1933–1939*, 65–81. Berlin, 2002.

Schilde, Kurt, and Joahnnes Tuchel. *Columbia-Haus: Berliner Konzentrationslager, 1933–1936*. Berlin, 1990.

Schmiechen-Ackermann, Detlef, ed. *Volksgemeinschaft: Mythos, wirkungsmächtige soziale Verheissung oder soziale Realität im Dritten Reich?* Paderborn, 2012.

Schüler-Springorum, Stefanie. "Masseneinweisungen in Konzentrationslager: Aktion 'Arbeitsscheu Reich,' Novemberpogrom, Aktion 'Gewitter.'" In Wolfgang Benz and Barbara Distel, eds., *Der Ort des Terrors: Geschichte der nationalsozialistischen Konzentrationslager*, vol. 1: *Die Organisation des Terrors*, 156–164. Munich, 2005.

Schwarz, Gudrun. *Die nationalsozialistischen Lager*. Frankfurt, 1990.

Sofsky, Wolfgang. *The Order of Terror: The Concentration Camp*. Princeton, NJ, 1997.

Steber, Martina, and Bernhard Gotto, eds. *Visions of Community in Nazi Germany: Social Engineering and Private Lives*. Oxford, 2014.

Stein, Harry. "Das Sonderlager im Konzentrationslager Buchenwald nach den Pogromen 1938." In Monica Kingreen, ed., *Nach der Kristallnacht: Jüdisches Leben und antijüdische Politik in Frankfurt am Main, 1938–1945,* 19–54. Frankfurt, 1999.

———. *Juden in Buchenwald, 1937–1942.* Weimar, 1992.

Steinbacher, Sybille. *Dachau: Die Stadt und das Konzentrationslager in der NS-Zeit; Die Untersuchung einer Nachbarschaft.* Frankfurt, 1993.

Steinbacher, Sybille, and Nikolaus Wachsmann, eds. *Die Linke im Visier: Zur Errichtung der Konzentrationslager 1933.* Göttingen, 2014.

Steinweis, Alan E. *Kristallnacht 1938.* Cambridge, MA, 2009.

Tuchel, Johannes. "Die Kommandanten des Konzentrationslagers Dachau." *Dachauer Hefte* 10 (1994): 69–90.

———. *Konzentrationslager. Organisationsgeschichte und Funktion der "Inspektion der Konzentrationslager," 1934–1938.* Boppard, 1991.

———. "Selbstbehauptung und Widerstand in nationalsozialistischen Konzentrationslagern." In Jürgen Schmädeke and Peter Steinbach, eds., *Der Widerstand gegen den Nationalsozialismus: Die deutsche Gesellschaft und der Widerstand gegen Hitler,* 938–953. Munich, 1985.

Tutas, Herbert E. *Nationalsozialismus und Exil: Die Politik des Dritten Reiches gegenüber der deutschen politischen Emigration.* Munich, 1975.

The United States Holocaust Memorial Museum Encyclopedia of Camps and Ghettos, 1933–1945, vol. 1: *Early Camps, Youth Camps, and Concentration Camps and Subcamps under the SS-Business and Administration Main Office (WVHA),* 2 parts, ed. Geoffrey P. Megargee. Bloomington, IN, 2009.

Wachsmann, Nikolaus. "The Dynamics of Destruction: The Development of the Concentration Camps, 1933–1945." In Jane Caplan and Nikolaus Wachsmann, eds., *Concentration Camps in Nazi Germany: The New Histories,* 17–43. London, 2010.

———. "KL: A History of the Nazi Concentration Camps." (Unpublished manuscript.)

———. "Looking into the Abyss: Historians and the Nazi Concentration Camps." *European History Quarterly* 36:2 (2006): 247–278.

———. "The Policy of Exclusion: Repression in the Nazi State, 1933–1939." In Jane Caplan, ed., *Short Oxford History of Germany: The Third Reich,* 122–145. Oxford, 2009.

Walk, Joseph. "Das Ende des Jüdischen Jugend- und Lehrheims Wolzig (1933)." *Bulletin des Leo Baeck Instituts* 66 (1983): 3–22.

White, Joseph Robert. "Introduction to the Early Camps." In *The United States Holocaust Memorial Museum Encyclopedia of Camps and Ghettos, 1933–1945,* vol. 1, pt. 1, 3–16, ed. Geoffrey P. Megargee. Bloomington, IN, 2009.

Wildt, Michael. "Volksgemeinschaft: Eine Antwort auf Ian Kershaw." *Zeithistorische Forschungen/Studies in Contemporary History* 8:1 (2011); http://www.zeithistorische -forschungen.de/16126041-Wildt-1-2011.

——. *Volksgemeinschaft als Selbstermächtigung: Gewalt gegen Juden in der deutschen Provinz, 1919 bis 1939*. Hamburg, 2007.

Wünschmann, Kim. "Die Konzentrationslagererfahrungen deutsch-jüdischer Männer nach dem Novemberpogrom 1938: Geschlechtergeschichtliche Überlegungen zu männlichem Selbstverständnis und Rollenbild." In Susanne Heim et al., eds., *"Wer bleibt opfert seine Jahre, vielleicht sein Leben": Deutsche Juden, 1938–1941*, 39–58. Göttingen, 2010.

——. "Jüdische politische Häftlinge im frühen KZ Dachau: Widerstand, Verfolgung und antisemitisches Feindbild." In Sybille Steinbacher and Nikolaus Wachsmann, eds., *Die Linke im Visier: Zur Errichtung der Konzentrationslager 1933*. (Forthcoming.)

——. "Männlichkeitskonstruktionen jüdischer Häftlinge in NS-Konzentrationslagern." In Anette Dietrich and Ljiljana Heise, eds., *Männlichkeitskonstruktionen im Nationalsozialismus: Formen, Funktionen und Wirkungsmacht von Geschlechterkonstruktionen im Nationalsozialismus und ihre Refelxion in der pädagogischen Praxis*, 201–219. Frankfurt, 2013.

——. "'Natürlich weiss ich, wer mich ins KZ gebracht hat und warum . . .': Die Inhaftierung von Juden im Konzentrationslager Osthofen 1933/34." In Andreas Ehresmann et al., eds., *Die Erinnerung an die nationalsozialistischen Konzentrationslager: Akteure, Inhalte, Strategien*, 97–111. Berlin, 2011.

——. "The 'Scientification' of the Concentration Camp: Early Theories of Terror and Their Reception by American Academia." *Leo Baeck Institute Year Book* 58 (2013): 111–126.

Yahil, Leni. "Jews in Concentration Camps in Germany Prior to World War II." In Israel Gutman and Avital Saf, eds., *The Nazi Concentration Camps: Structure and Aims, the Image of the Prisoner, Jews in the Camps; Proceedings of the Fourth Yad Vashem International Historical Conference, Jerusalem, January 1980*, 69–100. Jerusalem, 1984.

Zámečnik, Stansilav. *Das war Dachau*. Frankfurt, 2007.

ACKNOWLEDGMENTS

It is my great pleasure to acknowledge the people and institutions that have supported me in researching and writing this book. Thanks to them, the history of the Jews in the prewar Nazi concentration camps can be told, and it is my modest hope that this book will help to keep alive and honor the memory of the persecuted.

My study began at Birkbeck College, University of London, as a part of a larger research project, funded by the Arts and Humanities Research Council, on the Nazi concentration camps before the Second World War. It would not have taken shape, developed, and finally materialized in book form without the unflagging support, critical advice, and constant encouragement of Nikolaus Wachsmann, who has supervised both the research project as a whole, and my own work, every step of the way. I am extremely grateful to him, as well as to my colleagues Christopher Dillon and Paul Moore, for carefully reading multiple drafts of the whole manuscript and for offering much-needed feedback. Likewise, I was very fortunate to have wise advice from Jane Caplan and David Cesarani. Their astute comments, original insights, and broad expertise have helped me tremendously, and I extend my heartfelt thanks to them.

This book has also benefited from the exchange of ideas with many other scholars who have shared with me their deep knowledge of the history of German Jewry, National Socialism, and the Holocaust. For generously listening to, reading, and discussing my findings, and for guiding me toward valuable source material, I would like to express my appreciation in particular to Frank Bajohr, Michael Berkowitz, David Feldman, Robert Gellately, Susanne Heim, Dietfrid Krause-Vilmar, Birthe Kundrus, Beate Meyer, Stefanie Schüler-Springorum, Yfaat Weiss, and Michael Wildt. My sincere gratitude also goes to Carina Baganz and Angelika Königseder for offering important expert advice based on their vast knowledge of the history of the concentration camps, as well as to Edith Raim and Andreas Eichmüller for assisting me in the search for the legal files of postwar German prosecutions of camp perpetrators. Joseph Robert White has introduced me to the holdings of the International Tracing Service, for which I am most grateful. I am also extremely thankful to Knut Bergbauer, David Jünger, Sven Langhammer, and Julia Pietsch, who have kindly made the results of their own research available to me and have pointed me toward precious sources. Heartfelt thanks go to Birute Stern who has generously shared with me her memories of Hans Litten and her parents Margot and Max Fürst. For their helpful suggestions, challenging questions, and stimulating discussions of my work, I would like to thank those young scholars who participated in the research colloquium of Birthe Kundrus and Michael Wildt, in the Workshops on the History and Memory of the Nazi Concentration Camps held in 2006–2008, and in the Annual Conferences at the German Historical Institute London, 2007–2009. In the course of this project, some colleagues have become dear friends. They have not only engaged closely and critically with my research, but also shared many concerns, doubts, hopes, and joys generated by our common experience as young researchers but extending far beyond that academic realm. For their support and inspiration, I owe warmest thanks to Irene Aue-Ben-David Stefanie Fischer, Katharina Friedla, Maria Fritsche, Cornelia Geissler, Christiane Hess, Julia Hörath, Tomaz Jardim, Laura Jockusch, Dominique Schröder, Veronika Springmann, and, again, to Paul Moore and Chris Dillon, who, along with so many other things, have also helped me to navigate the troubled waters of the English language by painstakingly proofreading my texts. Needless to say, in spite of all the support I received from colleagues and friends, any flaws that remain in this book are solely my own responsibility.

Like every historical study, my research on Jews in the Nazi concentration camps very much depended on the knowledgeable assistance and expert guidance of the staff of numerous archives, libraries, museums, and memorial sites. For helping me find and access the documents that form the basis for this study, I am grateful to them all, but I would like to thank in particular Angelika Arenz-Morch of NS-Dokumentationszentrum Rheinland-Pfalz/Gedenkstätte KZ Osthofen; Fietje Ausländer and Kurt and Marianne Buck of Dokumentations- und Informationszentrum Emslandlager; Sabine Stein of the Gedenkstätte Buchenwald Archives; Monika Liebscher of Gedenkstätte and Museum Sachsenhausen Archives; Robert Bierschneider of Staatsarchiv München; Ingrid Heeg-Engelhart of Staatsarchiv Würzburg; and above all Albert Knoll of the KZ-Gedenkstätte Dachau Archives, who has, over the years, most competently and patiently answered all of my many research inquiries about Jewish prisoners in Dachau.

At Harvard University Press, I wish to thank Kathleen McDermott for taking on this project and for seeing it through to publication with her expert editorial guidance. Thanks are due to Andrew Kinney for most helpful support and advice, and to Wendy Nelson for attentive copyediting. I am also grateful to the anonymous readers whose erudite and perceptive comments have greatly helped to give the manuscript its final shape.

This book would not have seen the light of day without the generous financial support of several fellowship and grant organizations. I wish to thank Birkbeck College, University of London, for a College Research Studentship. I am extremely grateful for the vital support provided by the Leo Baeck Fellowship Programme of the Studienstiftung des deutschen Volkes, the Fondation pour la Mémoire de la Shoah, and the Saul Kagan Fellowship in Advanced Shoah Studies awarded by the Conference on Jewish Material Claims Against Germany. I am also indebted to the Franz Rosenzweig Minerva Research Center for German-Jewish Literature and Cultural History for granting me a research fellowship and thereby the unique chance to come back to the Hebrew University of Jerusalem. It is here, in this city unlike any other, that this book has been completed in the wonderfully collegial environment of the Martin Buber Society of Fellows in the Humanities and Social Sciences. I am deeply grateful for all the support and advice I received there. Finally, I wish to thank the German History Society, the Holocaust Educational Foundation, and the German Academic Exchange Service (DAAD) for travel grants that have allowed me to present and discuss my research at the Eleventh Biennial Lessons and Legacies Conference on the Holocaust in Boca Raton, Florida, and at the 37th Annual German Studies Association Conference in Denver, Colorado.

Last but not least, I am very happy to share the joy of publishing this book with my family and friends. For their all-important support I wish to thank Lisa, Mona, Herbert, Elisabeth, Bärbel, Klaus-Peter, Thomas, and Anton, the newest member of our family. During various research trips, I enjoyed the hospitality and close friendship of Oliver Glatz; Jürgen Grzondziel; Ada, Konrad, and Magdalene Linkies; Jürgen Mai, and Noa Seidel. My greatest debt is to the friends who have sustained me through this project. Though often geographically removed, they have most closely accompanied me, both intellectually and emotionally, at every step of this long journey. I owe much more than can be conveyed to Hanne Dahl, Maria Hilltorp, Kerstin Hünefeld, Zdenek Hrabec, Patrick Neumann, Luise Tremel, and Mayte Zimmermann. For his loving companionship and his indispensable presence all through the writing process I passionately thank Dani Uziel. This book is dedicated to my grandparents, Elfriede "Friede" and Josef "Jupp" Kramm, who have given me more than words can say. Their memory continues to burn bright.

INDEX